Lecture Notes in Computer Science 9604

Commenced Publication in 1973
Founding and Former Series Editors:
Gerhard Goos, Juris Hartmanis, and Jan van Leeuwen

More information about this series at http://www.springer.com/series/7410

Jeremy Clark · Sarah Meiklejohn
Peter Y.A. Ryan · Dan Wallach
Michael Brenner · Kurt Rohloff (Eds.)

Financial Cryptography and Data Security

FC 2016 International Workshops
BITCOIN, VOTING, and WAHC
Christ Church, Barbados, February 26, 2016
Revised Selected Papers

 Springer

Editors
Jeremy Clark
Concordia University
Montreal, QC
Canada

Dan Wallach
Rice University
Houston, TX
USA

Sarah Meiklejohn
University College London
London
UK

Michael Brenner
Leibniz Universität Hannover
Hannover
Germany

Peter Y.A. Ryan
Université du Luxembourg
Luxembourg
Luxembourg

Kurt Rohloff
New Jersey Institute of Technology
Newark, NJ
USA

ISSN 0302-9743 ISSN 1611-3349 (electronic)
Lecture Notes in Computer Science
ISBN 978-3-662-53356-7 ISBN 978-3-662-53357-4 (eBook)
DOI 10.1007/978-3-662-53357-4

Library of Congress Control Number: 2016949126

LNCS Sublibrary: SL4 – Security and Cryptology

Printed on acid-free paper

This Springer imprint is published by Springer Nature
The registered company is Springer-Verlag GmbH Berlin Heidelberg

BITCOIN 2016: Third Workshop on Bitcoin and Blockchain Research

We were pleased to once again hold a Bitcoin Workshop at Financial Cryptography and Data Security 2016. In the year leading up to our third workshop, many financial institutes—including banks, insurance companies, and security exchanges—began demonstrating interest in adapting Bitcoin's blockchain data structure for applications relevant to them. To capitalize on this expanding focus, we tweaked the name of the workshop to include "Blockchain Research" that utilizes Bitcoin's flagship component for broader or competing applications.

After completing the peer-review process, with gratitude to our outstanding Program Committee (listed herein), we selected ten papers for the workshop out of the 25 submissions we received. In addition to our program, we note that Financial Cryptography itself accepted six papers on Bitcoin; thus our joint conference remains a strong venue with a high concentration of new academic research into Bitcoin. Our programs contained a range of subjects but particular attention was paid to scalability issues in Bitcoin, as well as to the Ethereum platform.

We were pleased to have an insightful keynote presentation from Nathaniel Popper of the *New York Times* and author of *Digital Gold* touching on the history of Bitcoin and the people involved early in its development. We also had a rich security exposition of the Ethereum protocol and client by Gustav Simonsson of the Ethereum project. Finally, we witnessed a small sliver of Bitcoin history when Sean Bowe from zcash received the first zero-knowledge contingent payment live on the Bitcoin network from Gregory Maxwell in California.

We again extend our gratitude to our Program Committee for doing the hard work of selecting a strong set of papers for the workshop. Thanks in particular to Nicolas Christin for setting us up with a HotCRP server that made all of our lives easier, and to Joseph Bonneau for being the first PC member to complete all their reviews (his award is to be chair next year). We thank each of our invited speakers for taking the time to attend, interact, and give compelling talks. We thank all the attendees for their interest, questions, and interactions during the reception and breaks. We thank the organizers of Financial Cryptography, in particular the general chair, Ray Hirschfeld, for guiding us through the process and executing a flawless conference in a beautiful location. Finally we thank all of the sponsors of Financial Cryptography and, by extension, ourselves.

July 2016

Sarah Meiklejohn
Jeremy Clark

Program Committee

VOTING 2016: First Workshop on Advances in Secure Electronic Voting Schemes

In the summer of 2015 we were approached by the organizers of Financial Crypto with the suggestion to submit a proposal for a workshop on secure voting systems to contribute to marking the 20th anniversary of FC. We took up the invitation and the resulting proposal was duly accepted. This led to a rather shorter lead time for advertisement etc. than we would ideally have liked, but nonetheless the workshop was a success in terms of the number and quality of submissions, attendance, and the quality of presentations and the discussions.

Voting forms the foundation of democracy and as such voting systems constitute part of a democratic nation's critical infrastructure, albeit one that is only deployed periodically. Moves to use digital technologies in voting introduce a whole raft of new, poorly understood threats, especially when it comes to voting over the Internet. This has prompted the security and crypto communities to address the challenges of making voting technologies and systems that are really secure, principally ensuring that the outcome is demonstrably correct while guaranteeing the secrecy of votes.

We received 13 submissions, all of which had at least three reviews and several of which provoked lively debate among the reviewers. Six paper were accepted, leaving space for a keynote talk and a panel. We invited Glen Weyl of Microsoft Research New England and the University of Chicago to present his idea of quadratic voting and discuss the security aspects. The panel was organized by Mark Ryan of the University of Birmingham: "On the Possibility of Ever Deploying Internet-Based Voting," a discussion of the challenges and obstructions to developing secure and usable Internet voting systems.

We should like to thank the organizers of FC for inviting us to organize the workshop in association with the conference and for all their support throughout the process. We also thank all the authors who submitted papers but especially those who came to present the accepted papers. We also thank the PC for their sterling efforts, especially those who performed shepherding duties.

April 2015

Peter Y.A. Ryan
Dan Wallach

Program Committee

Michael Alvarez	California Institute of Technology, USA
Roberto Araujo	Universidade Federal do Pará, Brazil
Jeremy Clark	Concordia University, USA
Veronique Cortier	LORIA, CNRS, France
Jeremy Epstein	SRI, USA
Aleksander Essex	Western University
Kristian Gjosteen	Norwegian University of Science and Technology, Norway
Rajeev Gore	The Australian National University, Australia
Jeroen van de Graaf	Universidade Federal de Minas Gerais, Brazil
Rolf Haenni	Bern University of Applied Sciences, Switzerland
Reto König	Bern University of Applied Sciences, Switzerland
Steve Kremer	Inria Nancy, France
Robert Krimmer	Tallinn University of Technology, Estonia
Olivier Pereira	Universite Catholique de Louvain, Belgium
Ron L. Rivest	MIT, USA
Alon Rosen	IDC Herzliya, Israel
Mark Ryan	University of Birmingham, UK
Steve Schneider	University of Surrey, UK
Berry Schoenmakers	Eindhoven University of Technology, The Netherlands
Carsten Schuermann	IT University of Copenhagen, Denmark
Philip B. Stark	University of California, Berkeley, USA
Vanessa Teague	The University of Melbourne, Australia
Melanie Volkamer	TU Darmstadt, Germany
Poorvi Vora	The George Washington University, USA

WAHC 2016: 4th Workshop on Encrypted Computing and Applied Homomorphic Cryptography

Cloud hype and the recent leakage of private information show there is a demand for secure and practical computing technologies. The WAHC workshop addresses the challenge in safely outsourcing data processing onto remote computing resources by protecting programs and data even during processing. This allows users to outsource computation over confidential information independently from the trustworthiness or the security level of the remote delegate. The workshop serviced these research needs by collecting and bringing together some of the top researchers and practitioners from academia, government, and industry to present, discuss, and share the latest progress in the field relevant to real-world problems with practical approaches and solutions.

The workshop was uniformly attended by academia, government, and industry, with attendees both from prior years with experience in the domain and new attendees learning from the community. Specific encrypted computing technologies focused on homomorphic encryption and secure multiparty computation. The technologies and techniques discussed in this workshop are key to extending the range of applications that can be securely and practically outsourced.

Presentations and discussions at the workshop were of the high quality and deep insight we have come to expect from our community. Topics of conversation included insights and lessons learned from experience implementing encrypted computing schemes, and experience reports on applying these technologies. Special thanks to the invited speaker: Erman Ayday from Bilkent University, who shared experience from a recent encrypted computing projects applied to genetic testing.

This year we accepted demo papers for consideration. We had a strong inaugural demo paper presentation from Mamadou Diallo of SPAWAR System Center Pacific, who discussed applying homomorphic encryption technologies to support use cases for the US Navy.

All of the 11 submission contained unique and interesting results. Each was reviewed by at least three Program Committee members. While all the papers were of high quality, only five papers were accepted for the workshop. We thank the authors for their submissions, the members of the Program Committee for their effort, the workshop participants for attending, and the FC organizers for supporting us.

February 2016

Michael Brenner
Kurt Rohloff

Program Committee

Dan Bogdanov	Cybernetica, Estonia
Marten van Dijk	UConn, USA
Joan Feigenbaum	Yale, USA
Rosario Gennaro	CCNY, USA
Sergey Gorbunov	MIT, USA
Aggelos Kiayias	UConn, USA
Vlad Kolesnikov	Bell Labs, USA
Kim Laine	Microsoft, USA
Tancrède Lepoint	CryptoExperts, France
David Naccache	ENS, Paris, France
Michael Naehrig	Microsoft, USA
Pascal Paillier	CryptoExperts, France
Benny Pinkas	Bar-Ilan University, Israel
Yuriy Polyakov	NJIT, USA
Berk Sunar	WPI, USA
Mehdi Tibouchi	NTT, Japan
Yevgeniy Vahlis	Amazon, USA
Fré Vercauteren	KU Leuven, Belgium
Adrian Waller	Thales, UK

Contents

**4th Workshop on Encrypted Computing and Applied Homomorphic
Cryptography, WAHC 2016**

Third Workshop on Bitcoin and Blockchain Research, BITCOIN 2016

Stressing Out: Bitcoin "Stress Testing"

Khaled Baqer[1(✉)], Danny Yuxing Huang[2], Damon McCoy[3],
and Nicholas Weaver[4]

[1] Computer Laboratory, University of Cambridge, Cambridge, UK
khaled.baqer@cl.cam.ac.uk
[2] University of California, San Diego, La Jolla, USA
[3] New York University, New York, USA
[4] International Computer Science Institute, Berkeley, USA

Abstract. In this paper, we present an empirical study of a recent spam campaign (a "stress test") that resulted in a DoS attack on Bitcoin. The goal of our investigation being to understand the methods spammers used and impact on Bitcoin users. To this end, we used a clustering based method to detect spam transactions. We then validate the clustering results and generate a conservative estimate that 385,256 (23.41 %) out of 1,645,667 total transactions were spam during the 10 day period at the peak of the campaign. We show the impact of increasing non-spam transaction fees from 45 to 68 Satoshis/byte (from $0.11 to $0.17 USD per kilobyte of transaction) on average, and increasing delays in processing non-spam transactions from 0.33 to 2.67 h on average, as well as estimate the cost of this spam attack at 201 BTC (or $49,000 USD). We conclude by pointing out changes that could be made to Bitcoin transaction fees that would mitigate some of the spam techniques used to effectively DoS Bitcoin.

1 Introduction

The Bitcoin network [9] was subjected to a major spam campaign during the summer of 2015 that caused degraded performance of Bitcoin. The likely intent of the incident (advertised as a "stress test") was to Denial of Service (DoS) Bitcoin with spam transactions, in order to expose the vulnerability of Bitcoin to spam attacks and to garner support for a proposed change to increase the number of transactions that the Bitcoin network can verify, which is currently approximately 3 transactions per second. DoS attacks against Bitcoin have been theorized. However, to date there has been little empirical analysis of DoS attacks launched directly against Bitcoin.

In this paper, we conduct an empirical analysis of this spam based DoS attack launched against Bitcoin. To enable our analysis, we use k-means clustering and a set of features we identified to differentiate spam from non-spam transactions. We validate the results of our clustering technique and are able to identify that 385,256 (23.41 %) out of 1,645,667 total transactions were spam between July 7th and July 17th, which corresponds to the peak of the spam based DoS attack.

© International Financial Cryptography Association 2016
J. Clark et al. (Eds.): FC 2016 Workshops, LNCS 9604, pp. 3–18, 2016.
DOI: 10.1007/978-3-662-53357-4_1

Further analysis of transactions in these clusters allowed us to identify four distinct motifs of spam transactions. Based on our identification of spam and non-spam transactions we are able to measure the cost of this spam campaign and impact on non-spam transactions in terms of delay and increased fees.

Our study makes several contributions, including proposing and empirically validating a method to identify spam transactions, characterizing the spam transactions, and measuring the impact of this spam campaign on Bitcoin. Finally, in our discussion section we propose changes to transaction fees that would mitigate the effectiveness of DoS attacks that use spam motifs similar to those used in this attack.

2   Background

Bitcoin transactions are chained signed receipts, consisting of one or more signed inputs to spend, and one or more outputs. The outputs of the transaction are normally assigned to Bitcoin addresses; the hash of a public key that has the authority to use the particular output as an input to another transaction. Transactions are included in *blocks*, with each block also including the hash of the previous block to create a *blockchain*. A block results from verifying all included transactions, with a hash of the data creating a digest with a network-determined prefix of zeros. The latter constitutes the difficulty of the network which is automatically tuned to ensure that the network expects that each block takes 10 min to create, and the effort exerted to create the correct digests is Bitcoin's Proof-of-Work (PoW). The blockchain represents Bitcoin's global ledger, and miners compete to create blocks and broadcast them to the network to claim their rewards. Currently the network only creates and accepts blocks of 1 MB or less, limiting global transaction rate to less than 3 transactions per second.

The main components of a transaction, relevant to our analysis, are the transaction ID (*txid*), the inputs to the transaction (*vin*), and the outputs (*vout*). A transaction includes inputs that reference outputs of one or more older transactions. That is, each input includes, *inter alia*, a reference to an older transaction and the index in the list of outputs (of the referenced transactions) to be used. Bitcoin transactions vary in their inputs and outputs, which determine the size of a transaction.

Transactions are broadcasted to other peers in the Bitcoin P2P network, who perform local verifications to prevent DoS attacks, and the transaction propagates the entire network within a few seconds [3]. Received transactions are maintained in a node's own local memory pool (*Mempool*). Here, transactions remain in limbo until confirmed and included in a block; once a transaction is included in a block, a node removes the transaction from its Mempool. Although a node tends to maintain unconfirmed transactions for a very long period of time, memory pressure may cause a node to evict old entries from the Mempool if it grows sufficiently large.

Nodes also maintain an unspent transaction output set (UTXO) to easily verify inputs to newly received transactions. Therefore, an increase in the UTXO adds memory pressure on nodes which currently hold the UTXO set in RAM. Unlike the Mempool, memory pressure on the UTXO set cannot be relieved by eviction, but requires changing the node's implementation.

In the reference implementation, a Bitcoin miner calculates a priority and uses this to determine which transactions to include in the block. To calculate transaction priority (P), the node considers all inputs to the transaction as well as its size. P is defined in Bitcoin as $\sum_{i=0}^{n}(value_i \times age_i) \div S$, where n is the number of inputs to the transaction, $value$ is the value of input i (in Satoshis[1]), age is defined as the difference between the current block's height and the input's block height, and S is the transaction's size. The value of P determines a transaction's fate; there are three possibilities:

1. Include transactions in the high-priority section of a block (50 KB); no transaction fee is necessary. The following conditions must be satisfied, the transaction must be:
   - smaller than 1 KB
   - all output values are at least 0.01 BTC
   - P is high as determined by $value_i$ and age_i
2. Transactions that pay fees are prioritized by highest mBTC per KB.
3. The remaining transactions are maintained in the Mempool until one of the two conditions above is satisfied.

In the latter case, age is the determining factor for P since everything else is constant. It's of particular note that miners prioritize for higher fees.

2.1 DoS Targets Inherent in Bitcoin

Spam can be detrimental to the Bitcoin network by outcompeting legitimate transactions for inclusion in a block, delaying other transactions. We define the following types of spam:

1. **Fan-out:** Transactions that split a few inputs into many outputs occupy space in the blocks and also increase the UTXO set.
2. **Fan-in:** Transactions which absorb a large number of inputs reduce the UTXO set but still occupy substantial space in the blocks.
3. **Dust output:** Transactions that create very small "dust" outputs convey a trivially small amount of value but occupy the same amount of resources in the Bitcoin network.

The spam campaigns in the "stress test" target one or more aspects of the Bitcoin environment, including the block size limit, the UTXO set, and the computational cost for verification. All these limited resources represent potential targets.

The primary publicly stated motivation behind the stress test campaign was to provide a justification for raising the Bitcoin block size limit before organic

---

[1] 1 Satoshi = 10^{-8} bitcoins. We follow the convention of referring to the protocol as *Bitcoin*, the currency and its units as *bitcoin* or BTC.

demand limits the ability of Bitcoin to process payments. The current Bitcoin block size of 1 MB globally supports less than 3 Bitcoin transactions per second. Since this is three orders of magnitude lower than Visa's sustained rate of 150M transactions per day (and peak processing ability of 24,000 transactions per second) [10], it's clear that the current Bitcoin payment processing is insufficient to meet the ambitions of the Bitcoin community. The public intent was to demonstrate the impact of this limit by squeezing out normal transactions.

Raising the block size, however, opens up a different DoS vulnerability: a long term growth DoS on the Blockchain itself. Since the Blockchain records all previous transactions, an attacker could perform low fee transactions simply to consume space. Thus if Bitcoin raised the block limit to 20 MB, and an attacker can cheaply consume 10 MB of data per block, this causes the Blockchain to increase in size by half a terabyte a year.

Since valid transactions can only spend unspent outputs, most full Bitcoin nodes keep the UTXO set in memory to speed transaction validation. The memory requirements for the UTXO set are solely based on the number of unspent outputs, so the inclusion of dust outputs in the stress test adds memory pressure to the UTXO set. A better designed Bitcoin node should not have this vulnerability.

Another DoS attack occurred on October 7th and 8th, which also put a significant amount of pressure on the Mempool memory, raising the Mempool to nearly a GB, with a transaction backlog of nearly a week. Since there are a large number of nodes running on Raspberry Pi and other constrained systems, this large Mempool managed to crash over 10 % of all Bitcoin nodes[2]. Most of the spam itself, however, was of low priority. Such spam does not put pressure on block inclusion, but neither does it cost the spammer any bitcoins; transactions that are never confirmed do not incur a cost for the sender.

An inadvertent CPU DoS occurred due to a mining-pool's "cleanup" block, a single 1 MB transaction that served to remove a massive number of unspent transactions sent to crackable "Brain wallet" addresses (which use a passphrase, instead of private keys, to create Bitcoin addresses and spend bitcoins). Other nodes required substantial CPU time to validate this block, as the current implementation required $O(n^2)$ time to validate a transaction. There may be other CPU DoS possibilities inherent in the Bitcoin protocol that attackers can exploit.

Another DoS is inherent in "transaction malleability". Someone can take a valid transaction, permute it so it has a different *txid*, and broadcast that modified transaction to the network. If the attacker's transaction is accepted into the blockchain, this can disrupt wallet services, hardware wallets, and other systems tracking *txids* to determine when a transaction commits to the blockchain. Recently, an attacker performed this DoS "because I am able to do it."[3]

Finally, a later (failed) spam campaign attempted to flood the network with invalid transactions, perhaps intending either a traffic DoS or a CPU DoS. The

---

[2] https://www.reddit.com/r/Bitcoin/comments/3ny3tw/with_a_1gb_mempool_1000_n odes_are_now_down.

[3] https://bitcointalk.org/index.php?topic=1198032.msg12579271.

"money drop", a public release of private keys by one of the purported instigators of the stress test, seems intended to cause a big race which would cause a large number of "double-spend" transactions. This did not produce a meaningful disruption of the network, although it was probably intended to introduce computational load.

One aspect not encountered during the stress test was the effect of filtering valid but spammy transactions. The introduction of spam filters, if an unknown attacker continued a longer term DoS attempt, could in itself be a DoS. If the attacker adapts to the filters, eventually the filters will either fail to stop the spam or incur false positives. Even a small false positive rate might be disruptive: could a payment network tolerate a 1–2 % transaction failure rate due to spam filters?

3 Data Collection

In our study, we set up a server connected to a public-facing network. We installed Bitcoin Core 0.11 and kept it running between June 19 and September 23, 2015. We collected three main data sets using Bitcoin daemon's JSON-RPC interface.

1. Bitcoin Blockchain: On September 23, we downloaded the entire blockchain using the `getblock` and `getrawtransaction` methods. This returned details for all blocks and transactions, such as the timestamps of blocks, the timestamps at which we received the transactions, the number of transaction inputs and outputs, as well as the input and output amount. We stored the data as plain-text JSON strings. As a result, the total data size is 350 GB.

2. Mempool: Between June 19 and September 23, the `getrawMempool` method was invoked every minute. This returned a list of unconfirmed *txid*s currently in the Mempool. These would be either committed to the blockchain or later discarded by the P2P network. We saved this list of *txid*s, along with the timestamp of the RPC call, on the Hadoop file system. During this period, we captured 12 million distinct *txid*s in the Mempool, which amounts to 250 GB of plain-text data.

3. Unconfirmed transactions: For every unconfirmed transaction that we had obtained above, we *immediately* looked up the transaction details using the `getrawtransaction` method, since the Mempool could discard the transaction any moment. To optimize for speed and storage, we ignored transactions that we had previously seen. Finally, we saved all the transaction details, along with the data collection timestamp, on Hadoop. Between June 19 and September 23, we captured 1.3 TB of unconfirmed transactions in plain text.

The total size of the data collected is 2 TB, which we saved as plain-text JSON strings on the Hadoop file system and analyzed with Spark. We summarize our data sets in Table 1.

As we collected data using only a single node, our perspective of the P2P network—and thus the transactions in the Mempool—is potentially biased. In

Table 1. Data sets. All data sets cover a period between June 19 and September 23.

Data	Period	Size
Blockchain	Between Jan 9, 2009 and Sept 23, 2015	350 GB
Memory pool	Between June 19 and Sept 23, 2015	250 GB
Unconfirmed transactions	Between June 19 and Sept 23, 2015	1.3 TB

particular, network propagation takes time. For transactions in the Mempool, the timestamps that we observed may be later than the originating timestamps. Furthermore, whether a transaction is relayed is up to individual nodes. A transaction created a few hops away is not guaranteed to reach our node. It is, however, beyond the scope of this paper to adjust for such biases. We assume that our observation of the network is largely consistent with the rest of the network.

4   Spam Clustering

We use an unsupervised machine learning method, k-means clustering, to find similarities and evaluate our findings. This is not necessarily a perfect filter, but as we manually verify, this does efficiently detect the spam transactions in the "stress test".

To use k-means clustering, we create a multi-dimensional vector representing features of a Bitcoin transaction. We include in Table 2 the list of features and follow up with defining features that were not previously discussed.

Table 2. Transaction features

Feature	Notation	Description
Inputs	I	Number of inputs
Outputs	O	Number of outputs
Ratio	R	$I \div O$
Priority	P	Value-weighted measurement
Size	S	Size (bytes)
Size and ratio	$S \times R$	Emphasize fan-in and fan-out
Fees	F	Value of unclaimed outputs
Coin days destroyed	CDD	Coin age and spending velocity
Value	V	Total output value
Fees to values ratio	$F \div V$	Emphasize fee differences

R is necessary to highlight the difference between fan-in and fan-out transactions. We further highlight this difference by multiplying the size of the transaction by its ratio (otherwise, transactions with clear differences in R are clustered together based on similarities in S). We include another property to highlight the velocity of spending bitcoins represented as CDD^4. This feature gives more weight to older coins, and can be calculated as $\sum_{i=0}^{n}(value_i \times age_i)$. Unlike P, CDD does not consider S, age is measured in number of days rather than blocks (an estimate of 144 blocks are produced each day), and $value$ is in bitcoins.

4.1   Methodology

Since spam campaigns may not link transactions and addresses together, parsing the blockchain to look for linked transactions might be a futile process. Our approach is different: we cluster transactions based on their motifs (trends in the Bitcoin network), and disregard transactions' identifying information (output addresses, *txid*, etc.). Our main assumptions at this stage echo those required for machine learning algorithms: a pattern exists, we cannot mathematically point out differences in patterns (without data visibility), and we have a large trove of data to show the patterns exist. We assume motifs do exist because spam requires construction in-bulk to have a measurable effect on the network. Thus spammers naturally create large numbers of transactions that "look similar". We also expect that such groups of transactions may have different motifs compared with normal Bitcoin behavior, since spammers want to minimize the cost and maximize the impact, producing different types of transactions (e.g. very high fan-out or dust output) that particularly stress the network.

What we seek is a high-level interpretation of the data into distinct clusters that we can then use to label transactions as spam and validate our results. Thus, to investigate our main goal of identifying spam motifs, we consider the entire Bitcoin network as an entity, rather than analyzing features of a transaction independently from network norms. The latter process relies heavily on what features should be considered to identify spam, which might assign more weight to some features while disregarding others that are more influential.

We use k-means clustering, as provided in Spark's machine learning library (`MLlib`). k-means clustering is a type of machine learning algorithm for unsupervised learning. This algorithm is particularly useful to cluster similar data together when it is non-trivial to define *similarity* using the unlabeled data. Similarity of vectorized data is determined using k-means by minimizing the Within-Cluster Sum of Squares (WCSS); the data is matched to the cluster centroid with the closest mean. The following equation is used to iterate over the data to get optimal cluster centroids in order to minimize WCSS: $min \sum_{i=1}^{k} \sum_{x \in S_i}^{n} \|x - \mu_i\|^2$, where k is the number of clusters, x is the data element (in vector form), S_i is the set containing n elements, and μ_i is the mean of S_i (i.e. the mean of all the elements in vector form that are contained in S_i).

To reproduce the results discussed in this paper, the following properties of k-means must be considered: the number of clusters k was set to 10, the number of `maxIterations` was set to 100, and `initializationMode` was set to `random`. The silhouette coefficient measures the homogeneity of the data in a cluster.

---

[4] This feature is used by Bitcoin block explorers, see for example: https://blockr.io.

This is performed by measuring the average dissimilarity (defined in terms of distance between data elements) between a given element within its cluster, and comparing the result with the average dissimilarity between that same element and elements of another cluster considered to be the next best-fit. However, in our case, our aim is to show general transaction motifs, rather than to show detailed transaction differences or find anomalies. We arrive at $k = 10$ after testing multiple values for k to show enough visibility of transaction patterns. If we choose $k = 11$ for example, we obtain a new cluster where the average of transaction outputs is 8 rather than 11 (as shown in cluster 9 in Table 3). Instead, we accept that the clustering algorithm groups these transactions together in cluster 9, given that they are similar in other features. Conversely, with $k < 10$, clusters contain transactions that differ in most of their features; this does not enable us to inspect the clusters to easily determine which of them fit our definitions of spam. With $k = 10$, we see the "outliers" visible in a dedicated cluster (cluster 8 in Table 3), whereas with $k < 10$ these outliers are included in other clusters that do not match well.

The initial step for processing data was weeding out some transactions that alter the clustering results. To set a starting point, we create two checks to filter transactions. First, we check if the transaction creates dust output (we explain this check in details later). The second check determines if the transaction's fan-out ratio is unusual (a threshold is set at 0.3). The rationale for these two checks is as follows: If a fan-in transaction creates dust output, then it qualifies as spam, otherwise it is minimizing the set of UTXOs that must be maintained to verify transactions. Moreover, if a fan-out is unusual, this is enough to qualify a transaction for clustering, and we later determine if the transaction is spam by inspecting clustering results, and checking for dust outputs in clusters that seem to contain normal transactions.

We analyze confirmed transactions that occurred between June 24th and July 17th, 2015. The total number of transactions in this epoch is 3,321,429. To obtain k-means clusters, we perform k-means training on all transactions that were confirmed during the July spam campaign epoch, that occurred between July 7th and 17th, the total number of transactions in this training epoch is 1,645,667. Using the cluster centroids from the spam epoch, we analyze the pre-spam epoch to validate our results.

4.2   Results and Motifs

We now discuss motifs found in more than 1.6M transactions that occurred during the spam epoch. Table 3 shows each cluster centroid's features. As discussed earlier, these centroids are the result of optimizing WCSS, and are represented as the means of the values of all transactions in the corresponding cluster. Table 4 shows the standard deviation of the cluster centroids[5].

---

[5] The notation used in the tables corresponds to the notation used for the transaction features defined earlier. Note that both tables include rounded values, while attempting to maintain distinctions for small values with the minimum amount of rounding necessary. For better presentation, we omit some features.

Table 3. Cluster centroids (*confirmed transactions*)

C	TXs	I	O	R	P	S	F	CDD	V
0	48K	1.35	46	0.06	0.74	1.8K	0.0004	0.195	4.06
1	28	4.4K	1	4.4K	0.001	645K	0.04	0.06	0.0
2	896	106	1	103	0.17	16K	0.001	0.34	0.13
3	20	1.1K	1	1.1K	0.0008	162K	0.01	0.012	0.0
4	13.5K	31	1	31	0.04	4.7K	0.0002	0.02	0.006
5	16	1.4	13	0.15	535K	668	0.0004	25K	1K
6	9.5K	20	17	19	0.4	3.5K	0.0004	0.14	1.4
7	425K	1.1	2	0.8	1	224	0.0001	0.022	1.43
8	2	1	19	0.05	136M	787	0.0002	740K	3K
9	117K	1.2	11	0.14	72.43	561	0.0002	2.7	6.5

Table 4. Standard deviation of selected features (*confirmed transactions*)

C	I	O	R	P	S	F	CDD	V
0	4	104	0.77	27	3.6	0.002	17	40
1	1.2K	0	1.2K	0	176	0.012	0.05	0
2	43	0.2	35	2	6	0.0005	4	1.8
3	403	0	403	0	60	0.004	0.02	0
4	8	0.1	8	0.8	1.2	0.0002	0.5	0.24
5	1	7	0.1	0.35M	0.38	0.0001	26K	1.2K
6	2	0.4	2	1.65	0.35	0.0002	0.5	4
7	0.4	0.9	0.4	9	0.1	0.0002	0.2	15
8	0.0	0.5	0	3M	0.02	0	0.2M	748
9	0.5	6	0.2	2K	0.2	0.9μ	177	70

1. **Fan-in. Clusters 2 and 4** include about 14K fan-in transactions. The pattern is distinct: large I and one O (in rare cases O is for two addresses). The transactions vary in S due to variations in I, and a notable distinction is in CDD. Cluster 2 includes larger values for CDD, which indicates that the inputs are not used for rapid transfer of value. Moreover, these transactions may not have been used as spam *per se*, but are rather part of tumblers or mixers where a large number of inputs are collated into single outputs and the chain continues, in order to mix coins together and obtain relatively better privacy. These transactions involve long chains of many inputs to a single address, the last address then transfers funds to multiple outputs in fan-out transactions, and so on. A large number of fan-in transactions impact the Mempool, but minimize the UTXO set.

2. **Fan-out.** The fan-out pattern involves one or two addresses sending funds to many addresses, as shown in **Clusters 0, 5, 8 and 9**; the total number of transactions in these clusters is about 165K. These transactions increase the UTXO set. This pattern was dominant in the clustering results; it resulted in multiple clusters for fan-out transactions that differ in features other than R. A low value for CDD indicates a fast movement of coins. Note that Cluster 0 includes transactions that have a single address sending small amounts to more than 3K addresses.

3. **Unable-to-decode.** With 425K transactions, **Cluster 7** includes the largest number of transactions. The distinct feature of most of these transactions is a one-to-one mapping: one address sending to a single output that cannot be decoded. Moreover, the fees paid for these transactions (which are collected by miners since the output cannot be decoded) equal the default fee value of 0.1 mBTC per KB. Another feature of this cluster is the zero value for CDD (and low P), which indicates rapid movement of bitcoins.

4. **Dust.** The final motif of the analyzed spam campaign is the dust transactions we had previously discussed. **Cluster 7** contains non-spam transactions; normal transactions are matched to this cluster since they look similar to unable-to-decode transactions (low values for most features). It is not straightforward to visually inspect the cluster samples and determine if they are indeed spam. Therefore, we parse the transactions in this cluster to determine which of them fit our definition of dust spam. We explain in a later section how we parse the results to find dust spam transactions.

5. **UTXO cleanup. Clusters 1 and 3** include 'clean-up' transactions, created by miners to collate spam transactions to minimize the UTXO, thereby decreasing the spam impact on the network. The output addresses value of these transactions may be zero, meaning that all the inputs are collected as fees by the miner who includes the transaction in a block. Clean-up transactions include 'Brain wallet' addresses (discussed earlier). These two clusters are not categorized as spam, and the transactions are a consequence of the spam campaign. The number of inputs to these transactions range between 1K and 5K (resulting in a large standard deviation).

Note that clusters 5 and 8 contain few transactions due to their unusually high P. Cluster 8, which contains only two transactions, is indeed interesting and earns its unique cluster: along with high P, the values of these transactions are around 2,500 and 3,995 bitcoins (that is almost \$0.6M and \$0.96M in USD respectively). Both transactions include a generous fee of 0.002 BTC.

In summary **Clusters 0, 2, 4, 6, 7, and 9** correspond to our definition of Bitcoin spam, including dust transactions and unusual ratios, while clusters 1 and 3 are a consequence of spam and not spam motifs.

4.3 Validation

It is important to note that we lack an external source to create ground truth for our results. Without a labeled data set, or a third-party spam list, we cannot measure the clustering results to be spam more accurately than matching the results to our definitions of spam.

In order to find dust transactions, we check if P is low (less than 57M) and whether the transaction creates any outputs of 0.1 mBTC (about \$0.02), which is the default fee value. We consider this a conservative estimate of the dust transactions involved in the spam campaign, and at the same time we consider the 0.01 BTC normally involved in dust checks to be too large.

We also applied clustering to transactions that occurred in the pre-spam epoch, between June 24th and July 7th (after filtering for dust and unusual ratios). The results are discussed in the next section, where we see a difference in the intensity of motifs before and during the spam epoch. This validates our clustering results: we find that the centroids obtained from training k-means, using the spam epoch data, can also detect spam patterns in non-spam epochs.

5   Impact on Bitcoin

We now describe the effects of spam campaigns on the Bitcoin network—especially on users who send non-spam transactions, as well as the miners. For the users, we measure the change in transaction fees and transaction delays (i.e. the time between when we first observe a transaction in the Mempool and when the transaction is committed to the blockchain). A large amount of spam is likely to increase the backlog of unconfirmed transactions. As a result, transactions are delayed for longer time periods. With more intense competition, senders pay higher fees, in the hope that their transactions will be included in blocks sooner. For the miners, we measure the corresponding increase in the block reward.

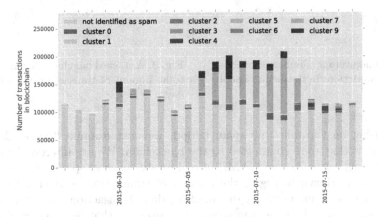

Fig. 1. A stacked bar chart that shows the number of transactions per day in the blockchain. Note that the spam period is from July 7th to 17th.

Figure 1 shows the clustering results in the non-spam and spam epochs. Note that in the pre-spam epoch (before July 7th), clustering results show

Cluster 1 transactions (UTXO-cleanup motif). This does not mean that miners were cleaning up spam; these transactions are similar to UTXO-cleanup transactions in terms of high I and low O, and similar P values.

To highlight periods of the spam campaign, we measure the number of unconfirmed transactions in the Mempool, which indicates the amount of backlog in the network. Every minute, we take a snapshot of the Mempool and count the number of unconfirmed transactions. We take the average on a daily basis and plot the result in Fig. 2.

Each major spike in the graph refers to a period of significant backlog. The first spike, which happened between July 7th and 17th, corresponds to the spam campaign in our study. There are sporadic spikes between July and August, but we do not have sufficient insight on the cause. Finally, a spike appeared around September 13, when an anonymous group conducted another stress-test on the network with their "money drop" (as discussed earlier). As a result, a large number of transactions were created to compete for the free bitcoins, although only a few of them would be included in the blockchain eventually. Such a deluge of transactions caused the second backlog in Fig. 2. We do not, however, consider these transactions as spam.

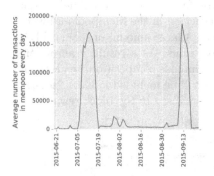

Fig. 2. The average number of unconfirmed transactions in the memory pool every day.

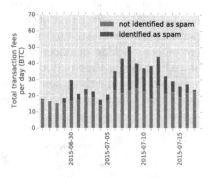

Fig. 3. A stacked bar chart showing the total amount of transaction fees every day.

Focusing on the mid-July spam period, we next examine the number of transactions that were committed to the blockchain. We are interested in how each block allocates its scarce 1 MB of real-estate space to spammers and non-spammers. As shown in Fig. 3, the number of transactions surged during the spam epoch. Between a quarter to half of the daily transactions have been identified as spam. As a baseline comparison, we also show that the number of spam transactions before the spam period is significantly lower, with the exception of June 30. Based on anecdotal evidence, some users were attempting to stress-test the Bitcoin network on a small scale, which resulted in a brief rise in spam.[6]

---

[6] http://motherboard.vice.com/read/wikileaks-is-now-a-target-in-the-massive-spam-attack-on-bitcoin.

For the non-spammers, the spam period was a time when both transaction fees and delays were higher than normal. We show the comparison in Figs. 4 and 5. On average, the delays in processing non-spam transactions increases by 7 times, from 0.33 to 2.67 hours. Likewise, the average non-spam transaction fees also surged, increasing from 45 to 68 Satoshis for every byte of transactions (or from $0.11 to $0.17 USD per kilobyte of transactions)—an uptick of 51 %.

While non-spammers suffered, miners slightly benefit from the fee hike. As shown in Fig. 3, miners were earning twice their normal fee-based revenue during the mid-July spam period, as compared with the non-spam period. However, even on days with maximum fees, the amount of extra mining income from fees was less than 1 % of the block reward (which is 25 BTC per block, and about 3,600 BTC per day). The total transaction fees that spam transactions paid amounted to 201 BTC (or about $49,000 USD) over a 10 day time period—a modest sum that caused a rather noticeable disruption to the network.

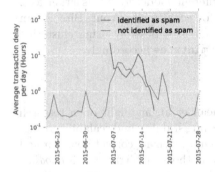 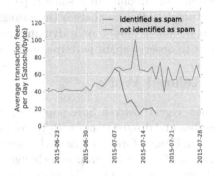

Fig. 4. Average transaction delay between when a transaction appears in the Mempool and when it is committed to the blockchain.

Fig. 5. Average transaction fees per transaction per day. Note that the fees are normalized against the size of each transaction.

6   Discussion

The spam campaign happened when the Bitcoin network is divided regarding a critical component of the protocol: the block size limit of 1 MB. The result was a recent fork between two camps: some want to raise the limit while others refuse to alter the rules set by Satoshi Nakamoto (Bitcoin's creator). We can speculate that the spammer was motivated to launch a DoS attack to demonstrate the fragility of Bitcoin's resilience if the block size limit is not raised. This is supported by an earlier spam campaign, where an online Bitcoin wallet service claimed responsibility under the pretext of "stress testing".

With regards to the methodology proposed in this paper, we do not suggest that this model can be used to prevent Bitcoin spam completely, nor should it be used as such. It was used to measure and analyze spam after the fact, without the spammers being aware that they are being measured. Spammers can learn from this paper what heuristics and features we used, to alter their motifs and adapt accordingly.

Although we used dust checks to validate our results, this is not a fool-proof measurement to accurately validate spam in Bitcoin. It is trivial to create a transaction that does not generate any dust outputs. However, if a transaction does not create dust, then the clustering algorithm matches that transaction to a cluster that highlights other features, particularly differences in ratio. We use dust validation when there is a possibility a cluster contains normal transactions. Since we defined unusual fan-out ratios to constitute spam transactions (and they are gathered in distinct clusters), along with our conservative measurement of dust, we believe that the results we had shown earlier provide a good estimate of the July spam campaign.

It is important to note that the July spam campaign on Bitcoin would be infeasible on altcoins since some deploy a different model for transaction fees. For example, Litecoin charges the `mintxfee` for *each* small output. Bitcoin can adopt a similar model, or a dynamic model for fees, possibly using clustering results to observe spam patterns, and change `mintxfee` accordingly.

7   Related Work

In their recent Bitcoin SoK paper [2], Bonneau et al. highlight open research questions and discuss issues with Bitcoin regarding stability and scalability, ranging from Bitcoin forks and network analysis to incentivizing correct behavior and adding resilience with proposed changes. The authors highlight *penny flooding*, as discussed in [8], which is related to our discussion of dust transactions. In the Appendix of the extended version of their SoK paper, the authors discuss in more details Bitcoin's stability and transaction validity. The extended version includes a discussion outlining options to overcome the drawbacks of maintaining the entire UTXO to process new transactions: using a *statefile*, updated incrementally with new data, it is possible to more efficiently retrieve transactions for verification using a transaction's hash in $O(log\ M)$, where M is the number of unspent transactions. It also possible to further minimize the data structure required to validate transactions using hash-based authenticated data structures as proposed in [5].

Becker et al. [1] discuss the possibility of denying service to the Bitcoin network using a virtual protest: protestors join forces to collectively execute a DoS attack by overwhelming the network and depleting precious block space (these transactions are much larger than normal Bitcoin transactions). If a protest is ongoing, this can frustrate non-protestors and decrease faith in the resilience of Bitcoin to process transactions in a timely manner (Bitcoin's main features include processing payments in minutes, as well as low transaction fees). This virtual protest attack was labeled 'Occupy Bitcoin' by Kroll et al. [4].

Our clustering approach is different than previous work aiming to find patterns in Bitcoin: we strip away identifying information (such as *txid*, addresses, etc.), and cluster transaction features in order to determine patterns, rather than linking transactions together to de-anonymize users. For example, in [6], researchers cluster transactions based on determining shared authority properties, while using similar transaction features used in this research.

Other empirical research determining detrimental affects on the Bitcoin network measure the lifetime of Bitcoin exchanges [7], through analyzing daily transaction volumes and how exchange breaches affect survival time. Running a profitable exchange logically results in a more lucrative target, hence a breach is more likely which leads to the eventual shutdown of an exchange. Another approach is to parse online forums to obtain data indicators of possible attacks on the network, as was done in [11].

8 Conclusion

We have presented an empirical study of a spam based "stress test" DoS attack against Bitcoin. Using our clustering based approach we find that 385,256 (23.41 %) out of 1,645,667 total Bitcoin transactions were spam during a 10 day period at the peak of the spam campaign. We also show that this attack had a negative impact on non-spam transactions, increasing average fees by 51 % (from 45 to 68 Satoshis/byte) and processing delay by 7 times (from 0.33 to 2.67 hours). This shows that an adversary who is willing to expand modest amounts of bitcoin (at least $49,000 USD), to pay higher fees, can DoS Bitcoin. Follow up DoS attacks against Bitcoin have used other methods, such as "money drops", and transaction malleability to degrade the operation of Bitcoin. We point out that changes to Bitcoin's minimum fees could mitigate some of the spam motifs we witnessed. Our results show that exploration into Bitcoin transaction spam filtering techniques, and other Bitcoin DoS mitigation approaches, merit further investigation.

Acknowledgements. This work was supported by US National Science Foundation grant CNS-1619620.

References

1. Becker, J., Breuker, D., Heide, T., Holler, J., Rauer, H.P., Böhme, R.: Can we afford integrity by proof-of-work? Scenarios inspired by the Bitcoin currency. In: Böhme, R. (ed.) The Economics of Information Security and Privacy, pp. 135–156. Springer, Heidelberg (2013)
2. Bonneau, J., Miller, A., Clark, J., Narayanan, A., Kroll, J.A., Felten, E.W.: SoK: Research perspectives and challenges for Bitcoin and cryptocurrencies. In: IEEE Symposium on Security and Privacy (2015)
3. Decker, C., Wattenhofer, R.: Information propagation in the Bitcoin network. In: IEEE Thirteenth International Conference on Peer-to-Peer Computing (P2P), pp. 1–10 (2013)
4. Kroll, J.A., Davey, I.C., Felten, E.W.: The economics of Bitcoin mining, or Bitcoin in the presence of adversaries. In: Proceedings of WEIS 2013 (2013)

5. Maxwell, G.: Merkle tree of open transactions for lite mode? bitcointalk.org (2011)
6. Meiklejohn, S., Pomarole, M., Jordan, G., Levchenko, K., McCoy, D., Voelker, G.M., Savage, S.: A fistful of Bitcoins: characterizing payments among men with no names. In: Proceedings of the Conference on Internet Measurement Conference, pp. 127–140. ACM (2013)
7. Moore, T., Christin, N.: Beware the middleman: empirical analysis of Bitcoin-exchange risk. In: Sadeghi, A.-R. (ed.) FC 2013. LNCS, vol. 7859, pp. 25–33. Springer, Heidelberg (2013)
8. Möser, M., Böhme, R.: Trends, tips, tolls: a longitudinal study of Bitcoin transaction fees. In: Brenner, M., Christin, N., Johnson, B., Rohloff, K. (eds.) FC 2015 Workshops. LNCS, vol. 8976, pp. 19–33. Springer, Heidelberg (2015)
9. Nakamoto, S.: Bitcoin: a peer-to-peer electronic cash system. Consulted 1(2012), 28 (2008)
10. Trillo, M.: Stress Test Prepares VisaNet for the Most Wonderful Time of the Year (2013). http://www.visa.com/blogarchives/us/2013/10/10/stress-test-prepares-visanet-for-the-most-wonderful-time-of-the-year/index.html
11. Vasek, M., Thornton, M., Moore, T.: Empirical analysis of denial-of-service attacks in the Bitcoin ecosystem. In: Böhme, R., Brenner, M., Moore, T., Smith, M. (eds.) FC 2014 Workshops. LNCS, vol. 8438, pp. 57–71. Springer, Heidelberg (2014)

Why Buy When You Can Rent?

Bribery Attacks on Bitcoin-Style Consensus

Joseph Bonneau[✉]

Stanford University and Electronic Frontier Foundation, Stanford, USA
jbonneau@gmail.com

Abstract. The Bitcoin cryptocurrency introduced a novel distributed consensus mechanism relying on economic incentives. While a coalition controlling a majority of computational power may undermine the system, for example by double-spending funds, it is often assumed it would be incentivized not to attack to protect its long-term stake in the health of the currency. We show how an attacker might purchase mining power (perhaps at a cost premium) for a short duration via bribery. Indeed, bribery can even be performed in-band with the system itself enforcing the bribe. A bribing attacker would not have the same concerns about the long-term health of the system, as their majority control is inherently short-lived. New modeling assumptions are needed to explain why such attacks have not been observed in practice. The need for all miners to avoid short-term profits by accepting bribes further suggests a potential tragedy of the commons which has not yet been analyzed.

1 Introduction

Bitcoin [6], launched as a cryptocurrency in 2009, has rocketed to popularity with a monetary base nominally worth over US\$6 billion at the time of this writing. Any cryptocurrency must prevent double-spending. Bitcoin relies on a public, distributed ledger called the blockchain which logs all transactions to ensure that funds may only be spent once. Bitcoin uses a computational puzzle system (often called "proof-of-work"[1]) to maintain consensus on this ledger and continually add new *blocks* of transactions.

The scheme is frequently claimed to be *incentive-compatible* in that stability is maintained assuming miners behave "rationally", though this was not formally defined (let alone proved) in the system's original design [6] and does not have a consistently agreed-upon definition [1]. A key assumption, dating to Nakamoto's original white paper [6], is that any party controlling a majority of mining capacity is likely to maintain significant capacity and hence has a large expected future revenue stream. The risk of compromising this earning potential is believed to discourage any attacks which may harm Bitcoin's exchange rate. Our contribution is to show that this assumption might fail in the case that a miner *temporarily* obtains a majority of mining power through bribery. Such a

---

[1] Bitcoin's mining puzzle is not a strict *proof-of-work* scheme but a probabilistic one.

© International Financial Cryptography Association 2016
J. Clark et al. (Eds.): FC 2016 Workshops, LNCS 9604, pp. 19–26, 2016.
DOI: 10.1007/978-3-662-53357-4_2

miner would know this majority to be fleeting and hence would not have future earnings to protect. There are plausible assumptions under which this attack is still not feasible or at least not lucrative, but they are much stronger than those used thus far to argue that Bitcoin is incentive compatible.

2   Renting Mining Capacity

There are multiple ways in which an attacker might obtain a *temporary majority* of mining capacity not through the traditional route of buying and owning mining power, but by renting this capacity from the nominal owners. We will discuss three such scenarios in turn, some are known in Bitcoin folklore but none has been explicitly discussed in formal Bitcoin research. Note that in every scenario, the attacker will have to pay some premium ϵ to rent mining capacity; the attacker would expect to recoup this through double-spending profits.

2.1   Out-of-Band Payment

The simplest mechanism is to directly pay the owners of mining capacity to work on blocks of the attacker's choosing. This payment may be in bitcoins or any outside (state) currency. Multiple online "cloud mining exchange" services have arisen in the past year which allow exactly that, including cex.io, pow88.com, and bitfinex.com. Relatively little has been published on the extent or efficacy of such mining exchange services, although they typically charge a premium of up to $\epsilon = 3\%$ over the expected earning capacity of rented mining power.

The downside of this arrangement is it lacks enforcement: a miner can accept payment and then mine independently for its own benefit. Both sides need to trust each other or a third-party exchange to enforce their agreement. Because of the lack of built-in trust, it is also difficult for the attacker to bribe anonymously.

2.2   Negative-Fee Mining Pool

A second approach is to establish a mining pool paying an above-market return. Mining pools exist to allow miners to share risk. Participants try to find blocks paying rewards to the pool manager, who then disburses the profits amongst members. Accounting is done by reporting *shares* or near-blocks. For example, if the current probability of finding a Bitcoin block is 2^{-d} (that is, the block's hash must begin with at least d zero bits), participants will report any blocks found with a hash starting with $s < d$ zero bits, drastically lowering the variance in earnings by the participants as many more shares will be found than blocks.

Popular mining pools now offer a "0 % fee" meaning that participants earn as much on expectation as they would by mining solo. That is, for a block reward is B miners in a 0 %-fee pool will earn $B \cdot 2^{s-d}$ per share. There is no technical reason why an attacker can't start a pool offering a *negative fee*, that is, $(1 + \epsilon)B \cdot 2^{s-d}$ per share reported. Because such a pool would lose money on expectation, no honest pool should be able to match this reward. The larger the negative fee, the greater the interest such a pool should attract.

This setup has the advantage for the attacker of reducing trust-the accounting mechanism ensures they will only pay for legitimate mining work.[2] Alert miners would still have to trust the attacker to pay. However, this trust can be incrementally established as the attacker pays for valid shares, making the setup relatively low-risk for miners. Miners would of course know they were joining an attack pool attempting to double-spend which could harm them via an exchange rate crash, though as we will discuss this would require coordinated action by the miners to ensure no miners are tempted to defect and profit from the attack.

An open question is how "sticky" miner preferences are or how quickly they would move in practice to a pool offering a better return.

2.3   In-Band Payment via Forking

Finally, an attacker could attempt to bribe through Bitcoin itself by creating a fork containing bribe money freely available to any miners adopting the fork. Such an attacker would begin with a large pool of funds in address K_0 as of block B_{i-1}. The attacker would then broadcast a transaction moving all of these funds to address K_1 and wait for it to be included in block B_i. The attacker would then try to introduce a fork[3] by finding an alternate block B_i' (possibly using another bribery method), in which they would include a transaction moving the funds from K_0 into another address $K_1' \neq K_1$. Note that this transaction would conflict with the transaction in block B_i moving the same funds to K_0.

Once this fork occurs, the attacker broadcasts a transaction sending the funds from K_1' to a series of m addresses $K_2^1, \ldots, K_2^m$. Each address K_m^j is a script enabling anybody to claim the funds as of block[4] $i + j$, ensuring that miner finding the jth block in the fork can claim the funds in address K_m^j.

The attacker's fork of the blockchain now contains freely available bribe money as desired, incentivizing miners to forgo mining on the current longest branch in exchange for potentially higher rewards. There are several variants of this attack, for example simply broadcasting a stream of time-locked transactions paying a high fee on the attacker's branch, but this version is probably best as it commits the attacker to a fixed sequence of bribes in advance.

Note that if the attacker's fork never overtakes the main branch, this bribe money will not be valid and the miners will be left with nothing. Put another way, the attacker only pays if the attack succeeds. Thus, this method inherently transfers risk from the attacker to the miners accepting bribes.

---

[2] An issue remains that pool participants could report shares but withhold valid blocks. This is an issue for all mining pools and has been analyzed in the context of attacks between mining pools [2–4], however it is not profitable for individuals.

[3] If the attacker's attempt to introduce a fork fails and another block is found on the main chain, they can move the funds from address K_1 again. By cycling these funds every block they can ensure their fork is arbitrarily close to the longest chain.

[4] This script would be achieved using a single OP_CHECK_LOCK_TIME_VERIFY command, which has been standard in Bitcoin since mid-2015.

In practice, most miners today run default node software which would ignore any such attack branch completely. Even if all miners were able to spot the attempted branch and detect the additional available bribe money, they would still be taking a risk by participating in the attack. Unlike the mining pool approach or direct payment, participating miners would not be paid if the attack fails. The attacker could try to accommodate this by making a larger proportion of the bribery money available in earlier blocks when it is less clear the attack will succeed. Still, it remains unclear how much of a risk premium the attacker would have to pay with this method to attract significant interest.

3   Bribery Attacks

Given the above methods for renting mining capacity, we can assume our attacker is able to rent an arbitrary amount of capacity at a cost of $\approx \epsilon \cdot B$ per block mined, where B is the mining reward for one block. Note that ϵ might vary based on the attack method and how deep the attempted fork is.

Given this capability, a bribery attack is straightforward: the attacker publishes a transaction T in block B_i, waits until k follow-up blocks have been published so that some irreversible action is taken as a result of T, introduces a new block B_i' with a conflicting transaction T', and then rents sufficient capacity (at least a majority of the network) to extend the branch containing B_i' until it becomes the longest branch. The attacker has double-spent the funds in transactions T and can potentially earn a profit equal to the entire value of T.

In a very simple model, such an attack would offer profits bound only by the quantity of currency in circulation. Assuming there is no inherent limit on the size of transactions or special security restrictions for large transactions, the size of T is unbounded. The attacker's cost is $k \cdot \epsilon \cdot B$, but with perfectly rational miners ϵ should trend towards zero as accepting any bribe would be more profitable for miners than mining directly. Therefore, in the simplest model the attacker's benefits could be unbounded and costs would a small constant, making the attack infinitely profitable.

3.1   Counter-Bribing by Miners

In the simple model above, there is no inherent lower limit to the amount the attacker must pay. If miners detect that this attack is occurring, however, miners who have already mined (and tentatively received mining rewards) for the current longest branch would be incentivized to oppose the attacker by *counter-bribing* to encourage miners to continue building on the current longest chain to ensure their mining rewards don't disappear.

If the attacker is attempting to institute a k-block fork, this would mean some miners are poised to lose (at least) $k \cdot B$ if the attack succeeds. They might be willing to spend nearly all of this money to oppose the attacker, as it would disappear if the attack succeeds. In this scenario, the attacker would need to pay at least $k \cdot B$ in bribes (instead of $k \cdot \epsilon \cdot B$ in the case of no counter-bribing). The attack may still be infinitely profitable as long as the amount T which the attacker stands to gain is unbounded while mining rewards are capped.

Limiting the attack requires offering larger mining rewards to ensure a high-incentive for counter-bribing, but this is likely impractical. Preventing the attack would require that the block reward B for each block was at least V, where V is the total amount transacted in each block (all of which could be funds the attacker is attempting to double spend). This would effectively mean a transaction fee rate of 50 % (paid through inflation), making the currency impractical.

4 Analysis of Mitigating Factors

Despite the apparently lucrative opportunity to perform a bribery attack, there is no evidence that this has ever been seriously attempted. We rule out explanations based on "good will" or lack of motivation given the track record of significant thefts of Bitcoin in practice [5]. We instead consider a number of factors which may hinder this attack in practice, which we will outline in rough order from least to most plausible. None of these explanations is completely satisfactory and all represent stronger assumptions than have previous been made when arguing that Bitcoin-style consensus is incentive-compatible.

4.1 Miners May Be Too Simplistic to Recognize or Accept Bribes

Today, it might not be possible to rent any significant mining capacity through bribes as a potentially large portion of miners are not technically capable of running any algorithm besides the default. They may be unwilling or unable to change pools even at the promise of higher fees, unable to rent their capacity on a mining exchange, or unable to detect in-band bribes. This mitigation goes against the very notion of incentive compatibility, which ensures the system is stable assuming miners behave rationally. Furthermore, as miners become more professional and technically capable this is likely to be less true in practice.

4.2 The Attack Requires Significant Capital and Risk-Tolerance

Profiting from the attack requires creating a very large transaction T. The attacker needs this capital available up front and, while the attacker won't necessarily lose the value of T if the attack fails, the bribes may not be recovered if the attack fails.[5] While this may be a practical limitation for many attackers, it appears to be a poor assumption to build into a mathematical model of Bitcoin.

4.3 Profit from Double-Spends May Not Be Frictionless or Boundless

Our analysis assumed the attacker could turn the opportunity to double-spend into "pure" profit of an unlimited amount. Double-spending in Bitcoin doesn't

---

[5] As mentioned in Sect. 2.3, bribers placed in band will not be at risk if the attack fails, though this method may be the most difficult to execute.

actually create additional currency, it simply gives an attacker the opportunity to temporarily deceive some other party into believing they have received funds which will later be taken back. Profiting from this capability requires a counterparty the attacker can swindle that will immediately (after k blocks of confirmation) transfer something of equal value to the attacker. In some scenarios (e.g. exchanges, mixing services), this might be an equal value of Bitcoin. In other cases, it might be physical goods whose shipment may be reversed.

Either way, in practice the attacker might not be able to double-spend without paying transaction fees to the counterparty, or may not be able to double-spend a sufficient amount to make the relative cost of bribes negligible. This seems a poor mitigation as it is relatively fragile and difficult to analyze. In any case, it probably only adds a small constant amount of overhead to the attack.

More practically, infinitely-sized double spends are of course not possible. Bounds exist both due to the limited amount of Bitcoin currency in existence and the amount that victims are willing to exchange. Thus, the profit potential is not infinite, although this is also an inadequate mitigation as in practice it is likely that profits from a double spend will be orders of magnitude higher than mining rewards (and hence the volume of bribes required).

4.4   Extra Confirmations for Large Transactions

Recipients may require more confirmations for larger transactions. This makes the attack more difficult because as the number of blocks in the attempted fork k increases, the attacker's bribery costs increase linearly. Unfortunately, the attack may make many smaller transactions simultaneously and attempt to double-spend all of them. Thus it appears impractical for this approach to have much impact. Furthermore it would require the confirmation time would need to grow linearly with the value of the transaction.

4.5   Counter-Bribing by the Intended Victim

In addition to counter-bribing by miners, the attacker's victim may be willing to counter-bribe to prevent the attack. Note that the attacker's profit is completely derived from the losses incurred by one or more specific parties. Assuming they detect the attack, they may be willing to spend significant money to fight back.

In general, any party receiving funds on the main chain but not on the attacker's branch may counter-bribe, but the attack can easily neutralize all non-targeted recipients by including their transactions on the attack branch as well. Therefore we only need to consider counter-bribing by the intended victim.

In the limit, they should be willing to spend up to the entire value of transaction T in counter-bribes, because if the attack succeeds they will lose this entire value. The attacker would then have to spend this same amount in bribes (plus ϵ), making the attack unprofitable.

This mitigation is undesirable as it significantly changes the security model of Bitcoin, with all parties receiving funds needing to scan for potential bribery attacks and be prepared to fight them off. It also implies recipients must be willing to effectively spend protection money (which miners would ultimately pocket) to protect their transactions' integrity.

4.6   Miners May Refuse to Help an Attack Against Bitcoin

The purpose of a bribery attack would be visible to any miners participating in it. It would also invariably damage the reputation of Bitcoin if successful. This is a very similar argument to the general argument that a 51 % attacker would be unwise to actually attack the network in practice: miners should be incentivized against accepting short-term bribery if it damages their long-term earning potential.

While this is the most plausible explanation, this suggests a looming tragedy of the commons, particularly in the case of a negative-fee mining pool. The security and reputation of Bitcoin (which maintain the strength of its exchange rate by attracting users) can be viewed as a *common good* shared by miners. All miners might recognize their long-term shared incentive is to resist joining the attacker's negative-fee pool which might damage Bitcoin's reputation. However, any miners who joined would immediately see their profits rise in this scenario, even if the attack failed, providing a direct incentive for miners to defect by accepting bribes to attack. SMiners generally have the capability to mine anonymously (by using new addresses in the coinbase transaction of any block they find), making it impractical to punish miners who defect and accept bribes without radically changing the protocol. This tragedy of the commons suggests it might be hard for small miners without effective political organization to prevent successful bribery attacks, whereas a monolithic majority miner is protecting its own self-interest by not attacking.

5   Concluding Remarks

We have outlined the possibility of a bribery attack on Bitcoin and discussed the potential implications. Bribery is possible in Bitcoin and indeed it can be facilitated in several surprising ways by the Bitcoin protocol, namely negative-fee mining pools and anybody-can-spend transactions. Requiring all miners to avoid short-term profits to protect the long-term health of the system appears to introduce a tragedy of the commons.

We do not claim this is currently a practical attack. Our aim was merely to demonstrate that, assuming this attack is not being observed because it is not practical, any model attempting to show that Bitcoin-style consensus is incentive-compatible must be strong enough to rule out such bribery attacks. From our initial analysis of possible new modeling assumptions, none seem highly desirable. This may put the security of Bitcoin's consensus protocol on weaker footing than previously believed.

References

1. Bonneau, J., Miller, A., Clark, J., Narayanan, A., Kroll, J.A., Felten, E.W.: Research perspectives and challenges for bitcoin and cryptocurrencies. In: 2015 IEEE Symposium on Security and Privacy, May 2015
2. Courtois, N.T., Bahack, L.: On subversive miner strategies and block withholding attack in bitcoin digital currency. arXiv preprint arXiv:1402.1718 (2014)
3. Eyal, I.: The Miner's Dilemma. In: IEEE Symposium on Security and Privacy (2015)
4. Luu, L., Saha, R., Parameshwaran, I., Saxena, P., Hobor, A.: On power splitting games in distributed computation: the case of bitcoin pooled mining. Technical report, Cryptology ePrint Archive, Report 2015/155 (2015). http://eprint.iacr.org
5. Moore, T., Christin, N.: Beware the middleman: empirical analysis of bitcoin-exchange risk. In: Sadeghi, A.-R. (ed.) FC 2013. LNCS, vol. 7859, pp. 25–33. Springer, Heidelberg (2013)
6. Nakamoto, S.: Bitcoin: a peer-to-peer electionic cash system (2008)

Automated Verification of Electrum Wallet

Mathieu Turuani[1]([✉]), Thomas Voegtlin[2], and Michael Rusinowitch[1]

[1] INRIA Nancy–Grand Est, Villers-lès-Nancy, France
mathieu.turuani@inria.fr, rusi@loria.fr
[2] Electrum Technologies GmbH, Berlin, Germany
thomasv@electrum.org

Abstract. We introduce a formal modeling in ASLan++ of the two-factor authentication protocol used by the Electrum Bitcoin wallet. This allows us to perform an automatic analysis of the wallet and show that it is secure for standard scenarios in Dolev Yao model [Dolev 1981]. The result could be derived thanks to some advanced features of the protocol analyzer such as the possibility to specify (i) new intruder deduction rules with clauses and (ii) non-deducibility constraints.

1 Context

Electrum is a popular Bitcoin Wallet. Thanks to a deterministic key derivation algorithm (BIP32), users can regenerate their wallet from a secret seed phrase, which protects them in case of loss or computer failure. It is a lightweight client, which means that it does not need to download the whole Bitcoin blockchain. Instead, the client communicates with a set of servers, and retrieves only needed information. The private keys used to sign Bitcoin transactions are never communicated to the servers, and servers do not store users accounts.

In order to protect users from Bitcoin theft, Electrum provides two-factor authentication, implemented using multi-signature addresses (P2SH) and an external co-signer (TrustedCoin). Our objective is to initiate the verification of Electrum's two-factor authentication protocol in order to increase user confidence or detect potential weaknesses and rise warnings.

Several tools have been recently developed to perform fully automated analysis of cryptographic protocols (e.g. [Proverif]). Some have been able to discover new flaws and most of them rely on symbolic models where messages are considered as terms in some abstract algebra as opposed to sequences of bits in more concrete models. In these tools generally no properties are assumed (and exploited) about cryptographic primitives besides the fact that when a message has been encrypted by some key, it can be recovered by applying the inverse key to the ciphered text. Although symbolic analysis relies on high-level protocol abstractions it has been able to discover important flaws in real-world protocols [Armando 2008]. Moreover, under some suitable hypothesis these analyses are cryptographically sound, i.e. from the absence of flaws at the symbolic level we can derive the correctness of the protocol w.r.t. cryptographic models too.

This work has received funding from the European Research Council (ERC) under the European Union's Horizon 2020 research and innovation program (grant agreement No. 645865-SPOOC).

© International Financial Cryptography Association 2016
J. Clark et al. (Eds.): FC 2016 Workshops, LNCS 9604, pp. 27–42, 2016.
DOI: 10.1007/978-3-662-53357-4_3

For this analysis we have employed Cl-Atse, a state-of-the-art protocol analyzer efficient and complete for bounded number of sessions [Turuani 2006]. It is compliant with ASLan++ specification language [von Oheim 2010], which allowed us to model relevant properties of the BIP32 key-derivation functions. Moreover, Cl-Atse's unique ability to handle so-called non-deducibility constraints over the agent's knowledge was fundamental in this analysis.

There exists a huge number of works on formal verification of security protocols. For instance, Bitcoin contracts have been modeled and verified using timed automata [Andrychowicz 2014]. However, to our knowledge previous verification works have not considered Bitcoin wallets.

2   Electrum Wallet

Electrum users may decide to enable two-factor authentication on their wallet. In that case, transactions will be signed by both the Electrum client and a cosigning server (TrustedCoin), if the user authenticates himself using a one-time password generated by Google Authenticator. The user (the human who owns the electronic wallet) keeps an offline copy of the wallet initialization data (seed phrase), in order to regenerate their wallet in case of data loss or disappearance of the cosigning service. A key feature of Electrum's two-factor authentication protocol is that the wallet regeneration procedure only requires the seed phrase, and does not need the cosigning server.

The cosigning server, however, has no way to use the wallet without the client's signature. Electrum's two factor authentication uses Bitcoin Pay-to-Script-Hash addresses (P2SH), and the BIP32 standard for deterministic generations of keys. BIP32 allows the cosigning server to deterministically generate new private keys - following a 'path' from a root key - which is needed to sign Bitcoin transactions, while the client alone is able to generate the corresponding public keys, which are needed in order to create new P2SH addresses.

The interactions between agents are described by four sequences of actions: initialisation (user/client), registration and confirmation (client/server), and (recurring) transaction phase. Authentication is carried out via the Google OTP function using a secret and the current time. BIP32 extended keys are denoted by k, K, C for private/public keys and the associated chain parameter. Personal data are denoted by: *email* for the client's e-mail (public); *time* for the current time (public); *database* for the server's database (private); and a, b, c, d, ... for some paths (public) used to build child keys in the BIP32 structure.

User and Client's Initialization.

Initial knowledge	: Both knows Ks, Cs;	
User generates two fresh seeds	: Seed1 and Seed2;	-secret-
User extracts the priv./public	: k1,K1,C1 from Seed1;	-secret-
keys and chain parameters	k2,K2,C2 from Seed2;	-secret-
User $* \rightarrow *$ Client	: email.k1.C1.K1.C2.K2	
Client computes the user IDs	: LongUserID from K1,C1,K2,C2;	-secret-
	UserID prefix of LongUserID;	

This sequence of actions simulates an exchange between a user and his client to model initialization. In practice, the Electrum client generates and shows to the user a sequence of English words called the seed phrase. Two independent BIP32 seeds are derived from this phrase, and only one of the private keys derived from them is stored by the client. To avoid the trivial case of a client already compromised when the seed phrase is generated, we model a user who generates both BIP32 seeds and sends only one of the corresponding extended private keys to the client. Let $A \to B : M$ denote a message M sent from A to B. This is decorated by stars when the channel is secured, i.e. protected against eavesdropping or modification. The concatenation of messages is written with a dot, as in $email.k1$. Finally, the long user ID is a hash of the public keys and parameters, and the (short) user ID is built from its first-10 characters.

New User Registration.

Initial knowledge	: Client was initialized; Server knows ks, Ks, Cs;
Client opens a channel	: Session key Sk shared with Server; -secret-
Client $\to$ Server	: {|register.{email.K1.C1.K2.C2}_Ks|}_Sk;
Server gets the user IDs	: LongUserID from K1, C1, K2, C2; -secret-
	UserID prefix of LongUserID;
Server builds the secret	: Sec from UserID, ks and Cs; -secret-
Server adds to database	: UserID.email.K1.C1.K2.C2.false
Server $\to$ Client	: {|**{Sec}_K1**|}_Sk;

This describes how a new client registers to the server, with new data later confirmed. The client uses the (known) server's public key to open a secure channel with a fresh symmetric key Sk. We denote the symmetric and asymmetric encryptions of M by $\{|M|\}\_Sk$ and $\{M\}\_Ks$ respectively. Then the client sends its registration query, allowing the server to rebuild its IDs and fill the database. Finally, for future authentications a secret data is returned to the client.

New User Confirmation.

Initial knowledge	: Client was registered; Server knows ks, Ks, Cs;
Client opens a channel	: Session key Sk shared with Server; -secret-
Client builds the OTP	: OTP = googleOTP(Sec,time) -secret-
Client $\to$ Server	: {|confirm.UserID.OTP|}_Sk;
Server reads database	: UserID.email.K1.C1.K2.C2.false
Server builds the Secret	: Sec from UserID, Ks and Cs; -secret-
Server tests the OTP	: OTP ?= googleOTP(Sec,time)
if data not found	
Server $\to$ Client	: {|false|}_Sk; *exit*;
if OTP differ	
Server del. from database	: UserID.email.K1.C1.K2.C2.false
Server $\to$ Client	: {|false|}_Sk; *exit*;
otherwise	
Server updates database	: UserID.email.K1.C1.K2.C2.true
Server $\to$ Client	: {|true|}_Sk;

Now, the client must confirm his registration before signing transactions. The Electrum client does not store the OTP secret, but displays it to the user who stores it on an external device with Google Authenticator. However, this cannot be modeled directly since the D.Y. intruder rather concentrates on internet communications between the client and the server. Therefore, this step is abstracted by a client who generates the OTP himself. The confirmation phase starts with the client opening a secure channel as before to send his request and OTP. Depending on server's agreement, *true* or *false* is returned and the client data is either confirmed or deleted from the database. The *exit* keyword indicates procedure termination for both parties when the server disagrees.

Signing a Transaction with the Server.

Initial knowledge	: Client was confirmed; Server knows ks, Ks, Cs;
Client opens a channel	: Session key Sk shared with Server; -secret-
Client creates a list	: SigList = empty list of signature requests;
Client iterates	
choose a path	: Path = sequence of a, b, c, d, ...
create a script	: Script using key from K1,C1 following Path;
add to the list	: Add Path.Script to SigList;
Client builds the OTP	: OTP = googleOTP(Sec,time); -secret-
Client → Server	: {|sign.UserID.tx_data.SigList.OTP|}_Sk;
Server reads database	: UserID.email.K1.C1.K2.C2.true
Server builds the Secret	: Sec from UserID, Ks and Cs; -secret-
Server tests the OTP	: OTP ?= googleOTP(Sec,time);
if data not found or OTP differs	
Server → Client	: {|false|}_Sk; *exit*;
otherwise Server iterates	
select element	: pick-up Path.Script from SigList;
derive new key	: k4 from ks,Cs following LongUserID.Path;
sign the transaction	: Sign tx_data and Script with k4 in signed_tx;
Server → Client	: {|**signed_tx**|}_Sk;

Once the client is registered, it is allowed to request transaction signatures. As before, this is done by opening a secure channel with the server, and sending a transaction request containing the one-time password generated with the current time. The request also includes the transaction data *tx_data* to be signed, along with a list *SigList* of signature requests. Each element in this lists consists in a Bitcoin script using a key derived from the client's root key $K1$ (plus $C1$) using the BIP32's CKD_pub (and CKD_priv) method. The path used to derive this key is also included in the list, so that the server can use it to derive his own key too. This method allows the client and the server to forget all the keys locally used in each transaction, as long as the root keys are safely stored along with the paths used to derive new keys. Moreover, the two keys used to sign transactions - client side and server side - are generated using the same, unique, path. On the server side, this path is extended with the long user ID so that all the keys used for all the clients are generated from one, single, root key pair

ks, Ks. Moreover, the server has no need to store key paths: the responsibility to keep these is left to the client. In practice, these paths are of length two and sequentially generated, so that a fast sieve allows the user to recover his keys in case of client loss. Once successful, the server returns the signed transaction to the client. While not modeled here, the Electrum server can also push the signed transaction to the Bitcoin network for the client.

3   Modeling BIP32

The BIP32 standard describes a hierarchy of keys derived from a single seed and by following paths, i.e. a sequences of integers. The master key generation function is a hash and does not require any specific construction. The Child Key Derivation (CKD) functions admit two variants: CKD_pub for deriving public keys and CKD_priv for private keys. Each one takes a public (resp. private) key, a chain parameter, and a path to follow, and produces the child public (resp. private) key. Consequently the algebraic relation linking CKD_pub and CKD_priv is: $CKD\_priv(inv(K), C, S) = inv(CKD\_pub(K, C, S))$ where inv is the key inversion function, used here to specify the private key associated to the public key K or to $CKD\_pub(..)$. For simplicity we have omitted the chain parameter in our description: it will be modeled by a function called cCKD in our ASLan++ specification. In our model, each public key is either the root public key $pk(A)$ of some agent A, or a child public key derived with BIP32. Note that pk already exists in ASLan++ syntax and thus will not be redefined. The two CKD functions can be modeled by declaring a single $pCKD$ function which takes a private key (as would CKD_priv) but computes the corresponding public child key (as would CKD_pub):

```
noninvertible pCKD(private_key,message,message): public_key;
```

where *message* is the generic type (used for a chain parameter and a path here), and *noninvertible* ensures that this function can be freely used but the intruder cannot retrieve the arguments from the result.

In our protocol model every occurrence of $CKD\_pub(K, C, S)$ from the initial specification is represented by $pCKD(inv(K), C, S)$ and every occurrence of $CKD\_priv(K, C, S)$ is represented by $inv(pCKD(K, C, S))$. This modeling ensures the validity of the above algebraic relation since for all K, C, S:

$$CKD\_priv(inv(K), C, S) = inv(pCKD(inv(K), C, S)) = inv(CKD\_pub(K, C, S))$$

The intruder deduction ability should be extended to take into account the CKD functions from BIP32. Therefore we define these two new intruder deduction rules expressed by Horn Clauses in ASLan++:

```
iknows(pCKD(inv(K),C,S))    :- iknows(K.C.S);   \% for CKD\_pub
iknows(inv(pCKD(K,C,S)))    :- iknows(K.C.S);   \% for CKD\_priv
```

The ability for the intruder to deduce a public key from its inverse (private) key is expressed using two Horn Clauses:

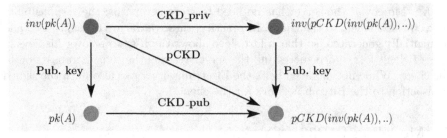

Fig. 1. Example of key derivations with fixed chain and path

```
iknows(pk(A))          :- iknows(inv(pk(A)));
iknows(pCKD(K,C,S))  :- iknows(inv(pCKD(K,C,S)));
```

These functions are summarized in Fig. 1, where each arrow represents an operator over keys, where both the chain parameter and the path are fixed.

4   ASLan++ Wallet Model

The ASLan++ model for the Electrum wallet is detailed here. It specifies the user agent and his client software (separately), plus the three server agents described previously. It also specifies the security properties to be preserved in any run, plus the intruder capabilities. Conforming to BIP32's modeling from Sect. 3, the CKD_priv and CKD_pub function are replaced by combining $pCKD$ and inv. Note that $pCKD$ is universally known and thus can be used by the intruder. The list containing the elements that the client want to be signed, and the list of these elements once they are signed by the server, are represented with concatenation of pairings. While the model contains variants for choosing $Input\_info$ (the list of signature requests), only the most general one where the intruder has full control over it is used for the analysis. Moreover, the ASLan++ syntax uses names starting with a non-capital letter to denote constants, e.g. atoms/nonces/..., and names starting with a capital letter for variables. Therefore, a key pair denoted by Ks, ks (public/private) in the description of the protocol will now be written $Ks/inv(Ks)$ instead, with Ks a variable of type $public\_key$ and $inv(Ks)$ the inverse of its value, thus the associated private key.

4.1   Attacker Model and Assumptions

Our analysis relies on the perfect cryptography hypothesis: no information about the content of a ciphertext can be derived by agents that do not possess the decryption key. Fresh random numbers used in a ciphering algorithm cannot be derived either. Random numbers cannot be predicted by the intruder. A ciphertext is in general not malleable and therefore cannot be used to generate a different ciphertext without being decrypted first. This can be slightly relaxed when the protocol uses specific operators (Xor, exponentiation, ..): the algebraic properties of these operators that can be exploited are made explicit. Horn Clauses are also used to express agent capabilities to modify or learn messages that goes beyond the perfect cryptography hypothesis.

A honest agent follows the protocol specification and is assumed to be *prudent*, that is, the agent decrypts as soon as possible every part of a received message, checks the content by relating it to its known data. In the same way signatures are verified by agents whenever possible.

4.2 Security Properties

While the built-in ASLan++ security properties are fine for protecting objects with scope larger than just one session, they were not adequate for protecting local objects inside sessions where one agent (e.g., the server) has no idea, and do not truly care, if he is speaking to a honest client or not. The server has to serve any client, honest or not, and he has no idea which one will contact him. Therefore, instead of tweaking the built-in properties, we have designed new specific ones for this kind of model:

```
uSecret (message , message )                          : fact;
uChecks (agent , message , message , message , message) : fact;
```

which associated security properties are:

```
uSecret: [](forall M K.        (!uSecret(M,K)      |
    !iknows(M) | iknows(K)        ));
uChecks: [](forall A M K U V. (!uChecks(A,M,K,U,V) | A=i
          | K=M        | !U=V));
```

where [] means 'in every trace at any moment' and ! denotes the negation. The first one, $uSecret(M, K)$, ensures that the message M remains unknown for the intruder, unless he can build or deduce K. This is widely used to preserve the security of some data inside a session, where K will be the session key. This way, an attack is raised on a local data, or a data transmitted during a session, only if the intruder has no access to the main key protecting it. Naturally, the session key itself has its own security property, to check whether it can be captured by the intruder. This method builds an interesting hierarchical structure among security properties reflecting the dependencies between data and the means used to protect them. This was made possible only thanks to the recent extension of Cl-Atse (the analysis backend used for this study) that allows it to check for non-deducibility constraints over the intruder knowledge. Indeed, this does not simply require that the key K was received by the intruder, but that among the infinite set of possible intruder knowledge solutions of some set of constraints, only those where he is unable to deduce that key, or to rebuild it from pieces, are kept.

The second property, $uChecks(A, M, K, U, V)$, ensures that if the agent A is not played by the intruder, then either the message M and K are equal, or the messages U and V differ. This is widely used to check the server's responses to the client's requests. Therefore, in this context an attack is conservatively raised iff: (i) the agent A was an honest agent; (ii) the response M from the server differs from the expected result K; (iii) the request (list of) parameter U was correct, i.e. identical to its expected value V.

4.3   User Role

The ASLan++ *User* role models human owner(s) of an Electrum wallet to be distinguished from a role played by software client(s), that owns only a subset of User's knowledge. The User role appears only during the initialization phase as described in Sect. 2. Thus, he will first generate two seeds using the *fresh*() nonce generator, and declares them as secrets:

```
secret_Seed1 : (Seed1)  := fresh();
secret_Seed2 : (Seed2)  := fresh();
```

Then, he derives two key pairs $K1/inv(K1)$ and $K2/inv(K2)$ from the seeds, plus their associated chain parameters $C1$ and $C2$, and declares the private keys as secrets. The chain parameters (or the public keys) being sent to the server, they can also be declared as secrets (for testing, as they are not critical) but under the assumption that the server was not compromised (actively or passively), i.e. that its root key remains private:

```
K1 := pk(Seed1); uSecret(inv(K1),Seed1);
K2 := pk(Seed2); uSecret(inv(K2),Seed2);
C1 := cp(Seed1); C2 := cp(Seed2);
uSecret(C2,inv(pk(server)));
```

Finally, he gives these initialization data to his client, necessarily through a secure channel:

```
Actor *->* Client : email.inv(K1).C1.K1.C2.K2;
```

The secure channel is specified in ASLan++ syntax by arrow decorations: left star for origin authenticity, and right-star for read-protection and guaranty of delivery to the correct recipient.

4.4   Client Role

The *Client* role is played by Electrum software client on behalf of the user. After a first initialization phase:

```
User *->* Actor : ?Email.inv(?K1).?C1.?K1.?C2.?K2;
```

where it receives its parameters from the User role, it computes the long user ID (*Long_ID*) and declares it as secret, truncates it to UID, and deduces the main server's public key $K3$ and chain parameter $C3$ devoted to this user. Also non essential or obviously public data are leaked to the intruder, in case some real user would do so involuntarily:

```
K3   := pCKD(inv(pk(server)),cp(server),Long_ID);
C3   := cCKD(    pk(server) ,cp(server),Long_ID);
Actor -> ? : Email.K1.C1.K2.K3.C3;
```

Then, the clients starts a registration process to the server. To do so, it first generates a fresh session key Sk and declares it as secret, then transmits it to the server through a read-protected channel followed by the registration request protected by that key:

```
secret_Sk:(Sk) := fresh();   Actor ->* Server : Sk;
Actor -> Server :
   {|register.{Email.K1.C1.K2.C2}_pk(server)|}_Sk;
```

After processing the request, the servers gives its answer protected by the session key too:

```
Server -> Actor : {|{?Secret}_K1|}_Sk; uSecret(Secret,Sk);
```

This answer contains the *Secret* that will be used for further authentication using the google_OTP function. Naturally *Secret* is declared as a secret w.r.t. the session key Sk. This goal is made inactive if the intruder can deduce or compute Sk, namely if the session officially involves an intruder (but this is not an attack) or if the session was compromised (but the goal associated to Sk must trigger instead). Then, following the same method and using an OTP declared as secret and generated through *google_otp*(*Secret*, *Time*) with *Time* being the current time of the client (correct or not), it casts the confirmation request (with a new session key) and gets the server *Result*, that could be *true* or *false*. This response is checked for validity:

```
uChecks(Server,true,Result,ctime,Time);
```

i.e. the *Result* must be *true* unless the client did not use the current time properly. This may generate an attack, see Sect. 5.2. Finally, the client casts a signature request. This request uses a *Raw_transaction* which is some fresh data leaked to the intruder, plus a list of signature requests called *Input_info* which must be as general as possible, and thus, directly provided by the intruder at its own discretion. This way, the intruder can choose the most dangerous values for the client. At the end, the client checks the server's response similarly as before.

4.5   Server Registration Role

The registration role is the first of the three server roles. Its goal is to record new user's registration data. The model does not even need to check if a previous user was already registered with the same ID, since the probability to find hash collisions by chance is considered to be negligible. Therefore, this role first opens a new connection to a client by receiving a session key, though a read-only channel, followed by the request itself:

```
Client ->* Actor : ?Sk;
Client ->  Actor :
    {|register.{?Email.?K1.?C1.?K2.?C2}_pk(server)|}_Sk;
```

This allows him to rebuild the long and short user ID in the same way as the client did on his side, along with the OTP's secret which is an hash over the user's short ID, the private server's key, and the server's chain parameter:

```
Secret := hash(UID.inv(pk(server)).cp(server));
uSecret(Long_ID,Sk); uSecret(Secret,Sk); uSecret(Long_ID,C2);
```

Naturally these data are also declared as secrets, w.r.t. the session key Sk since the data allowing to rebuild $Long\_ID$, and $Secret$, are both transmitted in a channel protected by Sk. However, we can notice that losing the session key Sk here does not necessarily implies losing the long user ID, since the data building it are also protected by the server's public key. Therefore, it is declared as secret a second time, but w.r.t. one of its element that was already declared as secret by the User (c.f. Sect. 4.3), i.e. $C2$. We note here that this study does not consider cryptographic attacks on the primitives. In particular, the server and the hashing method must be resistant by other means to an intruder performing e.g. huge series of (fake) client/server registrations to retrieve many pairs of UID and $Secret$ with the objective of rebuilding the secret associated to a known, honest, user ID. Finally, the server adds the client's data to its database, and sends the $Secret$ back for further authentication:

```
database->add(UID.Email.K1.C1.K2.C2.false);
Actor -> Client : {|{Secret}_K1|}_Sk;
```

where $false$ refers to the unconfirmed status, and the secret is protected by both the session key and an encryption with the public key $K1$.

4.6   Server Confirmation Role

The confirmation role is mandatory to allow the client to send further requests. It ensures that Google OTP can be used for authentication and if so, switch its status from unconfirmed to confirmed. The server starts this role as before, by receiving a new session key though a read-only channel, followed by the request itself containing the user ID from which the secret can be rebuilt:

```
Client ->* Actor : ?Sk;
Client ->  Actor : {|confirm.?UID.?OTP|}_Sk;
Secret := hash(UID.inv(pk(server)).cp(server));
```

This way, the server does not need to store each user's secret in the database. Then, the server has three choices, depending on the validity of the one-time password and the content of the database for this user ID:

– Either the database contains a non-confirmed user under that ID, and the provided password was correct. Then the server validates the request by switching the user status to confirmed in the database, and sending back the $true$ response:

```
database->remove(UID.Email.K1.C1.K2.C2.false);
database->add(   UID.Email.K1.C1.K2.C2.true );
Actor -> Client : {|response.true|}_Sk;
```

– Or the database contains a non-confirmed user under that ID, but the provided password was not correct. Then the server deletes (yes, it does!) the unregistered user account from the database, and sends back a *false* response. Whatever the reason was, a user mistake or an intruder trying to interfere with a wrong password, in both cases the client has to register again:

```
database->remove(UID.Email.K1.C1.K2.C2.false);
Actor -> Client : {|response.false|}_Sk;
```

– Or the database does not contains any non-confirmed user under that ID. If there exists some user registered and already confirmed under that ID, it is not seen here and thus it remains unchanged. Then the server simply sends back a *false* answer:

```
Actor -> Client : {|response.false|}_Sk;
```

Moreover, in all three cases above, the server also declares the local data as secrets within the session, i.e.:

```
uSecret(Secret,Sk); uSecret(OTP,Sk);
```

Other cases than these three could be introduced in future protocol variants. For example, the server could send an adequate response when the user is already registered. Depending of these future improvements on the server's tests and actions on data, a new analysis would be necessary.

4.7   Server Signature Role

The signature role is the master piece of the Electrum two factor authentication protocol. It allows the client to cast Bitcoin transactions signed both by him and the server. This is the most complex part of the protocol since the number of signatures to perform for one single request is not fixed, and thus requires an iterative process. The server starts this role as usual by receiving the session key followed by the request and uses it to rebuild the user secret and query the database:

```
Client   ->* Actor : ?Sk;
Client   ->  Actor :
    {|sign.?UID.?Raw_transaction.?Input_info.?OTP|}_Sk;
Secret := hash(UID.inv(pk(server)).cp(server));
if (database->contains(UID.?Email.?K1.?C1.?K2.?C2.true)
      & OTP = google_otp(Secret,ctime)) { ...
```

Similarly to the confirmation role, the server tests the database content and one-time password for user authentication. If this test is positive then the server processes *Input_info*, i.e. the list of objects that must be signed, by the server for some of them, and not for some others. This list is modeled by right-parenthesised pairings, and the server iterates the process until no more pairing is found (the last element in the list is supposed to be *end*):

```
while (Input_info = ?Elem.?Next) {
  if (Elem = mustSign(?A.?B.?Script)) { ...
```

The list elements of the form *mustSign(..)* are objects that the server is asked to sign. Others are objects that can be simply ignored. For each object of this kind found in the list, thus for each elementary signature request *A.B.Script* found inside, the server computes the key pair $K3/inv(K3)$ derived from his private root key using BIP32 and following the long user ID plus A and B as path. For readability, this is decomposed in two steps here:

```
K3 := pCKD(inv(pk(server)),cp(server),Long_ID);
C3 := cCKD(    pk(server) ,cp(server),Long_ID);
K4 := pCKD(inv(pCKD(inv(K3),C3,A)),cCKD(K3,C3,A),B);
C4 := cCKD(    pCKD(inv(K3),C3,A) ,cCKD(K3,C3,A),B);
```

An implementation of the server would certainly build $K3/inv(K3)$ before the loop, but this has no impact on the analysis. The server can now use $inv(K4)$ to sign the requested element, and add it to the list of signatures that he is building, and proceed to the next element:

```
Signatures := Signatures.{Raw_transaction.Script}_inv(K4);
Input_info := Next; secret_K4p:(K4p) := inv(K4);
Empty := false;
```

The private key $inv(K4)$ is also declared as secret, but this time, for the server: it is used for signing, so it must remain perfectly private to the server even if this one communicates with a compromised client. The *Empty* variable records the information that the signature list is not empty anymore. This is used right after the end of the iterative process, to declare the final signature list as a secret w.r.t. the session key (since it is transmitted during the session):

```
if (Empty=false) { uSecret(Signatures,Sk); }
```

Note that this secrecy goal would be trivially invalidated without the condition. Finally, the server can send back the signed list to the client:

```
Actor -> Client : {|response.Signatures|}_Sk;
```

If the password is incorrect or if the database does not contain a confirmed used of that ID, then the server simply replies *false* instead of the signature list. In both cases (correct or not), the secrecy of the local data (such as the user IDs or the OTP secret) is ensured w.r.t. the session key, in the same way as in the previous roles.

5 Results

We have performed several analyses using our ASLan++ model of Electrum's two factor authentication protocol. We first tested the executability of the protocol, i.e. to make sure that participants can truly run their parts as expected. Second we present a replay attack on the confirmation message that was unveiled by the tools. This attack does not threaten private data but makes the client erroneously believe that it is in some state with the server and this may block him in future actions. Finally we evaluate the protocol security according to several scenarios and show that no attack is possible for these configurations (beside the previously mentioned one). The investigated scenarios cover standard uses of the protocol (with honest server and client) but also critical cases where the client or the server is dishonest. We have employed a computer cluster for increasing the number of protocol sessions considered during our experiments.

5.1 Executability Checking

To check the absence of blocking during protocol execution and therefore that the protocol can reach a successful final state, we have considered several scenarios too. We consider here the case of a single honest client and a single honest server. Hence the *body* section contains:

```
newSession(alice,client1,server,inv(pk(server)));
```

Moreover the fact that a client role receives a correct final answer from the server is encoded with an ASLan property added at the end of the client role.

```
uChecks(Actor,true,false,Signatures,
        start.{Raw_transaction.Script2}_inv(SerKey2).
        none.{Raw_transaction.Script1}_inv(SerKey1) );
```

This property requires that the signature *Signature* sent by the server is exactly *data*. For the server to provide this signature, the client request must be properly constructed. Cl-Atse generates this request. Signatures are built from paths a, b and c, d that have been used to compute the public keys $SerKey1$ and $SerKey2$ with the corresponding scripts, i.e.:

```
K3   := pCKD(inv(pk(server)),cp(server),Long_ID);
C3   := cCKD(    pk(server)  ,cp(server),Long_ID);
SerKey1 := pCKD(inv(pCKD(inv(K3),C3,a)),cCKD(K3,C3,a),b);
SerKey2 := pCKD(inv(pCKD(inv(K3),C3,c)),cCKD(K3,C3,c),d);
```

5.2 Attack by Confirmation Replay

In a scenario where the client and the intruder have each one an open session with the server, the intruder has the possibility to replay the registration confirmation sequence of the client towards the server. This is possible since the server authenticates the client solely by its transmitted information, basically $UserID$ and OTP. The fact that the same session key is reused is neither detected by the server in our modeling, nor in real implementations. The fact that the OTP password used in a first request does not expire instantaneously and therefore remains valid for a second immediately following a session is not exploited here. However if an already confirmed client send a new confirmation request then according to the technical documentation the server will check whether the client is already recorded with *not confirmed* tag in the database. Hence the test will fail since the client is recorded with another tag. By consequence the second session fails and the server returns *false*. Then the intruder needs only to replace the positive answer to the first request by the negative answer to the second one to deceive the client into thinking that its confirmation was denied. Moreover, by believing so the client will probably not emit signature requests. If he tries again to get a confirmation he will be rejected again without any action from the intruder. This forces the client to initiate a new registration. In order to correct this protocol behavior the server should check after a confirmation request if the client is already confirmed and reply positively in that case.

Cl-Atse has generated automatically the following attack trace that corresponds. Agents between brackets < and > are controlled by the intruder. We note that *client*1 sends a request to the server that is duplicated, and he only receives the second answer.

```
 client1     ->    <server>  : _msg
<client1>    ->*    server    : n19(Sk)
<client1>    ->     server    : _msg
 server      ->    <client1>  : {|response.true|}_n19(Sk)
<i>          ->*    server    : n19(Sk)
<i>          ->     server    : _msg
 server      ->    <i>        : {|response.false|}_n19(Sk)
<server>     ->     client1   : {|response.false|}_n19(Sk)
```

where for readability *_msg* (and *_uid*) are shortened forms of:

```
_msg: {|confirm._uid.googleOTP(hash(_uid.inv(pk(server))).
                            cp(server)),time)|}_n19(Sk)
_uid: first10(hash(pk(n17(Seed1)).cp(n17(Seed1)).
                   pk(n17(Seed2)).cp(n17(Seed2))))
```

Suggestion: the server's answer could be more explicit to let the client understand that it is under attack. Also, the client must not accept a server's response if it arrives after the end of validity for the OTP, to prevent replay. The non-confirmed data deletion is acceptable if the client understands that he must restart from registration because an intruder interfered.

5.3 Security Analysis

Case of Dishonest Server: With a compromised server only few security properties can be preserved for the client. In particular, secrecy of $C2$, $LongUserID$, $Secret$, OTP is lost. However, the client's master private keys and their children should remain secret even with a compromised server. This includes $K1\_priv$ stored by the client and $K2\_priv$ stored by $Human$ role and the seeds that have been used for generating keys.

The model features a server that is compromised and thus, whose private root key is provided to the intruder. Therefore, its security properties are ignored and the intruder forces the server to follow or not the specification. The analysis of this specification by Cl-Atse shows that the client's security properties that are not related to data shared with the server are preserved.

Case of Honest Server: This is the main case. The number of honest clients running in parallel is a source of combinatorial explosion of the number of traces to analyze. To perform the analysis we have employed 50 nodes of a computation cluster. It appears that the limit was reached when analyzing this model for 2 to 3 concurrent sessions, each one being sequentially iterated 3 to 4 times. Each session is a block specifying one human owner and his software client, plus each of the three server's roles.

Finally, the scenarios containing two sessions featuring either two honest clients or one honest and one dishonest were found to be secure for up to four iterations (option '--nb 4' of the tool). We have tried to speed-up analysis by 'branching' the client sessions to specific server sessions (these are perfectly inter-changeable anyway) since this eliminates a large number of equivalent executions, but a scenario without this 'branching' was also tried and appeared to be truly difficult, when running on 30 nodes of the cluster for a week.

6   Conclusion

In this paper we have modeled Electrum's two factor authentication protocol using the ASLan++ language advanced features. Conditional security goals allow us to model several scenarios in one shot, without knowing beforehand which agent will be compromised. Horn Clauses allow us to model intruder capabilities (e.g. exploiting BIP32 related properties) in a flexible way and beyond standard Dolev Yao deduction rules. Our computer experiments have pointed a potential problem in the user registration process, and have shown that, assuming perfect cryptography, the protocol offers good security guarantees in standard scenarios. We have not studied privacy properties in this paper. In particular, a further analysis could check if an intruder is able to relate transactions that belong to the same user.

References

[Andrychowicz 2014] Andrychowicz, M., Dziembowski, S., Malinowski, D., Mazurek, Ł.: Modeling bitcoin contracts by timed automata. In: Legay, A., Bozga, M. (eds.) FORMATS 2014. LNCS, vol. 8711, pp. 7–22. Springer, Heidelberg (2014)

[Armando 2008] Armando, A., et al.: Formal analysis of SAML 2.0 web browser single sign-on: breaking the SAML-based single sign-on for Google apps

[Dolev 1981] Dolev, D., Yao, A.: On the Security of Public Key Protocols (Extended Abstract). In: FOCS, pp. 350–357 (1981)

[von Oheim 2010] von Oheimb, D., Mödersheim, S.: ASLan++ — a formal security specification language for distributed systems. In: Aichernig, B.K., Boer, F.S., Bonsangue, M.M. (eds.) Formal Methods for Components and Objects. LNCS, vol. 6957, pp. 1–22. Springer, Heidelberg (2011)

[Proverif] Proverif.   http://prosecco.gforge.inria.fr/personal/bblanche/proverif/

[Turuani 2006] Turuani, M.: The CL-Atse protocol analyser. In: Pfenning, F. (ed.) RTA 2006. LNCS, vol. 4098, pp. 277–286. Springer, Heidelberg (2006)

[Wuille 2012] Wuille, P.: Hierarchical Deterministic Wallets. Online specification for BIP32. https://github.com/bitcoin/bips/blob/master/bip-0032.mediawiki

Blindly Signed Contracts: Anonymous On-Blockchain and Off-Blockchain Bitcoin Transactions

Ethan Heilman[✉], Foteini Baldimtsi, and Sharon Goldberg

Boston University, Boston, USA
{heilman,foteini}@bu.edu, goldbe@cs.bu.edu

Abstract. Although Bitcoin is often perceived to be an anonymous currency, research has shown that a user's Bitcoin transactions can be linked to compromise the user's anonymity. We present solutions to the anonymity problem for both transactions on Bitcoin's blockchain and off the blockchain (in so called micropayment channel networks). We use an untrusted third party to issue anonymous vouchers which users redeem for Bitcoin. Blind signatures and Bitcoin transaction contracts (aka smart contracts) ensure the anonymity and fairness during the *bitcoin* ↔ *voucher* exchange. Our schemes are practical, secure and anonymous.

Keywords: Bitcoin · Blockchain · Smart contracts · Blind signatures · Anonymity

1 Introduction

When Bitcoin was first introduced in 2008, one of its key selling points was anonymity— users should be able to spend bitcoins "without information linking the transaction to anyone" [15]. In the last few years, however, researchers have shown that Bitcoin offers much weaker anonymity than was initially expected [12, 17], by demonstrating that they could follow the movement of funds on the Bitcoin blockchain. The community has reacted to this by proposing two key approaches to improve the anonymity of Bitcoin: (1) new anonymity schemes that are compatible with Bitcoin [1–3, 7, 11, 18, 19, 23, 24], and (2) new anonymous cryptocurrencies that are independent of Bitcoin [2, 14]. In this paper we take the former approach by developing new anonymity schemes that are compatible with Bitcoin via a soft fork. Our schemes offer a new trade-off between practicality (*i.e.*, transaction speed), security (*i.e.*, resistance to double-spending, denial of service (DoS) and Sybil attacks) and anonymity (*i.e.*, unlinkable transactions). As we will see below, previous work either provided schemes that are efficient but achieve limited security or anonymity [7, 18, 19, 23, 24] or schemes that provide strong anonymity but are slow and require large numbers of transactions [1, 3, 11].

Our first scheme is an "on-blockchain" scheme providing anonymity at reasonable speed, *i.e.*, requiring four transactions to be confirmed in three blocks (≈30 mins). Our protocol runs in epochs, and provides *set-anonymity within each epoch*. That is, while the blockchain publicly displays the *set* of payers and payees during an epoch, no one can tell which payer paid which payee. To do this,

© International Financial Cryptography Association 2016
J. Clark et al. (Eds.): FC 2016 Workshops, LNCS 9604, pp. 43–60, 2016.
DOI: 10.1007/978-3-662-53357-4_4

we introduce an untrusted (possibly malicious) intermediary $\mathcal{I}$ between all payers and payees.

Our second "off-blockchain" scheme uses a new payment technology called *micropayment channel networks* [9,16]. Micropayment channel networks use Bitcoin as a platform to confirm transactions within seconds, rather than minutes, and already provide a degree of anonymity—most of the transactions are made outside of the blockchain, and thus not shown to the public—but this anonymity is incomplete. Critically, because micropayment channel networks chain payments through pre-established paths of connected users (explained in Sect. 5.1), these users that participate in the path learn transaction details, including the cryptographic identities of the sending and receiving party. We provide anonymity against malicious users by using an *honest-but-curious* intermediary $\mathcal{I}$ (Sect. 5.3); set-anonymity within an epoch is preserved as long as $\mathcal{I}$ does not abort or deny service to payers or payees.

Our technique, inspired by eCash [8], works as follows. For a user $\mathcal{A}$ to anonymously pay another user $\mathcal{B}$, she would first exchange a bitcoin for an *anonymous voucher* through intermediary $\mathcal{I}$. $\mathcal{B}$ could then redeem the anonymous voucher with $\mathcal{I}$ to receive a bitcoin back. Our scheme overcomes two main challenges: (i) Ensuring that the vouchers are unlinkable (*i.e.*, hiding the link between the issuance and the redemption of a voucher), and (ii) enforcing fair exchange between participants (*i.e.*, users can redeem issued vouchers even against an uncooperative or malicious $\mathcal{I}$, and no party can steal or double-spend vouchers and bitcoins). We use *blind signatures* to achieve unlinkability, and the *scripting* functionality of Bitcoin transactions to achieve fair exchange via transaction contracts (aka smart contracts [20]).

We provide an overview of our scheme in Sect. 2 and define the required properties. We discuss our use of transaction contracts in Sect. 3. Our scheme for on-blockchain anonymous transactions is in Sect. 4. Our off-blockchain scheme which uses micropayment channel networks is in Sect. 5. Finally, we analyze the anonymity of our schemes in Sects. 4.2 and 5.3 and their security in Sect. 6.

1.1   Related Work

We now review some of the most representative related works in the literature.

Anonymous Payment Schemes.   Zerocash [2] and Zerocoin [14] provide anonymous payments through the use of a novel type of cryptographic proofs (ZK-SNARKs). Unlike our schemes, they are "stand-alone" cryptocurrencies and can not be integrated with Bitcoin. Meanwhile, [19] is an anonymous payment scheme that can offer anonymity protections to Bitcoin that provides excellent blockchain privacy and is very fast. However, the parties entrusted to anonymize transactions in [19] can still violate users' anonymity, even if they are honest-but-curious.

Mixing Services.   A bitcoin mixing service provides anonymity by transferring payments from an input set of bitcoin addresses to an output set of bitcoin addresses, such that is it hard to trace which input address paid which output address. Mixcoin [7] uses a trusted third party to mix Bitcoin addresses, but this third party can violate users privacy and steal users' bitcoins; theft is detected but not prevented. Blindcoin [23] improves on Mixcoin by preserving users privacy against the mixing service, as with Mixcoin, theft is still not prevented. CoinParty [24] is secure if 2/3 of the mixing parties are honest. CoinJoin [10] and CoinShuffle [18] improve on prior work by preventing theft. [13] shows a rigorous proof of anonymity for a scheme "almost identical" to CoinShuffle.

CoinShuffle's anonymity set is thought to be small due to coordination costs [3,6]; meanwhile, our schemes are not limited to small anonymity sets. Moreover, both CoinShuffle and CoinJoin run an entire mix in a single bitcoin transaction. Thus, a single aborting user disrupts the mix for all other users. Moreover, mix users cannot be forced to pay fees upfront, so that these schemes are vulnerable to DoS attacks [6,22] (where users join the mix and then abort) and Sybil attacks (where an adversary deanonymizes a user by forcing it to mix with Sybil identities secretly under her control) [3].

XIM [3] is a decentralized protocol which builds on the fair-exchange mixer in [1] and prevents bitcoin theft and resists DoS and Sybil attacks via fees. We also prevent bitcoin theft resist DoS and Sybil attacks with fees (Sect. 4.1). One of XIM's key innovations is a secure method for partnering mix users. Unfortunately, this partnering method adds several hours to the protocol execution because users have to advertise themselves as mix partners on the blockchain. Our schemes are faster because they do not require a partnering service.

CoinSwap [11] is a fair-exchange mixer that allows two parties to anonymously send Bitcoins through an intermediary. Like our schemes, the CoinSwap intermediary is prevented from stealing funds by the use of fair exchange. Unlike our schemes, however, CoinSwap does not provide anonymity against even a honest but curious intermediary. Our on-blockchain scheme takes $\approx$30 mins, slower than Coinshuffle's $\approx$10 mins. Off-blockchain however, our scheme is faster than CoinShuffle, since it only runs in seconds [16]; however, our off-blockchain only supports anonymity against a honest-but-curious intermediary[1].

2   Overview and Security Properties

We introduce two schemes: (a) on-blockchain anonymous payments and coin mixing, and (b) off-blockchain anonymous payments. By on-blockchain we denote the standard method of transferring bitcoins *i.e.,* using the Bitcoin blockchain, as opposed to the newly proposed "off-blockchain" methods that utilize micropayment channel networks.

On-Blockchain Anonymous Payments. We first consider the scenario where a user $\mathcal{A}$, the *payer* wants to anonymously send 1 bitcoin, BTC, to another user $\mathcal{B}$, the *payee*[2]. If $\mathcal{A}$ were to perform a standard Bitcoin transaction, sending

---

[1] Our off-blockchain scheme is fast because it uses micropayment channel networks. It's unclear how to retrofit prior work onto these networks, *e.g.,* mapping Coinshuffle's single atomic transaction onto the arbitrary graph topology of a micropayment channel network.

[2] We assume that all transactions in our schemes are of 1 bitcoin value.

1 bitcoin from an address $Addr_A$ (owned by $\mathcal{A}$) to a fresh ephemeral address $Addr_B$ (owned by $\mathcal{B}$) there would be a record of this transaction on Bitcoin's blockchain linking $Addr_A$ to $Addr_B$. Even if $\mathcal{A}$ and $\mathcal{B}$ always create a fresh address for each payment they receive, the links between addresses can be used to de-anonymize users if, at some point, they "non-anonymously" spend a payment (*e.g.*, buying goods from third party that learns their mailing address) or receive a payment (*e.g.*, a Bitcoin payment processor like BitPay) [12].

One idea $\mathcal{A}$ and $\mathcal{B}$ could use to protect their privacy is to employ an intermediary party $\mathcal{I}$ that breaks the link between them. $\mathcal{A}$ would first send one bitcoin to $\mathcal{I}$, and then $\mathcal{I}$ would send a different bitcoin to $\mathcal{B}$. Assuming that a sufficient number of users make payments through $\mathcal{I}$, it becomes more difficult for an outsider to link $\mathcal{A}$ to $\mathcal{B}$ by looking at the blockchain (more on this below). The downside of this idea, however, is that the intermediary $\mathcal{I}$ knows everything about all users' payments, violating their anonymity.

We could apply techniques used in online anonymous eCash schemes [8] to prevent $\mathcal{I}$ from learning who $\mathcal{A}$ wants to pay. The protocol is in Fig. 1. $\mathcal{A}$ pays one bitcoin to $\mathcal{I}$, and obtains an *anonymous voucher* $V = (sn, \sigma)$ in return. ($\mathcal{A}$ chooses a random serial number sn, blinds it to $\overline{sn}$ and asks $\mathcal{I}$ to compute a blind signature $\overline{\sigma}$ on $\overline{sn}$. $\mathcal{A}$ unblinds these

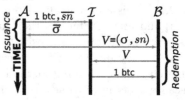

Fig. 1. Strawman eCash protocol.

values to obtain $V = (sn, \sigma)$. The blind signature requires only a minor change to Bitcoin and can be implemented using a soft fork (Sect. 3). Then $\mathcal{A}$ pays $\mathcal{B}$ using V, and finally $\mathcal{B}$ redeems V with $\mathcal{I}$ to obtain one bitcoin.

How do we ensure that $\mathcal{I}$ does not know who $\mathcal{A}$ wants to pay? This follows from the *blindness* of blind signatures—namely, that the signer ($\mathcal{I}$) cannot read the blinded serial number $\overline{sn}$ that it signs, and also cannot link a message/signature (sn, σ) pair to its blinded value $(\overline{sn}, \overline{\sigma})$. Blindness therefore ensures that even a malicious $\mathcal{I}$ cannot link a voucher it redeems with a voucher it issues. Blind signatures are also *unforgeable*, which ensures that a malicious user cannot issue a valid voucher to itself.

While this eCash-based approach solves our anonymity problem, it fails when $\mathcal{I}$ is malicious since it could just refuse to issue a voucher to $\mathcal{A}$ after receiving her bitcoin. To solve this, we use Bitcoin transaction contracts to achieve blockchain-enforced *fair exchange* (as in prior work, fair-exchange denotes an atomic swap). The key idea is that $\mathcal{A}$ transfers a bitcoin to $\mathcal{I}$ *if and only if* it receives a valid voucher V in return. Figure 2 presents the high-level idea, and full description is in Sect. 4.

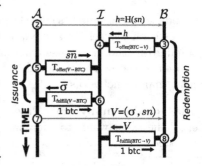

Fig. 2. Our protocol: circles (step numbers from Sect. 4), black arrows (objects transferred via transaction), grey arrows (messages).

At a high-level, our scheme consists of four blockchain transactions that are confirmed in three blocks on the blockchain, as shown in Figs. 2 and 3. The protocol involves two blockchain-enforced fair exchanges. The first is $V \rightarrow BTC$, which exchanges a voucher from $\mathcal{B}$ for a bitcoin from $\mathcal{I}$, and is realized using the following two transaction contracts: (1) $T_{offer(V \rightarrow BTC)}$, which is created by $\mathcal{I}$, confirmed in the first block on the blockchain and offers a fair exchange of one bitcoin (from $\mathcal{I}$) for one voucher (from $\mathcal{B}$), and (2) $T_{fulfill(V \rightarrow BTC)}$, which is created by $\mathcal{B}$ to fulfill the offer by $\mathcal{I}$ and is confirmed in the third block on the blockchain. These transaction contracts ensure that a malicious $\mathcal{I}$ cannot redeem $\mathcal{B}$'s voucher without providing $\mathcal{B}$ with a bitcoin in return (see Sects. 3 and 4). The second fair exchange is $BTC \rightarrow V$ and works in a similar fashion, fairly exchanging a bitcoin from $\mathcal{A}$ for a voucher from $\mathcal{I}$ via two transaction contracts: (1) $T_{offer(BTC \rightarrow V)}$, created by $\mathcal{A}$ and confirmed on the second block, and (2) $T_{fulfill(BTC \rightarrow V)}$, created by $\mathcal{I}$ and confirmed in the third block. These two fair exchanges are arranged to realize the anonymity protocol shown on the previous page; the fair exchange $BTC \rightarrow V$ stands in for the interaction between $\mathcal{A}$ and $\mathcal{I}$, while the fair exchange $V \rightarrow BTC$ stands in for the interaction between $\mathcal{B}$ and $\mathcal{I}$.

Mixing Service. A mixing service allows a user to move bitcoins from one address it controls to a fresh ephemeral (thus anonymous) address, without directly linking the two addresses on the blockchain. To use our on-blockchain anonymous payments as a mixing service, users can just anonymously pay themselves from one address to another fresh ephemeral address, thus playing the role of both $\mathcal{A}$ and $\mathcal{B}$ in the protocol above.

Off-Blockchain Payments. We also adapt our scheme to the recently proposed off-blockchain *micropayment channel networks*. Our off-blockchain scheme uses the same four transactions described above, but confirms them on a micropayment channel network. See Sect. 5 for details.

2.1   Anonymity Properties

In the strawman eCash protocol of Fig. 1, the anonymity level of users depends on the total number of payments using $\mathcal{I}$ as users can obtain or redeem vouchers at arbitrary times. However, our anonymous fair-exchange protocol of Fig. 2 provides anonymity only for payments starting and completing within an *epoch* (Fig. 3) *i.e.,* a three block window.

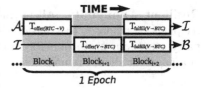

Fig. 3. Payment epoch

Assumptions. We make the following assumptions for our schemes:

1. We assume that all users coordinate on epochs (by *e.g.*, choosing the starting block to have a block height that is divisible by three).
2. As with traditional eCash schemes, we assume that if $\mathcal{A}$ pays $\mathcal{B}$, then $\mathcal{A}$ and $\mathcal{B}$ trust each other. (A malicious $\mathcal{A}$ or $\mathcal{B}$ could easily conspire with $\mathcal{I}$ to reveal the other party of the transaction; for instance, $\mathcal{A}$ could just tell $\mathcal{I}$ the serial number the voucher she was issued, and then $\mathcal{I}$ can identity $\mathcal{B}$ when he redeems that voucher.) This is a reasonable assumption in cases where $\mathcal{A}$ is purchasing goods from $\mathcal{B}$, since $\mathcal{A}$ is likely already trusting $\mathcal{B}$ with far more personal and identifying information including *e.g.*, her shipping address or IP address.
3. For our on-blockchain scheme only, payees $\mathcal{B}$ always receive payments in a fresh ephemeral Bitcoin address $Addr_B$ controlled by them. Any communication between $Addr_B$ and $\mathcal{I}$ is done anonymously (*e.g.*, using Tor). The payee can transfer the payment from $Addr_B$ to his long-lived Bitcoin address if the protocol successfully completes.
4. Payers only make one anonymous payment per epoch. Similarly, payees only accept one payment per epoch (*i.e.*, we assume they do not create multiple ephemeral addresses to receive multiple payments in one epoch).[3]

Given these assumptions, the anonymity properties of our on-blockchain scheme are:

Set-Anonymity Within an Epoch. Our assumptions imply that in every epoch there are exactly n addresses making payments (playing the role of payer $\mathcal{A}$) and n receiving addresses (playing the role of $\mathcal{B}$). All these Bitcoin addresses should belong to different users. Anyone looking at the blockchain can see the participating addresses of payers and payees, but should not be able to distinguish which payer paid which payee within a specific epoch. Thus, for all successfully completed payments within an epoch, the offered anonymity set has size n. In other words, the probability of successfully linking any chosen payer $\mathcal{A}$ to a payee should not be more than $1/n$ plus some negligible function. This means that an adversary (or a potentially malicious $\mathcal{I}$) can do no better than randomly guessing who paid whom during an epoch.

Resilient Anonymity. All payments should be totally anonymous until the recipient, $\mathcal{B}$, chooses to transfer them to an address linkable to $\mathcal{B}$. Even if a party *aborts* our protocol before it completes in an epoch, the *intended* recipient of a payment should remain totally anonymous.

Transparency of Anonymity Set. Users in our on-blockchain scheme learn the membership of their anonymity set after a transaction completes, just like

---

[3] We could allow users to perform multiple payments (by using multiple Bitcoin addresses that belong to them) but this would reduce their anonymity and make our analysis more complex.

anyone else who might be looking at the blockchain. This property is unusual for eCash schemes, but quite common for bitcoin mixes. Thus, if a particular B feels his anonymity set is too small in one epoch, he can increase the size of his anonymity set by remixing in a subsequent epoch. For instance, if $Addr_B$ gets paid in an epoch with $n = 4$, he can create a fresh ephemeral address $Addr'_B$ and have $Addr_B$ pay $Addr'_B$ in a subsequent epoch. If the subsequent epoch has a $n = 100$, then B increases the size of his anonymity set.

Our on-blockchain protocol achieves all the above anonymity properties, which also generalize to our mixing service (Sect. 4.2). Our mixing service has the additional advantage that A does not need to trust B since they are the same user. Our off-blockchain scheme only offers set-anonymity against $\mathcal{I}$ when $\mathcal{I}$ is honest-but-curious, rather than malicious (Sect. 5.3). Additionally, our off-blockchain scheme does not achieve the anonymity-set transparency or the anonymity resilience property.

Remark: Intersection Attacks. Anyone observing the anonymity-set membership in each epoch can attempt *intersection attacks* that de-anonymize users across epochs (*e.g.*, frequency analysis). This follows because we are *composing* set-anonymity across multiple epochs, and is a downside of any mix-based service that composes across epochs. ([3] has a detailed description of intersection attacks.) By anonymity transparency, anyone looking at the blockchain can attempt an intersection attack on our on-blockchain scheme. Our off-blockchain scheme (roughly) only allows $\mathcal{I}$ to do this (Sect. 5.3).

2.2 Security Properties

Fair-Exchange. There will always be a *fair-exchange* between $V \leftrightarrow BTC$. Our property ensures that: (i) malicious intermediary $\mathcal{I}$ cannot obtain a bitcoin from A unless it honestly creates a voucher for her, and (ii) malicious intermediary $\mathcal{I}$ cannot obtain a voucher V from B and refuse to pay a bitcoin back. This property is also true against malicious users: (iii) malicious A cannot refuse to give a bitcoin to $\mathcal{I}$ when receiving V, and (iv) malicious B cannot receive a bitcoin from $\mathcal{I}$ without presenting a (valid) V.

Unforgeability. A user cannot create a valid V without interacting with $\mathcal{I}$.

Double-Spending Security. A user can not redeem the same V more than once.

DoS Resistance. The intermediary $\mathcal{I}$ should be resistant to Denial of Service (DoS) attacks where a malicious user starts but never finishes many parallel fair exchanges (redemptions) of a V for a BTC.

Sybil Resistance. The protocol should be resistant to a Sybils (*i.e.*, identities that are under the control of single user) that attempt to de-anonymize a target user.

3 Implementing Fair Exchange via Scripts and Blind Signatures

We explain how the transaction contracts $T_{offer(BTC \to V)}$ and $T_{fulfill(BTC \to V)}$ implement the fair exchange $BTC \to V$ used in our protocol ($V \to BTC$ is analogous).

We start with some background on transaction contracts. Recall that Bitcoin has no inherent notion of an "account"; instead, users merely move bitcoins from old transactions to new transactions, with the blockchain providing a public record of all valid moves. To do this, each transaction contains a list of *outputs*. These outputs hold a portion of that transaction's bitcoins and a set of rules describing the conditions under which the portioned bitcoins in that output can be transferred to a new transaction. The rules for spending outputs are written in a non-Turing-complete language called *Script*. One transaction *spends* another transaction when it successfully satisfies the rules in a script. Transaction contracts (aka smart contracts [20]) are written as scripts, *e.g.*, $\mathcal{A}$ will only pay $\mathcal{B}$ if some condition is met. Using the CHECKLOCKTIMEVERIFY feature [21] of scripts, we can *timelock* a transaction, so that funds can be reclaimed if a contract has not been spent within a given time window tw.

We use timelocking to implement the $BTC \to V$ fair exchange. The fair exchange begins when a user $\mathcal{A}$ generates (and the blockchain confirms) a transaction contract $T_{offer(BTC \to V)}$ which says that $\mathcal{A}$ offers one bitcoin to $\mathcal{I}$ under the condition "$\mathcal{I}$ must compute a valid blind signature on the blinded serial number $\overline{sn}$ within time window tw"; if the condition is not satisfied, the bitcoin reverts to $\mathcal{A}$. More precisely, $\mathcal{A}$ first chooses a random serial number sn, blinds it to $\overline{sn}$, and then uses $\overline{sn}$ to create a transaction contract $T_{offer(BTC \to V)}$ with an output of one bitcoin that is spendable in a future transaction T_f if one of the following conditions is satisfied:

1. T_f is signed by $\mathcal{I}$ and contains a valid blind signature $\overline{\sigma}$ on $\overline{sn}$[4], or
2. T_f is signed by $\mathcal{A}$ and the time window tw has expired.

The contract $T_{offer(BTC \to V)}$ is *fulfilled* if $\mathcal{I}$ posts a transaction $T_f = T_{fulfill(BTC \to V)}$ that contains a valid blind signature $\overline{\sigma}$ on $\overline{sn}$. This would satisfy the first condition of $T_{offer(BTC \to V)}$ and so the offered bitcoin is transferred from $\mathcal{A}$ to $\mathcal{I}$. If $\mathcal{I}$ does not fulfill the contract within the time window tw, then $\mathcal{A}$ signs and posts a transaction T_f that returns the offered bitcoin back to $\mathcal{A}$, thus satisfying the second condition of $T_{offer(BTC \to V)}$.

---

[4] $\mathcal{I}$ signs T_f to stop a malicious miner that learns $\overline{\sigma}$ from stealing the bitcoin $\mathcal{A}$ gives $\mathcal{I}$.

Blind Signature Scheme. Our fair exchange requires blind signatures with exactly two rounds of interaction. We use Boldyreva's [4] scheme, instantiated with elliptic curves for which the Weil or Tate pairing are efficiently computable and the computational Diffie-Hellman problem is sufficiently hard. While bitcoin supports elliptic curve operations, it uses a curve (Secp256k1) that does not support the required bilinear pairings. Thus, we need a soft fork to add an opcode that supports elliptic curves with efficient bilinear pairings (*i.e.*, supersingular curves of the type $y^2 = x^3 + 2x \pm 1$ over $\mathbb{F}_{e^\ell}$).

We use standard multiplicative notation and overlines to denote blinded values. Let $\mathbb{G}$ be a cyclic additive group of prime order p in which the gap Diffie-Hellman problem [5] is hard and $\mathbb{G}'$ a cyclic multiplicative group of prime order q. By e we denote the bilinear pairing map: $e : \mathbb{G} \times \mathbb{G} \to \mathbb{G}'$. Let g be a generator of the group and H be a hash function mapping arbitrary strings to elements of $\mathbb{G}\backslash\{1\}$. Let (p, g, H) be public parameters and $(sk, pk = g^{sk})$ be the signer's secret/public key pair.

- To blind sn, user $\mathcal{A}$ picks random $r \in \mathbb{Z}_p^*$ and sets $\overline{sn} = H(sn)g^r$.
- To sign $\overline{sn}$, signer $\mathcal{I}$ computes $\overline{\sigma} = \overline{sn}^{sk}$.
- To unblind the blind signature $\overline{\sigma}$, user $\mathcal{A}$ computes $\sigma = \overline{\sigma} pk^{-r}$.
- To verify the signature σ on sn, anyone holding pk checks that the bilinear pairing $e(pk, H(sn))$ is equal to $e(g, \sigma)$.
- To verify that the *blinded signature* $\overline{\sigma}$ on the blinded $\overline{sn}$, anyone holding pk can verify that this is valid (intermediate) signature by checking if $e(pk, \overline{m}) = e(g, \overline{\sigma})$.

4   On-Blockchain Anonymous Protocols

We now discuss the details of on-blockchain protocol depicted in Figs. 2 and 3.

As shown in Fig. 2, our protocol interleaves two fair exchanges $BTC \to V$ (implemented using $T_{offer(V \to BTC)}$ and $T_{fulfill(V \to BTC)}$) and $V \to BTC$ (implemented using $T_{offer(BTC \to V)}$ and $T_{fulfill(BTC \to V)}$). The interleaving is designed to ensure that a malicious $\mathcal{I}$ cannot issue a voucher V to $\mathcal{A}$ and then subsequently refuse to redeem V from $\mathcal{B}$. The key idea is that it is in the interest of both $\mathcal{A}$ and $\mathcal{B}$ to force $\mathcal{I}$ to *commit* to redeeming the voucher $V = (sn, \sigma)$. To do this $\mathcal{A}$ starts by choosing the serial number sn for the voucher and sending its hash $h = H(sn)$ to $\mathcal{B}$; notice that h hides the value of sn and thus does not harm anonymity. Then, $\mathcal{B}$ uses h to force $\mathcal{I}$ to commit to redeeming a voucher with serial number sn. Specifically, $\mathcal{B}$ asks $\mathcal{I}$ to create the transaction contract $T_{offer(V \to BTC)}$ that offers one bitcoin to $\mathcal{B}$ under the condition "$\mathcal{B}$ must provide a *valid* voucher V with serial number sn such that $h = H(sn)$ within time window tw". To prevent double-spending, $\mathcal{I}$ agrees to create $T_{offer(V \to BTC)}$ iff the hash value h does *not* match the h of any prior transaction contract that $\mathcal{I}$ has signed. Once $T_{offer(V \to BTC)}$ is on the blockchain, committing that $\mathcal{I}$ will redeem the voucher with serial number sn, our two fair exchanges proceed as in Fig. 2.

The details of the scheme are as follows. Let k be the security parameter. We assume that $\mathcal{I}$ performs a one-time setup by posting public parameters on the blockchain. These parameters include the public parameters for the blind signature scheme, the fee value f and reward value w, and the time windows (tw_1, tw_2). (We define f, w below.)

1. $\mathcal{B}$ creates a fresh ephemeral Bitcoin address to receive the payment.
2. $\mathcal{A}$ randomly chooses $sn \xleftarrow{r} \{0,1\}^k$, computes $h \leftarrow H(sn)$ and sends h to $\mathcal{B}$.
3. $\mathcal{B}$ sends h to $\mathcal{I}$ and asks $\mathcal{I}$ to create transaction contract $T_{offer(V \rightarrow BTC)}$ offering one bitcoin to $\mathcal{B}$ under condition: "$\mathcal{B}$ must provide a *valid* voucher V with serial number whose hash is equal to h within time window tw_2".
4. If h does *not* match any h from prior transaction contracts signed by $\mathcal{I}$, then $\mathcal{I}$ creates the requested contract $T_{offer(V \rightarrow BTC)}$ and posts it to the blockchain.
5. $\mathcal{A}$ blinds sn to obtain $\overline{sn}$ and waits for $T_{offer(V \rightarrow BTC)}$ to be confirmed on the blockchain. Then $\mathcal{A}$ creates transaction $T_{offer(BTC \rightarrow V)}$, offering a $1 + w$ bitcoins to $\mathcal{I}$ under the condition "$\mathcal{I}$ must provide a valid blind signature on the blinded serial number $\overline{sn}$ within time window tw_1" (where $tw_1 > tw_2$ so that $\mathcal{I}$ cannot cheat by waiting until $T_{offer(BTC \rightarrow V)}$ expires but $T_{offer(V \rightarrow BTC)}$ has not).
6. To prevent $\mathcal{A}$ from double-spending the bitcoin offered in $T_{offer(BTC \rightarrow V)}$, $\mathcal{I}$ waits until the blockchain confirms $T_{offer(BTC \rightarrow V)}$. $\mathcal{I}$ then fulfills the $BTC \rightarrow V$ fair exchange by creating transaction $T_{fulfill(BTC \rightarrow V)}$ which contains the blinded signature $\overline{\sigma}$ on $\overline{sn}$. $T_{fulfill(BTC \rightarrow V)}$ is posted to the blockchain, and transfers $(1 + w)$ bitcoins from $T_{offer(BTC \rightarrow V)}$ to $\mathcal{I}$.
7. $\mathcal{A}$ learns $\overline{\sigma}$ from $T_{fulfill(BTC \rightarrow V)}$, unblinds $\overline{\sigma}$ to σ and sends $V = (sn, \sigma)$ to $\mathcal{B}$.
8. $\mathcal{B}$ creates a transaction $T_{fulfill(V \rightarrow BTC)}$ which contains the voucher $V = (sn, \sigma)$, and thus transfers the bitcoin in $T_{offer(V \rightarrow BTC)}$ to $\mathcal{B}$. $T_{fulfill(V \rightarrow BTC)}$ is posted to the blockchain and confirmed in the same block as $T_{fulfill(BTC \rightarrow V)}$.

Rewards. $\mathcal{A}$ offers $1 + w$ bitcoins to $\mathcal{I}$ in $T_{offer(BTC \rightarrow V)}$, but $\mathcal{I}$ only offers $\mathcal{B}$ 1 bitcoin in $T_{offer(V \rightarrow BTC)}$. The remaining w bitcoin is kept by $\mathcal{I}$ as a "reward" for completing its role in the protocol. $\mathcal{I}$ cannot steal w because w is paid via a fair exchange.

4.1   Anonymous Fee Vouchers

Bitcoin transactions include a transaction fee that is paid to the miner who confirms the transaction in the blockchain; if this transaction fee is not paid or is too low, it is extremely unlikely that this transaction will be confirmed. Since $\mathcal{I}$ can not trust $\mathcal{B}$ or $\mathcal{A}$, $\mathcal{I}$ should not be required to cover the cost of the transaction fee for first transaction contract $T_{offer(V \rightarrow BTC)}$ that $\mathcal{I}$ posts to the blockchain.

Following ideas from [3], we have $\mathcal{A}$ buy a special *anonymous fee voucher* V' of value f bitcoin from $\mathcal{I}$. The value $f \ll 1$ should be very small and is set as a public parameter. Since fee vouchers are anonymous and have low value, A should buy them out-of-band in bulk with cash, credit or bitcoin. Then, whenever A wishes to mix or make an anonymous payment, A sends an anonymous fee voucher V' to B, who in turn sends it to I with a request that I initiate the protocol. All this happens out-of-band. Note though, that the fee voucher V' is *not* created with a fair exchange, and thus I could steal f bitcoin by accepting V' but refusing to initiate the protocol. However, we argue that I has very little incentive to do this if, upon completing the protocol, I obtains a reward w that is significantly larger than f.

DoS Resistance. Fees raise the cost of an DoS attack where B starts and aborts many parallel sessions, locking I's bitcoins in many $T_{offer(V \rightarrow BTC)}$ transaction contracts. This is because B must forward an anonymous fee voucher V' from A to I every time B wishes to initiate our protocol. This method also works for our mixing service, where A and B are the same user. Moreover, if a party aborts a run of our protocol during an epoch, this has no affect on other runs in that epoch. This is in contrast to [10,18] where a single aborting player terminates the protocol for all parties in that mix.

Sybil Resistance. In a sybil attack, the adversary creates many sybil identities secretly under her control, and deanonymizes a target user by forcing the target to mix only with sybils [3,22]. To launch this attack on our protocol, the attacker could create m runs of our protocol (*i.e.,* m payers and payees) that occupy most of the intermediary I's resources, leaving only a single slot available for the targeted payer and payee. Again, we use fees to raise the cost of this attack, by requiring each of the m Sybil runs to pay a fee voucher of value f. If I performs a sybil attack, I avoids paying f but must pay all four transaction fees.

4.2 Anonymity Analysis

Before discussing the anonymity properties of our scheme we start by noting that in the first step of our protocol, B is always required to create a fresh ephemeral Bitcoin address $Addr_0$. Upon creation, this address is *completely anonymous*, in the sense that there is no way to link it to B's identity; this is a much stronger notion than the set anonymity defined in Sect. 2.1. Now suppose that A uses our protocol to pay a bitcoin to $Addr_0$. Then, as we will argue below, $Addr_0$ is now linkable to A with probability $1/n$ (if n payments happened in that epoch). However $Addr_0$ is still completely anonymous with respect to B's "Bitcoin identity", *i.e.,* the long-lived Bitcoin address that B uses to send and receive payments. If the funds from $Addr_0$ were paid into another fresh ephemeral Bitcoin address $Addr_1$ controlled by B, these funds would still be unlinkable to B. Indeed, the funds in $Addr_0$ only become linkable to B if they are transferred to an address controlled by B that already contains some bitcoins.

Set-Anonymity Within an Epoch. Our on-blockchain payment scheme achieves an anonymity set of size n within an epoch, as defined in Sect. 2.1. Suppose that n payments successfully complete during an epoch, and recall that each payer may only perform one payment per epoch and each payment is made to a fresh ephemeral address. It follows that there are n payers and n payees during the epoch. Any adversary (including $\mathcal{I}$) observing the blockchain can see the following: n payers' addresses, n payees' addresses, and n sets of transactions of the type $T_{offer(BTC \to V)}$, $T_{fulfill(BTC \to V)}$, $T_{offer(V \to BTC)}$, $T_{fulfill(V \to BTC)}$. For the adversary to link a payer to a payee, it would need to link a $T_{offer(BTC \to V)}$, $T_{fulfill(BTC \to V)}$ pair $(BTC \to V)$ to a $T_{offer(V \to BTC)}$, $T_{fulfill(V \to BTC)}$ pair $(V \to BTC)$. Let us first examine what do these pairs of transaction contracts reveal on the blockchain. The $BTC \to V$ pair reveals a blinded serial number $\overline{sn}$ and the corresponding intermediate (blinded) blind signature $\overline{\sigma}$. Meanwhile, the $V \to BTC$ pair reveals a serial number sn and the corresponding signature σ. As long as the blinding factor of sn is not revealed, the blind signature ensures that no one can link an sn to an $\overline{sn}$. The signatures $\overline{\sigma}$ and σ are similarly unlinkable (except with some negligible probability $\nu(k)$). Thus, the adversary's best strategy is to randomly link a payer to a payee, which succeeds with probability $1/n + \nu(k)$.

The same analysis applies to our mixing service. Moreover, mix users can repeatedly rerun the mix over several epochs, thus boosting the size of their anonymity set beyond what could be provided during a single epoch.

Resilient Anonymity and Transparency of Anonymity Set. Ephemeral addresses prevent $\mathcal{I}$ from de-anonymizing a payment from $\mathcal{A}$ to $\mathcal{B}$ by aborting or denying service. Suppose $\mathcal{I}$ aborts by refusing to issue $T_{fulfill(BTC \to V)}$ to $\mathcal{A}$ (Fig. 2). If this happens, $\mathcal{A}$ does not obtain voucher $V = (sn, \sigma)$ and cannot pass V on to $\mathcal{B}$. By the unforgeability of vouchers, it follows that $\mathcal{B}$ will not be able to issue a valid $T_{fulfill(V \to BTC)}$ that fulfills $T_{offer(V \to BTC)}$. Thus, $\mathcal{I}$ can de-anonymize the payment between $\mathcal{A}$ and $\mathcal{B}$ by matching the aborted exchange with $\mathcal{A}$ with the incomplete exchange with $\mathcal{B}$. As another possible attack, malicious $\mathcal{I}$ could instead refuse service to all payers apart from a target $\mathcal{A}$, and then identify $\mathcal{B}$ by finding the single $V \to BTC$ exchange that completes during the epoch. Fortunately, however, anonymity-set transparency allows $\mathcal{B}$ to detect these attacks. $\mathcal{B}$ can recover by discarding the ephemeral address it used in the attacked epoch, and chose a fresh ephemeral address in a subsequent epoch.

Note that for both our payment and mixing service one could attempt an intersection attack as discussed in Sect. 2.1.

5 Off-Blockchain Anonymous Payments over Micropayment Channel Networks

We start by reviewing off-blockchain transactions via micropayment channel networks and then describe how to make our protocol faster by adapting it to work with them.

5.1   Micropayment Channel Networks

Micropayment Channels. To establish a pairwise micropayment channel, $\mathcal{A}$ and $\mathcal{B}$ each pay some amount of bitcoins into an *escrow transaction* T_e which is posted to the blockchain. This escrow transaction is on-blockchain and therefore slow (≈ 10 mins), but all subsequent transactions are off-blockchain and therefore fast ($\approx$seconds). T_e ensures that no party reneges on an off-blockchain transaction. Suppose x bitcoins are paid into T_e. T_e offers these x bitcoins to be spent under condition: "The spending transaction is signed by both $\mathcal{A}$ and $\mathcal{B}$". Then, the spending transaction T_r has the form: "a bitcoins are paid to $\mathcal{A}$ and b bitcoins are paid to $\mathcal{B}$" where a and b reflect the agreed-upon balance of bitcoins between $\mathcal{A}$ and $\mathcal{B}$.

Once T_e is confirmed on the blockchain, $\mathcal{A}$ and $\mathcal{B}$ can transfer funds between themselves off-blockchain by signing a spending transaction T_r. Importantly, T_r is *not* posted to the blockchain. Instead, the existence of T_r creates a credible threat that either party can claim their allocated bitcoins by posting T_r to the blockchain; this prevents either party from reneging on the allocation reflected in T_r. To continue to make off-blockchain payments, $\mathcal{A}$ and $\mathcal{B}$ just need to sign a new transaction T_r' that reflects the new balance of bitcoins a' and b'. Micropayment channels have mechanisms that ensure that this later transaction T_r' always supersedes an earlier transaction T_r. Our protocol applies generically to any micropayment channel with such a mechanism, *e.g.*, Lightning Network [16], Duplex Micropayment Channels (DMC) [9].

Micropayment Channel Networks. Micropayment channel networks are designed to avoid requiring each *pair* of parties to pre-establish a *pairwise* micropayment channel between them. Indeed, such a requirement would be infeasible, since it requires each pair of users to lock funds into many different escrow transactions T_e on the blockchain. Instead, suppose a pair of users $\mathcal{A}$ and $\mathcal{B}$ are connected by a path of users with established pairwise micropayment channels (*i.e.*, $\mathcal{A}$ has a channel with $\mathcal{A}_1$, $\mathcal{A}_1$ has a channel with $\mathcal{A}_2$, ..., $\mathcal{A}_{m-1}$ has a channel with $\mathcal{A}_m$, $\mathcal{A}_m$ has a channel with $\mathcal{B}$). Then, the path of users can run a protocol to transfer funds from $\mathcal{A}$ to $\mathcal{B}$. However, it will not suffice to simply have each user $\mathcal{A}_i$ create a transaction paying the next user $\mathcal{A}_{i+1}$ in the path, since a malicious user $\mathcal{A}_k$ could steal funds by failing to create a a transaction for $\mathcal{A}_{k+1}$. Instead, the Lightning Network and DMC use a protocol based on *hash timelocked contracts* or HTLCs. A transaction T is an HTLC if it offers bitcoins under the condition: "The spending transaction must contain the preimage of y and be confirmed within timewindow tw", where $y = H(x)$ and x is a random value, *i.e.*, the preimage. We say that T is *locked under the preimage of y*.

Micropayment channels use HTLCs as follows. Suppose the existing balance between $\mathcal{A}$ and $\mathcal{B}$ is a bitcoin for $\mathcal{A}$ and b bitcoin for $\mathcal{B}$. Now suppose that $\mathcal{A}$ wants to transfer ϵ bitcoin to $\mathcal{B}$, updating the balances to $a - \epsilon$ and $b + \epsilon$. First, $\mathcal{B}$ chooses a random value x, computes $y = H(x)$, and announces y to everyone in the path. Then, $\mathcal{A}$ asks each pair of parties $(\mathcal{A}_i, \mathcal{A}_{i+1})$ on the path to transfer ϵ bitcoin *locked under the preimage of y* using the micropayment channel from

$\mathcal{A}_i$ to $\mathcal{A}_{i+1}$. The mechanics of the transfer between $\mathcal{A}_i$ and $\mathcal{A}_{i+1}$ are as follows. Suppose the existing balance between $\mathcal{A}_i$ and $\mathcal{A}_{i+1}$ is c bitcoin for $\mathcal{A}_i$ and d bitcoin for $\mathcal{A}_{i+1}$. Then $\mathcal{A}_i$ and $\mathcal{A}_{i+1}$ jointly sign a new spending transaction T_r' of the form "$c - \epsilon$ bitcoins are paid to $\mathcal{A}_i$ and $d + \epsilon$ bitcoins are paid to $\mathcal{A}_{i+1}$" under the condition "the spending transaction contains the preimage of y within timewindow tw". Once $\mathcal{A}$ sees that all the transactions on the path have been signed, it releases the preimage x to the path and the funds flow from $\mathcal{A}_i$ to $\mathcal{A}_j$. If any user refuses to sign a transaction, the timelock tw allows all signing users to reclaim their funds. The timelock is decremented along the path to prevent race conditions. This entire protocol occurs off-blockchain, with x and the HTLCs creating a credible threat that users can reclaim their funds if they are posted to the blockchain.

5.2 Anonymizing Micropayment Channel Networks

As a strawman for anonymous transactions in micropayment channel networks, we can replace the hash lock with the transaction contracts conditions in that we use in $T_{offer(V \to BTC)}$ and $T_{offer(BTC \to V)}$ (see Sect. 4). The protocol assumes paths of intermediate channels $(path_1, path_2)$ connecting $\mathcal{A}$ to $\mathcal{I}$ and $\mathcal{I}$ to $\mathcal{B}$ respectively, and has *Setup* phase as in our original on-blockchain protocol.

1. $\mathcal{A}$ chooses a random serial number sn, hashes it to $h = H(sn)$ and sends h to $\mathcal{B}$.
2. $\mathcal{B}$ uses h to lock a path of micropayment channels $(path_2)$ to $\mathcal{I}$ under the condition: "The spending transaction must provide a *valid* voucher V with serial number whose hash is equal to h within time window tw_2."
3. $\mathcal{A}$ blinds the serial number sn to obtain $\overline{sn}$. $\mathcal{A}$ asks $\mathcal{B}$ to confirm that each party on $path_2$ from $\mathcal{A}$ to $\mathcal{I}$ has properly locked the path. Then, $\mathcal{A}$ asks $\mathcal{I}$ to lock a path $path_1$ of micropayment channels between $\mathcal{A}_i$ and $\mathcal{I}$ under the condition: "The spending transaction must provide a valid blind signature on the blinded serial number $\overline{sn}$ within time window tw_1" where $tw_1 > tw_2$.
4. $\mathcal{I}$ then reveals $\overline{\sigma}$ to every party on $path_1$, unlocking the path from $\mathcal{I}$ to $\mathcal{A}$. $\mathcal{A}$ obtains $\overline{\sigma}$, unblinds it to σ and thus obtains the voucher $V = (\sigma, sn)$. $\mathcal{A}$ sends $V = (\sigma, sn)$ to $\mathcal{B}$ who releases it to every party on path $path2$, unlocking the path from $\mathcal{I}$ to $\mathcal{B}$.

We again need the notion of an epoch. Since we do not have blocks to coordinate these epochs, we instead use synchronized clocks. We break an epoch of q seconds into three equal divisions of $\frac{q}{3}$ seconds long. $path_2$ is set up in first division, $path_1$ is set up second and $path_1$ and $path_2$ are resolved in third division. Also, we can add anonymous fee vouchers to this protocol, since fee vouchers are redeemed out of band (Sect. 4.1).

5.3 Anonymity Analysis

Of the properties in Sect. 2.1, our off-blockchain scheme only supports set anonymity within an epoch (as discussed in Sect. 4.2) when $\mathcal{I}$ is *honest-but-curious*. That is, $\mathcal{I}$ follows the protocol without aborting or denying services to other payers and payees, but is still curious to learn which payer is paying which payee. However, we still support fair-exchange against a malicious $\mathcal{I}$ (Sect. 6) as well as set-anonymity within an epoch against malicious third parties.

We only support anonymity against honest-but-curious $\mathcal{I}$ because we cannot use fresh ephemeral addresses in this off-blockchain context. This follows because choosing a fresh address amounts to establishing a fresh micropayment channel. Because this requires a fresh escrow transaction T_e to be posted on the blockchain (taking $\approx$10 mins), it obviates the speed benefits of the off-blockchain scheme. Recall that $\mathcal{B}$ discards its ephemeral address in order to recover from an epoch where a malicious $\mathcal{I}$ de-anonymized the payment from $\mathcal{A}$ to $\mathcal{B}$ by aborting or denying service (Sect. 4.2).

We have also given up on anonymity transparency. Because transactions are no longer posted on the blockchain, even users that participate in the protocol cannot learn the size or membership of their anonymity set.

Proxy Addresses. We need the notion of *proxy addresses* to ensure that no parties (other than $\mathcal{I}$) can break anonymity by behaving maliciously. Notice that in a micropayment channel network, a malicious user $\mathcal{A}_i$ along the path $path_1$ from $\mathcal{A}$ to $\mathcal{I}$ can abort the protocol by refusing to create the appropriate transactions. Now if $\mathcal{A}_i$ is also on the path $path_2$ from $\mathcal{I}$ to $\mathcal{B}$, then $\mathcal{A}_i$ can abort the protocol and de-anonymize $\mathcal{A}$ and $\mathcal{B}$ in the same way that $\mathcal{I}$ can. To prevent this attack, we need to make sure that $\mathcal{I}$ is the only party that is on both $path_1$ and $path_2$. The idea is that every user $\mathcal{B}$ of our system has an additional proxy address $Addr_B^{px}$, and uses this address to establish, just once, a (reusable) micropayment channel directly to $\mathcal{I}$. This ensures that $path_2$ consists of only $\mathcal{I}$ and $Addr_B^{px}$. Then, $\mathcal{B}$ will receive payments to its proxy address $Addr_B^{px}$ using the strawman protocol of Sect. 5.2 in a one epoch. In the subsequent epoch, $\mathcal{B}$ will rerun the strawman protocol to transfer funds from $Addr_B^{px}$ (acting as user $\mathcal{A}$) to its long-lived address $Addr_B$ (acting as user $\mathcal{B}$).

Intersection Attacks. The lack of anonymity set transparency and the use of proxy addresses implies that only $\mathcal{I}$ can observe the full membership of the anonymity set during each epoch. As payments between proxy $Addr_B^{px}$ and identity $Addr_B$ addresses occur in contiguous epochs, $\mathcal{I}$ could use an intersection attack [3] to infer their relationship. Other adversaries only observe off-blockchain transactions flowing through them.

6 Security Analysis

Fair-Exchange. Our schemes prevent parties from stealing from each other.

1. The $BTC \rightarrow V$ fair exchange (Sect. 3) ensures that (1) $\mathcal{I}$ cannot steal $\mathcal{A}$'s bitcoin without issuing her a valid voucher V, and (2) $\mathcal{A}$ cannot refuse to pay $\mathcal{I}$ a bitcoin upon receiving a V. (Fair exchange properties (i) and (iii) from Sect. 2.2.)

2. The $V{\rightarrow}BTC$ fair exchange ensures that $\mathcal{B}$ cannot steal $\mathcal{I}$'s bitcoins without actually redeeming V. Also, $\mathcal{I}$ cannot refuse to redeem a $V = (sn, \sigma)$ that it issued to $\mathcal{A}$. This follows because, as discussed in Sect. 4, $\mathcal{I}$ commits to the redemption of V when it posts $T_{offer(V \rightarrow BTC)}$ (which contains h, where $h = H(sn)$). Moreover, recall that $T_{fulfill(BTC \rightarrow V)}$ is transaction where (a) $1 + w$ bitcoin are transferred from $\mathcal{A}$ to $\mathcal{I}$, and (b) $\mathcal{I}$ issues V by providing the blind signature $\overline{\sigma}$. Since $T_{offer(V \rightarrow BTC)}$ is posted to the blockchain before $T_{offer(V \rightarrow BTC)}$, it follows that $\mathcal{A}$ does not pay $\mathcal{I}$ for V until $\mathcal{I}$ has committed to redeeming V. (Fair exchange properties (ii) and (iv) from Sect. 2.2.)

3. $\mathcal{I}$ cannot prevent $\mathcal{B}$ from redeeming V by issuing V just before $T_{offer(V \rightarrow BTC)}$ expires. This follows because $\mathcal{A}$ choose tw_1 such that $tw_1 > tw_2$ which ensures that $T_{offer(BTC \rightarrow V)}$ expires earlier that $T_{offer(V \rightarrow BTC)}$. This way, if $\mathcal{I}$ takes too long to issue $T_{offer(BTC \rightarrow V)}$, $\mathcal{A}$ will have already reclaimed her refunds. (Fair exchange property (ii) from Sect. 2.2.)

Unforgeability and Double-Spending. Unforgeability follows from the underlying blind signature scheme, which ensures that only the intermediary $\mathcal{I}$ can issue vouchers $V = (sn, \sigma)$. Moreover, vouchers cannot be double-spent because if $\mathcal{I}$ has previously seen $h = H(sn)$, $\mathcal{I}$ will refuse to post $T_{offer(V \rightarrow BTC)}$.

DoS and Sybil Resistance. Both our on- and off-blockchain schemes support anonymous fee vouchers, and thus resist DoS and sybil attacks (Sect. 4.1).

7   Conclusion

In this work we developed an eCash inspired technique that can be used to enhance anonymity in Bitcoin transactions that happen on the blockchain or via micropayment channel networks (off-blockchain). Both our schemes provide fair-exchange security, forgery and double-spending security and moreover are resistant to DoS and Sybil attacks. Regarding anonymity, our on-blockchain scheme is anonymous against malicious users or a malicious intermediary $\mathcal{I}$. Our off-blockchain scheme is still anonymous against malicious users but is only anonymous against an honest-but-curious $\mathcal{I}$. Achieving anonymity against a malicious intermediary for off-blockchain schemes is left as an interesting open problem.

Acknowledgments. We thank Dimitris Papadopoulos, Ann Ming Samborski and the anonymous reviewers for comments on this draft. This work was funded by the National Science Foundation under grants 1012910 and 1350733.

References

1. Barber, S., Boyen, X., Shi, E., Uzun, E.: Bitter to better — how to make bitcoin a better currency. In: Keromytis, A.D. (ed.) FC 2012. LNCS, vol. 7397, pp. 399–414. Springer, Heidelberg (2012)

2. Sasson, E.B., Chiesa, A., Garman, C., Green, M., Miers, I., Tromer, E., Virza, M.: Zerocash: decentralized anonymous payments from bitcoin. In: IEEE Security and Privacy (SP), pp. 459–474 (2014)

3. Bissias, G., Ozisik, A.P., Levine, B.N., Liberatore, M.: Sybil-resistant mixing for bitcoin. In: Workshop on Privacy in the Electronic Society, pp. 149–158. ACM (2014)

4. Boldyreva, A.: Threshold signatures, multisignatures and blind signatures based on the gap-diffie-hellman-group signature scheme. In: PKC, vol. 2567, pp. 31–46 (2003)

5. Boneh, D., Lynn, B., Shacham, H.: Short signatures from the Weil pairing. In: Boyd, C. (ed.) ASIACRYPT 2001. LNCS, vol. 2248, p. 514. Springer, Heidelberg (2001)

6. Bonneau, J., Miller, A., Clark, J., Narayanan, A., Kroll, J.A., Felten, E.W.: Sok: research perspectives and challenges for bitcoin and cryptocurrencies. In: IEEE Security and Privacy (SP) (2015)

7. Bonneau, J., Narayanan, A., Miller, A., Clark, J., Kroll, J.A., Felten, E.W.: Mixcoin: anonymity for bitcoin with accountable mixes. In: Christin, N., Safavi-Naini, R. (eds.) FC 2014. LNCS, vol. 8437, pp. 481–499. Springer, Heidelberg (2014)

8. Chaum, D.: Blind signature system. In: Chaum, D. (ed.) CRYPTO. Springer, New York (1983)

9. Decker, C., Wattenhofer, R.: A fast and scalable payment network with bitcoin duplex micropayment channels. In: Pelc, A., Schwarzmann, A.A. (eds.) SSS 2015. LNCS, vol. 9212, pp. 3–18. Springer, Heidelberg (2015)

10. Maxwell, G.: Coinjoin: bitcoin privacy for the real world (2013)

11. Maxwell, G.: Coinswap: transaction graph disjoint trustless trading (2013)

12. Meiklejohn, S., Pomarole, M., Jordan, G., Levchenko, K., Voelker, G.M., Savage, S., McCoy, D.: A fistful of bitcoins: characterizing payments among men with no names. In: Proceedings of the ACM SIGCOMM Internet Measurement Conference, IMC, pp. 127–139 (2013)

13. Meiklejohn, S., Orlandi, C.: Privacy-enhancing overlays in bitcoin. In: Brenner, M., Christin, N., Johnson, B., Rohloff, K. (eds.) FC 2015 Workshops. LNCS, vol. 8976, pp. 127–141. Springer, Heidelberg (2015)

14. Miers, I., Garman, C., Green, M., Rubin, A.D.: Zerocoin: anonymous distributed e-cash from bitcoin. In: IEEE Security and Privacy (SP), pp. 397–411 (2013)

15. Nakamoto, S.: Bitcoin: a peer-to-peer electronic cash system. Consulted 1(2012), 28 (2008)

16. Poon, J., Dryja, T.: The bitcoin lightning network: scalable off-chain instant payments. Technical report (2015). https://lightning.network

17. Ron, D., Shamir, A.: Quantitative analysis of the full bitcoin transaction graph. In: Sadeghi, A.-R. (ed.) FC 2013. LNCS, vol. 7859, pp. 6–24. Springer, Heidelberg (2013)

18. Ruffing, T., Moreno-Sanchez, P., Kate, A.: Coinshuffle: practical decentralized coin mixing for bitcoin. In: Kutyłowski, M., Vaidya, J. (eds.) ICAIS 2014, Part II. LNCS, vol. 8713, pp. 345–364. Springer, Heidelberg (2014)

19. Saxena, A., Misra, J., Dhar, A.: Increasing anonymity in bitcoin. In: Böhme, R., Brenner, M., Moore, T., Smith, M. (eds.) FC 2014 Workshops. LNCS, vol. 8438, pp. 122–139. Springer, Heidelberg (2014)

20. Szabo, N.: Formalizing and securing relationships on public networks. First Monday 2(9) (1997)

21. Todd, P.: BIP 65: OP CHECKLOCKTIMEVERIFY. Bitcoin improvement proposal (2014)
22. Tschorsch, F., Scheuermann, B.: Bitcoin and beyond: a technical survey on decentralized digital currencies
23. Valenta, L., Rowan, B.: Blindcoin: blinded, accountable mixes for bitcoin. In: Brenner, M., Christin, N., Johnson, B., Rohloff, K. (eds.) FC 2015 Workshops. LNCS, vol. 8976, pp. 112–126. Springer, Heidelberg (2015)
24. Ziegeldorf, J.H., Grossmann, F., Henze, M., Inden, N., Wehrle, K. Coinparty: secure multi-party mixing of bitcoins. In: Proceedings of the 5th ACM Conference on Data and Application Security and Privacy, pp. 75–86. ACM (2015)

Proofs of Proofs of Work with Sublinear Complexity

Aggelos Kiayias, Nikolaos Lamprou[(✉)], and Aikaterini-Panagiota Stouka

National and Kapodistrian University of Athens, Athens, Greece
aggelos@di.uoa.gr, nikolaoslabrou@yahoo.gr, katerinastou21@yahoo.gr

Abstract. In the setting of blockchain based transaction ledgers we study the problem of "simplified payment verification" (SPV) which refers to the setting of a transaction verifier that wishes to examine the last k blocks of the blockchain (e.g., for the purpose of verification of a certain transaction) using as only advice the genesis block (or some "checkpoint" block that is known to it).

The straightforward solution to this task requires the delivery of the blockchain, the verification of the proof of work it contains, and subsequently the examination of the last k blocks. It follows that the communication required to complete this task is linear in the length of the chain.

At first thought the above seems the best one can hope: a sublinear in the length of the chain solution to the problem will be susceptible to an attacker that, using precomputation, can fool the verifier.

Contrary to this intuition, we show that with a suitable modification to the current Bitcoin blockchain protocol (that incurs a single hash expansion in each block and gives rise to the notion of an *interconnected blockchain*) we can produce *proofs of proof of work* with sublinear complexity in the length of the chain hence enabling SPV to be performed much more efficiently.

1 Introduction

Bitcoin, introduced by Nakamoto [10], and other numerous decentralized cryptocurrencies that were developed using the same codebase, have at their core a blockchain-based ledger of transactions. In these systems the ledger is a distributed data structure where transactions are organized into blocks. The blocks themselves form a hash chain so that each block is associated with a proof of work puzzle [1,4,7,11] and it points to a single previous block. A valid blockchain is rooted at a genesis block that is hard-coded into the client software that supports the distributed ledger.

The blockchain is maintained by a dynamically changing set of players that are called miners. The main task of each miner is to solve a proof of work and thus produce the next block. A transaction is validated when it is added to the blockchain. The certainty placed upon a certain transaction is associated to

This research was supported by ERC project CODAMODA, # 259152.

J. Clark et al. (Eds.): FC 2016 Workshops, LNCS 9604, pp. 61–78, 2016.
DOI: 10.1007/978-3-662-53357-4_5

the depth that is found in the blockchain. The deeper a transaction is placed in the blockchain the more certain it becomes that it will remain there. This was originally argued in [10] in a simplified model where the honest players are assumed to act in unison and the adversary follows a specific strategy. Security in the setting where the honest players are distributed and the adversary may exploit this was subsequently formally considered and proven in [6]. In this latter work two properties are introduced: common prefix and chain quality, and it is shown that with overwhelming probability in a parameter k, honest players will agree on the same prefix of the blockchain (after k blocks are pruned) and such chain will contain a certain percentage of blocks produced by honest players. These two properties were shown to imply that transactions in the ledger are "persistent" and that the ledger itself has "liveness" i.e., it is impossible for the adversary to stifle new transactions indefinitely.

In this work we study the problem of simplified payment verification or SPV. Introduced in [10], this problem considers a verifier that wishes to examine the ledger for a recent transaction. The verifier has as input a transaction identifier, say tx as well as the genesis block.[1] The verifier, with only this information, wishes to verify with high probability that the transaction has been included in the ledger and be sure that it will remain there with high probability. Based on the results stated above it is simple to implement such SPV verification as follows: the verifier will query the network and receive various blockchains (possibly some generated by an adversary that wishes to fool him) containing only the block headers for most blocks except the last k ones that are provided with all transactions (such communications have been referred as "SPV proofs"); the verifier will verify the integrity of the received chains and will select the one with the most proof of work. Finally, if the transaction with identifier tx is found at a depth say k it will conclude that the transaction is valid (with a probability of error as detailed by the persistence property of [6]). This SPV operation is more efficient than running a "full node" since not all transaction history needs to be received and verified.

An important observation regarding the above solution is that it is seemingly impossible to improve to below linear complexity in the length of the blockchain. Indeed, if a verifier is only allowed sublinear complexity it will not be able to verify that all the proofs of work in the received blockchains are valid. In this way it will only be able to verify fragments of given blockchains at best and this may open the door to potential attacks by an adversary that prepares ahead of time suitable blockchain fragments that are unrelated to the genesis block but are otherwise seemingly valid portions of the main blockchain.

Our Results. In this work, we present a method to construct *proofs of proof of work* that have sublinear complexity in the blockchain length. These proofs are capable of enabling "lite" SPV verification that is substantially more efficient compared to the full SPV verification described above. Our solution requires a modification in the current Bitcoin codebase that incurs a small overhead per each block that never exceeds a logarithmic function in the length of the

---

[1] Or a checkpoint block, if the verifier is in possession of such a block.

blockchain and can be compressed to a single hash value; this gives rise to a special type of blockchain that we call an *interconnected* blockchain.

In our solution the lite verifier receives a pair $(\mathcal{X}, \pi)$, where $\mathcal{X}$ is a blockchain fragment corresponding to the rightmost k blocks of the senders' chain and π is a proof of the proof of work that the pruned chain (denoted by $\mathcal{C}^{\lceil k}$) represents. Constructing the proof π is achieved via the following mechanism.

Recall that each block in a blockchain is associated with a proof of work which corresponds to a suitably formed value w that satisfies the inequality $H(w) < T$ where H is a hash function (e.g., SHA-256 in the case of Bitcoin) and T is a target value which is determined via a target calculation function (this function takes into account the rate of growth of the blockchain and reflects the size of the set of miners that participate in the protocol).

Our new mechanism operates as follows: whenever a block with a lower than usual hash is created we mark this in the next block as a continuation of a "deeper" chain that we call the inner chain of depth i where i is the greatest integer for which it holds $H(w) < T/2^i$. Specifically, each block carries a vector of pointers (which can be thought of expanding the standard reverse pointing link in a blockchain across multiple levels). In this way, in our modified blockchain, a block will have a vector of pointers denoted as interlink $= \langle s_0, \ldots, s_l \rangle$ such that s_0 points to the genesis block and for $i = 1, \ldots, l$, s_i points to the previous block with hash value smaller than $T/2^i$. Note that l would be the largest integer for which a hash in the blockchain is less than $T/2^l$ (and s_l is a pointer to the most recent such hash).

The construction of the proof π is as follows: the sender will remove the k-suffix from its local chain $\mathcal{C}$ and denote it as $\mathcal{X}$. Then, in the remaining prefix denoted as $\mathcal{C}^{\lceil k}$, he will attempt to find the deepest inner chain π that is of length at least m (the value m is a security parameter). The pair $(\mathcal{X}, \pi)$ will be the proof and will be transmitted to the lite verifier. In the optimistic scenario where the adversary does not actively interfere there is no further interaction between the lite verifier and the prover. In the general case, the adversary may invest hashing power in order to produce blocks with very low target, with the only purpose to increase the communication complexity between a lite verifier and a prover. In such case, the lite verifier engages in further interaction with the provers in order to be fully convinced.

Finally, we present a formal treatment of security for lite SPV proofs. Our argument is a *simulation-based* one. Security for a lite verifier is captured by the following statement: for any adversary that produces an SPV proof directed to a lite verifier there is an adversary producing an SPV proof directed to a regular SPV verifier that produces the same outcome. We establish the above security condition with overwhelming probability in m where m is a parameter of the lite verification protocol.

In our construction the complexity of the lite verifier will be shown to be $O(m \log n)$ in the optimistic case which can be improved in a straightforward manner to be $O(m \log \log n)$ where n is the blockchain length using Merkle trees.

Related Work. The first suggestion we are aware of[2] regarding the use of low hash values that appear naturally in the blockchain as an indicator of total proof of work was in a post in the Bitcoin forum [9]. A suggestion for a modification of the Bitcoin protocol was made in this post to include in each block a single "back-link" to the most recent block with a hash value less than half that of the previous block. Potential benefits of this modification were discussed including the possibility of using such pointers in SPV proofs.

In a short article posted in the Bitcoin-development list [5] this idea was taken further by suggesting to include a data structure containing various such back-links to previous blocks. An exact form of the data structure was not described and it was suggested that further research would be required to determine the most suitable data structure. A number of use-cases were discussed including the possibility of constructing compact SPV proofs as well as the design of "symmetrical two-way pegging schemes" between Bitcoin and side-chains. This latter concept, formulated in [2], enables the transfer of ledger assets from one main chain (say Bitcoin) to pegged side-chains. It is argued that such side-chains enable experimentation with new features in blockchain design and hence pegging them to, say, the Bitcoin blockchain enables the fluid transition of assets to these alternative blockchains (that potentially offer enhanced functionality or robustness features that are difficult to be assessed ahead of time). The pegging operation itself requires the main blockchain to enable transactions that move assets to special outputs that can only be "unlocked by an SPV proof of possession in the side-chain." This effectively enables the transfer of assets from the main chain to the side-chain as well as their return to the main chain in case the owner of the assets wishes to do that. Building efficient SPV proofs is an important aspect of this mechanism and a suggestion along the lines of [5] is presented in [2]. The possibility of exploiting the SPV proof mechanism by an adversary is recognized and some countermeasures are briefly discussed however without any formal analysis or the conclusion to an explicit data structure and a proof construction algorithm.

Finally, we note that the Bitcoin modifications related to SPV node verification do not affect the operation of the full nodes of the blockchain protocol and thus are of a different nature to chain selection and reward mechanism modifications such as those suggested in the GHOST rule for blockchain selection [12] or the inclusive blockchain protocols of [8].

2 Preliminaries

We follow the same notation as the Bitcoin backbone protocol, [6]. Below we introduce some basic notation and terminology.

- $G(.), H(.)$ are cryptographic hash functions with output in $\{0,1\}^{\kappa}$.
- A block B has the following form: $B = \langle s, x, ctr \rangle$ where $s \in \{0,1\}^{\kappa}, x \in \{0,1\}^{*}, ctr \in \mathbb{N}$.

---

[2] We thank the anonymous reviewers of the 3rd Workshop on Bitcoin and Blockchain Research for providing pointers to the relevant forum posts.

- A round is the period during which all the parties in the network are able to synchronize and obtain each other's messages. The scheduling of messages is controlled by the adversary. Furthermore, in each round, the adversary is able to introduce arbitrary number of messages and deliver them selectively to the parties.
- The rightmost block of the chain $\mathcal{C}$ is the head $(\mathcal{C})$ and $\mathcal{C}^{\lceil k}$ is the chain $\mathcal{C}$ without the rightmost k blocks. If we suppose that head $(\mathcal{C}) = \langle s, x, ctr \rangle$ and the previous block is $\langle s', x', ctr' \rangle$ then it holds $s = H(ctr', G(s', x'))$; in general every block has a reference to the previous block and thus all the blocks form a chain.
- The block header can be defined as $\langle ctr, G(s, x) \rangle$.
- A proof of work is finding a value $ctr : 0 \leq ctr < 2^{32}$ so that $H(ctr, G(s, x)) < T$ where $T \in \{0, 1\}^{\kappa}$ is the target of the block.
- The value x is the information is stored in the a block. In the case of the Bitcoin protocol this information is a sequence of transactions (organized in the form of a Merkle tree).

3   Interconnected Blockchains

In order to produce a proof of proof of work, the prover with local chain $\mathcal{C}$ will produce the pair $(\mathcal{X}, \pi)$ by setting the $\mathcal{X}$ to be the k-suffix of its local chain $\mathcal{C}$ and computing the proof π. The proof π constitutes a collection of blocks that are part of chain $\mathcal{C}^{\lceil k}$ and are collected in a specific way detailed below.

A proof π is associated with an integer $i \in \mathbb{N}$ which is the *depth* of the proof. The blocks contained in the proof are determined by a special type of chain that we will call innerchain$_i$.

Definition 1. *An* innerchain$_i$ *parameterized by an index $i > 0$ is a valid chain derived from a chain $\mathcal{C}$ that has the feature that each block $B = \langle s, x, ctr \rangle$ satisfies $H(ctr, G(s, x)) < T/2^i$.*

In an innerchain$_i$ we observe that, intuitively, each block represents as much proof of work as 2^i blocks with target T of the parent chain $\mathcal{C}$. As a result, if the proof π consists of m blocks, then the innerchain$_i$ represents proof of work as much as $m \cdot 2^i$ blocks of target T.

In our system, in order to produce the proof, provers should extract innerchain$_i$ for some $i > 0$ from $\mathcal{C}^{\lceil k}$. This means that for every $i \in \mathbb{N}$ all blocks with hash value smaller than $T/2^i$ should form a chain. This leads to the notion of an *interconnected blockchain*.

Every block with hash value smaller than $T/2^i$ needs a pointer to the previous block with hash value smaller than $T/2^i$. This does not exist in regular blockchains of Bitcoin, so a suitable modification with a sequence of pointers in each block in $\mathcal{C}$ is needed. The addition of this data structure inside each block, that we will call interlink[] will give rise to an "interconnected blockchain." A graphical description of an interconnected chain is shown in Fig. 1.

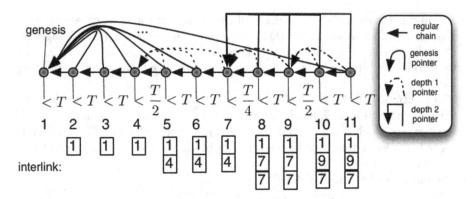

Fig. 1. A graphical depiction of an interconnected blockchain of 11 blocks that contains an inner chain of depth 1 (comprised of blocks $(1, 4, 7, 9)$) and an inner chain of depth 2 (comprised of blocks $(1, 7)$. The value of the interlink vector for each block is also shown.

The interlink data structure which should be included in each block B is *dynamic* and we formally define it below. Note that a block will be defined as $B = \langle s, x, ctr, \text{interlink} \rangle$ and the blockheader as $\langle ctr, G(s, x, \text{interlink}) \rangle$.

Definition 2. interlink *is a vector, which is included in each block B and for which it holds that, for all $i > 0$, interlink[i] is the hash of the previous block of B in chain C with hash value smaller than $T/2^i$. interlink[0] is the hash of the genesis block.*

Note that the length of the vector depends on the type of blocks that exist in chain C. Suppose that $B = \langle s, x, ctr, \text{interlink} \rangle$ is the head of the chain and $B' = \langle s', x', ctr', \text{interlink}' \rangle$ is the previous block; then interlink is equal to interlink$'$ after being updated with the algorithm we describe next.

3.1 Description of the Interlink-Update Algorithm

The purpose of this algorithm is to determine the operation that is needed in order to properly form an interconnected chain. When mining a new block, we must determine the appropriate set of pointers that will be used. Given the hash of the previous block denoted by s, the algorithm performs the following.

- Finds *max i*, so that $s = H(ctr', G(s', x', \text{interlink}')) < T/2^i$.
- Extends the size of interlink$'$ by adding $i - i'$ elements where the value i' equals *sizeof*(interlink$'$) (only if $i' < i$).
- Assign $H(ctr', G(s', x', \text{interlink}')) = s$ to interlink[1], ..., interlink[i].

Algorithm 1. Interlink-Update

    Input : $B' = \langle s', x', ctr', \text{interlink}' \rangle$
    Output: interlink
1 dynamic data structure interlink;
2 int $entry, i = 0$;
3 interlink = interlink$'$;
4 **while** $(H(ctr', G(s', x', \text{interlink}')) < \dfrac{T}{2^i})$ **do** ;   // finds vector's max length

5
6     $entry = i$;
7     $i = i + 1$;
8 **if** $entry = 0$ **then**
9   return interlink;
10 **else**
11   **for** $(i = 1, i \le entry, i + +)$ **do**
12   **if** $i > sizeof(\text{interlink})$ **then**
13        $sizeof(\text{interlink})+ = 1$;
14   interlink$[i] = H(ctr', G(s', x', \text{interlink}'))$;
15   return interlink;

---

4 Proving Proof of Work with Sublinear Complexity

4.1 Description of the Prover

When a prover with a local chain $\mathcal{C}$ receives a request from a lite verifier that asks for the rightmost k blocks, then it constructs a proof π of the proof of work in $\mathcal{C}^{\lceil k}$ using the algorithm ConstructProof.

This algorithm's input is $\mathcal{C}^{\lceil k-1}$ and its output is innerchain$_i = \pi$, where i is the max i so that there are at least m (security parameter) blocks with hash value smaller than $T/2^i$ in $\mathcal{C}^{\lceil k}$. The algorithm ConstructProof (which we will describe below) calls the next algorithm, which is ConstructInChain.

This algorithm uses a hash table, which is a data structure that stores (key, value) pairs. In our case, the hash table stores blocks with their hash values.

The algorithm ConstructInChain has as input a chain $\mathcal{C}$ and an i. Its output is a chain with all the blocks with hash value smaller than $T/2^i$ in $\mathcal{C}^{\lceil 1}$.

4.2 Description of the Lite Verifier

We consider the case when a lite verifier has received $(\mathcal{X}_A, \pi_A)$ and $(\mathcal{X}_B, \pi_B)$ from provers A, B respectively that supposedly hold chains $\mathcal{C}_A$ and $\mathcal{C}_B$. Its purpose is to find which proof represents the chain with the most proof of work.

– Without loss of generality, let $\pi_A = \text{innerchain}_\mu$, so its blocks have hash value smaller than $T' = T/2^\mu$ and $\pi_B = \text{innerchain}_{i+\mu}$, so its blocks have hash value smaller than $T/2^{i+\mu} = T'/2^i$ with $i \geq 0$.

Algorithm 2. ConstructInChain

Input : $\mathcal{C}, i$
Output: $InnerChain[\ ]$
1 data structure hashtable;
2 int $x, y = 0$;
3 int $j = \mathcal{C}.length$;
4 int $inner = 0$;
5 block B ;   // as it is defined above
6 $B = \mathcal{C}[j]$;
7 $x = B.\text{interlink}[i]$;   // B.interlink is interlink in block B
8 $y = B.\text{interlink}[i]$;
9 initialize $hashtable(\cdot)$ with all pairs (s, B) from $\mathcal{C}$;
10 **while** $(x != 0)$ **do**
11 | $x = B.\text{interlink}[i]$;
12 | **if** $x != 0$ **then**
13 | | $B = hashtable(x)$;
14 | | $inner = inner + 1$;

15 int $c = inner$;
16 chain $InnerChain[c]$;   // data structure which stores blocks
17 **while** $(y != 0)$ **do**
18 | $y = B.\text{interlink}[i]$;
19 | **if** $y != 0$ **then**
20 | | $B = hashtable(y)$;
21 | | $InnerChain[c] = B$;
22 | | $c = c - 1$;

23 **return** $InnerChain$;

Firstly the lite verifier examines whether the length of π_A and π_B is more than m without the genesis and whether the length of the suffixes is k respectively. If a proof does not satisfy the above properties, it is rejected.

Next, the lite verifier examines whether there is a common block x in $\mathcal{X}_A$ and $\mathcal{X}_B$, because in this case the lite verifier can find which chain represents more proof of work easily. Specifically this means that there is a fork between $\mathcal{C}_A$ and $\mathcal{C}_B$ in the last k blocks. So the lite verifier chooses the suffix that represents the most proof of work (more blocks after x since we assume the same T).

If there is no common block in the suffixes then the lite verifier will execute the algorithm MaxChain$[\pi_A, \pi_B]$ which will decide which proof represents the chain with the most proof of work. This algorithm may require additional interaction with A, B and operates as follows.

MaxChain uses two sub-procedures called RemoveCPhigh and RemoveCPlow. The RemoveCPlow algorithm with input (π_A, π_B) just prunes the common blocks, sets π'_A, π'_B to be the proofs without these common blocks and sets b to be the most recent common block in π_A, π_B.

Algorithm 3. ConstructProof

   Input : $C^{\lceil k-1}$
   Output: $Proof[\,]$
1 int $size = C^{\lceil k-1}.length$;
2 int $maxtarget = 0$;
3 chain $Proof[\,]$;
4 **while** $(C[size].\text{interlink}[maxtarget + 1]\;!= 0)$ **do**
5    $\lfloor$ $maxtarget = maxtarget + 1$;

6 int $i = maxtarget$;
7 **if** $maxtarget > 0$ **then**
8    $Proof[\,] = $ ConstructInChain $[C^{\lceil k-1}, i]$;
9   **while** $(Proof.length < m \wedge i > 0)$ **do**
10      $i = i - 1$;
11      $\lfloor$ $Proof[\,] = $ ConstructInChain $[C^{\lceil k-1}, i]$;

12   **if** $(i > 0)$ **then**
13      $|$ return $genesis\|Proof$;
14   **else**
15      $\lfloor$ return $C^{\lceil k-1}$;

16 return $C^{\lceil k-1}$;

The RemoveCPhigh on input (π_A, π_B) will actively query B for the chain with blocks with hash value smaller than $T/2^\mu$ that is omitted in π_B. Formally, it will return (π'_A, π'_B, b), where π'_A, π'_B are the proofs without the common prefix and b is the most recent common block with hash value smaller than $T/2^\mu$ in $\mathcal{C}_A$ and $\mathcal{C}_B$. In more detail, it operates as follows:

- We suppose that the proofs are stored in two arrays respectively. The algorithm looks for block $\pi_B[1]$ in π_A and it continues until it finds a $\pi_B[i']$ that it is not in π_A. As $\pi_B[i'-1]$ is included in π_A, there is a j, so that $\pi_A[j] = \pi_B[i'-1]$.
- It asks B for an array V with blocks with hash value smaller than $T/2^\mu$ between $\pi_B[i'-1]$ and $\pi_B[i']$. RemoveCPhigh will fail in case the array V is not returned by B.
- It finds min $j' \geq j+1$ so that $\pi_A[j']$ differs from $V[j'-j]$.
- $\pi_{B'}$ is π_B without the first $i'-1$ blocks and $\pi_{A'}$ is π_A without the first $j'-1$ blocks.
- $b = \pi_A[j'-1]$.
- Return (b, π'_A, π'_B).

Next we describe the algorithm MaxChain. Given diverging π_A, π_B, the algorithm will select the proof with the most proof of work as long as the diverging suffix is long enough (as determined by a parameter m). In case the algorithm cannot make a decision it will recurse, requesting proofs with lower depths from A, B as needed, until it reaches level 0 where a decision will be made independently of the parameter m. During these recursion steps if one of the communicating nodes, A, B, fails to support its proof (by providing the extra blocks that the lite node requests) the MaxChain algorithm will conclude that the opposing chain is the correct one (or it will inevitably fail in case no node is responding to its requests). In more detail the algorithm operates as follows:

- Firstly, the algorithm calls RemoveCPlow to obtain the pruned suffixes (this does not require interaction). Then, it checks whether $i > 0$. In this case, the proofs have different depths and the algorithm checks whether $\pi'_B.pow \geq \pi'_A.pow$ and simultaneously $\pi'_B.length \geq m$. If these two conditions hold, the lite verifier will choose π_B. Otherwise the algorithm uses RemoveCPhigh in order to discover the common prefix from the proofs π_A, π_B (this will require interacting with B).
- Secondly the algorithm checks which of the proofs represents the most proof of work. The proof with the most proof of work is returned if it has length at least m for π'_B and $2^i m$ for π'_A. Note that in this case a decision is made whose security hinges on the parameter m.
- If the proof with the most proof of work is not long enough the algorithm asks B or both A, B for a proof with a lower depth of the part of the chain ($\mathcal{C}_A^{\lceil k}$ or $\mathcal{C}_B^{\lceil k}$) without the common prefix and continues recursively. We use Request$_B[b, y]$ to denote a request from B for a proof with hash value smaller than $T/2^y$ of the chain $\mathcal{C}_B^{\lceil k}$ that is rooted at block b. Similarly, Request$_A[b, y]$ functions in the same way for player A.[3]

Eventually, the algorithm will either obtain diverging suffixes that are long enough or will reach the depth 0 (where the actual target T is used) where a decision will be made based solely on the amount of proof of work. This will determine the winning proof and the lite verifier may proceed to execute another comparison or conclude the process.

5   Efficiency Analysis

In this section we present the efficiency analysis of the proof system: first we discuss space complexity, i.e., the expansion that is required in the local storage of the full nodes due to the data structure of the interconnected blockchain. Then, we analyze the communication that is required to send the proof and the verification complexity of the lite verifier.

5.1   Space Complexity

We first show a suitable upper bound on the vector interlink that is the only addition in each block of the interconnected blockchain.

---

[3] We note that there is no provision for authenticated channels in the Bitcoin setting; hence when we refer to a request for information from a certain player this is not performed in an authenticated fashion.

Algorithm 4. MaxChain

Input : π_A, π_B chains consisted of blocks with hash value smaller than $T/2^\mu, T/2^{i+\mu}$ resp., s.t. $i \geq 0$, or *fail*

Output: $Max[\ ]$

1 chain $Max[\ ], Proof_A[\ ], Proof_B[\ ]$;
2 block b;
3 **if** *either of* π_A, π_B *equals fail* **then**
4 | return the other one ;
5 **else**
6 | $(b, \pi'_A, \pi'_B) = $ RemoveCPlow$[\pi_A, \pi_B]$;
7 | **if** $(i > 0)$ **then**
8 | | **if** $((\pi'_B.pow \geq \pi'_A.pow) \wedge (\pi'_B.length \geq m))$ **then**
9 | | | return π_B
10 | | **else**
11 | | | response:= RemoveCPhigh$[\pi_A, \pi_B]$;
12 | | | **if** *response* = *fail* **then**
13 | | | | return π_A
14 | | | **else**
15 | | | | parse response as (b, π'_A, π'_B);

16 | **if** $(\pi'_B.pow \geq \pi'_A.pow)$ **then**
17 | | **if** $((\pi'_B.length \geq m) \vee (i + \mu = 0))$ **then**
18 | | | return π_B
19 | | **else**
20 | | | **if** $(i > 0)$ **then**
21 | | | | $Proof_B = $ Request$_B[b, \mu]$;
22 | | | | $Proof_A = b \| \pi'_A$;
23 | | | **else**
24 | | | | $Proof_A = $ Request$_A[b, \mu - 1]$;
25 | | | | $Proof_B = $ Request$_B[b, \mu - 1]$;

26 | **else**
27 | | **if** $((\pi'_A.length \geq 2^i \cdot m) \vee (i + \mu = 0))$ **then**
28 | | | return π'_A
29 | | **else**
30 | | | **if** $(i > 0)$ **then**
31 | | | | $Proof_B = $ Request$_B[b, \mu]$;
32 | | | | $Proof_A = b \| \pi'_A$;
33 | | | **else**
34 | | | | $Proof_A = $ Request$_A[b, \mu - 1]$;
35 | | | | $Proof_B = $ Request$_B[b, \mu - 1]$;

36 | return MaxChain$[Proof_A, Proof_B]$;

Theorem 1. *Let n be the length of a chain C that is consisted of blocks with hash value smaller than $T = 2^f$. Then the expected size of the dynamic vector interlink, is $f - \sum_{i=1}^{f}(1 - \frac{1}{2^i})^n$.*

Proof. We define a discrete random variable $X_j \in \{0, \ldots, f\}$ associated with each block $C[j]$ so that

$$X_j = i \Longleftrightarrow \frac{T}{2^{i+1}} \leq H_B < \frac{T}{2^i}, i \in \{0, \ldots, f-1\}$$

$$X_j = f \Longleftrightarrow 0 \leq H_B < \frac{T}{2^f}$$

(H_B is the hash value of $C[j]$).

The hash value of each chain's block H_B follows the uniform discrete distribution on $\{0, \ldots, T-1\}$. So

$$\Pr(X_j = i) = \Pr(\frac{T}{2^{i+1}} \leq H_B < \frac{T}{2^i}) = \frac{1}{2^{i+1}}, i \in \{0, \ldots, f-1\}$$

$$\Pr(X_j = f) = \Pr(0 \leq H_B < \frac{T}{2^f}) = \frac{1}{2^f}$$

It holds:

$$\sum_{i=0}^{f} \Pr(X_j = i) = 1$$

Then the size of the interlink follows $Y = max\{X_1, \ldots, X_n\}$ distribution.

If $0 \leq y < f$ then:

$$\Pr(Y \leq y) = (\Pr(X_j \leq y))^n = (\sum_{i=0}^{y} \frac{1}{2^{i+1}})^n = (1 - \frac{1}{2^{y+1}})^n$$

$$\Pr(Y = y) = \Pr(Y \leq y) - \Pr(Y \leq y-1) = (1 - \frac{1}{2^{y+1}})^n - (1 - \frac{1}{2^y})^n$$

It also holds: $\Pr(Y \leq f) = 1$ and $\Pr(Y = f) = 1 - (1 - \frac{1}{2^f})^n$

We have:

$$E(Y) = \sum_{y=0}^{f-1} y \cdot [(1 - \frac{1}{2^{y+1}})^n - (1 - \frac{1}{2^y})^n] + f \cdot [1 - (1 - \frac{1}{2^f})^n]$$

$$= (f-1) \cdot (1 - \frac{1}{2^f})^n - \sum_{i=1}^{f-1} (1 - \frac{1}{2^i})^n + f \cdot [1 - (1 - \frac{1}{2^f})^n]$$

$$= f - \sum_{i=1}^{f} (1 - \frac{1}{2^i})^n$$

$\square$

In Fig. 2 we demonstrate a graph that shows that the size of interlink is logarithmic in n when n ranges in the current Bitcoin blockchain length and the target is kept stable at 2^{200}.

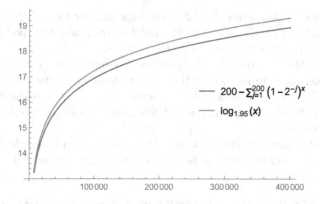

Fig. 2. Size of interlink as a function of blockchain length when target is $T = 2^{200}$.

Compressing the Interlink Vector Using Merkle Trees. To reduce the storage per block it is possible to compress the interlink vector using a Merkle tree. In more detail, instead of storing the whole interlink in each block we can organize the vector in a Merkle tree and store only the root hash in each blockheader. This demands the addition of only a hash value in each block instead of the sequence of hash values in interlink. The modifications needed in the ConstructProof algorithm are straightforward and we omit them.

5.2 Communication and Time Complexity

We will analyze now the size of the proof π. We will focus in the optimistic scenario, where the adversary does not create deep forks that cut into the proofs of the honest parties, i.e., when the k-suffix that the adversary sends has a common block with the suffix of the proofs sent by the honest provers. Note that the honest parties will not fork in the part of the chain before the k-suffix with overwhelming probability in k [6]. In such case the lite verifier chooses the chain with the most proof of work without having to perform any extra interaction with the provers (performing the Request steps in the MaxChain algorithm). Therefore the size of the proof will be the output of the ConstructProof algorithm.

Let $C^{\lceil k}$ be the pruned local chain without the k-suffix of a prover that a lite verifier has asked, n the length of the chain and m the security parameter. Firstly we will prove that the probability with which a block of $C^{\lceil k}$ has hash value smaller than $\dfrac{T}{2^i}$ is $\dfrac{1}{2^i}$.

If H_B is the hash value of a block B and $j \in \mathbb{N}$, $j < T$ then $\Pr(H_B = j \mid H_B < T) = 1/T$. It follows,

$$\Pr(H_B < T/2^i \mid H_B < T) = \sum_{j=0}^{T/2^i - 1} \Pr(H_B = j \mid H_B < T) = \frac{T/2^i}{T} = \frac{1}{2^i}$$

The number of blocks in $C^{\lceil k}$ with hash value smaller than $T/2^i$ is a discrete random variable D_i that follows the Binomial distribution with parameters $(n, p_i = 1/2^i)$ and its expected value is $E(D_i) = n \cdot p_i$.

Recall that the ConstructProof algorithm has output the innerchain$_{i_0} = \pi$, where i_0 is the maximum i so that there are at least m blocks with hash value smaller than $T/2^i$ in $C^{\lceil k}$. As a result we must examine what is the depth i_0 of the proof that the algorithm returns and how many blocks (denoted by D_{i_0}) the proof π will contain.

In the next lemma we establish that the depth of the inner chain that the ConstructProof algorithm returns is quite close to the optimal value (which is roughly $\log(n/m)$).

Lemma 1. *Let n be the size of the local pruned chain $C^{\lceil k}$ of the prover. Assume that $n < Tm$ and define i so that $2^i m \leq n < 2^{i+1}m$. Then it holds $\Pr(D_{i-1} \leq m - 1) \leq \exp(-\Omega(m))$.*

Proof. Observe that $n \cdot p_{i-1} = n/2^{i-1} \geq 2^i m/2^{i-1} = 2m > m - 1$. So according to the Chernoff bound[4] for the Binomial distribution it holds that:

$$\Pr(D_{i-1} \leq m - 1) \leq \exp(-(np_{i-1} - (m - 1))^2/2np_{i-1})$$
$$\leq \exp(-1/(2/(2^{i-1})) \cdot (n(1/(2^{i-1})) - (m - 1))^2/n))$$
$$\leq \exp(-(2m - m + 1)^2/2^3 m) \leq \exp(-\Omega(m))$$

This completes the proof. □

Armed with this lemma we next observe that the length of the inner chain for the suitable index is not going to be substantially larger than m.

Lemma 2. *Let $n < Tm$ and define i so that $2^i m \leq n < 2^{i+1}m$. It holds that $\Pr(D_{i-1} \geq 5m) \leq \exp(-\Omega(m))$.*

Proof. Observe first that $2m/n \leq p_{i-1} = 1/2^{i-1} < 4m/n$. Consider the Chernoff bound on the upper tail that states $\Pr[X \geq (1 + \delta)\mu] \leq \exp(-\delta^2\mu/3)$ when X is a Binomial distribution with mean μ and $\delta \in (0, 1]$. It follows that $\Pr[D_{i-1} \geq 5m] \leq \Pr[D_{i-1} \geq (1 + 1/4)p_{i-1}n] \leq \exp(-p_{i-1}n/48) \leq \exp(-m/24)$. □

We are now ready to state the theorem that establishes the efficiency of the proof that is constructed and communicated to the lite verifier.

Theorem 2. *The size of the proof π that the prover sends in response to a lite verifier in the optimistic case is $O(m)$ with overwhelming probability in m.*

Proof. In the optimistic case the proof π that the prover sends to the lite verifier is the output of the ConstructProof algorithm. If n is the length of the local chain from which the prover constructs the proof and we have $2^i m \leq n < 2^{i+1}m$ for an $i \geq 1$ then it holds that: The ConstructProof algorithm will return

---

[4] Here we use the following variant: $\Pr(X \leq k) \leq \exp(-(np - k)^2/2np)$, where $k \leq np$.

a proof of depth $i - 1$ with overwhelming probability in m, as we proved in Lemma 1. Furthermore, the size D_{i-1} of the proof π will be bounded by $5m$ with overwhelming probability in m, as we proved in Lemma 2. This completes the proof. □

The above completes the argument for the optimistic case, where the adversary does not explicitly interfere and attempts to increase the complexity of the lite verifier. We note that in the case that the adversary interferes and makes the lite node to engage in extra communication by issuing the Request commands, he can only succeed in this with significant effort (by mining very low target blocks) and with bounded, albeit non-negligible, probability. It seems unlikely that an adversary will engage in this effort for the sole purpose of delaying a lite verifier and for this reason, we consider the optimistic efficiency analysis performed above to be quite indicative of the actual performance of the protocol.

Finally with respect to time complexity observe that in the optimistic case, the verifier will have to perform a number of verification steps that are proportional to the size of the proof that is received. It follows that the complexity of the verifier is also $O(m \log n)$.

Complexity When Using a Compressed Interlink Vector. The communication and time complexity in this case can be improved since in each block from the interlink vector committed in the Merkle root hash only a path in the tree needs to be transmitted. It follows easily that the complexity of the lite verifier in the optimistic case will be $O(m \log \log n)$.

6   Security Analysis

A successful attack against our lite verification mechanism suggests that a lite verifier reaches a different conclusion about a certain transaction compared to a full verifier. The proof argument for security is as follows: given an adversary $\mathcal{A}$ that responds to a lite verifier we construct an adversary $\mathcal{A}^*$ that responds to a full verifier. We will argue that with high probability the full verifier operating with $\mathcal{A}^*$ reaches the same conclusion as the lite verifier operating with $\mathcal{A}$.

Intuitively the above means that for any proof that a lite verifier accepts and processes there exists a full chain that can be recovered and produces the same output behavior for a regular SPV verifier.

The description of $\mathcal{A}^*$ is as follows:

1. $\mathcal{A}^*$ simulates the operation of $\mathcal{A}$ while additionally in each round acts as a full verifier and requests the chains from all the honest nodes denoted by $\mathcal{C}_1, \ldots, \mathcal{C}_e$ for some integer e. It maintains a "block tree" BT containing all blockchains and adds there any blocks that are produced by the adversary. Note that it is possible to $\mathcal{A}^*$ to perform this since in the random oracle model (that we adopt from [6]) it is possible for $\mathcal{A}^*$ to monitor all queries of $\mathcal{A}$ to the hash function $H(\cdot)$. Any queries made by $\mathcal{A}$ that do not correspond to valid blocks are ignored.

2. When $\mathcal{A}$ responds to a lite verifier with a pair $(\mathcal{X}, \pi)$, $\mathcal{A}^*$ searches in BT for a chain $\mathcal{C}$ that is consistent with $(\mathcal{X}, \pi)$, i.e., $\mathcal{X}$ is the suffix of $\mathcal{C}$ and π is a sub-chain of $\mathcal{C}$. If such a chain is found, then $\mathcal{A}^*$ response to a full verifier with $\mathcal{C}$. If no chain is found then $\mathcal{A}^*$ returns no response to the full verifier.

We perform our analysis in the model of [6]. Recall that in their model, there are n parties maintaining the blockchain, each allowed q queries to the hash function (thought of as a random oracle) and t of the parties are controlled by the adversary. The probability of finding a proof of work with a single hash query is $T/2^\kappa$ (recall that the target is T and is stable). We use the same notation as [6] and we denote $\alpha = (n - t)pq$, $\beta = pqt$ and $\gamma = \alpha - \alpha^2$. Intuitively, the parameter α represents the hashing power of the honest parties; it is also an upper bound on the expected number of solutions that the honest parties will obtain in one round; on the other hand β is the expected number of solutions that the adversary may produce in one round. Finally, γ is a lower bound on the expectation of a uniquely successful round, i.e., a round where a single honest party finds a proof of work solution.

We are now ready to formulate the theorem that establishes the security of lite verification. The theorem is conditioned on $\gamma > (1 + \delta)\beta$ which roughly[5] corresponds to the setting where the honest parties command the majority of the hashing power.

Theorem 3. *(Security of lite verification) Let $\gamma > (1 + \delta)\beta$ for some $\delta > 0$. A full verifier interacting with $\mathcal{A}^*$ reaches the same conclusion as the lite verifier operating with $\mathcal{A}$ with probability $1 - \exp(-\Omega(\delta^2 m))$.*

Proof. (Sketch). We compare any execution with $\mathcal{A}$ where a lite verifier requests a proof to an execution where a full verifier requests a proof from $\mathcal{A}^*$. We define an event BAD to be the event that the two verifiers report a different conclusion. An event BAD would necessarily correspond to the case 2 above in the definition of $\mathcal{A}^*$ when the latter fails to reconstruct a chain $\mathcal{C}$ from BT that corresponds to the proof $(\mathcal{X}, \pi)$ that the adversary $\mathcal{A}$ produces. Let NOWIT be this latter event and observe BAD $\subseteq$ NOWIT. We will argue that whenever NOWIT happens then with overwhelming probability in m it holds that a proof originating from an honest party will win the comparison performed by the MaxChain. Let this event be HWIN. In more detail we will prove that $\Pr(\neg \mathsf{HWIN} \wedge \mathsf{NOWIT})$ drops exponentially in m. Observe that this is sufficient since BAD $\subseteq \neg$HWIN and hence it will follow that $\Pr(\mathsf{BAD})$ drops exponentially in m.

The event $\neg$HWIN suggests that the adversary $\mathcal{A}$ has managed to produce a proof for which no honest party could outperform in the view of the MaxChain procedure. Furthermore, if NOWIT happens also, it follows that it is impossible for $\mathcal{A}^*$ to reconstruct a chain that corresponds to the proof that wins the MaxChain algorithm. This suggests that the winning proof $(\mathcal{X}, \pi)$ contains blocks that were impossible to attach to the blockchain tree BT by $\mathcal{A}^*$, due to the fact

---

[5] Roughly because $\gamma = \alpha - \alpha^2$ and thus this condition approximates the "honest majority" condition only if α^2 is close to 0. See [6] for more details.

of not being valid extensions of a (level-0) chain. It follows that in the response $(\mathcal{X}, \pi)$, the proof π should diverge from all chains that belong to an honest party (otherwise all the blocks in $\mathcal{X}$ would have been attached to BT and a witness for $(\mathcal{X}, \pi)$ would be reconstructed by $\mathcal{A}^*$). Let b be the most recent common honestly generated block of π with the longest chain $\mathcal{C}$ from BT that belongs to an honest party. Given that MaxChain elected $(\mathcal{X}, \pi)$ over the proof provided by the owner of $\mathcal{C}$ it holds that π contains a sequence of at least m blocks starting from b (or later) that are of target $T/2^i$ where $i > 0$ is the depth of π. Let r be the round that block b was created. We will next show that the probability that $\mathcal{A}$ obtains m blocks with hashes less than $T/2^i$ faster than the honest parties' chains advance by $2^i m$ blocks is negligible in m. It follows that it will be with negligible in m probability that $\mathcal{A}$ can produce a proof that will be selected by MaxChain.

Let X_r be the random variable that is equal to 1 if r is a successul round (following the terminology of [6]). In [6] it is shown that in any s rounds following round r it holds that the length of the honest parties' chains will be at least $\ell + \sum_{l=r}^{s} X_l$ where ℓ is the length of an honest parties' chain at round r.

The number of rounds that will be required for the adversary to compute m blocks with hash less than $T/2^i$ follows a negative binomial distribution. The expectation for the number of rounds is $2^i \beta^{-1} m$ where $p = T/2^\kappa$ and $\beta = pqt$. By applying a tail bound for the negative binomial distribution we obtain that the probability the number of rounds is less than $(1 - \delta/4)2^i \beta^{-1} m$ is $\exp(-\Omega(\delta^2 m))$.

On the other hand, in $(1 - \delta/4)2^i \beta^{-1} m$ rounds, by applying a Chernoff bound, the probability that the honest parties will produce less than $(1 - \delta/4)^2 \gamma 2^i \beta^{-1} m$ blocks is bounded by $\exp(-\Omega(\delta^2 m))$.

Observe now that $\gamma > (1 + \delta)\beta$ implies $\gamma(1 - \delta/4)^2 \beta^{-1} > 1$ and thus the probability that the proof of work of the chains owned by the honest parties will exceed that of the adversary is $1 - \exp(-\Omega(\delta^2 m))$. $\square$

On the Feasibility and Infeasibility of Non-interactive and/or Constant Size Proofs. Observe that our security parameter for the proof is m and the size of the proof in the optimistic case is $O(m)$. In our construction, the lite verifier may require further interaction with the provers if it discovers forks in the inner chains that it receives. This leaves open the question whether shorter proofs can be achieved (e.g., constant size) or whether it is possible to obtain non-interactive proofs, i.e., proofs that require always a single message from the full nodes to the lite verifier. With respect to constant size proofs it is unlikely that the techniques like the ones we consider here would provide such an improvement: for instance, if a single block of exceptionally low hash value is transmitted as a proof of many proofs of work of proportional length, concentration bounds will not be able to provide a sufficiently low probability of attack. In other words, such short proofs might be exploitable by an attacker in very much the same way that the difficulty raising attack of [3] operates and hence they will not be secure. Similarly, given any non-interactive proof that goes arbitrarily low in terms of the inner chain it selects, one can always imagine an attacker that attempts to fork in the very last block of the inner chain and thus gain an unfair advantage compared to the honest parties even in the honest majority setting. However this may be countered by requiring sufficient number of blocks following such low hash blocks; we leave for future work the feasibility of investigatng the design of short and secure non-interactive SPV proofs.

The Dynamic Setting. To account for a dynamically changing population of miners, in Bitcoin and related blockchain protocols, the target is recalculated at regular intervals. It is possible to build our interconnected blockchains in the dynamic setting as well; some care needs to be applied during verification of proofs however since target recalculation will need to be performed over the inner chains. We leave the analysis in the dynamic setting for future work.

Acknowledgement. The authors wish to thank Giorgos Panagiotakos for helpful discussions as well as the anonymous referees of the 3rd Workshop on Bitcoin and Blockchain Research for their valuable comments.

References

1. Back, A.: Hashcash (1997). http://www.cypherspace.org/hashcash
2. Back, A., Corallo, M., Dashjr, L., Friedenbach, M., Maxwell, G., Miller, A., Poelstra, A., Timn, J., Wuille, P.: Enabling Blockchain Innovations with Pegged Sidechains (2014). https://blockstream.com/sidechains.pdf
3. Bahack, L.: Theoretical bitcoin attacks with less than half of the computational power (draft). Cryptology ePrint Archive, Report 2013/868 (2013). http://eprint.iacr.org/
4. Dwork, C., Naor, M.: Pricing via processing or combatting junk mail. In: Brickell, E.F. (ed.) CRYPTO 1992. LNCS, vol. 740, pp. 139–147. Springer, Heidelberg (1993)
5. Friedenbach, M.: Compact SPV proofs via block header commitments, Bitcoin-development mailing list post (2014). https://lists.linuxfoundation.org/pipermail/bitcoin-dev/2014-March/004727.html
6. Garay, J., Kiayias, A., Leonardos, N.: The Bitcoin backbone protocol: analysis and applications. In: Oswald, E., Fischlin, M. (eds.) EUROCRYPT 2015. LNCS, vol. 9057, pp. 281–310. Springer, Heidelberg (2015)
7. Juels, A., Brainard, J.G.: Client puzzles: a cryptographic countermeasure against connection depletion attacks. In: NDSS. The Internet Society (1999)
8. Lewenberg, Y., Sompolinsky, Y., Zohar, A.: Inclusive block chain protocols. In: Böhme, R., Okamoto, T. (eds.) FC 2015. LNCS, vol. 8975, pp. 528–547. Springer, Heidelberg (2015)
9. Miller, A.: The high-value-hash highway, Bitcoin forum post (2012). https://bitcointalk.org/index.php?topic=98986.0
10. Nakamoto, S.: Bitcoin: a peer to peer electronic cash system (2008). http://bitcoin.org/bitcoin.pdf
11. Rivest, R.L., Shamir, A., Wagner, D.A.: Time-lock puzzles and timed-release crypto. Technical report, Cambridge, MA, USA (1996)
12. Sompolinsky, Y., Zohar, A.: Secure high-rate transaction processing in bitcoin. In: Böhme, R., Okamoto, T. (eds.) FC 2015. LNCS, vol. 8975, pp. 507–527. Springer, Heidelberg (2015)

Step by Step Towards Creating a Safe Smart Contract: Lessons and Insights from a Cryptocurrency Lab

Kevin Delmolino[1]([✉]), Mitchell Arnett[1], Ahmed Kosba[1], Andrew Miller[1,2], and Elaine Shi[2]

[1] Department of Computer Science, University of Maryland, College Park,
College Park, USA
del@terpmail.umd.edu, marnett@umd.edu, {akosba,amiller}@cs.umd.edu
[2] Initiative for Cryptocurrencies and Contracts (IC3),
Department of Computer Science, Cornell University, Ithaca, USA
elaine@cs.cornell.edu

Abstract. We document our experiences in teaching smart contract programming to undergraduate students at the University of Maryland, the first pedagogical attempt of its kind. Since smart contracts deal directly with the movement of valuable currency units between contractual parties, security of a contract program is of paramount importance.

Our lab exposed numerous common pitfalls in designing safe and secure smart contracts. We document several typical classes of mistakes students made, suggest ways to fix/avoid them, and advocate best practices for programming smart contracts. Finally, our pedagogical efforts have also resulted in online open course materials for programming smart contracts, which may be of independent interest to the community.

1 Introduction

Completely decentralized cryptocurrencies like Bitcoin [18] and other altcoins [5] have captured the public's attention and interest, and have been much more successful than any prior incarnations of electronic cash. Many would call the rise of these electronic currencies a technological revolution, and the "wave of the future" [3]. Emerging altcoins such as Ethereum [23] and Counterparty [14] extend Bitcoin's design by offering a rich programming language for writing "smart contracts." Smart contracts are user-defined programs that specify rules governing transactions, and that are enforced by a network of peers (assuming the underlying cryptocurrency is secure). In comparison with traditional financial contracts, smart contracts carry the promise of low legal and transaction costs, and can lower the bar of entry for users.

In Fall 2014, at the University of Maryland, we organized a new, hands-on smart contract programming lab in our undergraduate-level security class – the first of its kind that has ever been attempted.

J. Clark et al. (Eds.): FC 2016 Workshops, LNCS 9604, pp. 79–94, 2016.
DOI: 10.1007/978-3-662-53357-4_6

Smart Contract Programming: Unique Challenges and Opportunities.
Although smart contract programming in many ways resembles traditional programming, it raises important new security challenges. Contracts are "play-for-keeps", since virtual currencies have real value. If you load money into a buggy smart contract, you will likely lose it. Further, smart contract programming requires an "economic thinking" perspective that traditional programmers may not have acquired. Contracts must be written to ensure fairness even when counterparties may attempt to cheat in arbitrary ways that maximize their economic gains.

As an outcome of our lab, we observed several classes of typical mistakes students made. In contrast to traditional software development tasks where bugs such as buffer overflows are often benign (except in rare or contrived scenarios), in our lab, we observed several bugs and pitfalls that arise due to the unique nature of smart contract programs and lead to clear and immediate exploits (e.g., theft or loss of money).

Our lab experiences show that even for very simple smart contracts (e.g., a "Rock, Paper, Scissors" game), designing and implementing them correctly was highly non-trivial. This suggests that extra precautions and scrutiny are necessary when programming smart contracts.

In this paper, although we adopt Ethereum's Serpent language, most of the the insights we gain are not language-specific, but can be generalized to smart contract programming under a broad model.

Open-Source Course and Lab Materials. Based on lessons and insights drawn through this experimental lab, we have designed new, open course materials and lab designs for smart contract programming [4]. We hope that these open-source course materials and labs will aid both instructors who wish to teach smart contract programming and students/developers who wish to teach themselves smart contract programming.

Broader Insights Gained. Inspired by our experimental smart contract lab, we argue why cryptocurrency and smart contracts will serve as a great pedagogical platform for Cybersecurity education. We also draw from our experiences why the "build, break, and amend your own program" approach is beneficial to instructing adversarial thinking and incentivizing a student-driven learning atmosphere.

Roadmap. In the remainder of this paper, we will first give more background on cryptocurrency and smart contracts (Sect. 2). We will then detail experiences with our lab (Sect. 3), the typical pitfalls we observed in smart contract programming (Sect. 4), and the insights and lessons learned.

2   Background

In this section, we provide some background on cryptocurrencies and the programming model of smart contracts.

2.1   Background on Decentralized Cryptocurrencies

Smart contracts are built on top of an underlying cryptocurrency platform. A cryptocurrency is a decentralized system for interacting with virtual money in a shared global ledger. Users transfer money and interact with contracts by publishing signed data called *transactions* to the cryptocurrency network. The network consists of nodes (called miners) who propagate information, store data, and update the data by applying transactions. A high-level schematic is shown in Fig. 1.

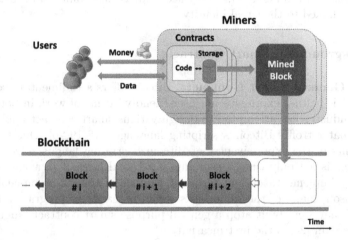

Fig. 1. Schematic of a decentralized cryptocurrency system with smart contracts. A smart contract's state is stored on the public blockchain. A smart contract program is executed by a network of miners who reach consensus on the outcome of the execution, and update the contract's state on the blockchain accordingly. Users can send money or data to a contract; or receive money or data from a contract.

Although the ideas behind cryptocurrencies date back at least twenty-five years (e.g., cryptographic e-cash [13]), a recent surge of interest in this technology has been incited by the success of Bitcoin [18]. For a comprehensive survey on Bitcoin and other cryptocurrencies, see [7,9].

The main interface provided by the underlying cryptocurrency is an append-only log called a *blockchain*, which imposes a partial or total ordering on transactions submitted by users. The data in the blockchain is guaranteed to be *valid* according to certain predefined rules of the system (e.g., there are no double-spends or invalid signatures). All of the data in the blockchain is public, and every user can access a copy of it. No one can be *prevented* from submitting transactions and getting them included in the blockchain (with at most some small delay). There is global agreement among all nodes and users about the contents of the blockchain, except for the most recent handful of blocks which have not yet settled.

For simplicity, we also assume that the built-in currency has a stable monetary value. Users therefore have an incentive to gain more of (and avoid losing) units of this currency. Anyone can acquire the virtual currency by purchasing or trading for it using other fiat currencies (e.g., US dollars) or virtual currencies. The currency is assumed to be fungible; one unit of Ether (the currency unit of Ethereum) is exactly as valuable as any other, regardless of the currency's "history."

The system keeps track of "ownership" of the currency by associating each unit of currency to an "address". A user address is a hash of a public key; whoever knows the corresponding private key can spend the money associated to that address. Users can create as many accounts as they want, and the accounts need not be linked to their real identity.

2.2 Background on Smart Contracts

Need for General Smart Contracts. Bitcoin offers a rudimentary scripting system that is neither expressive nor user-friendly. A line of work in both academia and industry has attempted to design various smart contract applications in a way that retrofits Bitcoin's scripting language [6,8,19,20]. Due to fundamental limits of the expressiveness of Bitcoin's scripting language, retrofitting the language is not only time consuming, but can also result in asymptotically more costly implementations in terms of number of rounds or on-chain cost. In comparison, many of the same tasks would be easier to program and more efficient, if they were built atop a general purpose smart contract language (of which Ethereum [23] is the first incarnation).

Smart Contract Model. A contract is an instance of a computer program that runs on the blockchain, i.e., executed by all consensus nodes. A smart contract consists of program code, a storage file, and an account balance. Any user can create a contract by posting a *transaction* to the blockchain. The program code of a contract is fixed when the contract is created, and cannot be changed.

As shown in Fig. 1, a contract's storage file is stored on the public blockchain. A contract's program logic is executed by the network of miners who reach consensus on the outcome of the execution and update the blockchain accordingly. The contract's code is executed whenever it receives a message, either from a user or from another contract. (A user can sends a message to a contract by including the message data and the address of the contract in her transaction; one contract can send a message to another using a special instruction in its program code.) While executing its code, the contract may read from or write to its storage file. A contract can also receive money into its account balance, and send money to other contracts or users.

Conceptually, one can think of a contract as a special "trusted third party" – however, this party is *trusted only for correctness and availability but not for privacy*. In particular, a contract's entire state is visible to the public.

Contract Invocation. A contract's code will be invoked whenever it receives a message. A contract can define multiple entry points of execution – in Ethereum's

Serpent language, each entry point is defined as a function. A message contents will specify the entry point at which the contract's code will be invoked. Therefore, messages act like function calls in ordinary programming languages. After a contract finishes processing a message it receives, it can pass a return value back to the sender.

Gas. Ethereum uses the concept of "gas" to discourage over-consumption of resources (e.g., a contract program that causes miners to loop forever). The user who creates a transaction must spend currency to purchase gas. During the execution of a transaction, every program instruction consumes some amount of gas. If the gas runs out before the transaction reaches an ordinary stopping point, it is treated as an exception: the state is reverted as though the transaction had no effect, but the Ether used to purchase the gas is not refunded! When one contract sends a message to another, the sender can offer only a *portion* of its available gas to the recipient. If the recipient runs out of gas, control returns to the sender, who can use its remaining gas to handle the exception and tidy up.

Ethereum Specifics. Our lab employs Ethereum's Serpent language to illustrate smart contract programming, although the lessons apply more generally to other cryptocurrencies and smart contract systems as well. We only define as much Ethereum-specific terminology as needed to understand our examples. In particular, the built-in currency of Ethereum is called Ether, and an Ether can be divided into smaller currency units such as "wei".

2.3 A Taste of Smart Contract Design

In this section, we will give the reader a brief overview of smart contract design by describing the Ethereum implementation of a simple, yet useful, motivating example – the financial swap instrument. This contract allows two parties, Alice and Bob, to take opposing bets about the price of a stock at some future time. Both parties initially deposit equal amounts of money (as units of Ether currency). After a deadline has passed, the current price of the stock is queried by interacting with a designated stock price authority (which would itself be implemented as a smart contract - we refer to this contract as `StockPriceAuthority`). Depending on the price at that time, the entire combined deposit is awarded to either Alice or Bob.

The contract's storage allocates space for the following data on lines 1 and 2: (1) the public keys of Alice and Bob; and (2) the deadline and threshold of the swap contract. The contract also defines a function `determine_outcome`, which any party may invoke. This example serves as motivation of the useful aspects of smart contracts as financial instruments. In our other examples, we will tend to focus on gambling games. It also serves to illustrate several low level aspects of Serpent programming.

3   A Recount of Our Smart Contract Programming Lab

In our undergraduate security class at the University of Maryland, students were asked to develop smart contract applications of their choice atop Ethereum [23], using its expressive Serpent [22] programming language for composing smart contracts (Fig. 2).

```
1   data Alice, Bob
2   data deadline, threshold
3
4   # Not shown: collect equal deposits from Alice and Bob
5   # We assume StockPriceAuthority is a trusted third party contract
    ⌐   that can give us the price of the stock
6
7   def determine_outcome():
8     if block.timestamp > deadline:
9       price = StockPriceAuthority.price()
10      if price > threshold:
11        send(Alice, self.balance)
12      else:
13        send(Bob, self.balance)
```

Fig. 2. This Serpent program implements a simple financial "swap" instrument, illustrating that smart contracts are a powerful and useful tool for programming with money.

Students were divided into groups of four. Due to the experimental nature of the lab, the instructor assigned one of her Ph.D. students to closely supervise each group, to ensure that students could obtain hands-on help. The lab proceeded in two phases.

Creation Phase. The first phase is a creation phase where each group created a smart contract application of their own choice. The students created a variety of applications, including games (e.g., Rock-Paper-Scissors, Russian Roulette, custom-designed games), escrow services, auctions (e.g., sealed auctions, silent auctions), a parking meter service, and stock market applications.

At the end of the first phase, each group made a short presentation of their contract application in class. The instructor, TAs, and students jointly observed numerous issues with the programs that students created (see Sect. 4 for a detailed discussion).

Amendment Phase. Therefore, we extended the project to a second phase, called an amendment phase. The goal of this phase was for students to critique their programs, find bugs, and amend their designs. The instructor and TAs had in-person meetings with each project group to help them amend their smart contract programs. Students also formed pair groups to critique and help the other group.

4   Pitfalls of Smart Contract Programming

In this section, we will demonstrate some of the typical pitfalls we observed for smart contract programming. For ease of exposition, we will use a simple "Rock, Paper, Scissors" example to illustrate three classes of typical mistakes. Similar mistakes were commonly observed in various other applications developed by the students.

Quick Overview of Our Running Example. We will first give a quick overview of the structure of our buggy "Rock, Paper, Scissors" program before we go on to diagnose the bugs. In this contract, two players will play a simple "Rock, Paper, Scissors" for money. The contract program consists of two main functions:

- **player_input**: The players register with the contract and deposit money to play. Each player also provides input to the contract in the form of their choice of rock, paper, or scissors.
- **finalize**: The contract decides a winner and sends the proceeds to the winner.

As we show below, surprisingly, *even for a very simple smart contract it is difficult to create it correctly!*

4.1   Errors in Encoding State Machines

Programming smart contracts typically involves encoding complex state machines. Logical errors in encoding state machines were commonly observed. The simplest type of logical error is a contract that leaks money in corner cases.

To illustrate this, let us look at our buggy "Rock, Paper, Scissors" example. Figure 3 shows the **player_input** function where players register with the contract and deposit money to play. The contract would then store the players' public keys, inputs, and coins deposited (Lines 14–17). This contract exhibits several mistakes:

- If a *third* player attempts to join and sends money to the contract, that money becomes inaccessible (Line 20). Neither the player nor anyone else can ever recover it.
- Similarly, if a player sends an amount of money that is not exactly 1000 wei, the contract also leaks the money.

Note that while a careful player can protect herself from the second problem by never sending the incorrect amount, *she cannot always protect herself from the first problem.* In a decentralized cryptocurrency like Bitcoin or Ethereum, multiple parties may be sending inputs to the contract simultaneously. In this case, it is up to the miner who mines this block to decide how to order these transactions.

To fix these bugs, the contract should *refund* the money back to a player unless the player is successfully registered in the game. This approach is taken in our improved contract (Fig. 4, Lines 17 and 20).

```
1   # A two-player game with a 1000 wei prize
2
3   data player[2](address, choice)
4   data num_players
5   data reward
6   data check_winner[3][3] # a ternary matrix that captures the rules
     ↪  of rock-paper-scissors game
7
8   def init():
9     num_players = 0
10    # code omitted: initialize check_winner according to the game
     ↪  rules
11
12  def player_input(choice):
13    if num_players < 2 and msg.value == 1000:
14      reward += 1000
15      player[num_players].address = msg.sender
16      player[num_players].choice = choice
17      num_players = num_players + 1
18      return(0)
19    else:
20      return(-1)
21  def finalize():
22    p0 = player[0].choice
23    p1 = player[1].choice
24    # If player 0 wins
25    if check_winner[p0][p1] == 0:
26      send(0,player[0].address, reward)
27      return(0)
28    # If player 1 wins
29    elif check_winner[p0][p1] == 1:
30      send(0,player[1].address, reward)
31      return(1)
32    # If no one wins
33    else:
34      send(0,player[0].address, reward/2)
35      send(0,player[1].address, reward/2)
36      return(2)
```

Fig. 3. Pitfalls in smart contract design. This buggy contract illustrates a few pitfalls:
Pitfall 1 (Lines 19 and 20): If a third player attempts to join the contract, his money effectively vanishes into a blackhole.
Pitfall 2 (Line 16): Players send their inputs in plaintext to the contract. A malicious player can wait to see his opponents choice before deciding on his own input.

What is shown here is merely the simplest example of a logical error when encoding the state machine. In our lab, students created contracts that are far more sophisticated (e.g., stock market applications, various flavors of auctions) that required the design of much more complex state machines. Failure to encode the correct state machine (e.g., omitting certain transitions, neglecting to check the current state) was among the most commonly observed pitfalls.

4.2   Failing to Use Cryptography

Another mistake is more subtle: Players send their inputs in cleartext. Since transactions are broadcast across the entire cryptocurrency network, a cheating player may wait to see what his opponent chooses before providing his own input.

Players in a smart contract are typically anonymous, and can be reasonably expected to act selfishly to maximize their financial gains, even if it means deviating from the default or "honest" behavior.

Cryptography is often the first line of defense against potentially malicious parties. Here, the obvious remedy is to use cryptographic commitments. Both players can commit to their inputs in one time epoch, and then in a later epoch open the commitments and reveal their inputs. A standard commitment satisfies two properties, *binding* and *hiding*. Binding ensures that a player cannot change their input after committing to it. Hiding ensures that a party learns nothing about the others input choice even after observing the commitment. In our application, the commitment must also be *non-malleable*, i.e., a player should not be able to maul a previous player's commitment into a related value (e.g., one that will allow her to win). In general, for secure composition of computationally sound primitives, we would recommend the usage of universally composable commitments [10–12]. In this paper, we will use a simple, hash-based commitment that is secure under the random oracle model. To commit a message m, first pick a random nonce that is sufficiently long, and then compute the commitment $H(m, \text{nonce})$. The opening and verification algorithms are obvious.

In Fig. 4, we show a fixed contract that properly uses commitments. The previous player_input function is broken up into two phases: in the new player_input function, each player provides a commitment; after both commitments are received, the open function is used to reveal their commited inputs.

Opportunity to Teach Cryptography. As students realized and sought to fix bugs in their own programs, the opportunity arose to teach them cryptography as a *well-motivated solution to their immediate practical problems*. The instructor seized this opportunity, and the amendment phase of the project, students were indeed able to implement cryptographic commitments to secure their smart contracts!

4.3   Misaligned Incentives

More subtle bugs remain, even for the improved contract in Fig. 4.

```
1   data player[2](address, commit, choice, has_revealed)
2   data num_players
3   data reward
4   data check_winner[3][3]
5
6   def init():
7     num_players = 0
8     # code omitted: initialize check_winner according to the game
      ↪   rules
9
10  def player_input(commitment):
11    if num_players < 2 and msg.value >= 1000:
12      reward += msg.value
13      player[num_players].address = msg.sender
14      player[num_players].commit = commitment
15      num_players = num_players + 1
16      if msg.value - 1000 > 0:
17        send(msg.sender, msg.value-1000)
18      return(0)
19    else:
20      send(msg.sender, msg.value)
21      return(-1)
22
23  def open(choice, nonce):
24    if not num_players == 2: return(-1)
25    # Determine which player is opening
26    if msg.sender == player[0].address:
27      player_num = 0
28    elif msg.sender == player[1].address:
29      player_num = 1
30    else:
31      return(-1)
32    # Check the commitment is not yet opened
33    if sha3([msg.sender, choice, nonce], items=3) ==
      ↪   player[player_num].commit and not
      ↪   player[player_num].has_revealed:
34      # Store opened value in plaintext
35      player[player_num].choice = choice
36      player[player_num].has_revealed = 1
37      return(0)
38    else:
39      return(-1)
```

Fig. 4. An improved but nonetheless buggy contract. This contract fixes a subset of the problems identified in the original (Fig. 3). When an edge case occurs, the contract refunds the players rather than leaking money (Lines 17 and 20). A cryptographic commitment scheme is used to offer privacy of users' inputs before they are revealed for the winner determination (Line 14 and 33–36). As mentioned in Sect. 4.3, this improved contract is still not safe due to misaligned incentives.

```
44   def finalize():
45     #check to see if both players have revealed answer
46     if player[0].has_revealed and player[1].has_revealed:
47       p0 = player[0].choice
48       p1 = player[1].choice
49       #If player 0 wins
50       if check_winner[p0][p1] == 0:
51         send(player[0].address, reward)
52         return(0)
53       #If player 1 wins
54       elif check_winner[p0][p1] == 1:
55         send(player[1].address, reward)
56         return(1)
57       #If no one wins
58       else:
59         send(player[0].address, reward/2)
60         send(player[1].address, reward/2)
61         return(2)
62     else:
63       return(-1)
```

Fig. 4. (*continued*)

For example, one party can wait for the other to open its commitment. Upon seeing that he will lose, that party may elect to abort (i.e., not to send any further messages) – thus denying payment to the other player as well. It may seem at first glance like the losing party should be indifferent to revealing his committed input or not (regardless, we would prefer to have a clear positive preference for revealing it); however, the reality is slightly worse, since that party must incur a *gas* cost to even submit a transaction that opens his commitment.

This generalizes to a broader question of how to ensure the incentive compatibility of a contract. Can any player profit by deviating from the intended behavior? Does the intended behavior have hidden costs?

In this specific example, we can remedy the problem by setting a deadline before which the second player has to reveal, otherwise the player who revealed first will be able to get the reward. This will protect the first player when the second player aborts. The modifications needed to protect against that case are shown in Fig. 5. Furthermore, we can have both players include an additional security deposit in the first stage, which they forfeit unless they open their commitments in a timely manner. This way, even the losing player has a stronger motivation to open his bid, but this change is not included here for simplicity.

```
# Declare a timer variable in the beginning
data timer_start
#### < Code omitted. Same as Figure 4 lines (1-22) >

def open(choice, nonce):
  #### < Code omitted. Same as Figure 4 lines (24-32)>
  if sha3([msg.sender, choice, nonce], items=3) ==
  ↪   player[player_num].commit and not
  ↪   player[player_num].has_revealed:
    player[player_num].choice = choice
    player[player_num].has_revealed = 1
    # Keep track of the first reveal time. The other player should
    ↪   reveal before 10 blocks are mined.
    if not timer_start:
      timer_start = block.number
    return(0)
  else:
    return(-1)

def finalize():
  # Check timer: Wait 10 blocks for both players to open
  if block.number - timer_start < 10:
    return(-2)

  if player[0].has_revealed and player[1].has_revealed:
    #### < Code omitted. Same as Figure 4 lines (47-61)>
  # Check for abort: If p1 opens but not p2, send money to p1
  elif player[0].has_revealed and not player[1].has_revealed:
    send(player[0].address, reward)
    return(0)
  # If p2 opens but not p1, send money to p2
  elif not player[0].has_revealed and player[1].has_revealed:
    send(player[1].address, reward)
    return(1)
  else:
    return(-1)
```

Fig. 5. Modifications required to the contract of Fig. 4 to protect against an aborting player.

4.4 Ethereum-Specific Mistakes

Several subtle details about Ethereum's implementation make smart contract programming prone to error.

Call-Stack Bug. Without going into too much detail, contracts must be written "defensively" to avoid exceptions that can occur when multiple contracts interact. One Ethereum contract can send a message to another contract, which can in turn send a message to another. However, Ethereum limits the resulting call-stack to a fixed size of 1024. For example, if the callstack depth is already at this limit when the **send** instruction on Line 59 of Fig. 4 is reached, then that instruction will be skipped and the player will not get paid. Furthermore, a **send** instruction sends by default the maximum available gas to the recipient. If the recipient of the **send** instruction on Line 59, for example, is a contract with buggy code that raises an exception, then Line 60 is never executed and the other player loses out. We stress that the same bug was later manifested in Etherpot [2], a lottery application built atop Ethereum and released to the public. In our online course materials [4] we offer guidance on how to avoid this call-stack bug in Ethereum.

Blockhash Bug. Another Ethereum-specific quirk is that the `block.prevhash` instruction supports only the 256 most recent blocks, presumably for efficiency reasons. This limitation also affected Etherpot [2] and potentially other contracts that went into production. Miller proposed one potential fix to this problem by implementing a global "blockhash service" contract that allows other contracts to retrieve block hashes beyond 256 blocks [1].

Incentive Bugs. Ethereum's underlying mining protocol can introduce subtle, incentive-related bugs. We again use Etherpot [2] as an example. Etherpot uses the hash of a block in the blockchain (e.g., at height T) as a random beacon value to pick the lottery winner. However, by selectively withholding blocks, miners can bias this value, gaining an unfair advantage in the lottery - the miner who first finds a block at height T can check whether this results in them winning the lottery – if not, they can withhold the block until another block is found, gaining a "second chance" to win. To combat this, Etherpot makes sure the prize value of each lottery is less than the base block reward. Thus a miner who withholds a block must sacrifice the block reward they would have earned. However, Ethereum implements a protocol variation called GHOST [17, 21], which allows miners who temporarily withhold blocks to still get a (discounted) reward for their block, even if the block is revealed later. Thus Etherpot's reward limit is set too loose.

4.5 Complete, Fixed Contract

Due to space constraints, we provide a fully working, incentive compatible, and secure contract for the "Rock, Paper, Scissors" game in our online course materials [4].

5 Conclusion

5.1 Open-Source Course and Lab Materials

Our smart contract programming lab was an audacious, original attempt at instructing a technology of in-development nature. Ethereum and its Serpent language have only recently emerged, and are rapidly undergoing changes.

The Serpent language is not well documented and development environment support (e.g., debugging tools) is also rudimentary. Therefore, several students struggled in installing the simulation environment and getting up to speed. To facilitate future pedagogical endeavors on smart contract programming, we have released open course materials on smart contract programming [4]. The course materials comprise the following:

- A detailed language reference guide for Ethereum's Serpent programming language.
- A virtual machine image with a snapshot of `pyethereum` and `serpent` compiler installed, providing a simulator environment for experimentation. Since the Ethereum's Serpent language is constantly under development, our Serpent language reference matches the snapshot installed in this VM.
- A tutorial that builds on our "Rock, Paper, Scissors" example, intended to walk the student through the typical pitfalls in programming safe smart contracts. The student is presented with the buggy version of the contract and asked to fix the bugs in a step-by-step, guided manner.

These materials are available at https://mc2-umd.github.io/ethereumlab/.

5.2   Cryptocurrency and Smart Contracts as a Cybersecurity Pedagogical Platform

Our experiences also led us to conclude that cryptocurrency and smart contracts are a great platform for cybersecurity pedagogy. First, cryptocurrency and smart contracts, like other interesting emerging technologies, could easily capture the students' attention and imagination. Second, cybersecurity is a science that is interdisciplinary in nature; and cryptocurrency is a platform that captures multiple core cybersecurity notions, e.g., cryptography, programming languages, and game theory. Third, cryptocurrency and smart contracts easily motivate "adversarial thinking." For example, in our lab, students had to analyze their own smart contracts and reason how other selfish players can harm honest participants and maximize their own financial gains.

5.3   The "Build, Break, and Amend Your Own Programs" Approach to Cybersecurity Education

Inspired by our smart contract programming lab, we also feel that the "Build, break, and amend your own programs" approach is very helpful for cybersecurity education. In our labs, students learned why security is difficult and learned adversarial thinking by analyzing and breaking their own programs. Students initially failed to make proper use of cryptography in their smart contracts (see Sect. 4). But then, by realizing why their smart contracts are not safe, they become self-driven in learning cryptographic building blocks.

In future work, we plan to further extend these pedagogical ideas, such that students can learn through hands-on, creative experiences, and learn adversarial thinking through attacking and amending their own code.

5.4   Subsequent Pedagogical Efforts and Research

Based on insights gained through our experiences, one of the co-authors of this paper, Miller, gave a smart contract programming tutorial at 1st Cyberport FinTech Programming Workshop. This lab has also inspired later research on cryptocurrencies and smart contracts. Juels et al. [15] recently demonstrated how smart contracts can be leveraged to facilitate criminal activities and create incentive compatible underground eco-systems. They then discuss countermeasures and advocate the responsible deployment of technology. Their paper would be the criminal counterpart of our "step by step" paper. Finally, Kosba et al. propose a general formal model for the "blockchain model of computation" which captures the formal abstraction of smart contract programming [16].

Acknowledgements. We thank the anonymous reviewers for their insightful feedback. This work is funded in part by NSF grants CNS-1314857, CNS-1453634, CNS-1518765, CNS-1514261, a Packard Fellowship, a Sloan Fellowship, two Google Faculty Research Awards, a VMWare Research Award, and by Maryland Procurement Office contract H98230-14-C-0137, ARO grants W911NF11103, W911NF1410358, and W911NF09102.

References

1. Blockhash Contract. https://github.com/amiller/ethereum-blockhashes
2. Etherpot. https://etherpot.github.io/
3. The rise and rise of bitcoin. Documentary. http://bitcoindoc.com/
4. Smart Contract Programming Open Course Materials. http://mc2-umd.github.io/ethereumlab/
5. Ahamad, S., Nair, M., Varghese, B.: A survey on crypto currencies. In: International Conference on Advances in Civil Engineering (2013)
6. Andrychowicz, M., Dziembowski, S., Malinowski, D., Mazurek, L.: Secure multiparty computations on bitcoin. In: IEEE Symposium on Security and Privacy (2013)
7. Barber, S., Boyen, X., Shi, E., Uzun, E.: Bitter to better — how to make bitcoin a better currency. In: Keromytis, A.D. (ed.) FC 2012. LNCS, vol. 7397, pp. 399–414. Springer, Heidelberg (2012)
8. Bentov, I., Kumaresan, R.: How to use bitcoin to design fair protocols. In: Garay, J.A., Gennaro, R. (eds.) CRYPTO 2014, Part II. LNCS, vol. 8617, pp. 421–439. Springer, Heidelberg (2014)
9. Bonneau, J., Miller, A., Clark, J., Narayanan, A., Kroll, J.A., Felten, E.W.: SoK: research perspectives and challenges for bitcoin and cryptocurrencies. In: IEEE Symposium on Security and Privacy, SP, San Jose, CA, USA, pp. 104–121, 17–21 May 2015
10. Canetti, R.: Universally composable security: a new paradigm for cryptographic protocols. In: IEEE Symposium on Foundations of Computer Science (FOCS) (2001)
11. Canetti, R., Dodis, Y., Pass, R., Walfish, S.: Universally composable security with global setup. In: Vadhan, S.P. (ed.) TCC 2007. LNCS, vol. 4392, pp. 61–85. Springer, Heidelberg (2007)

12. Canetti, R., Rabin, T.: Universal composition with joint state. In: Boneh, D. (ed.) CRYPTO 2003. LNCS, vol. 2729, pp. 265–281. Springer, Heidelberg (2003)
13. Chaum, D., Fiat, A., Naor, M.: Untraceable electronic cash. In: Goldwasser, S. (ed.) CRYPTO 1988. LNCS, vol. 403, pp. 319–327. Springer, New York (1990)
14. Dermody, A.K.R., Slama, O.: Counterparty Announcement, January 2014. https://bitcointalk.org/index.php?topic=395761.0
15. Juels, A., Kosba, A., Shi, E.: Rings of gyges: using smart contractsfor crime. Manuscript (2015)
16. Kosba, A., Miller, A., Papamanthou, C., Shi, E., Wen, Z.: Hawk: the blockchain model of cryptography and privacy-preserving smart contracts. https://eprint.iacr.org/2015/675.pdf
17. Lewenberg, Y., Sompolinsky, Y., Zohar, A.: Inclusive block chain protocols. In: Financial Cryptography and Data Security (FC) (2015)
18. Nakamoto, S.: Bitcoin: a peer-to-peer electronic cash system (2008)
19. Pass, R., Shelat, A.: Micropayments for decentralized currencies. In: Proceedings of 22nd ACM SIGSAC Conference on Computer and Communications Security, CCS 2015, pp. 207–218 (2015)
20. Ruffing, T., Kate, A., Schröder, D.: Liar, liar, coins on fire! Penalizing equivocation by loss of bitcoins. In: Proceedings of 22nd ACM SIGSAC Conference on Computer and Communications Security, CCS 2015 (2015)
21. Sompolinsky, Y., Zohar, A.: Accelerating bitcoin's transaction processing. Fast money grows on trees, not chains. IACR Cryptology ePrint Archive 2013:881 (2013)
22. Etheruem Wiki: Serpent (2015). https://github.com/ethereum/wiki/wiki/Serpent
23. Wood, G.: Ethereum: a secure decentralized transaction ledger (2014). http://gavwood.com/paper.pdf

EthIKS: Using Ethereum to Audit a CONIKS Key Transparency Log

Joseph Bonneau[✉]

Electronic Frontier Foundation, Stanford University, Stanford, USA
jbonneau@gmail.com

Abstract. CONIKS is a proposed key transparency system which enables a centralized service provider to maintain an auditable yet privacy-preserving directory of users' public keys. In the original CONIKS design, users must monitor that their data is correctly included in every published snapshot of the directory, necessitating either slow updates or trust in an unspecified third-party to audit that the data structure has stayed consistent. We demonstrate that the data structures for CONIKS are very similar to those used in Ethereum, a consensus computation platform with a Turing-complete programming environment. We can take advantage of this to embed the core CONIKS data structures into an Ethereum contract with only minor modifications. Users may then trust the Ethereum network to audit the data structure for consistency and non-equivocation. Users who do not trust (or are unaware of) Ethereum can self-audit the CONIKS data structure as before. We have implemented a prototype contract for our hybrid EthIKS scheme, demonstrating that it adds only modest bandwidth overhead to CONIKS proofs and costs hundredths of pennies per key update in fees at today's rates.

1 Introduction

Distribution and verification of public keys for end-to-end encrypted communication remains a challenging problem. In terms of deployment, the most successful model has been centralized services which serve as trusted public key directories [10], such as those used by iMessage and WhatsApp. This model is also employed by security-focused messaging applications such as Signal (TextSecure), Silent Circle, Telegram or Threema. These apps additionally allow users to verify public keys manually, although experience suggests few actually do so.

These services might try to launch a man-in-the-middle attack by serving keys maliciously. That is, instead of serving Alice's true public key PK_A to Bob, the server might serve a public key PK_S for which it knows the private key. Such attacks are facilitated in centralized applications since the server typically routes and/or stores all communication for efficiency, making it is straightforward to decrypt traffic if the keys are known. Many applications also enable users to register multiple public keys to support multiple devices, making it easy to add an "interception key" which simply looks like an extra device.

An essential requirement of this attack is that the key directory interacts inconsistently between Alice and Bob. If Alice queries her own public key, it

© International Financial Cryptography Association 2016
J. Clark et al. (Eds.): FC 2016 Workshops, LNCS 9604, pp. 95–105, 2016.
DOI: 10.1007/978-3-662-53357-4_7

should respond with the correct result or else Alice's device may automatically detect the attack (since it knows which public keys it has uploaded). A key server with global consistency would therefore be a significant security upgrade: as long as Alice verifies that her own entry in the directory is correct, she can be sure that she is not being attacked. Furthermore, if Bob trusts that Alice is regularly monitoring her own entry, Bob can accept whatever public keys the directory returns for Alice and trust that she will detect if an attack has taken place. While this setup will only detect attacks (without preventing them), it is far more lightweight for users than manually verifying all public keys out-of-band.

CONIKS [7] (CONsistent Identity Key Service) is a concrete proposal for a key server with consistency while also protecting users' privacy. This approach is currently being adapted by Google and Yahoo! for use in their prototype end-to-end encrypted email systems. The key data structure in CONIKS is a signed hash chain of roots of Merkle prefix trees.

Ethereum [11] is a "secure decentralized transaction ledger." Inspired by Bitcoin [9], Ethereum adds support for long-lived, stateful "contracts" with a Turing-complete scripting language. Under the hood, Ethereum uses data structures similar to CONIKS, including a blockchain with snapshots of the entire Ethereum system using Merkle Patricia trees to store the state of each contract.

These similarities are not coincidental. While the two systems were designed for very different purposes, both require a globally consistent data structure supporting efficient updates and proofs of inclusion. In this paper we show that, with minor modifications, a CONIKS directory can be "wrapped" inside an Ethereum contract in a hybrid scheme we call EthIKS. This allows it to piggyback on Ethereum's consensus protocol to prevent equivocation, potentially obviating the need for a separate gossip protocol to ensure consistency. It also enables increased efficiency for clients willing to trust the Ethereum network.

We have implemented a prototype Ethereum contract to measure the cost of EthIKS both in terms of transaction fees paid to the Ethereum network ("gas") and bandwidth overhead compared to the original CONIKS design.

2   CONIKS Overview

We provide a brief overview of CONIKS here [7]. The key data structure in CONIKS is a chain of directory snapshots, or *signed tree roots* (STRs). Each STR commits to the entire directory, which is a binary Merkle prefix tree containing the current mapping from users to public keys.

Merkle Prefix Trees. The tree in CONIKS maps arbitrary indices[1] to data. It is a radix tree; each branch of the tree represents either a "0" or "1" in the binary representation of an index. Each leaf of the tree stores data mapped to the index represented by its complete path from the root. To reduce the length of paths in the tree, subtrees with only one non-null leaf are collapsed into a single leaf marked with the unique suffix of this single non-null index. The data structure

---

[1] The term "key" is avoided to prevent confusion with cryptographic keys.

is authenticated in that each non-leaf node includes the hash of its children. The root of the tree thus uniquely commits to the entire data structure, assuming the hash used is collision-resistant [8].

Private Bindings. To ensure privacy, CONIKS generates the index for each user's data using a verifiable unpredictable function (VUF). The CONIKS provider generates a VUF private key which can be used to deterministically derive the index for any username and provide a publicly-verifiable proof that this index was generated correctly. Furthermore, each leaf in the CONIKS tree stores a commitment to a user's data rather than the data itself. Thus, to verify a (username, data) binding in the CONIKS tree, one must verify both that the index produced by the VUF for that username is present in the tree and that the commitment at that leaf commits to the claimed data. Without the VUF proofs or commitment randomness, the CONIKS tree reveals no information about any usernames or their data beyond the number of users in the tree.[2]

Key Binding Proofs. To communicate in CONIKS, Alice requests Bob's key binding from the CONIKS provider as of the latest STR. The provider responds with Bob's key data, a Merkle proof of inclusion in the STR's tree root, the VUF proof of Bob's index and the randomness to open the commitment to Bob's data.

Non-equivocation. To assure that all users see a consistent version of the CONIKS tree, the root is included in a chained sequence of STRs. Each STR commits to the hash of the previous version of the tree (and hence the entire history of the directory) as well as a timestamp and other metadata, and is signed by the CONIKS provider. While the CONIKS provider is able to sign two inconsistent versions of the tree, if they are ever discovered this will provide non-repudiable proof that the provider is malicious. To discourage such equivocation, the original CONIKS proposal assumes that users will participate in a gossip protocol to share STRs they have observed. It also suggests that STRs might be embedded in an external append-only log such as the Bitcoin blockchain.

Key Updates and Revocation. By default, the CONIKS provider can change a user's key binding at any time. This enables recovery from lost or stolen keys by traditional backup authentication means such as password reset questions or telephone helplines. Optionally, CONIKS users may request that their leaf be marked with a *strict* flag meaning that updates must be signed by a designated user-controlled key. This option enables preventive (rather than purely detective) defense against unauthorized key changes, at the price of burning the username forever if the update key is lost. There is no special notion of revocation of CONIKS: the old key is simply replaced in the next version of the tree.

---

[2] The number of valid users in the system can be obscured by adding dummy users at random indices with random data, which will be indistinguishable from real users.

Auditing and Monitoring. Each CONIKS user *audits* the provider for consistency, checking that each STR forms a chain and potentially checking for equivocation with third parties (i.e. gossip). Auditing can also be done by any third-party. Each user also *monitors* their own entry in the tree for correctness based on the key changes they have actually requested from the server. If an unexpected key change occurs, the user's software should show a warning message.[3]

Efficiency Considerations. In the process of auditing and monitoring, each user must download every STR from the server and check that their binding is correctly included. While these checks are all logarithmic in the number of users, if STRs are issued frequently users must download and verify a large number of signatures. However, if STRs are issued slowly, the time to add a new key binding (or equivalently, revoke an old one) will be long. The original CONIKS proposal suggested STRs being issued on the order of hours, with a secondary system of auditable "promises" to include data in the next STR to enable faster enrollment (similar to signed certificate timestamps in Certificate Transparency [4]).

In development at Google and Yahoo!, promises were scrapped in favor of faster STR updating times. To mitigate the cost of verifying that a user's binding has stayed consistent in n consecutive STRs, an update count is added to each leaf, enabling users to simply verify that their update count was not incremented at in the most recent STR. However, this assumes the existence of third party auditors to verify that update counts are incremented if and only if the committed data is actually changed.

Our goal in wrapping CONIKS in an Ethereum contract is to maintain the advantages of frequent STRs, while relying on the Ethereum network to audit that update counts are incremented correctly. We also use Ethereum to gain confidence in non-equivocation.

3   Ethereum Overview

While it is often described as being "like Bitcoin with a Turing-complete scripting language," Ethereum [11] is perhaps more accurately described as a *consensus computer*. Unlike Bitcoin, in which each block contains a set of transactions updating an implicit global state, each block in the Ethereum blockchain explicitly commits to the complete state of the system which includes both user accounts and *contracts*, which represent a running process in the system with code, memory state and a monetary balance. Each contract's code describes an API which users of the system can call to cause the contract to execute some code which may update its state and/or transmit money to other contracts or users. An API call is called a *transaction*. Transactions must be signed by a specific sender and may contain a payment and an arbitrary amount of data.

---

[3] Note that in CONIKS, warning messages are only intended when the user's own key has changed unexpectedly at the server. If their peer's keys change, this is ignored as it is assumed the peer will monitor this change themselves.

A simple example is a game of chess between strangers with a binding monetary bet. A contract representing a chess game can be sent to the network. Its code should initialize the contract state to represent an empty board and no players. Two players may then join by sending a message to the contract along with a deposit equal to the betting stake. While the game is underway, the deposits will be owned by the contract itself. Each player will then submit moves in turn, with the contract updating the board after each move and rejecting any invalid moves. When one player wins the game, the contract would then send its entire value to the winner and close.[4]

Programming Ethereum contracts correctly has already proven quite subtle [2], requiring defensive programming and extensive sanity checks to ensure no API calls can corrupt the contract state. For example, in the chess game, the contract must implement a timeout rule where players lose by default if they don't submit a move within a required time, to avoid simply stalling a lost game forever (sometimes called a "rage quit").

Contract Fees. The state of every contract in the system (as well as each user account) must be tracked by every miner. Every miner must also validate all transactions in every block to see that they execute each contract's code correctly and update the global state accordingly. This presents an obvious denial-of-service avenue as contracts may contain infinite loops, allocate an arbitrary amount of storage, or perform other resource-intensive computations. Thus, every instruction executed requires a fee, referred to as *gas*. Gas is the same currency used for sending value between users and/or contracts in the system; it is simply called gas when it is being used to pay for executing a transaction.

At prices planned for the "Homestead" Ethereum release, simple instructions (e.g. addition) cost 2–10 gas whereas more complex instructions may cost significantly more (e.g. computing a SHA-3 hash costs 30 gas). Writing to storage is particularly costly, at 20,000 gas per 256-bit word. Any transaction must send sufficient gas to pay for all of the instructions executes. If a contract runs out of gas while executing a transaction, execution halts with all changes to the state undone and the gas being kept by the miners. Thus it is critical both to write programs which are efficient in their gas costs and to ensure transactions contain sufficient gas to pay for the instructions they execute.

Storage Model. Each block in the Ethereum blockchain contains a "Merkle Patricia tree" with the state of each contract and user account stored in the leaves. Each contract or user account is represented by a unique 160-bit address (either the hash of the user's public key or a hash of the contract's code plus a nonce). Unlike the prefix tree used in CONIKS, in Ethereum the Patricia tree is 16-ary (hexary), although the suffix-compression is similarly applied.

Each leaf contains a hash of that addresses state, including its current balance within the system. For addresses representing contracts (as opposed to simply

---

[4] In Ethereum parlance, the contract closes by calling a special SUICIDE opcode which enables the network to permanently delete its storage.

user accounts) the state also includes the root of a Merkle Patricia tree representing that contract's persistent storage. The storage model is very simple: each contract has a memory space of 2^{256} 256-bit words, each representing a 256-bit address. The contract's storage is thus a function $\{0,1\}^{256} \rightarrow \{0,1\}^{256}$. Leaves are inserted into the tree for any address with a non-zero word stored; addresses which are not in the storage tree are interpreted to have a value of 0.

This storage model makes implementing hash tables extremely simple in Ethereum: the value v associated to a key k is simply stored at the memory address $H(k)$, with the storage tree handling this efficiently under the hood. Most high-level Ethereum languages (including Solidity) expose this $\{0,1\}^{256} \rightarrow \{0,1\}^{256}$ map as a built-in type.

4   EthIKS

Given the contract execution model of Ethereum, we can implement a close variant of CONIKS. The goal will be to ensure EthIKS is as secure as CONIKS for clients which ignore Ethereum completely and interact directly with the EthIKS log, while Ethereum-aware clients will gain greater trust and efficiency.

Core Data Structure. EthIKS implements the core data structure of CONIKS, the tree mapping user indices to user data, in the persistent storage of a single Ethereum contract. This contract allows the service provider to update the tree by sending messages from a designated address. The service provider can send the contract an index i and a commitment c, which will then be stored (or updated) in the tree by simply writing the value c to memory address i. These values will be the VUF-derived private index for a given user and the commitment to the user's public-key data. A side-effect of this design is that the Ethereum blockchain will contain a record of each update to the tree, something that is not normally published in CONIKS.

Key Bindings. As in plain CONIKS, a key binding will include the VUF proof that an index i corresponds to a username u, as well as the randomness required to open the commitment c to the user's data. Because these values are now stored in an Ethereum contract rather than a separate CONIKS-specific prefix tree, the key binding must include the proof that the address c has the value i in the contract's persistent storage. This is simply a proof-of-inclusion for the contract's storage tree plus a proof-of-inclusion that this storage tree is currently mapped to the contract as of the most recent block in the Ethereum block chain. Notice that each Ethereum block is effectively a signed tree root (STR) in EthIKS.

Backwards-Compatible Proofs. To maintain the normal CONIKS interface for clients which wish to ignore Ethereum, the provider still publishes signed tree roots after every update to the tree. In EthIKS the tree root to be signed is the root of the Merkle Patricia tree representing its EthIKS contract's storage after each update. These tree roots are implicitly "signed" by the Ethereum network through their inclusion in a block. The provider additionally signs the tree root, combined with a pointer to the previous version of the tree and publishes this chain of signatures separately. For non-Ethereum-aware clients, this chain of signed roots functions exactly as in plain CONIKS.

Update Frequency. In CONIKS, the tree is updated (by publishing a new STR) at a provider-chosen frequency. In EthIKS, the tree can be updated in every Ethereum block. The Ethereum block frequency, targeted currently at one block per 13 s, is a lower-bound on the epoch length.[5] The provider may choose to sign the tree less frequently than once per block to reduce the length of its owned chain of signed tree roots. Legacy clients would only see updated versions at this slower rate. However, Ethereum-aware clients would see new updates rapidly (and may rapidly update their own entries).

Update Counts. The EthIKS contract maintains an *update counter* for each index in the tree. Any update to this index's data must increments the counter; the contract's code which allows no other API for updating the tree. The benefit of this counter is that Ethereum-aware clients can be sure that their data in the tree has not changed if their counter has not changed, allowing them to skip monitoring every version of the tree and simply check the counter value in the most recent version of the tree.

User-Controlled Addresses. EthIKS supports a comparable feature to CONIK's strict mode: each leaf in the tree has an associated owner (by default the service provider) which is the only address allowed to send updates to this leaf in the tree. Updates may include changing the owner; the provider must do this initially to create a new leaf and then transfer control to its owner if requested. Security-conscious users may request the service provider change their leaf's owner address to a public key of their choosing.

Unlike in CONIKS, users who opt for control of their own leaf can then update it directly by communicating with the Ethereum contract themselves, they no longer need to route updates through the service provider. However, if they update their data and don't send the commitment randomness to the provider, the provider can no longer answer queries about this user's public key.

Revoked Usernames. EthIKS also retains CONIKS' ability to permanently remove a user's data by replacing it with a special *tombstone* value. In EthIKS, tombstoned users simply have their owner set to a dummy address for which the private key clearly does not exist (e.g. the public key whose hash equals zero). Note that this is not the same as setting a user's data to be zero; this removes their data from the tree but enables this username to be later reincarnated.

---

[5] Currently, the mean time between blocks is about 50 % higher due to network latency.

5   Implementation and Costs

We have implemented a prototype of EthIKS by modifying the prototype CONIKS implementation [7] and writing an Ethereum contract to handle the core tree updates. The EthIKS contract is contains fewer than 100 SLOC in Solidity, Ethereum's most popular high-level language for writing smart contracts. The contract exposes only a single API call (besides the constructor), `updateMappings` which takes a list of indices, data values, and (possibly null) addresses. Each index is updated to the new data value and its counter incremented after checking that the owner of this index is the party sending the message.

Table 1. Transaction fees (gas costs) for different update types in EthIKS, along with the current price in ether (the base currency of Ethereum), millibitcoin (mBTC), and US dollars as of January 2016 exchange rates and the default gas price of 1 gas = $5 \cdot 10^{-8}$ ether. Ethereum transactions also incur an overhead cost of 21,000 gas, but this can be amortized by batching multiple updates in a single transaction so we ignore it here.

Operation	Gas cost			
	Gas	Ether	mBTC	US dollar
Create tree	367535	3.675	1.838	0.0036
Insert new user	42042	0.420	0.210	0.0004
Update mapping	12042	0.120	0.060	0.0001
Delete user data	12042	0.120	0.060	0.0001
Change ownership	17382	0.174	0.087	0.0002
Tombstone user	17382	0.174	0.087	0.0002

Gas Costs. The transaction costs (in gas) of updating the EthIKS tree through the EthIKS contract are listed in Table 1. These are based on our Solidity implementation, a hand-coded byte code might achieve better efficiency. The main cost in all operations is writing to permanent storage; the current implementation of Solidity invokes several writes at 100 gas each for every update to the tree. Still, the contract costs on the order of hundredths of pennies per update to the tree. At current rates, these costs would be significant for a large provider, which might be required to handle millions of key updates per day (costing tens of thousands of dollars in gas). However, we note that the future value of gas (and ether) is very difficult to project. The current Ethereum network (Frontier) would not handle a provider with billions of users due to limits on the size and number of transactions per block, but these limits are expected to be increased in the future as Ethereum scalability improves.

Bandwidth Costs. EthIKS re-uses the same construction for the VUF and hash commitment as plain CONIKS does. In our prototype implementation, we use the elliptic-curve based VUF and signature scheme (EC-Schnorr) proposed with CONIKS (CONIKS also can be implemented with RSA or BLS, but we ignore these to match the cryptography used in Ethereum). We consider two cases for EthIKS: clients which trust the Ethereum network and clients which ignore the Ethereum network (legacy clients). We simulated the same scenario used as a benchmark in CONIKS: $N = 2^{32}$ total users, $n = 2^{21}$ user updates per epoch and k epochs per day.

For legacy clients, the performance is asymptotically equivalent to that of plain CONIKS. Each binding proof requires verifying one path in the tree, one VUF, one commitment opening and one signature on the root which require a constant 192 bytes. However, Ethereum's Merkle tree structure is known to be slightly inefficient in being hexary. Assuming N total users and n updates per epoch ($n \leq N$), the binary prefix tree in CONIKS requires a path of length $\lg_2 N$ with 256 bits of data per node to reconstruct the path. By contrast, the Ethereum tree requires a path of length $\lg_{16} N = \frac{\lg_2 N}{4}$, but each node requires up to $(N - 1) \cdot 256$ bits of data per node. At our simulated size, this increases the path representation from 1024 bytes to 3840 bytes, and the overall binding proof size from 1216 bytes to 4032 bytes.

Ethereum-aware clients can save greatly on monitoring costs by only receiving updated paths when their data actually changes (or at a sampling frequency of their choice). If clients are tracking all of the block headers in Ethereum, this requires downloading at least 220 bytes per 13 s or 1.4 MB per day.[6] They might also get this data for selected blocks only by querying one or more trusted sources. The complete proof will also require proof that the EthIKS tree is correctly included in the current block, the size of which will depend on the number of contracts in existence. Currently this is less than 1000 so this proof is relatively short, but it might be considerably larger in the future. To be conservative, we assume 2^{32} Ethereum contracts exist, requiring an additional 3840 bytes of data.

We combine these numbers in Table 2 comparing a user in a plain CONIKS system, a legacy user in an EthIKS system, an Ethereum-aware user in EthIKS

Table 2. Client bandwidth requirements, in kB, assuming a $\approx 2^{32}$ total users, $\approx 2^{21}$ changes per epoch, 24 epochs per day, and $\approx 2^{32}$ total Ethereum addresses. A legacy client ignores Ethereum completely and simply uses the EthIKS provider's signed tree roots. A light client trusts Ethereum and relies on a third party to give it the latest Ethereum block header when needed. A full client trusts Ethereum but downloads all Ethereum block headers locally.

	CONIKS	EthIKS		
	Default	Legacy client	Light client	Full client
Lookup (per binding)	1.2	4.0	7.9	7.9
Monitor (per epoch)	0.7	2.6	5.0	5.2
Monitor (daily)	17.6	62.4	7.9	1401
Audit (per epoch)	0.1	0.1	0	60
Audit (daily)	2.3	2.3	0	1394

---

[6] This lower bound does not include block's timestamp and difficulty (which can be compressed), or the bloom filter whose size will vary based on usage.

willing to trust a third party to deliver the current Ethereum block header (a light client) and an EthIKS client which downloads all Ethereum block headers locally. Note that this requires a large amount of bandwidth (1.4 MB per day) but might be useful for other purposes.

6   Concluding Discussion

Our analysis shows that EthIKS is a natural extension of CONIKS: it is simple to implement and can be used by legacy clients with minor modifications and only a small performance overhead compared with CONIKS. This performance overhead would be reduced to near-zero by the adoption of a more efficient binary Merkle prefix tree by Ethereum; the adoption of a hexary tree has already been recognized as a regrettable design error [1] that may be fixed in future versions.

For Ethereum-aware clients, superficially additional bandwidth must be used to track the chain of Ethereum block headers. However, this might be useful on its own or be outsourced to a third party. These clients gain a significant advantage over plain CONIKS: keys can be updated very rapidly (bound only by Ethereum's 13 s block generation time). These updates are also independent of the service provider for user-controlled bindings. Furthermore, these clients gain the full security of the Ethereum consensus protocol against equivocation of the provider's state or corruption of the update counters. Overall, this greatly simplifies the service as promises to update are no longer needed (due to the fast update time) and a separate gossip protocol can be eliminated.

The idea of building a naming system on top of Ethereum or other cryptocurrencies is not new. Namecoin [5] was the first formal fork of Bitcoin, designed to provide a distributed naming system, and the simplicity of implementing Namecoin in Ethereum (requiring only a few lines of code in the simplest form) has even been used as a "Hello world!" teaching example of Ethereum programming. However, Namecoin has struggled to gain any significant use, with nearly all registered names currently held by squatters [3] and no clear economic model for assigning valuable names. It also offers no privacy for users, making it difficult to retrofit to existing communication services. CONIKS (and in turn EthIKS) addresses these problems by assuming a centralized service, which controls the assignment of names and maintains privacy by managing a secret VUF key to obscure name-key bindings. However, the central provider in CONIKS is not fully trusted to avoid inserting spurious keys or equivocating about the state of the system. This is prevented by public monitoring and auditing.

Our contribution is EthIKS, which improves on this design by leveraging the Ethereum network to do this checking. Assuming Ethereum proves to be a secure consensus computer in practice [6], EthIKS can enable greatly improved efficiency for clients willing to trust the integrity of Ethereum, while enabling normal CONIKS-like operation for legacy clients. We have implemented this and shown that it is possible today for small providers, costing hundredths of pennies per update to the tree. While the current network may not scale to large providers requiring millions of updates, our work shows that it is asymptotically efficient and therefore possible as the Ethereum network itself scales.

References

1. Ethereum Design Rationale (2016). https://github.com/ethereum/wiki/wiki/Design-Rationale
2. Delmolino, K., Arnett, M., Kosba, A., Miller, A., Shi, E.: A Programmers Guide to Ethereum and Serpent, May 2015
3. Kalodner, H., Carlsten, M., Ellenbogen, P., Bonneau, J., Narayanan, A.: An empirical study of Namecoin and lessons for decentralized namespace design. In: Workshop on the Economics of Information Security (WEIS), June 2015
4. Laurie, B., Langley, A., Kasper, E.: Google Inc. RFC 6962 Certificate Transparency, June 2013
5. Loibl, A.: Namecoin (2014). namecoin.info
6. Luu, L., Teutsch, J., Kulkarni, R., Saxena, P.: Demystifying incentives in the consensus computer. In: ACM Conference on Computer and Communications Security (CCS) (2015)
7. Melara, M.S., Blankstein, A., Bonneau, J., Freedman, M.J., Felten, E.W.: CONIKS: bringing key transparency to end users. In: USENIX Security, August 2015
8. Miller, A., Hicks, M., Katz, J., Shi, E.: Authenticated data structures, generically. In: ACM Conference on Principles of Programming Languages (POPL), January 2014
9. Nakamoto, S.: Bitcoin: A Peer-to-Peer Electronic Cash System (2008). http://bitcoin.org/bitcoin.pdf
10. Unger, N., Dechand, S., Bonneau, J., Fahl, S., Perl, H., Goldberg, I., Smith, M.: SoK: secure messaging. In: IEEE Symposium on Security and Privacy, May 2015
11. Wood, G.: Ethereum: a secure decentralized transaction ledger (2014). http://gavwood.com/paper.pdf

On Scaling Decentralized Blockchains

(A Position Paper)

Kyle Croman[1,2], Christian Decker[5(✉)], Ittay Eyal[1,2], Adem Efe Gencer[1,2],
Ari Juels[1,3], Ahmed Kosba[1,4], Andrew Miller[1,4], Prateek Saxena[7],
Elaine Shi[1,2], Emin Gün Sirer[1,2], Dawn Song[1,6], and Roger Wattenhofer[5]

[1] Initiative for CryptoCurrencies and Contracts (IC3), Ithaca, USA
[2] Cornell University, Ithaca, USA
[3] Jacobs, Cornell Tech, New York, USA
[4] UMD, College Park, USA
[5] ETH, Zürich, Switzerland
cdecker@tik.ee.ethz.ch
[6] UC Berkeley, Berkeley, USA
[7] NUS, Singapore, Singapore

Abstract. The increasing popularity of blockchain-based cryptocurrencies has made scalability a primary and urgent concern. We analyze how fundamental and circumstantial bottlenecks in Bitcoin limit the ability of its current peer-to-peer overlay network to support substantially higher throughputs and lower latencies. Our results suggest that reparameterization of block size and intervals should be viewed only as a first increment toward achieving next-generation, high-load blockchain protocols, and major advances will additionally require a basic rethinking of technical approaches. We offer a structured perspective on the design space for such approaches. Within this perspective, we enumerate and briefly discuss a number of recently proposed protocol ideas and offer several new ideas and open challenges.

1 Introduction

Increasing adoption of cryptocurrencies has raised concerns about their ability to scale. Since Bitcoin is a self-regulating system that works by discovering blocks at approximate intervals, its highest transaction throughput is effectively capped at maximum block size divided by block interval. The current trend of ever increasing block sizes on Bitcoin portends a potential problem where the system will reach its maximum capacity to clear transactions, probably by 2017 [46]. As a result, the cryptocurrency community has been discussing techniques for improving scalability of blockchains in general, and Bitcoin in particular, for some time. These debates have been vigorous, and at times acrimonious, and led to splits within the community, without a clear path forward on which technical measures ought to be deployed to address the scalability problem.

Today's representative blockchain such as Bitcoin takes **10 min** or longer to confirm transactions, achieves **7 transactions/sec** maximum throughput. In

J. Clark et al. (Eds.): FC 2016 Workshops, LNCS 9604, pp. 106–125, 2016.
DOI: 10.1007/978-3-662-53357-4_8

comparison, a mainstream payment processor such as Visa credit card confirms a transaction within seconds, and processes 2000 transactions/sec on average, with a peak rate of 56,000 transactions/sec [10]. Clearly, a large gap exists between where Bitcoin is today, and the scalability of a mainstream payment processor. Therefore, the key questions are,

Can decentralized blockchains be scaled up to match the performance of a mainstream payment processor? What does it take to get there?

This paper aims to place exploration of blockchain scalability on a scientific footing. We note that "scalability" is not a well-defined, singular property of a system, but a term that relates several quantitative metrics to each other.

We offer three contributions that illuminate the problem of scaling Bitcoin and blockchains generally to achieve high-performance, decentralized systems:

Measurement Study and Exploration of Reparametrization. We present experimental measurements of a range of metrics that characterize the resource costs and performance of today's operational Bitcoin network. As a first step toward better scalability in Bitcoin, the community has put forth various proposals to modify the key system parameters of block size and block interval. Through further experimental investigation, we show that such scaling by reparametrization can achieve only limited benefits given the network performance induced by Bitcoin's current peer-to-peer overlay network protocol while maintaining its current degree of decentralization, as measured by number of functioning peers in the overlay network.

Our results hinge on the key metric of *effective throughput* in the overlay network, which we define here as which blocks propagate within an average block interval period the percentage of nodes to. If the transaction rate exceeds the 90 % effective throughput, then 10 % of the nodes in the network would be unable to keep up, potentially resulting in denied services to users and reducing the network's effective mining power. To ensure at least 90 % of the nodes in the current overlay network have sufficient throughput, we offer the following two guidelines:

- **[Throughput limit.]** The block size should not exceed 4 MB, given today's 10 min. average block interval (or a reduction in block-interval time). A 4 MB block size corresponds to a maximum throughput of at most 27 transactions/sec.
- **[Latency limit.]** The block interval should not be smaller than 12 s, if full utilization of the network's bandwidth is to be achieved.

We stress that the above guidelines seem somewhat intuitive (especially in hindsight). The community has thus also proposed radically different scaling approaches, and introduced mechanisms such as Corallo's relay network, a centralized block-propagation mechanism. One of our contributions, however, is to *quantify* Bitcoin's current scalability limits within its decentralized components.

Note that as we consider only a subset of possible metrics (due to difficulty in accurately measuring others), our results on reparametrization may be viewed as upper bounds: additional metrics could reveal even stricter limits.

Painting a Broad Design Space for Scalable Blockchains. Our findings lead us to the position that *fundamental protocol redesign is needed for blockchains to scale significantly while retaining their decentralization.* We compile and review various technical approaches that can help blockchains scale. We lay out a broad design space that encompasses not just incremental improvements, but also radical rearchitecture. We frame a structured discussion of new protocol design strategies in terms of a partitioning blockchain systems into distinct planes, namely: Network, Consensus, Storage, View, and Side Planes. We discuss the properties of each plane and both recent and new proposals to improve each; we also discuss open research challenges.

Posing Open Challenges. Another goal of our paper is to articulate open challenges in the service of *(i)* better understanding of scalability bottlenecks; and *(ii)* the design of more scalable blockchains. As mentioned earlier, scalability is not a singular metric, but captures the tension between various performance and security metrics. So far, measurement and understanding of many important metrics (e.g., fairness and mining power utilization [25]) are lacking — partly because monitoring and measuring a decentralized blockchain from only a few vantage points poses significant challenges. We call for better measurement techniques such that we could continuously monitor the health of decentralized system such as Bitcoin, and answer key questions such as *"To what extent can we push system parameters without sacrificing security?" "How robust is the system when under attack?"* Finally, although we paint the broader design space for a scalable blockchain, instantiating and combining these ideas to build a full-fledged system with formally provable security is a non-trivial challenge.

2   Bitcoin Scalability Today: A Reality Check

We analyze some of the key metrics of the Bitcoin system as it exists today.

Maximum Throughput. The maximum throughput is the maximum rate at which the blockchain can confirm transactions. Today, Bitcoin's maximum throughput is 3.3–7 transactions/sec [1]. This number is constrained by the maximum block size and the inter-block time.

Latency. Time for a transaction to confirm. A transaction is considered confirmed when it is included in a block, roughly 10 minutes in expectation.[1]

---

[1] Although we define latency in Bitcoin as the time to obtain a single confirmation, some payment processors accept "zero-confirmation" transactions, while others follow common advice to wait for 6 confirmations before accepting a payment.

Bootstrap Time. The time it takes a new node to download and process the history necessary to validate the current system state. Presently in Bitcoin, the bootstrap time is linear in the size of the blockchain history, and is roughly **four days** (averaged over five fresh `t2.medium` Amazon EC2 nodes that we connected to the network running the most recent `master` software).

Cost per Confirmed Transaction (CPCT). The cost in USD of resources consumed by the entire Bitcoin system to confirm a single transaction. The CPCT encompasses several distinct resources, all of which can be further decomposed into operational costs (mainly electricity) and capital equipment costs:

1. *Mining:* Expended by miners in generating the proof of work for each block.
2. *Transaction validation:* The cost of computation necessary to validate that a transaction can spend the outputs referenced by its inputs, dominated by cryptographic verifications.
3. *Bandwidth:* The cost of network resources required to receive and transmit transactions, blocks, and metadata.
4. *Storage:* The cost (1) of storing all currently spendable transactions, which is necessary for miners and full nodes to perform transaction validation, and (2) of storing the blockchain's (much larger) historical data, which is necessary to bootstrap new nodes that join the network.

Table 1 presents our estimates of these various costs. As the table shows, the majority of the cost is attributable to mining. Our calculation suggests that, at the maximum throughput, the cost per confirmed transaction is **\$1.4 – \$2.9**, where 57 % is electricity consumption for mining. If the de facto Bitcoin throughput is assumed, the CPCT is as high as **\$6.2**. We proceed to explain our cost-estimation methodology.

To measure the cost per transaction for Bitcoin, we perform a back-of-the-envelope calculation by summing up the electricity consumed by the network as a whole, as well as the hardware cost of mining equipment. We project our estimates based on the AntMiner S5+ mining hardware [8], which is the currently available hardware that has the highest hash rate per joule, and the highest hash rate per dollar according to this comparison as of October 2015 [2]. We assume a 1 year effective lifetime for the hardware, and that the average hashing rate of the network is 450,000,000 GH/s based on statistics from October 2015 [3]. Based on the power consumption of the selected hardware (0.445 W/GH), the total power consumed by the network will be about 200 MegaWatt. Furthermore, we assume the average price per KWh is \$0.1 [48].

There are two interesting scenarios: The first scenario is when the Bitcoin network is operating at maximum throughput, namely 3.3–7 transactions/sec. This maximum throughput is mainly constrained by Bitcoin's 1 MB maximum block size and the variable transaction size. The lower bound of the maximum throughput is inferred from the current average transaction size, about 500 bytes, while the upper bound is based on an oft-cited estimate from [1] which corresponds to unusually small (250 byte) transactions. The second scenario is the de facto average throughput for the Bitcoin network, which is, based on statistics collected in October 2015, 1.57 transactions/sec [4].

Table 1 shows ballpark estimates for the transaction validation, storage, and bandwidth costs. These estimates are attained assuming that the entire network contains 5400 full nodes — a coarse-grained estimate obtained from https://bitnodes.21.co/. We assume that each full node incurs roughly the running cost of an EC2 micro-instance ($\sim$ \$0.01/h) to validate transactions; alternatively, assuming a \$500 processor with a 5-year life-time would yield the same ballpark estimate. We assume that transactions are stored on an SSD drive with a 5-year lifetime, costing about \$0.3/GB today. We also assume all nodes store the entire history, to maintain the system's security. We assume each node maintains a home-grade Internet connection (about \$100/month) whose cost is amortized over all transactions. We stress that an EC2 micro instance and a home-grade Internet connection provide sufficiently large computation/network bandwidth at the operating scale of today's Bitcoin.

Table 1. Bitcoin cost breakdown. Includes cost incurred by all nodes.

	At max throughput		At *de facto* throughput	
	Cost/tx	Percentage	Cost/tx	Percentage
Mining: proof-of-work	$\sim$\$0.8–\$1.7	$\sim$56 %	$\sim$\$3.6	$\sim$56 %
Mining: hardware	$\sim$\$0.6–\$1.3	$\sim$42 %	$\sim$\$2.7	$\sim$42 %
Transaction validation	$\sim$\$0.002	$\sim$0.2 %	$\sim$\$0.008	$\sim$0.2 %
Bandwidth	$\sim$\$0.02	$\sim$2 %	$\sim$\$0.08	$\sim$2%
Storage (running cost)	$\sim$\$0.0008/5years			

We note that it is a fallacy to assume that transaction costs necessarily have to be offset by transaction fees. In particular, the operational costs of running full nodes may be offset by financial externalities, such as being able to confirm one's own transactions without trusting third parties, or by network effects, such as selling items whose costs factor in the cost of operating a node. Miners, however, are bereft of these two factors and need to be compensated in the steady state, especially as the block subsidy is reduced over time.

Other Metrics. The above is of course not an exhaustive list of potentially interesting metrics. For example, while we have focused on Bitcoin's role as a transaction medium, it also serves as a store of value. We might therefore consider the *cost per stored dollar* as an alternative to CPCT. Many other metrics are of interest and it is an open research question which can best inform technical and policy decisions.

3   Scaling by Parameter Tuning and Fundamental Limits

The Bitcoin community has several propositions under discussion for increasing the maximum block size (or to remove the limit altogether [42]). Bitcoin Improvement Proposals (BIPs) 100, 101, 102, and 103, all involve a fork, triggered by a combination of time and miner buy-in as reflected in the blockchain [13,23,26,27,50]. These proposals differ primarily on the initial date of the first increase, the block size change strategy (none vs. linear vs repeated doublings vs optional reductions), and the percent of miner buy-in to trigger a change. The segregated witness proposal [23] amends the blocksize by less than a factor of 2 through a "soft fork" implementation, wherein legacy nodes do not need to upgrade, but end up implicitly trusting the miners with transaction validation. The developer community has been further fragmented into various proposals (Core, XT, Classic and Unlimited) that embody different combinations of features and rollout schedules. There is, as of yet, no clear winner, partly because it is difficult to determine, a priori, which change schedule will best fit future changes in node provisioning. It is an open question whether reparametrization alone can adequately address the growth needs of a medium-to-large transaction processing system. In the rest of this section, we explore its limitations.

3.1   Measurement Study

A critical reference point for Bitcoin's performance is Decker and Wattenhofer's 2012 measurement study of the Bitcoin network's block propagation [20]. At the time, the median and 90-percentile time for Bitcoin nodes to receive a block was 6.5 s and 26 s respectively. This study also showed that for small blocks, less than roughly 20 KB in size, latency was a significant factor in block propagation times. Beyond this size, throughput was the dominating factor, and was invariant in block size; thus they found that for large enough blocks *the block propagation times grew linearly with respect to the block size.*

At the time of their measurement, the average block size was 87 KB. This means that back in 2012, it would have taken 5 min for 90 % of the nodes to receive a full 1 MB block — a significant fraction of the block interval.

Since nodes' bandwidth provisioning and the network topology have evolved since 2012, we repeated their measurement recently in 2014 and 2015. Our measurement indicates that the 10 %, median, and 90 % block propagation times are 0.8 s, 8.7 s, and 79 s respectively. Further, the average block size is now roughly 540 KB. Projecting to a 1 MB block size, the 90 %, median, and 10 % block propagation times would be 2.4 min, 15.7 s, and 1.5 s respectively.

X% Effective Throughput. We define the metric "X% effective throughput" as X% effective throughput := (block size)/(X% block propagation delay).

Our measurement study suggests the following X% effective throughputs for the network (with translation to transactions/sec for 250-byte transactions):

X%	X% effective throughput	Translated to transactions/sec	*c.f.* Visa
50 %	496 Kbps	248 tx/sec	2000 tx/sec
90 %	55 Kbps	26 tx/sec	

We additionally performed experiments to determine the minimum block size for throughput to dominate over latency, similarly mirroring the 2012 study by Decker and Wattenhofer [20]. The results are depicted in Fig. 1. That figure shows the overall rate ("network propagation rate") at which blocks propagated to 50 %, 75 %, and 90 % of nodes, capturing the combined effects of latency plus throughput. As block sizes grow from zero, the network propagation rate increases until it levels off at roughly 80 KB, suggesting that when the block size is above 80 KB, throughput dominates over latency. At this point, the propagation rate for 90 % of nodes is about 55 Kbps, which is consistent with the 90 % effective throughput observed in the table above for the current overlay network.

As the data are noisy, we do not provide an estimate of the latency. As it is negligible for blocks of size above 80 KB, we disregard it elsewhere in the paper.

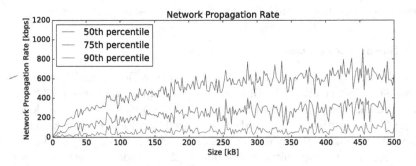

Fig. 1. Network propagation rate (capturing both latency and throughput) vs. block size.

3.2 Limits of Scalability by Reparametrization

We now explore the potential of reparametrization to scale Bitcoin. If the average block size reaches the X%-effective capacity during a block interval, then (100-X)% of the nodes on the network would be unable even to receive blocks as they arrive, and thus would be effectively disabled.

We assume that it is desired to maintain nearly the current degree of decentralization, as measured by the number of properly functioning nodes in the peer-to-peer overlay network. For the purpose of our study, we take 90 % to be our target. It is difficult to quantify what each node contributes towards the overall virtue implied by decentralization. Not all nodes are necessarily miners; and while some nodes can be associated with service providers and individual users, there is no absolute measure of the economic significance of each node. Our definition reflects an equal weighting of each node.

We also stress that our results assume the use of Bitcoin's current peer-to-peer overlay network. If the size or properties of the network change, that would affect the $X\%$ effective throughput. We note, however, that Bitcoin's overlay network has remained stable in size from Nov. 2014 to Nov. 2015 at between $\sim$4500 to $\sim$6300 full nodes [5]. For brevity, we use the term "current overlay network" to refer to these assumed conditions.

Throughput Limit. We observe that the block size and interval must satisfy:

$$\frac{\text{block size}}{X\% \text{ effective throughput}} < \text{block interval}.$$

Consequently, for a 10 min (or shorter) block interval, the block size should not exceed 4 MB for $X = 90\%$; and 38 MB for $X = 50\%$.

Observation 1 (Throughput Limit). *Given the current overlay network and today's 10 min average block interval, the block size should not exceed 4 MB. A 4 MB block size corresponds to a throughput of at most 27 transactions/sec.*

Latency Limit. To improve the system's latency, we can in principle simply reduce the block interval. To do so while retaining high effective throughput, however, would also require a reduction in the block size. Our experiments reflected in Fig. 1

Propagating a block of size smaller than 80 KB would not make full use of the network's bandwidth, as latency would still be a significant factor in the block's propagation time. To propagate a 80 KB block to 90 % of the nodes would take roughly 12 s, given that the 90 % effective throughput of the network today is 55 Kbps. Thus the following guideline.

Observation 2 (Latency Limit). *Given today's overlay network, to retain at least 90 % effective throughput and fully utilize the bandwidth of the network, the block interval should not be significantly smaller than 12 s.*

How to Interpret/Use These Numbers. We stress that the above are *conservative bounds* on the extent to which reparametrization alone can scale Bitcoin's peer-to-peer overlay network given its current size and underlying protocols. Other, more difficult-to-measure metrics could also reveal scaling limitations. One example is *fairness*. Our measurement results (see Sect. 3.1) suggest that in today's Bitcoin overlay network, when nodes are ordered by block propagation time, the top 10 % of nodes receive a 1 MB block 2.4 min earlier than the bottom 10 % — meaning that depending on their access to nodes, some miners could obtain a significant and unfair lead over others in solving hash puzzles. Due to complicating factors, e.g., the fact that many miners today do not rely on a single overlay node to obtain transactions (and indeed often rely on a separate, faster mining backbone to propagate blocks), we believe that this figure cannot directly inform reparametrization discussions. It is illustrative of other metrics, however, that may be important but difficult to measure. Consequently, until the Bitcoin system undergoes fundamental protocol changes, gradual or conservative parameter changes may be prudent. Finally, note that our throughput guidelines apply whether parameters are determined by market outcome or enforced by hard-coded limit.

3.3 Bottleneck Analysis

While scaling the blockchain protocol by parameter tuning is possible, we find that best achievable throughput is significantly smaller than the limit posed by the underlying infrastructure.

In Table 2a, we show results from our measurement study where we perform a per-node bandwidth measurement to more than 4000 Bitcoin nodes. Table 2a suggests that individual nodes are provisioned with significantly higher network bandwidth than the overall network throughput attained by Bitcoin today — recall that the 90 % effective throughput today is 55 Kbps (see Sect. 3.1). The reason why Bitcoin's network stack cannot reach the per-node link bandwidth is likely due to the combination of several factors. For example, each transaction is transmitted twice, first for gossiping the transaction; and then after a block is mined, the newly mined block will be propagated again including all transactions it contains. Moreover, due to lack of pipelining, propagation over multiple overlay hops introduce delay proportional to the length of the path. Finally, Table 2b shows that the cryptographic overheads associated with transaction verification, and disk I/O are unlikely the bottleneck.

Table 2. Per-node resource and bottleneck analysis.

%	Max. BW Mbps	Tx thruput tx/sec
90%	3.03	**758**
50%	33.03	8.3K
10%	186.10	46K

(a) Lower bound on per-node provisioned bandwidth: measuring 4565 Bitcoin nodes.

Resource	Max. thruput [1000 tx/sec]
Tx validation on a modern quad-core processor (2 signatures per Tx)	4
Disk I/O Rotational 100MB/sec	200
SSD 300MB/sec	600

(b) Maximum throughput analysis.

4   Rethinking the Design of a Scalable Blockchain

We discuss techniques that will allow blockchains to scale beyond the parameters of today's Bitcoin. They range from incremental changes atop today's decentralized blockchain to more radical redesigns. The goal of this section is not to propose an end-to-end system, but rather to paint the design space, suggest promising approaches, and pose open challenges to the community.

We organize our discussion around a decomposition of the Bitcoin system into a set of abstraction layers that we call *planes*. Ordered in a hierarchy of dependency from bottom to top, the five planes we consider are the Network, Consensus, Storage, View, and Side Planes.

In our exposition here, the *ledger* is the full history of the system, the complete output of the *Consensus Plane*, as we define it below. A more precise definition is possible that also specifies a particular confirmation policy, as ledger contents may be subject to change, as in decentralized cryptocurrencies. For simplicity, we do not model this feature of decentralized cryptocurrencies and instead treat writes to the ledger as confirmed.

4.1 Network Plane

The function of the Network Plane is to propagate transaction messages. It supports a broadcast abstraction in which a transaction message from any player is transmitted to all (full) nodes in the Bitcoin network. The Network Plane in Bitcoin is not a pure broadcast medium, however. Nodes only propagate messages that represent valid transactions and thus the abstraction only accepts valid transactions as inputs.

Our measurements have shown that Bitcoin's network protocol and implementation do not fully utilize underlying network bandwidth, making Bitcoin's Network Plane the bottleneck in transaction processing. A natural direction to improve scaling in Bitcoin is thus to improve the design of its Network Plane.

Two inefficiencies in Bitcoin's Network Plane stand out. First, to avoid denial-of-service by propagation of invalid transactions, a node must fully receive and validate a transaction before further propagating it. (To be deemed valid, a transaction must ingest and produce legitimate transaction outputs and not conflict with previous transactions.) This local validation of transactions contributes significantly to the overall propagation time. Second, Bitcoin's network-layer protocol first propagates all transactions, and then propagates a block (containing previously propagated transactions) again when it is mined. This effectively requires each transaction to be transmitted twice.

There have been several proposals to improve Bitcoin's network-layer protocol. One possibility, to avoid transferring each transaction twice, is to rely on a set reconciliation protocol in which nodes only fetch transactions that they do not possess in a newly mined block [6,31,38,47]. Another option, in use by miners today, is to use a dedicated, centralized, high-speed relay network for inter-miner communication [19].

A different direction is to improve the network layer's function as a broadcast channel. The Network Plane could be designed as a robust P2P overlay topology, with strong connectivity between honest nodes and a low diameter. Such overlay topologies are usually expander graphs, which have known low-latency broadcast protocols [28,32]. To limit influence of adversarial nodes, the overlay could randomize the location of all peers (outside of their control). Several previous distributed systems have adopted this approach [14,43]. To further limit denial-of-service, nodes could rate-limit transmissions from their peers. Designing such an overlay which maintains a strong connectivity between honest nodes (in the presence of byzantine adversaries) is well-known for static networks [22,35], but for highly dynamic networks is an active area of research [30].

A longstanding issue involving the Network Plane is the incentivization of the participants. Researchers have noted that Network Plane lacks an incentive structure for the dissemination of transactions, and have proposed a modified fee splitting structure to provide robust incentives. Many other aspects of the network protocol rely on voluntary participation and require ad hoc defenses to stem flooding and denial of service attacks.

4.2   Consensus Plane

The function of the Consensus Plane is to designate a globally accepted set of transactions for processing, as well as a total or partial order on these transactions. As a general abstraction, this plane ingests messages from the Network Plane and outputs transactions for insertion into the system ledger. In Bitcoin, the Consensus Plane is the functionality that mines blocks and reaches consensus on their integration into the blockchain.

Improving Proof-of-Work Protocols. Bitcoin's blockchain protocol introduces a tradeoff among consensus speed, bandwidth, and security. By improving the former two, one introduces an increased number of forks, leading to a loss of the mining power that secures the system and to reduced fairness [25]. Many cryptocurrencies (e.g. [9]) favor consensus speed over security, employing a standard Bitcoin blockchain with a high block-generation frequency.

This three-way tradeoff, however, is not inherent in decentralized cryptocurrencies. The GHOST protocol [45] of Sompolinsky et al. as well as Lewenberg et al. [36] demonstrate that fairness and mining power utilization can be improved by changing the chain selection rule, in particular, by being inclusive to forks outside the main chain as well. In more recent work, Bitcoin-NG [25] demonstrates that the inherent tradeoffs in Bitcoin can be eliminated with an alternative blockchain protocol, offering a consensus delay and bandwidth limited only by the Network Plane.

Proof of Stake. Various proposals (e.g. [11,33]) use *proof of stake* to achieve consensus, eliminating the computational expense of proofs of work. In proof of stake, principals gain the right to create blocks by depositing funds they own. These techniques, however, lack formal guarantees of system convergence [18].

Consortium Consensus. Decentralization carries a performance cost. A trust model with stronger assumptions than those in Bitcoin can support a more efficient consensus protocol, achieving better latency and throughput with less computation, bandwidth, and storage. Specifically, using a standard Byzantine Fault Tolerant (BFT) replication protocol with a small number of pre-designated trusted entities removes many of the scaling obstacles in Bitcoin.

Settings involving BFT protocols executed by small sets of trusted entities have received little treatment in the academic literature, but are of considerable interest in practice, and mainstream financial institutions are actively exploring their use [44]. They are sometimes referred to as "consortium blockchains."

Consortium blockchains are worth investigation both as an alternative to decentralized cryptocurrencies and to characterize the performance cost that decentralized blockchains incur by distributing trust. In Appendix A, we present performance figures and microbenchmarking results on experiments with a popular BFT protocol (PBFT) across a range of different system parametrizations and with nodes dispersed across eight geographies worldwide. Our results illustrate the attractiveness of BFT as a basis for the consensus layer in a cryptocurrency (given acceptance of its strong trust assumptions). Even with dozens of nodes, PBFT greatly outperforms Bitcoin in both transaction latency and throughput. For example, 64 nodes processing batches of 8192 transactions can achieve a throughput of **4.5 K tx/sec**, average transaction latency of **1.79 s**, and an estimated resource cost per transaction of just **$3.95 $\times$ 10^{-7}**.[2] Scaling to hundreds of nodes, however, would greatly degrade the performance of the system. As we now explain, a promising approach to scaling and an open research direction is how to *shard* a BFT protocol.

Sharding. One possible technique for improving the scalability of the Consensus Plane is to shard it, that is, split up the task of consensus among concurrently operating sets of nodes, with the aim of improving throughput and reducing per-node processing and storage requirements. Sharding is commonly employed in distributed databases, such as Dynamo, MongoDB, MySQL, and BigTable, although performance typically does not grow linearly with shard count. This is due to the need to reach consensus among the shards when operations span multiple shards. One possibility, explored in a non-Byzantine environment in past work [24,29,51], is to use a separate consensus protocol, such as Paxos, to achieve agreement among the shards. Such schemes, however, can incur substantial overhead when cross-shard coordination is required in a Byzantine setting, so sharding protocols for blockchains are an open area of research.

Delegation of Trust and a Hierarchy of Sidechains. Another technique for scaling is to create a hierarchy of lower-tier "consensus instances," commonly referred to as "sidechains." Sidechains can potentially have a lower degree of decentralization than the top-level blockchain. Sidechains may also run non-proof-of-work consensus protocols, such as BFT. One sidechain structure, proposed by Back et al. [15], permits transactions to move funds among independent chains.

---

[2] Transactions in our experiments are 190 bytes long, all that is needed for a basic money transfer; given the roughly 500 byte average size of Bitcoin transactions, the system would achieve 1.7 k tx/sec.

The introduction of sidechains raises three technical challenges. First, the sidechains must be secured independently of the main blockchain. Merged mining techniques [15] allow separate chains to share their mining power, but require miner coordination. Without such coordination, the maintenance of sidechains dilutes the mining power in the system, rendering the individual chains vulnerable. Second, if sidechains are widely adopted, the chances that a given source of funds and a desired destination are on the same sidechain are small, requiring inter-chain transactions. Inter-chain transactions will have to go through the main blockchain, possibly requiring two separate transactions, and therefore may place more of a burden on the main blockchain and thus have an adverse impact on scalability. Finally, transactions involving more than one decentralized chain may incur high latency. Decentralized blockchains require the accumulation of a number of blocks to ensure that a transaction will remain in the blockchain with high probability. Transactions among chains will require a sequence of such block accumulations, one per chain.

4.3   Storage Plane

The Storage Plane functions as a global memory that stores and provides availability for authenticated data produced by the Consensus Plane. It may be regarded as an abstraction with two interfaces: (1) It ingests and processes memory-modification instructions—write and (potentially) delete operations—from the Consensus Plane and (2) It services read requests from any entity in the system. The storage plane contains the ledger of the system but may also contain other state produced by consensus, such as smart contract state or "views" supported by the View Plane.

There are several ways to implement the Storage Plane in a cryptocurrency. In Bitcoin, the Storage Plane may be regarded as storing the Bitcoin ledger. The Bitcoin reference implementation today by default stores the entire ledger; as a result, the system stores many duplicates of the entire ledger. The Storage Plane in Bitcoin accepts only writes that append data, namely newly mined blocks, and does not support delete operations. The only generally supported read operation for the Bitcoin Storage Plane downloads the contents of the entire ledger, a process that requires four days (see Sect. 2). (Given the current height of the blockchain, a downloaded ledger may be authenticated by reference to the genesis block.) Thus, Bitcoin's Storage Plane has notable inefficiencies.

Other implementations of and interfaces for the Storage Plane are possible. The community has proposed interesting ideas that can essentially shard the storage of a UTXO data structure [37] (see below). It is not clear how these ideas would generalize to other forms of state that might go into the Storage Plane, e.g., the state associated with smart contracts. How to shard a general-purpose Storage Plane such that not all consensus nodes have to store it in its entirety and such that its contents can be authenticated during read operations is an open research challenge. Distributed Hash Tables (DHT) are a possible start, coupled with suitable data authentication techniques.

4.4 View Plane

For Bitcoin miners, it is unnecessary to operate on the full ledger that stores the entire transaction history. Thus miners and nodes in Bitcoin locally compute and operate on a view of the ledger called the *unspent transaction outputs* (UTXO) set, which in effect specifies the current balance of all entities in the system. Similarly, in Ethereum smart contracts can define state that resides in the ledger. Parties to a smart contract may wish to access and authenticate this state without reading other parts of the ledger. For this reason, a key performance requirement in cryptocurrencies (both decentralized and probably centralized) is support for *views*.[3]

A view is a data structure derived from the full ledger whose state is obtained by applying all transactions. For performance reasons, a view may be stored in the Storage Plane and distributed in an authenticated fashion — Bitcoin did not implement this optimization, and therefore new miners would now need four days to reconstruct the UTXO set (which can be considered as a view) from the beginning of time. In general, the view can be an arbitrary function of the full ledger, not necessarily the UTXO set. As a piece of data in the Storage Plane, a view must be determined either implicitly or explicitly by the Consensus Plane and must be authenticable by any entity executing a Read operation against it. There are a number of options for implementing a view, including the following.

Views via Replication. Bitcoin [39], Ethereum [49], and other popular decentralized cryptocurrencies require all consensus nodes to verify all transactions (and/or smart contracts), and based on the result of the computation, update their respective views, e.g., UTXO sets, locally. In this case, the view is an implicit output of the Consensus Plane and may be regarded as residing in the Storage output: provided that it is correctly computed, it represents the computation that an honest set of consensus nodes would produce, and of course it has high availability.

Outsourcing Views via Cryptography. It is possible to outsource the computation of a view to a third-party service provider. This provider may release a cryptographic digest (e.g., Merkle-tree root) of this view along with a proof of its correctness. By relying on verifiable computation techniques such as succinct non-interactive arguments of knowledge (SNARKs) [17,40], the provider can produce a proof of correctness for the digest, supporting authentication of the view. The view may then be inserted into the Storage Plane. If availability is not essential, the view can alternatively be stored within some other part of the system, e.g., by the provider itself, rather than in the Storage Plane.

One advantage of this approach is that consensus nodes now need not store the entire ledger. They can instead operate over suitably chosen views. A key question that must be answered, however, is whether cryptographic techniques such as SNARKs are practically viable. In the Appendix, we present

---

[3] We adapt the term "view" from its meaning in database theory, where it refers to the result set of a stored query.

experimental results showing that the amortized cost of employing SNARKs can be as low as **$0.0154** per transaction for computing a simple view that essentially stores all users' balances.

4.5   Side Plane

Much as sidechains allow off-the-main-chain consensus, we can consider off-chain functionalities. Off-chain transactions have been demonstrated in payment networks [12,21,41], in which payments are routed along paths of pre-established "collateral" channels. Each such channel represents a quantity of bitcoin reserves set aside, such that parties can repeatedly adjust their relative stake by exchanging out-of-band messages until the channel is finalized (and the reserves paid out). While payment networks have been heralded as a solution to Bitcoin's inherent limitations, much of their operation, and the guarantees they can offer, rely critically on the nature of the links formed between parties. Even when payment networks use the same underlying transaction format as Bitcoin, as do the Lightning Network [41] and full duplex channels [21], they essentially form a separate Network Plane as well as an independent, peer-to-peer Consensus Plane, backed by Bitcoin. As a result, their capacity, ability to find routes, achieved throughput, latency, and privacy guarantees depend fundamentally on emergent properties of the payment network graph, such as the value capacity of peer-to-peer channels, the discoverability of routes, the online status of nodes involved, and so on. Further, payment channels may embody a similar tradeoff between performance and centralization in the payment network; a centralized hub-and-spoke topology that simplifies routing embodies inherent problems with centralization, such as loss of privacy. The design of protocols for efficient, scalable, privacy-preserving payment networks is an ongoing area of research: it is far from a given that they can outperform Bitcoin's Network and Consensus layers overall.

5   Conclusion

This paper explored the challenges in scaling Bitcoin and blockchains in general. Supported by measurement studies, we showed that reparametrization of the block size and interval in Bitcoin is only a first step toward substantial throughput and latency improvements while retaining significant system decentralization. More aggressive scaling will in the longer term require fundamental protocol redesign. Through a structured presentation of the design landscape for blockchain protocols, we illustrated the variety of potentially successful approaches to such scaling, categorized a range of recently proposed and new ideas, and framed a number of important open technical challenges for the community.

Acknowledgements. This work is supported in part by NSF grants CNS-1314857, CNS-1453634, CNS-1518765, CNS-1514261, CNS-1518899, a Packard Fellowship, a Sloan Fellowship, two Google Faculty Research Awards, and a VMWare Research Award.

Appendix

A BFT Experiments (Consortium Consensus)

Table 3. Consortium blockchain scalability. Results of running PBFT over geographically distributed EC2 nodes for some representative (n, k) parameterizations. As for any BFT protocol, the throughput drops as the number n of nodes increases. Conversely, in this small experiment, enlarging the batch size k may be seen to increase throughput at the cost of a small increase in latency.

# of Nodes (n)	Batch size (k)	Latency	Throughput	Price per tx	500 byte tx
4 nodes (1 region)	32768	288 ms	113 K tx/sec	\$9.83 $\times 10^{-10}$	42.9 K tx/sec
8 nodes	8192	0.58 s	14.0 K tx/sec	\$1.59 $\times 10^{-8}$	5.3 K tx/sec
8 nodes	32768	1.48 s	22.2 K tx/sec	\$1.00 $\times 10^{-8}$	8.4 K tx/sec
16 nodes	8192	0.69 s	11.9 K tx/sec	\$3.73 $\times 10^{-8}$	4.5 K tx/sec
16 nodes	16384	1.04 s	15.8 K tx/sec	\$2.81 $\times 10^{-8}$	6.0 K tx/sec
32 nodes	2048	0.48 s	4.3 K tx/sec	\$2.07 $\times 10^{-7}$	1.6 K tx/sec
32 nodes	8192	0.925 s	8.8 K tx/sec	\$1.01 $\times 10^{-7}$	3.3 K tx/sec
64 nodes	2048	0.824 s	2.4 K tx/sec	\$7.40 $\times 10^{-7}$	0.9 K tx/sec
64 nodes	8192	1.79 s	4.5 K tx/sec	\$3.95 $\times 10^{-7}$	1.7 K tx/sec

Here we report on our experiments on BFT performance. Table 3 illustrates the attractiveness of BFT as a basis for the consensus layer in a cryptocurrency (given acceptance of its strong trust assumptions). Even with dozens of nodes, PBFT greatly outperforms Bitcoin in both transaction latency and throughput. Scaling to hundreds of nodes, however, would greatly degrade the performance of the system.

Experiments were conducted using t2.medium Amazon EC2 instances. The results are displayed in Table 3. The 4 node experiment represents a best-case setting; all nodes were located in the US East N. Virginia region. In all other experiments the nodes, plus a client furnishing transaction inputs but not participating in the consensus protocol, were evenly distributed across 8 geographical regions: Northern Virginia, Oregon, Northern California, Ireland, Frankfurt, Tokyo, Sydney, Sao Paulo. As instance costs vary by region, we conservatively assume each node incurs the highest observed fee of \$0.10 per hour. We experimented with several batch sizes in order to locate the point at which each configuration becomes bandwidth bound. Here, a transaction message is 190 bytes in length and is modeled after a Bitcoin transaction, including a pay-to-public-key-hash scheme and a digital signature.

We observed that configurations with a larger number of nodes became bandwidth bound at smaller batch sizes. This is due to the primary node broadcasting each batch to every other node participating in the protocol. Increasing the batch size beyond this bound for a given configuration increases latency while leaving throughput relatively unchanged. For smaller batch sizes the bottleneck was local processing, primarily signature verification for the batch as a whole. Once an ordering of batches has been agreed upon and committed, individual transactions may be processed and verified independently from the consensus protocol. However, we expect to see a much larger slowdown when scaling to hundreds of nodes, as the number of messages in standard BFT protocols grows quadratically in the number of nodes.

B   Use of SNARKs for Outsourcing View Computation

We now explain how SNARKs may be used to support computation of views by a service provider, rather than individually by every node in the network (as happens today). In our experiment, we assume that a simple view is adopted containing all users' account balances.

To support the secure outsourcing of view derivation, the provider (or prover, as we might call it) must store the balance for each Bitcoin address used in the transactions so far. As in Bitcoin, we assume 2^{160} possible public addresses. The prover will maintain a Merkle tree of height 160, where each leaf stores the balance of the public address identified by the path to the leaf. (Unused zero-balance leaves do not have to be stored explicitly.) Computing the initial digest of the tree when all balances are zero can be done by utilizing the similarity across levels. Later, when a transaction is received, the system checks the balance of the sender address, and if it is sufficient, transfers the desired amount to the receiver's balance. (In case of a mining reward, the initial check is not necessary.) The prover then updates the ledger digests accordingly.

Using SNARKs, the service provider will be able to prove the correct application of a set of transactions, and the correct update of digests. We evaluated a SNARK circuit that checks and applies 25 1-sender 1-receiver transactions to the ledger. Each transaction in that case specifies the desired amount of money to be transferred. This is equivalent to 1-input 2-output transactions in Bitcoin, where one of the outputs is a remainder going back to the sender's address, but the remainder does not have to be specified explicitly in our setting. The prover then outputs the modified digest with a vector representing which transactions were valid, and possibly the modified balances. To make the circuit efficient, we used a SNARK-friendly collision resistant function based on subset sum [16], at 80-bit of security as in [34]. To experiment at higher transaction rate, multiple circuits can be run in a nearly-parallel mode, by computing and feeding the next digest quickly from one circuit to the next one without waiting for the proof to complete.

Table 4 shows the estimated cost incurred by the prover (provider) and the verifiers (relying miners or consensus nodes) to produce the proof at multiple settings. We ran the experiment for the first case using an Amazon EC2 r3.8xlarge instance [7] (using 32-cores for the proof computation, and single core for verification) and using libsnark [17] as a backend, and estimated the overall performance and cost accordingly assuming throughputs of 7 tx/sec, and 10 tx/sec. The table shows that the computation cost for applying one transaction to the ledger is

Table 4. Verifiable outsourcing of ledger storage and maintenance using SNARKs

Rate tx/block	Total proof time (prover)	Verification time (verifiers)	Proof Size	# of EC2s	Total cost (prover)	Cost per tx (prover)
25	496 s	0.01 s	288 bytes	1	$0.385	$0.0154
4200 (7tx/sec)	588 s	1.68 s	48 kbytes	168	$64.68	
6000 (10tx/sec)	628 s	2.4 s	68 kbytes	240	$92.40	

about $0.0154, but at high throughput, the waiting time for proof computation is about or more than 10 min (implying a higher delay if higher security level is used).

By adopting SNARKs, miners no longer need to store the full ledger nor the necessary views to validate transactions. In this way, decentralized storage and replication of the ledger and views can be decomposed from the consensus protocol and the view computation. Additionally, in our current experiments, we assume that the consensus nodes are validating the signatures on the transactions, and this signature validation is not performed within SNARKs (otherwise the cost of SNARKs would be more expensive).

References

1. https://en.bitcoin.it/wiki/Scalability
2. https://en.bitcoin.it/wiki/Mining_hardware_comparison
3. https://blockchain.info/charts/hash-rate
4. https://blockchain.info/charts/n-transactions-per-block
5. https://bitnodes.21.co/dashboard/?days=365
6. https://gist.github.com/gavinandresen/e20c3b5a1d4b97f79ac2
7. Amazon EC2 pricing. http://aws.amazon.com/ec2/pricing/. Accessed 30 Oct 2015
8. Antminer S5+ hardware. https://bitmaintech.com/productDetail.htm?pid=0002015081407532655504JMKzsM067B. Accessed 30 Oct 2015
9. Litecoin, open source P2P digital currency. https://litecoin.org
10. How a Visa transaction works (2015). http://web.archive.org/web/20160121231718/http://apps.usa.visa.com/merchants/become-a-merchant/how-a-visa-transaction-works.jsp
11. NXT.org, Decentralized Financial Ecosystem (2015). http://nxt.org/
12. Shelat, A., Pass, R.: Micropayments for peer-to-peer currencies. In: CCS (2015)
13. Andresen, G.: Increase maximum block size (BIP 101). https://github.com/bitcoin/bips/blob/master/bip-0101.mediawiki. Accessed Oct 2015
14. Awerbuch, B., Scheideler, C.: Towards a scalable and robust DHT. In: SPAA (2006)
15. Back, A., Corallo, M., Dashjr, L., Friedenbach, M., Maxwell, G., Miller, A., Poelstra, A., Timón, J., Wuille, P.: Enabling blockchain innovations with pegged sidechains. https://www.blockstream.com/sidechains.pdf. Accessed 26 Nov 2015
16. Ben-Sasson, E., Chiesa, A., Tromer, E., Virza, M.: Scalable zero knowledge via cycles of elliptic curves. In: Garay, J.A., Gennaro, R. (eds.) CRYPTO 2014, Part II. LNCS, vol. 8617, pp. 276–294. Springer, Heidelberg (2014)

17. Ben-Sasson, E., Chiesa, A., Tromer, E. Virza, M.: Succinct non-interactive zero knowledge for a von neumann architecture. In: Security (2014)

18. Bentov, I., Lee, C., Mizrahi, A., Rosenfeld, M.: Proof of activity: extending bitcoin's proof of work via proof of stake. https://eprint.iacr.org/2014/452/

19. Corallo, M.: High-speed Bitcoin relay network, December 2015. https://github.com/TheBlueMatt/RelayNode

20. Decker, C., Wattenhofer, R.: Information propagation in the Bitcoin network. In: IEEE P2P, pp. 1–10. IEEE (2013)

21. Decker, C., Wattenhofer, R.: A fast and scalable payment network with bitcoin duplex micropayment channels. In: Pelc, A., Schwarzmann, A.A. (eds.) SSS 2015. LNCS, vol. 9212, pp. 3–18. Springer, Heidelberg (2015)

22. Dolev, S., Tzachar, N.: Spanders: distributed spanning expanders. Sci. Comput. Prog

23. Eric Lombrozo, P.W., Lau, J.: Segregated witness (consensus layer). https://github.com/CodeShark/bips/blob/segwit/bip-codeshark-jl2012-segwit.mediawiki

24. Escriva, R., Wong, B., Sirer, E.G.: Warp: Lightweight Multi-Key Transactions for Key-Value Stores. http://arxiv.org/abs/1509.07815

25. Eyal, I., Gencer, A.E., Sirer, E.G., van Renesse, R.: Bitcoin-NG: a scalable blockchain protocol. Technical report, CoRR (2015)

26. Garzik, J.: Block size increase to 2MB (BIP 102). https://github.com/bitcoin/bips/blob/master/bip-0102.mediawiki. Accessed Oct 2015

27. Garzik, J.: Making decentralized economic policy. http://gtf.org/garzik/bitcoin/BIP100-blocksizechangeproposal.pdf. Accessed Oct 2015

28. Georgiou, C., Gilbert, S., Guerraoui, R., Kowalski, D.R.: Asynchronous gossip. J. ACM 60(2) (2013)

29. Glendenning, L., Beschastnikh, I., Krishnamurthy, A., Anderson, T.: Scalable consistency in Scatter. In: SOSP (2011)

30. Guerraoui, R., Huc, F., Kermarrec, A.-M.: Highly dynamic distributed computing with byzantine failures. In: PODC (2013)

31. Johansen, H.D., Renesse, R.V., Vigfusson, Y., Johansen, D.: Fireflies: a secure and scalable membership and gossip service. ACM Trans. Comput. Syst. (2015)

32. Karp, R., Schindelhauer, C., Shenker, S., Vocking, B.: Randomized rumor spreading. In: FOCS (2000)

33. King, S., Nadal, S.: PPCoin: Peer-to-Peer Crypto-Currency with Proof-of-Stake, August 2012

34. Kosba, A., Zhao, Z., Miller, A., Qian, Y., Chan, H., Papamanthou, C., Pass, R., Shelat, A., Shi, E.: How to use snarks in universally composable protocols. Cryptology ePrint Archive, Report 2015/1093 (2015). http://eprint.iacr.org/

35. Law, C., Siu, K.-Y.: Distributed construction of random expander networks. In: IEEE INFOCOM, pp. 2133–2143 (2003)

36. Lewenberg, Y., Sompolinsky, Y., Zohar, A.: Inclusive block chain protocols. In: FC (2015)

37. Maxwell, G.: https://bitcointalk.org/index.php?topic=314467#msg3371194

38. Minsky, Y., Trachtenberg, A., Zippel, R.: Set reconciliation with nearly optimal communication complexity. IEEE Trans. Inf. Theory (2003)

39. Nakamoto, S.: Bitcoin: A Peer-to-Peer Electronic Cash System (2009). http://bitcoin.org/bitcoin.pdf

40. Parno, B., Howell, J., Gentry, C., Raykova, M.: Pinocchio: nearly practical verifiable computation. In: S&P (2013)

41. Poon, J., Dryja, T.: The bitcoin lightning network. https://lightning.network/lightning-network-paper.pdf. Accessed 26 Nov 2015

42. Rizun, P.: A transaction fee market exists without a block size limit (2015)
43. Sen, S., Freedman, M.J.: Commensal cuckoo: secure group partitioning for large-scale services. SIGOPS Oper. Syst. Rev. (2012)
44. Shin, L.: Bitcoin blockchain technology in financial services: how the disruption will play out. Forbes, 14 September 2015
45. Sompolinsky, Y., Zohar, A.: Secure high-rate transaction processing in bitcoin. In: FC (2015)
46. TradeBlock. Bitcoin network capacity analysis. https://tradeblock.com/blog/bitcoin-network-capacity-analysis-part-1-macro-block-trends
47. van Renesse, R., Dumitriu, D., Gough, V., Thomas, C.: Efficient reconciliation and flow control for anti-entropy protocols. In: LADIS (2008)
48. Wilson, L.: Average electricity prices around the world. http://shrinkthatfootprint.com/average-electricity-prices-kwh
49. Wood, G.: Ethereum: a secure decentralized transaction ledger (2014). http://gavwood.com/paper.pdf
50. Wuille, P.: Block size following technological growth (BIP 103). https://github.com/bitcoin/bips/blob/master/bip-0103.mediawiki. Accessed Nov 2015
51. Xie, C., Su, C., Littley, C., Alvisi, L., Kapritsos, M., Wang, Y.: High-performance ACID via modular concurrency control. In: SOSP (2015)

Bitcoin Covenants

Malte Möser[1]([✉]), Ittay Eyal[2], and Emin Gün Sirer[2]

[1] Department of Information Systems, University of Münster, Münster, Germany
malte.moeser@uni-muenster.de
[2] Initiative for Cryptocurrencies and Contracts (IC3),
Computer Science Department, Cornell University, Ithaca, USA

Abstract. This paper presents an extension to Bitcoin's script language enabling *covenants*, a primitive that allows transactions to restrict how the value they transfer is used in the future. Covenants expand the set of financial instruments expressible in Bitcoin, and enable new powerful and novel use cases. We illustrate two novel security constructs built using covenants.

The first, *vaults*, focuses on improving the security of private cryptographic keys. Historically, maintaining these keys securely and reliably has been a critical vulnerability for Bitcoin users. We show how covenants enable vaults, which disincentivize key theft by preventing an attacker from gaining full access to stolen funds.

The second construct, *poison transactions*, is a generally useful mechanism for penalizing double-spending attacks. Bitcoin-NG, a protocol that has been recently proposed to improve Bitcoin's throughput, latency and overall scalability, requires this feature. We show how covenants enable poison transactions, and detail how Bitcoin-NG can be implemented progressively as an overlay on top of the Bitcoin blockchain.

1 Introduction

Bitcoin is an innovative payment system built to enable a wide variety of financial contracts that are executed in a decentralized manner. Part of its power and expressiveness derives from the way transactions use a flexible script language to specify redemption criteria. The system ensures that subsequent transactions must fulfill the redemption criteria in order to unlock the embedded value. While traditional financial contracts rely on trust and after-the-fact enforcement, Bitcoin's scripting mechanism allows to enforce contracts within the currency system itself.

Yet, the functionality provided by the scripting language is characterized by an inherent trade-off between security, efficiency, and expressiveness. Currently, the expressiveness of the script language is limited, not only by the constricted operations of the language, but also by the information that can be accessed in or checked by a script program.

© International Financial Cryptography Association 2016
J. Clark et al. (Eds.): FC 2016 Workshops, LNCS 9604, pp. 126–141, 2016.
DOI: 10.1007/978-3-662-53357-4_9

To extend the capabilities of the system, we propose an extension to Bitcoin's script language that enables *covenants*[1]: transactions that are able to enforce restrictions on the composition of subsequent transactions (cf. Sect. 3). Covenants enable multiple novel and powerful use cases. We first illustrate the power of covenants by describing how colored coins, a well-established but ill-supported idea to attach meaning beyond nominal value to bitcoins, would benefit from the ability to prevent such coins from accidentally mixing into general circulation. We then focus on two new use cases.

First, we use covenants to implement secure vaults, which addresses one of the biggest problems of cryptocurrency security: the difficulty of secure key management. Vaults improve end-user security by disincentivizing theft of coins using a mechanism that prevents an attacker from gaining full control over funds despite stealing the private keys used to secure them (cf. Sect. 4).

Then, we describe how covenant functionality enables new overlays to be placed on top of the Bitcoin blockchain. Making changes to the consensus protocol of a cryptocurrency is a difficult process as it requires agreement by participants and stakeholders. Bitcoin-NG [16] is an alternative blockchain protocol that promises significant improvement in transaction throughput and confirmation delay. However, changing Bitcoin's blockchain protocol would require a change to Bitcoin's consensus protocol, a daunting task.

We use covenants to implement *poison transactions*, which invalidate a deposit using fraud proof. With poison transactions, we detail the implementation of Bitcoin-NG as an overlay on top of Bitcoin. This implementation can be progressively adopted, not requiring a change of the consensus rules (cf. Sect. 5) beyond the general functionality of covenants.

In summary, this paper makes the following contributions:

1. Covenants, a new script operation that enables novel security constructs,
2. Vaults, a construct that reduces private key theft incentives by prohibiting an attacker from gaining control of funds, and
3. An implementation of *Bitcoin-NG* as an overlay using covenant-enabled poison transactions.

We review related work in Sect. 6 and conclude in Sect. 7.

2 Preliminaries

Bitcoin is a distributed, decentralized cryptocurrency [23] that uses a probabilistic consensus protocol to serialize transactions of the currency among its users. We describe the elements of Bitcoin's design relevant to this work, a detailed description of the system can be found in [4, 26].

The novel data structure used in Bitcoin, and many other derived altcoins [14, 21], is the *blockchain*, an append-only log used to track and store currency

---

[1] A covenant is a special contract in property law that restricts the use of an object, typically restricting the use of land for certain purposes. We adopt the term from earlier discussions on related ideas [22], which are discussed in Sect. 6.

transactions. To serialize new transactions, *miners* aggregate transactions in a block and append the block to the ledger by solving a proof of work crypto puzzle. This process is financially rewarded by allowing the successful miner to mint new coins in a special *coinbase* transaction.

Rather than having a notion of accounts and transactions among accounts, as in earlier cryptocurrency systems [9,27], Bitcoin tracks the individual coins, or, more accurately, fractions of coins. Each transaction in Bitcoin describes the movement of coins from one logical location to another. Cryptographic tools allow only designated principals to move coins out of a location.

Transaction Structure. The logical locations are called *transaction outputs*. Each transaction contains an array of such outputs and specifies the amount of currency it places in each. A location is uniquely defined by the unique *transaction identifier* and the index of the output. The coins placed are moved, or *spent*, from their previous locations, namely transaction outputs of previous transactions. The sources are listed in the transaction in an array of *transaction inputs*. We note that there is no notion of individual coin tracking — there is no meaningful way to connect specific inputs to specific outputs.

The sum of values in the outputs referenced by a transaction's input array is the total input value of the transaction. The total output value, given by the sum of values in the transaction's output array, cannot be larger than the total input value. Any value not accounted for is transacted to an output specified by the miner who generated the block in the block's coinbase transaction.

Each transaction furthermore has a locktime field that determines the minimal time (block number or unix time) after which it can be placed.

Script. To make sure that funds can only be spent by designated principals, spending an output requires satisfying a predicate. Such a predicate is included in each output as a program written in a stack-based language called *Script* [23]. Inputs redeeming an output have to provide data to the output's program. A transaction is valid if its inputs yield true for all corresponding outputs.

In the common case, transactions are secured with public-key cryptography. The logical location of a coin is defined by the public key supplied in the output's script program. The owner, and only this owner, can move the coins by proving her control of the matching private key in the input.

Typical output script programs require the ownership of one or more private keys for successful validation by including public keys or hashes thereof. To validate signatures corresponding to the keys listed, the script language contains a CheckSig operation that accepts a signature and a public key, and then verifies the validity of the signature computed over the spending transaction. A detailed step-by-step execution of a script program can be found in [26].

The Bitcoin script language is intentionally restricted to a small set of opcodes, prioritizing security and efficiency over expressiveness and feature-completeness. A key limitation is that the scope of Bitcoin's script operations is restricted to the data provided in the output program and the data provided in the input script. This rule will, however, soon have an exception in the form of two new opcodes (which we will use) called CheckLockTimeVerify (CLTV) [25] and CheckSequenceVerify (CSV) [6]. These allow to make an output unspendable until a certain point in time is reached. This extends the awareness of the script to the current position of the transaction in the blockchain.

Algorithm 1. Specification of CheckOutputVerify

1 **On** CheckOutputVerify(*index, value, pattern*)
2   **if not exists** output at output *index* **then**
3   return False
4   **if** *value* $\neq 0$ **then**   (Check value)
5   **if** (value at output *index*) $\neq$ *value* **then**
6   return False
7   **if** *pattern* $\neq 0$ **then**   (Check pattern)
8   *sanitizedPattern* $\leftarrow$ *pattern*, replacing pattern-placeholders with *pattern*, then replacing key placeholders with 0's
9   *map* $\leftarrow$ 1's of length *sanitizedPattern*, but 0's at key placeholders
10   **if** (script at output *index* **bitwise-and** *map*) $\neq$ *sanitizedPattern* **then**
11   return False
12   return True

---

3   Covenants

Our main contribution is an extension of Bitcoin's script language to enable covenants: restrictions on future use of coins. Covenants enable a transaction output to restrict the outputs in its spending transaction. Using a form of reflection, a covenant can be specified recursively. This enables the enforcement of covenants across a potentially unlimited number of subsequent transactions.

In this section, we describe the operation of single-use covenants (Sect. 3.1) and show how to extend them into the future by applying them recursively (Sect. 3.2). As a running example, we use distinguished coins (Sect. 3.3). Inspired by colored coins [11], distinguished coins are tokens that correspond to real-world assets that should not be mixed or merged with others.

3.1   Basic Covenants

Each transaction output consists of an amount and an output script program. We enable covenants by adding a new operation to the scripting language that restricts both of these fields. Specifically, the operation takes an output index, an amount and a pattern. It verifies that the output at the given index exists, that it carries the required amount and that its script matches a given pattern. Algorithm 1 shows the formal specification.

We implement this operation as a patch of Bitcoin Core, the standard Bitcoin client, as an opcode, CheckOutputVerify. The opcode expects the index as the first parameter, allowing to place it in the input of the spending transaction. The creator of the spending transaction can therefore determine the output's position.

The script pattern is simply a script program with placeholders for variable parts. We make use of two placeholder opcodes that are already used internally by the client, namely PubKey and PubKeyHash, to represent arbitrary public keys or hashes of public keys within the pattern.

Both placeholders represent fields of static size. The script interpreter replaces each placeholder with the appropriate number of zero-bits. Separately, it creates a bitmask with the program's size that masks out these placeholder locations. A bitwise comparison of both programs sanitized with the bitmask then yields the verification results.

There may exist scenarios in which it is only necessary to check the value or the script program, but not both. In this case, either of those values can be set to 0. This prevents one from requiring that an output script is actually equal to False, which prevents any future spending of the output. It also prevents one from requiring that an output carries 0 value, which is not a useful notion either.

A toy example will lead us to the construction of the distinguished coins covenant. Here, we will let a specific 1 BTC stand in for the ownership of a real-world asset. The transaction output requires that the subsequent output sends exactly 1 BTC to an arbitrary public key. We supply CheckOutputVerify with (1) an output index of 0, (2) an amount of 1 BTC (specified as 100,000,000 units of 10^{-8} Bitcoin, called Satoshis) and (3) a pattern that contains a placeholder for a public key (*PubKey*) followed by the CheckSig opcode:

```
0 <100000000> <PubKey CheckSig> CheckOutputVerify.
```

This covenant ensures that the bitcoin corresponding to the asset can only be transferred in whole and cannot be mixed with other coins. This particular covenant, however, only holds for one transaction.

3.2   Recursive Covenants

It is critical to be able to apply covenants to an entire chain of transactions that derive from a covenant-bearing transfer. This section describes how this can be accomplished with recursive covenants.

We start by enforcing our example covenant over two subsequent transactions by including the covenant for the second output in the covenant for the first output. Modifying our example, the following script program not only enforces the first output in the next transaction to have a value of 1 BTC, but also puts the same restriction on the first output in the subsequent transaction (we omit the output's index hereinafter as they can be supplied in the input script).

```
<100000000> <<100000000> <PubKey CheckSig> CheckOutputVerify
     PubKey CheckSig> CheckOutputVerify <keyDest> CheckSig
```

To extend the sequence of outputs further, we could again include another CheckOutputVerify command in the innermost script pattern. Since we cannot repeat this infinitely, and instead of creating a self-reproducing script (a Quine), we use the interpreter to replace a dedicated keyword with the pattern itself.

We therefore add a new placeholder opcode called `Pattern` that allows to specify the occurrence of the pattern within itself. When evaluating a pattern, the `Pattern` opcode will be replaced by the pattern itself, thereby resolving the recursion one step at a time. The following example demonstrates the basic use of the `Pattern` opcode.

```
<100000000> <<100000000> Pattern CheckOutputVerify PubKey
    CheckSig> CheckOutputVerify <keyDest> CheckSig
```

When evaluating the pattern in this script program, the `Pattern` opcode will be replaced by the full pattern itself, yielding the exact same script as a pattern for comparison with the script program of the spending output.

3.3 Distinguished Coins

Many (most notably [11]) have noted that Bitcoin can be used as a digital asset exchange mechanism by associating a physical asset to a certain coin. For example, one could attach an arbitrary amount of bitcoins to a certain amount of gold, deposited with a trusted party. This coin could then be used to represent ownership of the gold and be easily traded.

However, as we noted above, bitcoin amounts are not separately tracked by the system, as every Bitcoin transaction inherently mixes all of its inputs' values. In contrast, covenants are carried from one input to a distinct set of outputs, thereby making it possible to meaningfully link currency flows. Our running example constructs distinguished coins by enforcing the coin to retain its distinguished status in all subsequent transactions.

A small security issue inherent to the script used so far is that a user can have multiple distinguished coins with the same value. When the output index is explicitly provided in the input, a user could reuse the same index for multiple covenants and thereby invalidate all but one of the distinguished coins. Solving this problem is straightforward as each distinguished coin can include a unique identifier in the script that prevents mapping multiple inputs to the same output, as in the following example. First, we define `patternDistinguishedWithId` as

```
<assetId> Drop <value> Pattern CheckOutputVerify PubKey
    CheckSig ,
```

and the distinguished coin covenant is

```
<assetId> Drop <value> <patternDistinguishedWithId>
    CheckOutputVerify <keyDest> CheckSig .
```

3.4 Overhead

The `CheckOutputVerify` opcode maintains Script's simplicity, and does not introduce excessive overhead. While `CheckOutputVerify` does not enable loops, a naïve implementation (verbatim following the specification of Algorithm 1) could cause the interpreter to form an excessively large final script program with repeated use of the Pattern opcode. To mitigate this concern, instead of first replacing all Pattern placeholder with the script itself, the interpreter incrementally expands the pattern and compares the prefix, thereby bounding the overhead to the parsing time of the output to be matched.

3.5 Discussion

Variants. There are a few design choices in our implementation of covenants. For instance, the covenant opcode could be made more flexible than a simple match. One option is that the opcode can return true or false on the stack, indicating the verification result. This would allow for elaborate combinations of validity conditions. Similarly, an opcode can return the output value, allowing arithmetic operations for validation.

Our current implementation allows covenants in different transaction inputs to refer to the same outputs, which requires some diligence of covenant programmers. This behavior can be removed by enforcing a one-to-one mapping of output checks to transaction outputs. Each transaction input can check any number of the outputs and map these outputs in order, according to the transaction input order and the access order with CheckOutputVerify. This alternative implementation introduces slightly more complexity, but is also more resilient to human error.

Covenant Termination. As part of the covenant programmer's responsibility, we note that in various cases covenants should enable an exit strategy, allowing to repurpose a coin, for example after a set time or with a specific private key.

4   Vault Transactions

Bitcoin funds are, by and large, protected by sets of cryptographic secret keys. Whoever knows those keys can instantly, anonymously, and irrevocably move the funds by spending the transaction outputs in which they are represented.

This makes Bitcoin private key theft an attractive target for thieves. A long list of thefts has been curated by the Bitcoin community [20], illustrating that attackers have been able to steal bitcoins worth millions of USD. Even major Bitcoin companies frequently fall prey to such attacks (e. g., [19]).

Correctly managing private keys is therefore one of the central challenges for client-side security in Bitcoin in order to protect users from both accidental loss and deliberate theft. A recent study by Eskandari et al. evaluated different methods of key management and concluded that each of them is vulnerable to a range of attacks [15].

A common approach for storing bitcoins in a secure manner is to put them into "cold storage", which means that their keys are stored on a device not connected to the Internet. However, in order to retrieve the coins, one must regularly (albeit infrequently) interact with those keys, which makes them vulnerable as well.

We now introduce recoverable vaults, which reduce the incentive for Bitcoin private key theft. Vaults provide two mechanisms to increase security. First, funds stored in a vault can be recovered using a recovery key in case the vault key is compromised. Second, in case the recovery key is compromised as well, the owner can still prevent the attacker from moving the coins; the worst the attacker can do is to prevent the owner from regaining full control over the funds. As this reduces the motivation for key theft, users can be more permissive in their storage of the private keys, reducing the chances of key loss.

Note. As explained below, vault transactions use a delay mechanism. We note that vault transactions cannot be implemented with existing timing mechanisms such as the `CheckLockTimeVerify` opcode or transaction locktime.

4.1 Overview

Vault transactions prevent an attacker from instantly moving funds from a victim's wallet by enforcing a delay for the transfer of those bitcoins. Coins placed in a vault transaction cannot be released immediately. The key idea of vaults is that the spending transaction has to be placed publicly on the blockchain, with its output locked for a specified amount of time. During this period, the owner of the coins can abort the release of the coins using a recovery key (preferably placed in cold storage) to send them to a different address in a new spending transaction, thereby denying the payout from the attacker. When the attacker also gains access to the recovery key, she can use the same recovery mechanism to again try to send the funds to her address. However, as the covenant is enforced recursively, the legitimate owner can again cancel the payout. Using a long locktime, it is cheap for the legitimate owner to maintain the block.

While ultimately the attacker can blackmail an owner, promising a share of the funds once they are released, this increases both the cost and the exposure of the attacker due to the need to communicate with the victim and provides a lead for criminal investigations.

4.2 Architecture

To secure an amount with a vault, a user sends it to a *vault fund* transaction. The output of this transaction requires a signature corresponding to the vault key and contains a covenant script program that enforces that the output cannot be spent directly, but must be spent through a *vault spend* transaction. The vault spend offers two possibilities to redeem its funds. First, the funds can be spent to a standard output, but only after a certain time has passed, e. g., 100 blocks using a locktime. This is the timer on the vault. When there is no attack, this simply delays the payout from a vault.

Alternatively, the funds can be spent at any time (without having to wait for the locktime to expire) using the recovery key in another vault spend, identical to the first one (cf. Fig. 1). This effectively resets the locktime of the funds.

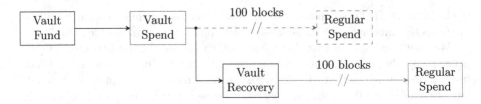

Fig. 1. The attackers spending attempt (red) is interrupted by a vault recovery issued by the legitimate owner, followed by a regular spend of the legitimate owner (green) (Color figure online)

4.3   Script Programs

In the following we provide the script programs implementing vault transactions. Beside our `CheckOutputVerify`, we assume the availability of another opcode that is currently being developed called `CheckSequenceVerify` (CSV) [6], which allows outputs to specify a locktime relative to the block height (or timestamp) when their containing transaction is committed to the blockchain.[2]

Vault Spend. Assume that 1 BTC has been locked in a vault. To spend this bitcoin, the payout transaction has to specify a relative locktime (using CSV) after which the coin can be redeemed with the signature belonging to a certain public key. Before the locktime expires, the funds can be moved to an output that retains the value and adheres to the vault pattern (which we describe below). This new output must be accompanied with a signature corresponding to the recovery key.

```
If
   <100> CheckSequenceVerify <keyDest> CheckSig
Else
   <100000000> <patternVault> CheckOutputVerify <keyRecovery>
      CheckSig
EndIf
```

Pattern. To enforce the above script program structure, we use the following pattern. Coins can be spent with an arbitrary public key (specified by the `PubKey` placeholder) after a relative locktime of 100 blocks has passed, or immediately respent in an output that adheres to the same pattern (enforced through the `Pattern` placeholder) and provides a valid signature with the recovery key.

```
If
   <100> CheckSequenceVerify PubKey CheckSig
Else
   <100000000> Pattern CheckOutputVerify <keyRecovery>
      CheckSig
EndIf
```

---

[2] We abstract from opcode behavior specific to Bitcoin's soft-fork upgrade mechanism, namely the need to drop items from the stack afterwards.

Vault Fund. To initially lock funds in a vault, we use a script program which specifies that an output in the redeeming transaction must adhere to the `patternVault`, have the same value (otherwise it would be possible to retrieve the money through another output) and that the transaction has to provide a valid signature corresponding to the vault key.

```
<100000000> <patternVault> CheckOutputVerify <keyVault>
    CheckSig
```

5 Bitcoin-NG Overlay

Bitcoin-NG is a blockchain protocol that offers major improvements of transaction bandwidth and latency in comparison to Bitcoin [16]. We explain how we can use covenants to deploy Bitcoin-NG's core features on top of Bitcoin, so users can benefit from improved efficiency. This allows to gradually deploy Bitcoin-NG, with nodes gradually adopting it.

In the following, we overview the Bitcoin-NG protocol (Sect. 5.1) demonstrate how such a deployment can be carried out (Sect. 5.2) and how covenants allow to implement Bitcoin-NG on top of Bitcoin by providing a mechanism to realize *poison transactions* (Sect. 5.3).

5.1 Preliminaries: Bitcoin-NG Operation

Bitcoin-NG's blockchain has two types of blocks. Key-blocks are generated with proof of work, like in Bitcoin, but contain no transactions. They serve as a leader election mechanism and contain a public key that identifies the chosen leader. Once a leader is elected, she publishes microblocks that contain transactions.

In order to motivate participants to follow the protocol, Bitcoin-NG uses the following mechanisms. As in Bitcoin, proof-of-work is motivated by a subsidy — a prize for mining. As in Bitcoin, each transaction pays a fee to the system, but unlike Bitcoin, this fee is distributed, with 40 % to the leader, and 60 % to the subsequent leader. Finally, if a leader forks the chain by generating two microblocks with the same parent, she is punished by revoking her subsidy revenue; whoever detects the fraud wins a nominal fee.

5.2 Overlaying Bitcoin-NG on Top of Bitcoin

Our goal is to have Bitcoin-NG nodes use the Bitcoin protocol when communicating with other Bitcoin nodes, but use the Bitcoin-NG protocol when talking to Bitcoin-NG nodes.

To achieve this, all the information in Bitcoin-NG blocks — both key-blocks and microblocks — must be translated into standard Bitcoin blocks for compatibility. Specifically, key-blocks are mapped to standard Bitcoin blocks. We start with the case where consecutive key-blocks are found by Bitcoin-NG miners. The second miner puts all transactions placed in microblocks by the previous miner into the mapped Bitcoin block. When Bitcoin-NG nodes communicate with each other, they exchange key-block and microblock data structures. A Bitcoin-NG node can reconstruct the standard Bitcoin blocks on demand. However, if a Bitcoin-NG node communicates with a standard Bitcoin node, it sends the standard blocks, which contain all the transactions. For both Bitcoin and Bitcoin-NG nodes, mining is performed on the standard Bitcoin blocks, again, for backward compatibility.

Recall that in Bitcoin-NG the transaction fees are distributed among the current and next leaders. In the overlay implementation, the microblock transactions are actually placed in the subsequent key-block, and their fees go to the subsequent leader. This key-block must therefore redistribute those fees. If the fees are not distributed correctly, the block is not a valid Bitcoin-NG key-block, and it is considered a standard block by the protocol.

However, if not all miners are running the Bitcoin-NG client, some blocks are found by non-NG miners. These do not respect the microblock chain of the current leader, and do not distribute the fees correctly. If a Bitcoin-NG key-block (and its microblocks) is followed by a standard block, Bitcoin-NG-miners discard the current microblock chain; the leader, previously chosen, remains leader and starts a new microblock chain on top of the standard block. This is illustrated in Fig. 2. A new leader will thus pay 40% of the fees in the latest microblock chain to the previous leader, no matter how many standard block separate its key-block from the previous leader's key-block. Keeping the leader across standard blocks has two objectives. First, the Bitcoin-NG fast transaction commitment can be used even after standard blocks. Second, it increases the incentive to run a Bitcoin-NG node, as the leader is guaranteed to win 40% of a subsequent epoch, even if not the immediate next one.

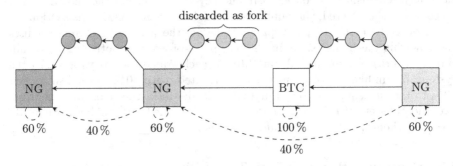

Fig. 2. Structure of a mixed Bitcoin and Bitcoin-NG blockchain

5.3 Poison Transactions

The missing piece towards deploying Bitcoin-NG on top of Bitcoin are poison transactions. Leaders commit to destroying a large share of their own coinbase reward if they produce a fork in their microblock chain. Destroying the value of the coinbase is enforced by a covenant. Without this commitment, the blocks are not accepted as valid Bitcoin-NG blocks.

Poison Structure. Bitcoin-NG's coinbase transactions need a time frame in which they are unspendable by the miner, but destroyable by a poison transaction. In Bitcoin, a consensus rule enforces that normal coinbase outputs can be spent after 100 confirmations [3]. Bitcoin-NG's coinbase transactions must therefore delay the ability to spend the coinbase output by an additional number of blocks t. We implement this using CLTV:

```
If
    <height+100+t> CheckLockTimeVerify <pkLeader> CheckSig
Else
    <90% of value > <Return > CheckOutputVerify
    <10% of value > 0 CheckOutputVerify
    <pkPoison> CheckSig
EndIf
```

Within these t blocks a poison transaction can destroy a significant share of the coinbase's value and reward the reporting user with the remainder of the funds. This mechanism is enforced by a covenant that ensures that most of the value is destroyed in an unspendable Return output and the rest of the funds can be claimed by the user reporting the misbehavior, who can choose her own output script program.

Fraud Detection. The crux of the fraud detection mechanism is to construct every microblock such that if the leader creates a fork with more than one microblock succeeding any block it is possible to extract the private poison key.

To achieve this, we use a property of the ECDSA signature scheme used for Bitcoin transaction signing. Each ECDSA signature created with a secret key d requires the signer to select an ephemeral key k, that is, a secret random number used in the signing process. This ephemeral key must not be reused with the same private key to sign another message as this allows to calculate d from the two signatures [18]. In fact, such operational security mistakes have led to theft of bitcoins [5].

Every ECDSA signature contains a value r that is computed based on k and otherwise fixed parameters. Computing k from r is believed to computationally infeasible [18]. We utilize this fact as follows.

Each key-block and microblock are published with a bundled value r, thereby committing to a certain ephemeral key for the *next* microblock. Each microblock is signed with the leader's poison key using the ephemeral key previously selected; if the r value of a microblock does not match the commitment in the previous block, it is considered invalid.

If the leader creates a microblock fork, she is forced to reuse the ephemeral key to sign the microblocks. This allows any party with access to both messages to calculate the private poison key. The leader can only profit from such forking by making one microblock public, as part of the main chain, and one microblock known to some defrauded party. Once this defrauded party learns about the fork, she can find the poison private key and expose the fraud.

Note that we use two different keys in the scheme as the leaked key should only enable the poison mechanism, but not to be useful to produce arbitrary microblocks on behalf of the leader.

6   Related Work

Covenants. The first mention of *covenants* in Bitcoin is due to Maxwell [22], who coined the term. Maxwell proposed using zero-knowledge succinct non-interactive arguments of knowledge (SNARKs) to place, and discharge, arbitrarily complicated constraints on any data in the blockchain. However, even assuming SNARKs can be implemented efficiently, the generality of this approach makes it difficult to reason about the system's security. Consequently, this idea was immediately dismissed by Maxwell himself. Ethereum [7] is a blockchain-based protocol that provides a Turing-complete programming language for writing arbitrary programs. The power of the scripts is limited in Ethereum through utility pricing to limit malicious use and to maintain fairness. While the programming language is universally expressive and can thus implement covenants, it offers no formal security guarantees. In contrast, the covenants implementation we propose requires only limited changes to Bitcoin's limited script language, accesses only designated outputs, and incurs nominal overhead.

Further discussion on the concept of covenants [2] focuses mostly on risks, such as potential impact on fungibility and the possibility to use covenants to enforce anti-money laundering (AML) regulation upon Bitcoin. Covenants do not necessarily impact fungibility if programmed properly, and it is the responsibility of the covenant programmer to lift a covenant when it makes sense to do so. In general, most general-purpose extensions, including the presence of unconfirmed transactions [13] as well as extensions such as CLTV, can pose problems for fungibility if not properly used. Overall, the political consequences of general-purpose technical features are beyond the scope of this paper.

Vault Transactions. In [10], a Bitcoin forum participant outlines a 4-line proposal to deter theft using restrictions on expenditures. This scheme uses a recursive covenant that allows the owner of funds to abort a theft transaction within a bounded time, and send the funds to a new output, secured by a different private key. While this scheme may be useful in certain scenarios, in essence, it simply secures the funds by an additional key. Multisignature transactions, which require m out of n keys to be used to sign a valid transaction, provide similar protections. Eskandari et al. [15] evaluate the usability of different key management schemes, and conclude that there is no silver bullet for private key storage. And while others have suggested more efficient threshold signature schemes based on ECDSA [17], with better privacy and smaller transaction size in comparison to standard multisignature transactions, these schemes all rely on the secrecy of the signing keys. In contrast, vaults prohibit a thief from taking possession of the funds even if she learns *all* the secret keys.

Fraud Proof. Fraud-proofs have gained attention with the introduction of cryptocurrencies due to the ability to use them against a security deposit. Fraud proofs similar to the one we use were suggested in the context of generic covenants by d'aniel and Todd [12]. Other instances are in the context of pegged sidechains [1], and proof-of-stake [8]. Ruffing, Kate, and Schröder [24] propose a general scheme for double-attestation proof, using a cryptocurrency as a primitive.

7   Conclusions

We showed how Bitcoin covenants can be added to the existing scripting language with a single simple opcode with nominal overhead. Overall, covenants introduce a novel functionality that opens the door to a wide range of security constructs and financial contracts. We demonstrate this with two novel and useful constructs.

The first, vault transactions, tackles cryptocurrency key security. Vault transactions significantly reduce theft in Bitcoin by removing the ability of a thief to keep the proceeds.

The second, poison transactions, enable automatic fraud-proof-based penalizing, a generally useful construct. We showed how covenant-enabled fraud-proofs can be used to progressively deploy Bitcoin-NG as an overlay on top of the Bitcoin blockchain, thereby enabling significant improvements in throughput, confirmation time and scalability.

Acknowledgments. The authors thank Glenn Willen for useful conversations, Tim Ruffing and Dominique Schröder for their advice on cryptographic primitives, and the anonymous reviewers for their valuable feedback.

This material is based upon work supported by a fellowship within the FITweltweit programme of the German Academic Exchange Service (DAAD), the German Bundesministerium für Bildung und Forschung (BMBF) under grant agreement No. 13N13505, and the National Science Foundation under Grant No. CNS-1518779 and Grant No. CNS-1561209. Any opinions, findings, and conclusions or recommendations expressed in this material are those of the author(s) and do not necessarily reflect the views of the funding organizations.

References

1. Back, A., Corallo, M., Dashjr, L., Friedenbach, M., Maxwell, G., Miller, A., Poelstra, A., Timón, J., Wuille, P.: Enabling Blockchain Innovations with Pegged Sidechains. https://blockstream.com/sidechains.pdf. Accessed 03 Nov 2015
2. #Bitcoin-Wizard IRC log. https://download.wpsoftware.net/bitcoin/wizards/2014/01/14-01-15.log. Accessed 28 Oct 2015
3. Block chain. https://en.bitcoin.it/w/index.php?title=Block_chain&oldid=59033. Accessed 19 Oct 2015
4. Bonneau, J., Miller, A., Clark, J., Narayanan, A., Kroll, J.A., Felten, E.W.: Research perspectives on bitcoin and second-generation cryptocurrencies. In: IEEE Symposium on Security and Privacy. IEEE, San Jose (2015)

5. Bos, J.W., Halderman, J.A., Heninger, N., Moore, J., Naehrig, M., Wustrow, E.: Elliptic curve cryptography in practice. In: Christin, N., Safavi-Naini, R. (eds.) FC 2014. LNCS, vol. 8437, pp. 156–174. Springer, Heidelberg (2014)

6. BtcDrak, Friedenbach, M., Lombrozo, E.: BIP 112: CHECKSEQUENCEVERIFY (2015). https://github.com/bitcoin/bips/blob/master/bip-0112.mediawiki. Accessed 08 Oct 2015

7. Buterin, V.: A Next Generation Smart Contract and Decentralized Application Platform (2013). https://www.ethereum.org/pdfs/EthereumWhitePaper.pdf/. Accessed Feb 2015

8. Buterin, V.: Slasher: A Punitive Proof-of-Stake Algorithm, January 2015. https://blog.ethereum.org/2014/01/15/slasher-a-punitive-proof-of-stake-algorithm/

9. Chaum, D., Fiat, A., Naor, M.: Untraceable electronic cash. In: Goldwasser, S. (ed.) CRYPTO 1988. LNCS, vol. 403, pp. 319–327. Springer, Heidelberg (1990)

10. Coastermonger: Thief's downfall covenant. https://bitcointalk.org/index.php?topic=278122.msg3164726#msg3164726. Accessed 16 Sept 2013

11. Colored Coins Project. Colored Coins. http://coloredcoins.org/. Accessed Sept 2015

12. d'aniel, Todd, P.: Security deposits (2013). https://bitcointalk.org/index.php?topic=278122.msg2973895#msg2973895. Accessed 20 Aug 2013

13. Decker, C.: [bitcoin-dev] [BIP] Normalized transaction IDs. https://lists.linuxfoundation.org/pipermail/bitcoin-dev/2015-November/011657.html. Accessed 03 Nov 2015

14. Dogecoin Project. Dogecoin. http://dogecoin.com/. Accessed Nov 2014

15. Eskandari, S., Barrera, D., Stobert, E., Clark, J.: A first look at the usability of bitcoin key management. In: NDSS Workshop on Usable Security (USEC) (2015)

16. Eyal, I., Gencer, A.E., Sirer, E.G., van Renesse, R.: Bitcoin-NG: a scalable blockchain protocol. In: Proceedings of the 6th USENIX Symposium on Networked Systems Design and Implementation, NSDI 16–18, 2016, Santa Clara, CA, USA, March 2016

17. Goldfeder, S., Gennaro, R., Kalodner, H., Bonneau, J., Kroll, J.A., Felten, E.W., Narayanan, A.: Securing Bitcoin Wallets Via a New DSA/ECDSA Threshold Signature Scheme (2015)

18. Hankerson, D., Menezes, A., Vanstone, S.: Guide to Elliptic Curve Cryptography (2004)

19. Higgins, S.: Bitstamp Claims $5 Million Lost in Hot Wallet Hack (2015). http://www.coindesk.com/bitstamp-claims-roughly-19000-btc-lost-hot-wallet-hack/. Accessed 16 Oct 2015

20. List of Major Bitcoin Heists, Thefts, Hacks, Scams, Losses. https://bitcointalk.org/index.php?topic=576337. Accessed 16 Oct 2015

21. Litecoin Project. Litecoin, open source P2P digital currency. https://litecoin.org. Accessed Nov 2014

22. Maxwell, G.: CoinCovenants Using SCIP Signatures, an Amusingly Bad Idea. https://bitcointalk.org/index.php?topic=278122.0. Accessed 25 Oct 2015

23. Nakamoto, S., Bitcoin: A Peer-to-Peer Electronic Cash System (2008). http://www.bitcoin.org/bitcoin.pdf

24. Ruffing, T., Kate, A., Schröder, D.: Liar, liar, coins on fire! — penalizing equivocation by loss of bitcoins. In: Proceedings of the 22nd Conference on Computer and Communications Security, CCS 2015, Denver, CO, USA. ACM, New York (2015)

25. Todd, P.: BIP 65: OP_CHECKLOCKTIMEVERIFY (2014). https://github.com/bitcoin/bips/blob/master/bip-0065.mediawiki. Accessed 08 Oct 2015

26. Tschorsch, F., Scheuermann, B.: Bitcoin and Beyond: A Technical Survey on Decentralized Digital Currencies. Cryptology ePrint Archive. Report 2015/464 (2015)
27. Vishnumurthy, V., Chandrakumar, S., Sirer, E.G.: Karma: a secure economic framework for peer-to-peer resource sharing. In: Workshop on the Economics of Peer-to-Peer Systems, Berkeley, California, vol. 35 (2003)

Cryptocurrencies Without Proof of Work

Iddo Bentov[1(✉)], Ariel Gabizon[1], and Alex Mizrahi[2]

[1] Department of Computer Science, Technion, Haifa, Israel
`idddo@cs.technion.ac.il`, `ariel.gabizon@gmail.com`
[2] Chromaway.com, Stockholm, Sweden
`alex.mizrahi@gmail.com`

Abstract. We study decentralized cryptocurrency protocols in which the participants do not deplete physical scarce resources. Such protocols commonly rely on *Proof of Stake*, i.e., on mechanisms that extend voting power to the stakeholders of the system. We offer analysis of existing protocols that have a substantial amount of popularity. We then present our novel pure *Proof of Stake* protocols, and argue that they help in mitigating problems that the existing protocols exhibit.

1 Introduction[1]

The decentralized nature of Bitcoin [7,12] means that anyone can become a "miner" at any point in time, and thus participate in the security maintenance of the Bitcoin system and be compensated for this work. The miners continuously perform *Proof of Work* (PoW) computations, meaning that they attempt to solve difficult computational tasks. The purpose of the PoW element in the Bitcoin system is to reach consensus regarding the ledger history, thereby synchronizing the transactions and making the users secure against double-spending attacks.

The miners who carry out PoW computations can be viewed as entities who vote on blocks of transactions that the users recently broadcasted to the network, so that the decision-making power of each miner is in proportion to the amount of computational power that she has. Thus, an individual miner who has a fraction p of the total mining power can create each new block with probability $\approx p$, though other factors such as "selfish mining" [1,5,6] can influence p.

Under the assumption that the majority of the PoW mining power follows the Bitcoin protocol, the users can become increasingly confident that the payment transactions that they receive will not be reversed [7,12,15].

By means of the PoW mechanism, each miner depletes physical scarce resources in the form of electricity and mining equipment erosion, and thereby earns cryptographic scarce resources in the form of coins that can be spent within the Bitcoin system.

Hence the following question is of interest: can a *decentralized* cryptocurrency system be as secure as Bitcoin even if the entities who maintain its security do not deplete physical scarce resources?

---

[1] The full version of this work includes extra material such as a section on the initial issuance of the money supply, and is available at http://arxiv.org/abs/1406.5694.

© International Financial Cryptography Association 2016
J. Clark et al. (Eds.): FC 2016 Workshops, LNCS 9604, pp. 142–157, 2016.
DOI: 10.1007/978-3-662-53357-4_10

Cryptocurrency protocols that attempt to avoid wasting physical scarce resources commonly rely on *Proof of Stake*, i.e., on mechanisms that give the decision-making power regarding the continuation of the ledger history to entities who possess coins within the system. The rationale behind *Proof of Stake* is that entities who hold stake in the system are well-suited to maintain its security, since their stake will diminish in value when the security of the system erodes. Therefore, in an analogous manner to Bitcoin, an individual stakeholder who possesses p fraction of the total amount of coins in circulation becomes eligible to create the next extension of the ledger with probability $\approx p$.

We use the terminology "pure" *Proof of Stake* to refer to a cryptocurrency system that relies on *Proof of Stake* and does not make any use of PoW. To the best of our knowledge, the idea of *Proof of Stake* in the context of cryptocurrencies was first introduced in [17], though that discussion focused on non-pure *Proof of Stake* variants (cf. [3]).

PoW based cryptocurrencies become insecure when a significant enough portion of the total mining power colludes in an attack. Likewise, the security of pure *Proof of Stake* cryptocurrencies deteriorates when enough stakeholders wish to collude in an attack. If the majority of the stake wishes to participate in attacks on a pure *Proof of Stake* system, it can be argued that there is no longer enough interest that this system should continue to exist, hence assuming that the majority of the stake will not participate in an (overt) attack is sensible. The same does not necessarily hold in a PoW based system, i.e., the majority of the mining power might be under the control of an external adversary during some time period, while the majority of the participants in this system still wish for it to remain sound. See [3] and Sect. 3 for additional considerations.

2 Pure *Proof of Stake*

There are two apparent hurdles with decentralized pure *Proof of Stake* systems: fair initial distribution of the money supply to the interested parties, and network fragility if the nodes are rational rather than altruistic. PoW offers an elegant solution to the first hurdle, by converting physical scarce resources into coins in the system. We provide here an analysis of the second hurdle in an existing pure *Proof of Stake* system, and also describe our novel CoA and Dense-CoA pure *Proof of Stake* systems that seek to mitigate this problem. Let us note that the second hurdle is less severe in PoW systems, though bribe attacks on Bitcoin have indeed been considered, for example in [16].

2.1 The PPCoin System

PPCoin is a pure *Proof of Stake* system, in the sense that PoW is used only[2] for distributing the initial money supply. Stakeholders in the PPCoin network can create the next block according to the following type of condition:

$$\texttt{hash}(\texttt{prev\_blocks\_data}, \texttt{time\_in\_seconds}, txout_A) \leq d_0 \cdot \texttt{coins}(txout_A) \cdot \texttt{timeweight}(txout_A) \quad (*)$$

---

[2] See http://peercoin.net/assets/paper/peercoin-paper.pdf.

In the inequality (*), `time_in_seconds` should correspond to the current time (with some leniency bounds), thus restricting hash attempts to 1 per second and preventing PoW use at creating the next block, because nodes will regard a new block as invalid unless the difference between its time and their local time is within the bounds. The notation $\texttt{coins}(txout_A)$ refers to the amount of coins of some unspent transaction output $txout_A$, hence if stakeholder A has the private key sk_A that controls $txout_A$ then she can create a valid block by signing the block with sk_A and attaching the signature as evidence that condition (*) holds. This means that a stakeholder who controls an output of e.g. 50 coins is 10 times more likely to create a block than a stakeholder who controls an output of 5 coins. See footnote 1 regarding $\texttt{timeweight}(txout_A)$, and Sect. 2.1.3 regarding `prev_blocks_data`. The constant d_0 is readjusted according to a protocol rule that dictates that blocks should be created in intervals of 10 min on average, i.e., if fewer stakeholders are online during a certain time period then d_0 gets increased. The winning blockchain is the one with the largest cumulative stake, i.e., the blockchain with the most blocks such that stake blocks are weighted according to their d_0 difficulties, and PoW blocks have a negligible weight.

Although the PPCoin cryptocurrency had a market cap of over \$100 million in 2014, the PPCoin protocol has the following problems:

2.1.1 Rational Forks.

On every second we have that $\Pr[\{\text{some block is solved}\}] \approx \frac{1}{600}$, therefore multiple blocks will be solved simultaneously every $\approx 360000\,\text{s} \approx 4$ days. Rational stakeholders can increase their expected reward by maintaining and trying to solve blocks on the multiple forked chains that were transmitted to them, which would lead to a divergent network. An individual stakeholder can either tie her hands behind her back by ignoring all the forked chains except for one, or opt to gain more rewards by keeping all the forked chains, which may render her entire stake worthless in case the network becomes divergent. The strategy of tying your hands behind your back is not a Nash equilibrium: if all the stakeholders follow this strategy then it is better for an individual stakeholder to deviate and maintain all the forked chains, as her influence on the overall convergence of the network is minor. Network propagation lag implies an even greater frequency of forks, as a stakeholder will get competing blocks sent to her even if those blocks were honestly solved a few seconds apart from one another. Worse still, when a rational stakeholder who currently tries to extend the block B_i receives B_{i+1} from her peers, she may opt to increase her expected reward by attempting to extend both the chain $\ldots, B_i, B_{i+1}$ and the chain $\ldots, B_i$ simultaneously. Rational stakeholders may thus prefer to reject blocks whose timestamp is later than another block that they currently try to extend, though an attempt to extend both $\ldots, B_i, B_{i+1}$ and $\ldots, B_i$ can still be possible if the rule that the stakeholders deploy does not retrace to an earlier chain that is received late due to propagation lag.

2.1.2   Bribe Attacks on PPCoin. An attacker can double-spend quite easily. After the merchant waits for e.g. 6 block confirmations and sends the goods, the attacker can publicly announce her intent to create a fork that reverses the last 6 blocks, and offer bribes to stakeholders who would sign blocks of her competing branch that starts 6 blocks earlier. The attacker may offer a larger bribe to stakeholders who sign only her branch, and may commit to giving bribes even after her competing branch wins, to encourage more stakeholders to participate in the attack. Notice that the stakeholders who collude with the attacker will not lose anything in case the attack fails. As long as the value of the goods is greater than the total value of the bribes, this attack will be profitable. Let us note that a bribe attack in a pure PoW network has to surmount far greater obstacles: miners who join the attack would deplete their resources while working on a fork with a 6 blocks deficit, and it is a nontrivial task to assess the success probability by measuring how many other miners participate in the attack. See also [3, Sect. 5.3].

2.1.3   Opportunistic Attacks in Relation to the Need to Disallow PoW. A stakeholder who holds a significant fraction of all the coins is able to generate a significant fraction of the blocks, as the probability to generate a block is proportional to the amount of coins that a stakeholder holds. Therefore, from time to time a stakeholder will be able to generate chains of consecutive blocks.

We can analyze this event by using a simplified model where stakeholders who own $\frac{1}{M}$ of all coins can generate a block with probability $\frac{1}{M}$, and the probability to generate k sequential blocks is $(\frac{1}{M})^k$. This approximation is accurate under the assumption that the stakeholder holds a number of unspent transaction outputs significantly larger than k, so that `timeweight` will have no impact. We can estimate the average number of blocks between groups of k sequential blocks generated by one stakeholder as a mean of exponential distribution, which would be equal to $1/(1/M)^k = M^k$.

If merchants wait for k confirmations before sending their goods, the stakeholder has a chance to attack the merchant when she is able to generate k sequential blocks, thus the mean number of blocks between such attacks is M^k. For example, a stakeholder who holds $\frac{1}{4}$ of all coins participating in stake mining will be able to carry out a 6-block reorganization each $4^6 = 4096$ blocks, i.e., approximately once per month if one block is generated every 10 min.

An attacker who is able to create k sequential blocks would prefer to know about it as early as possible, so that she has enough time to send the payment transaction (that she intends to reverse) to the merchant. If the possible stakeholders' identities who may create the next blocks are derived from a low entropy process that only takes into account the identities who created the previous blocks, then the attacker can "look into the future" by carrying out brute-force computations to assess the probabilities that she will be able to create the k consecutive blocks at certain points in time. In order to gain a measure of unpredictability, PPCoin re-calculates once every 6 h a "stake modifier" value that depends on the transactions that the previous blocks included, i.e., this stake modifier is part of `prev_blocks_data` in condition (*). Therefore, a stakeholder who obtains an opportunity to generate k blocks in a row can know about this approximately 6 h in advance, so she has plenty of time to mount an attack. If the protocol required the stake modifier to be re-calculated at a shorter time interval, this would open the door for a stakeholder to do PoW attempts at deriving herself as being able to create future blocks more frequently.

2.2   The CoA Pure *Proof of Stake* System

The Chains of Activity (CoA) system that we hereby present is a pure *Proof of Stake* protocol that aims to overcome the problem of rational forks (cf. Sect. 2.1.1) by dictating that only a single stakeholder identity may create the next block, and solidifying the random choices for these identities in the earlier ledger history via an interleaving mechanism.

The CoA protocol is based in part on the core element of PoA [3], i.e., on a lottery among the online stakeholders via the *follow-the-satoshi* procedure. This procedure takes as input an index of a satoshi (smallest unit of the cryptocurrency) between zero and the total number of satoshis in circulation, fetches the block of ledger data in which this satoshi was minted, and tracks the transactions that moved this satoshi to subsequent addresses until finding the stakeholder who can currently spend this satoshi (cf. [3, Sect. 3 and Appendix A]). Note that if for example Alice has 6 coins and Bob has 2 coins then Alice is 3 times more likely to be picked by *follow-the-satoshi*, regardless of how their coins are fragmented. This implies that a stakeholder who holds her coins in many Sybil addresses do not obtain any advantage with regard to *follow-the-satoshi*.

The CoA protocol is parameterized by an amount of minted satoshis 2^κ, a subgroup length $w \geq 1$, a group length $\ell = \kappa \cdot w$, a function **comb** $: \{0,1\}^\ell \rightarrow \{0,1\}^\kappa$, a minimal block interval time G_0, a minimal stake amount C_0, an award amount C_1 where $0 \leq C_1 < C_0$, and a double-spending safety bound T_0.

The blocks creation process of CoA assembles a blockchain that is comprised of groups of ℓ consecutive blocks:

$$\overbrace{\square\square\cdots\square}^{\ell}, \overbrace{\square\square\cdots\square}^{\ell}, \overbrace{\square\square\cdots\square}^{\ell}, \cdots$$

The rules of the CoA protocol are specified as follows:

The CoA Protocol

1. Each block is generated by a single stakeholder, whose identity is fixed and publicly known (as will be explained in the next steps). This stakeholder collects transactions that are broadcasted over the CoA network as she sees fit, and then creates a block B_i that consists of these transactions, the hash of the previous block, the current timestamp, the index i, and a signature of these pieces of data as computed with her private key.

2. Every newly created block B_i is associated with a supposedly uniformly distributed bit b_i that is derived in a deterministic fashion, for example by taking the first bit of $hash(B_i)$.

3. The time gap between B_i and B_j must be at least $|j - i - 1| \cdot G_0$. This means that if for example the next four blocks $B_i, B_{i+1}, B_{i+2}, B_{i+3}$ were supposed to be generated by the four stakeholders $A_i, A_{i+1}, A_{i+2}, A_{i+3}$ but A_{i+1} and A_{i+2} were inactive, then the difference between the timestamp of B_{i+3} and B_i must be at least $2G_0$. Nodes in the network will consider a newly created block to be invalid if its timestamp is too far into the future relative to their local time.

4. After a group of ℓ valid blocks $B_{i_1}, B_{i_2}, \ldots, B_{i_\ell}$ is created, the network nodes will form a κ-bit seed $S^{B_{i_\ell}} = \mathbf{comb}(b_{i_1}, \ldots, b_{i_\ell})$. The function $\mathbf{comb}$ can simply concatenate its inputs (if $w = 1$), and several other alternatives are explored in Sect. 2.2.1.

5. The seed $S^{B_{i_\ell}}$ is then used in an interleaved fashion to derive the identities of the *after* next ℓ stakeholders, via *follow-the-satoshi*. That is, if the next ℓ valid blocks are $B_{i_\ell + j_1}, B_{i_\ell + j_2}, \ldots, B_{i_\ell + j_\ell}$, then the nodes who follow the protocol will derive the identity of the stakeholder who should create the block $B_{i_\ell + j_\ell + z}$ by invoking *follow-the-satoshi* with $hash(i_\ell, z, S^{B_{i_\ell}})$ as input, for $z \in \{1, 2, \ldots\}$.

6. If the derived satoshi is part of an unspent output of $c < C_0$ coins, the stakeholder must also attach an auxiliary signature that proves that she controls another output of at least $C_0 - c$ coins, or else she will not be able to create a valid block. Neither the derived output nor this auxiliary output may be spent in the first T_0 blocks that extend the newly created block. In case the stakeholder A_i who should create the ith block signs two different blocks B_i, B_i', any stakeholder A_j among the next T_0 derived stakeholders can include it as evidence in the block that she creates, in order to confiscate at least C_0 coins that A_i possessed. The stakeholder A_j is awarded with C_1 of the confiscated coins, and the rest of the confiscated coins are destroyed.

7. If the network nodes see multiple competing blockchains, they consider the blockchain that consists of the largest number of blocks to be the winning blockchain.

The interleaving in step 5 is crucial as a cementing mechanism. Otherwise, competing last stakeholders may extend the chain with seeds that derive different ℓ next identities, introducing divergence risk because it is rational for the next identities to extend the different forks. This cementing process ensures that unless $\approx \ell$ stakeholders collude by bypassing their turn on the honest chain and creating a hidden fork instead, only a single stakeholder will be eligible to create each next block. Thus the rational forks hazard is avoided.

The punishment scheme in step 6 expires after T_0 blocks, because honest stakeholder must eventually regain control over their security deposit (see also Sect. 3). Note that a stakeholder can divide her coins among multiple outputs, so that only one of the outputs would become unspendable for T_0 blocks. If

$C_1 \approx C_0$, an attacker might double-sign and publish the double-signing evidence in a next block to recover her security deposit, so $C_1 \leq \frac{C_0}{2}$ is a better choice.

If ℓ is very large (in the extreme $\ell = \infty$, i.e., practically equivalent to selecting the identities of the stakeholders via a round-robin), then an attacker may try to gain possession of future consecutive satoshis to mount a double-spending attack (cf. Sect. 2.2.3). On the other hand, small ℓ makes it easier for coalitions to influence the future identities (cf. Sect. 2.2.1). Moreover, if the range of **comb** were $\kappa' < \kappa$, an attacker could more easily see into the future, e.g. with $\kappa' = 10$ the attacker could buy satoshis of consecutive identities in one possible next group and succeed with probability $1/1024$ to carry out a double-spending attack. A sensible recommendation for the CoA parameters can be $\kappa = 51$ (for ≈ 21 million coins of 10^8 satoshis each), $w = 9$ with **comb** as the iterated majority function (see Sect. 2.2.1), $\ell = 459$, $G_0 = 5\,\mathrm{min}$, and $T_0 = 5000$.

2.2.1   Using Low-Influence Functions to Improve Chain Selection.

To give an intuitive illustration of the advantages of different choices, we focus on the prominent case of analyzing the probability that the last stakeholder in the chain, A_ℓ, can choose herself again as one of the first possible stakeholders $A'_1, \ldots, A'_\ell$ of the next round (see Fig. 1). Denote this probability by μ. We also make the simplifying assumptions that the previous players have indeed picked their bits b_i randomly, and that the function $hash$ is a random oracle. Let us assume that A_ℓ has a q-fraction of the coins in the system, and denote $p = 1 - (1-q)^\ell$. Thus, $\mu = p$ in case A_ℓ picks a random bit.

Simple Concatenation: We let $\mathbf{comb}(b_1, b_2, \ldots, b_\ell) \triangleq b_1 \circ b_2 \circ \cdots \circ b_\ell$, where b_i is the supposedly random bit that stakeholder A_i provided. The probability μ that A_ℓ can choose herself in the next round is the probability that $\exists b' \in \{0,1\}, i \in \{1, \ldots, \ell\}$ such that $hash(i_0 + i, \mathbf{comb}(b_1, \ldots, b_{\ell-1}, b'))$ maps to a coin of A_ℓ under *follow-the-satoshi*. Using the simplifying assumption that these are random independent values we have $\mu = 1 - (1-p)^2 = 2p - p^2 \approx 2p$.

Combining Majority with Concatenation: Assume now that $\ell = \kappa \cdot w$ for positive integer w. We now split the ℓ stakeholders into groups of size w: $A_1, \ldots, A_w, A_{w+1}, \ldots, A_{2w}, \ldots, A_{(\kappa-1)\cdot w+1}, \ldots, A_{\kappa \cdot w} = A_\ell$. Each group will determine a bit of the seed using the majority function. That is, the ith bit of the seed, denoted s_i, will be the majority of the bits $b_{(i-1)\cdot w+1}, \ldots, b_{iw}$. And $s = \mathbf{comb}(b_1, \ldots, b_\ell) \triangleq s_1 \circ s_2 \cdots \circ s_\kappa$. Note first that when the bits b_i are all chosen randomly, s is random – as the majority of random inputs is a random bit. Now, we analyze again the probability μ that A_ℓ can choose herself in the next round. It can be shown, using Stirling's approximation, that with probability roughly[3] $1 - \sqrt{2/\pi w}$ the last bit of the seed, s_κ, will already be determined by the bits of the previous stakeholders. This is because when w players choose

---

[3] More precisely, as w goes to infinity this is the limit of the probability of the event.

a bit randomly, the probability that *exactly half* of the bits came out one tends to $\binom{w}{w/2}/2^w \approx \frac{2^{w+1/2}}{\sqrt{\pi w}}/2^w = \sqrt{2/\pi w}$. In the absence of this event we have $\mu = p$, "as it should be". When this event happens, as before A_ℓ can get to probability $\approx 2p$. In total we have $\mu \approx p \cdot (1 - \sqrt{2/\pi w}) + 2p \cdot \sqrt{2/\pi w}$. Taking a large enough w, this is much closer to the "correct" p than in the previous choice of **comb**.

Protection Against Larger Coalitions: Let us use the terminology that a function **comb** : $\{0,1\}^\ell \rightarrow \{0,1\}^\kappa$ is an *ε-extractor* if for any choice of the coalition C of size c, and any strategy of C to choose their input bits after seeing the bits of the honest players, **comb**$(b_1, \ldots, b_\ell)$ produces an output that is ε-close to uniform.

[9], using the analysis of [2], give the following construction of an ε-extractor – that is in fact the same one we described earlier when replacing the majority function with *iterated majority* (defined in [2] and illustrated in Fig. 1).

$KZ(b_1, \ldots, b_\ell)$:

- Choose $w = 3 \cdot (c/\varepsilon)^{1/\alpha}$, where $\alpha = \log_3 2$. Set $\ell = w \cdot \kappa$.
- Output κ bits via *iterated majority* of consecutive groups of w inputs.

Upon fixing ε as the desired statistical error, κ as the desired output length, and ℓ as the total number of players in a chain, KZ can handle a coalition of size $c \leq \varepsilon \cdot (1/3 \cdot \ell/\kappa)^\alpha$. On the other hand, [9] show that any such ε-extractor can handle coalitions of size at most $c \leq \varepsilon \cdot 10 \cdot \ell/(\kappa - 1)$.

Since $\alpha > 1/2$, it follows that this choice of **comb** is less than quadratically worse than the optimal choice. Notice that this assumes that stakeholders who are not honest are non-oblivious, i.e., that they see the choices of the honest stakeholders before they play. This conservative assumption makes a certain sense in our context, as it easier for stakeholders who play in the last locations to try to collude in order to influence the seed.

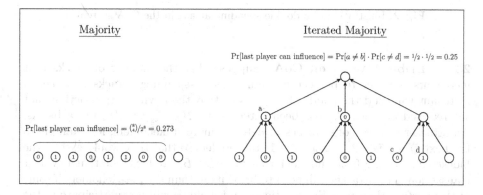

Fig. 1. Majority versus iterated majority.

2.2.2   Rational Collusions. Stakeholders may wish to collude and skip the last several blocks as if they did not exist, i.e., to extend the blockchain from an earlier block, in order to gain the fees that went to previous stakeholders. This can be mitigated by including in each transaction the index of the latest block that the user who made this transaction is aware of. For example, if the last block of the chain is B_i and it contains a transaction tx_0 that specifies that block $i-1$ exists, and a new transaction tx_1 that specifies that block i exists is broadcasted, then the stakeholder who creates B_{i+1} cannot reverse B_i to collect the fees of both tx_0 and tx_1, because B_i must exist in the chain that contains tx_1. The user can even specify in her transaction the index of the block that is currently being created, but this implies that the user will need to send another transaction in the case that the current stakeholder is offline. The colluding stakeholders diminish the overall value of their stake when they participate in such attacks, hence this strategy is not necessarily rational. It is also possible to reward stakeholders via monetary inflation and have the transaction fees destroyed to provide a counterbalance, though bribe attacks may then become more likely (see Sect. 2.2.3).

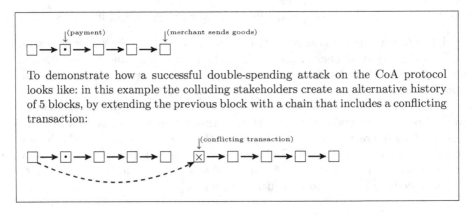

Fig. 2. Illustration of a double-spending attack in the CoA system.

2.2.3   Bribe Attacks on CoA. Suppose that the number of blocks that merchants consider to be secure against double-spending attacks is d, i.e., a merchant will send the goods after she sees that the payment transaction that she received in block B_{i_1} has been extended by $B_{i_2}, B_{i_3}, \ldots, B_{i_d}$ extra blocks. An attacker can now offer bribes to $d+1$ or more stakeholders, for example to the next $i_d+1, i_d+2, \ldots, i_d+d+1$ stakeholders so that they would extend the blockchain starting from the block that preceded B_{i_1} and exclude that payment transaction. The attacker will need to bribe more than $d+1$ stakeholders if some of them refuse the bribe. Since rational stakeholders will not participate in the attack without an incentive, the cost of the attack is at least $\mu(d+1)$ where μ is the average bribe amount that is given to each stakeholder.

Observe that $\Pr[\{\text{successful attack}\}] < 1$ since some of the stakeholders might be altruistic, some of the rational stakeholders may think that it would be unprofitable to participate in such attacks, and the attacker's funds are not unlimited. Hence, a rational stakeholder will choose to accept the bribe by weighing whether $(\mu + F') \cdot \Pr[\{\text{successful attack}\}] > F \cdot (1 - \Pr[\{\text{successful attack}\}])$, where F and F' are the fee amounts that this stakeholder will collect on the honest chain and the attacker's chain, respectively. Note that $F' = 0$ is likely when the safety mechanisms of Sect. 2.2.2 are deployed, since it is rational for users to continue to transact on the honest chain as long as the attacker's chain is inferior. Overall, the attacker may need to spend substantially more than $\mu(d + 1)$ coins for the attack to succeed.

In Fig. 2 we illustrate the nature of a double-spending bribe attack.

The above stands in stark contrast to Sect. 2.1.2, as the short-term dominant strategy of the PPCoin stakeholders is to participate in the attack, while the CoA stakeholders will forfeit their reward F if the attack fails. In our setting, the premise of a short-term strategy can be regarded to be that the utility per coin is constant, while the premise of a long-term strategy can be regarded to be that the utility per coin may change due to actions taken by the player.

Notice that the attacker cannot simply bribe the stakeholders who generated the blocks $B_{i_1}, B_{i_2}, B_{i_3}, \ldots, B_{i_d}$ to create an alternative history of length d in a risk-free manner, as their coins will be confiscated if they double-sign.

Formally, let us restrict ourselves to a limited strategy space (cf. [10]) in which players have to choose one of only these two actions (**),

1. Follow the protocol honestly by signing a block that extends the longest known chain.
2. Accept bribe and sign the attacker's block which extends the secretive chain that the attacker builds.

This restriction can be justified under plausible assumptions. In particular, the C_0 penalty can be assumed to be high enough to make the action of double-signing unappealing. This requires the presupposition that the double-signing punishment mechanism is effective in the sense that the evidence of double-signing will be recorded on every fork, and hence the utility of a player is the value of attacker's bribe minus the loss of her C_0 security deposit. This also implies that our analysis here only covers forks that are shorter than the T_0 deposit duration, in Sect. 3 we discuss attacks that involve longer forks.

Our objective is to show that the honest strategy is dominant. In fact, we will show that under further assumptions no attack will be initiated, thus only the honest action will be available to the players.

To analyse what merchants can consider to be an appropriate confidence level for security against double-spending in the CoA system, let us make a reasonable assumption regarding the participation rate of stakeholders in the CoA network.

Density Assumption. Let $\rho > 1/2$. In the longest blockchain, for every segment of K or more potential blocks, at least ρK of those blocks were created.

While this is a simplifying assumption, it is indeed reasonable, as our presupposition for the CoA network is that its security is derived from stakeholders' participation. Notice that we do not assume that the majority of stakeholders are altruistic (i.e., follow the CoA protocol even if it is against their self-interest). Although an altruistic majority would facilitate a system with better security, a rational majority is far more likely to capture reality.

Let B_0 be a block in which some particular payment transactions resides. Let δ denote the amount missing blocks in largest segment with participation rate $\leq 1/2$ prior to B_0, and let ρ' denote the density of the longest segment that follows B_0. In the illustration below, $\delta = 3$ and $\rho' = 10/14$.

Claim 1. Let ε be the average fee amount that a stakeholder earns for creating a block. Assume that stakeholders are restricted to the strategy space (**). Assume that reversing B_0 has a value of V coins to the attacker. If the attacker is rational in the sense that she does not wish to lose coins, then the merchant is safe by waiting until S blocks extend B_0 before sending the merchandise, for S that satisfies $V < \varepsilon(\rho'S - \delta + 1)$.

Proof. By using the safety extension that is described in Sect. 2.2.2, we may consider the blocks in a hostile competing fork to be void of transactions, and therefore it is rational of each colluding stakeholder who could otherwise earn ε coins to demand a bribe of more than this amount. There exist $(1 - \rho')S + \delta$ stakeholders who can contribute to the attack and have already forfeited their turn to create a block, thus the merchant may assume that in the worst case they will collude with the attacker for free. As the other $S + 1$ stakeholders need to be bribed with ε coins each, $V < \varepsilon(S - (1 - \rho')S - \delta + 1) = \varepsilon(\rho'S - \delta + 1)$ implies that the attack is unprofitable.   □

The above argument gives only a crude bound, since it does not capture all the relevant aspects w.r.t. the attack. In particular, the coins that the attacker recovers (in the case of a successful attack) may have less purchasing power, because the cryptocurrency system becomes less valuable whenever double-spending attacks take place.

Claim 2. If the density assumption holds in addition to the assumptions of Claim 1, then the merchant can be confident that it is irrational to carry out a double-spending attack after B_0 has been extended by S blocks, for S that satisfies $V < \varepsilon(\rho S - K + 1)$.

Proof. According to the density assumption, it holds that $K > \delta$, and since the merchant waited until more than K blocks extend B_0 it also holds that $\rho' \geq \rho$. Therefore, $(1 - \rho)S + K \geq (1 - \rho')S + \delta$, and the result follows from Claim 1.□

To get a better sense of things, let us substitute concrete numbers for the above parameters. Suppose for example that $\rho = 7/10$, $K = 20$, $\varepsilon = 10$ coins, and $V = 100$ coins. Hence $10 \cdot (7/10 \cdot S - 19) > 100$ implies that $S = 42$ blocks are sufficient. This means that the merchant will need to wait $\leq 42 \cdot 5\,\text{min}$ or $3.5\,\text{h}$ before sending the merchandise, in case CoA is parameterized according to $G_0 = 5\,\text{min}$.

2.2.4 Majority Takeover.

Consider some stakeholders $A_1, A_2, \ldots, A_m$ who control all of the first ℓ locations in the current round. Suppose that these m stakeholders possess p-fraction of the *total* stake, and they wish to collude and control all the locations in all of the next rounds, thereby creating a winning chain that consists of *only* their blocks. While this strategy may be irrational as it diminishes the value of their stake, perhaps the m stakeholders prefer a competing system and wish to destroy CoA.

Due to interleaving (cf. Sect. 2.2), the starting condition for this attack is more difficult to achieve, as these m stakeholders need to control 2ℓ locations.

Suppose that q-fraction of the honest stake is offline, hence the m stakeholders can give on average a head start of $(\frac{1}{(1-p)(1-q)} - 1)\ell$ blocks to a competing group in each round. Denote $\hat{q} \triangleq (\frac{1}{(1-p)(1-q)} - 1)$. Let Y be the random variable that counts how many of the first $(2+\hat{q})\ell$ locations of the next round will be controlled by the m stakeholders, so $E[Y] = (2 + \hat{q})\ell p$. Using tail inequality, it holds that

$$\Pr(Y > \ell) = \Pr(Y > \frac{1}{(2+\hat{q})p}E[Y]) \leq \exp\{-(\frac{1}{(2+\hat{q})p} - 1)^2 \cdot (2+\hat{q})\ell p \frac{1}{3}\}.$$

Thus, the amount of hash invocations that these m stakeholders need to compute tends toward infeasibility when p is smaller or when ℓ is larger. For example, with $\ell = 459, p = 1/10, q = 1/5$, the m stakeholders will need more than $e^{371} \approx 2^{535}$ hash attempts on average.

Compared with Bitcoin, in a *Proof of Stake* based system such as CoA it is less reasonable to assume that a large combined stake is an hostile external attacker (see [3, Sect. 2.1]), hence p is likely to be small.

2.3 The Dense-CoA Pure *Proof of Stake* Variant

The Dense-CoA pure *proof of stake* protocol is an alternative variant of CoA in which the identities of stakeholders who should create the next blocks are not known far in advance, with the objective of making collusions and bribe attacks more difficult. Another plus point of Dense-CoA is that it makes it more difficult for rational stakeholders to obtain disproportional rewards. The disadvantages of the Dense-CoA protocol are susceptibility to DoS attacks by large stakeholders, and greater communication and space complexities.

In Dense-CoA, each block is created by a group of ℓ stakeholders, rather than by a single stakeholder:

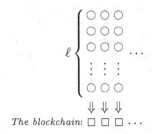

The blockchain: □ □ □ ···

Let $h : \{0,1\}^n \to \{0,1\}^n$ be a one-way permutation. Let us assume for a moment that the block B_{i-1} is associated with a seed $S^{B_{i-1}}$ that was formed by the ℓ stakeholders who created B_{i-1}. Now, the identity of the stakeholder A_ℓ who determines which transactions to include in a block B_i is derived by invoking *follow-the-satoshi* with $hash(i, \ell, S^{B_{i-1}})$ as input, and the identities of the rest of the stakeholders $A_1, A_2, \ldots, A_{\ell-1}$ who must participate in the creation of B_i are derived by invoking *follow-the-satoshi* with $hash(i, j, S^{B_{i-1}})$ for $j \in \{1, 2, \ldots, \ell - 1\}$. These ℓ stakeholders engage in a two-round protocol to create the current block B_i:

- In round 1, for every $j \in \{1, 2, \ldots, \ell\}$, the stakeholder A_j picks a random secret $R_j \in \{0,1\}^n$, and broadcasts $h(R_j)$ to the network.
- In round 2, for every $j \in \{1, 2, \ldots, \ell-1\}$, the stakeholder A_j signs the message $M \triangleq h(R_1) \circ h(R_2) \circ \cdots \circ h(R_\ell)$, and broadcasts her signature $\mathsf{sign}_{sk_j}(M)$ and her preimage R_j to the network.

We require Dense-CoA to use a signature scheme with multisignature [4,8, 11,13] support, therefore A_ℓ can aggregate the signatures $\{\mathsf{sign}_{sk_j}(M)\}_{j=1}^{\ell}$ into a single signature $\hat{s}(M)$. Note that the size of $\hat{s}(M)$ depends only on the security parameter of the signature scheme (and not on ℓ), and the verification time is faster than verifying ℓ ordinary (ECDSA) signatures.

Hence, the stakeholder A_ℓ signs and broadcasts a block B_i that consists of the (Merkle root of the) transactions that she wishes to include, the hash of the previous block B_{i-1}, the current timestamp, the index i, the ℓ preimages $R_1, R_2, \ldots, R_\ell$, and $\hat{s}(M)$. To verify that the block B_i is valid, the network nodes invoke h to compute the images $h(R_1), h(R_2), \ldots, h(R_\ell)$, then concatenate these images to form M, and then check that $\hat{s}(M)$ is a valid signature of M with respect to the public keys $pk_1, pk_2, \ldots, pk_\ell$ that control the winning satoshis of the stakeholders $A_1, A_2, \ldots, A_\ell$.

The seed S^{B_i} is defined as $hash(R_1 \circ R_2 \circ \cdots \circ R_\ell)$. Notice that S^{B_i} is computationally indistinguishable from random even if only a single stakeholder A_j picked a random R_j, under the assumption that n is sufficiently large so that the OWP h is resistant to preimage attacks.

If some of the ℓ stakeholders are offline or otherwise withhold their signatures, then after G_0 time the nodes who follow the protocol will set $t = 1$ and derive alternative ℓ identities from the previous block B_{i-1}, by invoking *follow-the-satoshi* with inputs $hash(i, t\ell+j, S^{B_{i-1}})$ for $j \in \{1, 2, \ldots, \ell\}$. The starting index

$t\ell + j$ should be specified in the new block B_i so that the verification of blocks will be simpler, and the gap between the timestamps of B_{i-1} and B_i must be at least tG_0. As with CoA, the honest nodes consider the blockchain with the largest amount of valid blocks to be the winning blockchain, and disregard blocks with a timestamp that is too far into the future relative to their local clock.

The parameters C_0, C_1, T_0 of the CoA protocol (cf. Sect. 2.2) are utilized by the Dense-CoA protocol in exactly the same way.

The parameter ℓ should be big enough in order to resist large stakeholders from controlling consecutive seeds $\{S^{B_i}, S^{B_{i+1}}, \ldots\}$ and re-deriving themselves. For example, to force a stakeholder who holds 5 % or 10 % of the total stake into making $\approx 2^{100}$ *hash* invocations on average until re-deriving herself as all of the ℓ identities of the next block, we need $\ell = 23$ or $\ell = 30$, respectively. However, if we set $G_0 = 5 \min$ and $\ell = 23$, a malicious stakeholder with e.g. 10 % of the total stake will have $1 - (90/100)^{23} \approx 91\,\%$ probability to be one of the derived stakeholders $A_1, A_2, \ldots, A_\ell$ and then refuse to participate in creating the next block, hence it will take $5 \cdot (1 - 91\,\%)^{-1} \approx 56 \min$ on average to create each next valid block while this attack is taking place (actually less than 56 min because chains that extend blocks prior to the last block can also become the longest valid chain).

Overall, the main difference between the Dense-CoA and CoA protocols is that Dense-CoA offers improved security over CoA in terms of double-spending attacks, but weaker security against DoS attacks by large stakeholders who wish to harm the cryptocurrency. Also, Dense-CoA prevents a rational stakeholder from influencing the seed in an attempt to earn more rewards than her fair share, unless she colludes with all the other $\ell - 1$ stakeholders who create the next block. The Dense-CoA protocol is less efficient than CoA due to the preimages $R_1, R_2, \ldots, R_\ell$ that need to be stored in each valid block, and the two-round protocol that requires a greater amount of network communication to create each successive block.

3   Solidification of the Ledger History

Any decentralized cryptocurrency system in which extending the ledger history requires no effort entails the danger of costless simulation [14], meaning that an alternative history that starts from an earlier point of the ledger can be prepared without depleting physical resources and hence without a cost. This is a problem because a rational adversary who has little or no stake in the system may try to attack by replacing an arbitrarily long suffix of the current ledger history with an alternative continuation that benefits her. Further, a malicious adversary who does not operate out of self-interest is also more likely to attempt this kind of an attack, as she would not incur a monetary loss for executing the attack.

In the case of pure *Proof of Stake* systems, this danger can manifest itself in the following form. Consider participants who held coins in the system a long time ago and have since traded those coins in exchange for other goods, so they are no longer stakeholders of this system. These participants can now collude to extend the ledger from the point at which they had control over the system, and it may indeed be rational for them to mount this attack because it is costless and would have no detrimental outcome from their standpoint, as they have no stake in the current system.

More specifically, let us examine how this attack looks like in the CoA or Dense-CoA systems. Even a single stakeholder with few coins can fork the blockchain and create an alternative branch with large enough time gaps as she re-derives herself to create subsequent blocks, but according to the timestamp rules for valid blocks, the other participants will reject this alternative branch (even though it contains more blocks) because the timestamps will be too far ahead in the future relative to their local time. Therefore, if the average participation level among current stakeholders is $p\%$, and the stakeholders who collude to carry out this attack have had control at the earlier history over $q\%$ of the coins, then $q > p$ implies that the attack will succeed. Because $p\% = 1$ is highly unlikely, and collusion among participants who held $q\% > p\%$ stake at an earlier point is costless and rational, this attack vector appears to be quite dangerous.

To mitigate this attack, we propose periodic checkpointing as a rigid protocol rule that extends the CoA and Dense-CoA protocols, as follows:

- Denote by $T_0 = 2T_1$ the double-spending safety bound of Sect. 2.2.
- The blocks at gaps of T_1 are designated as *checkpoint* blocks: the genesis block is a checkpoint block, and any block that extends a checkpoint block by exactly T_1 additional blocks is a candidate checkpoint block.
- When a node that follows the protocol receives for the first time a candidate checkpoint block B_j that extends the candidate checkpoint block B_i such that $j = i + T_1$ (or $j > i + T_1$ if stakeholders were inactive), she solidifies B_i meaning that she disallows any changes to the history from the genesis block until B_i, though B_j can still be discarded as a result of a competing fork.

Since the double-spending safety bound is T_0, a stakeholder who creates a block can spend the coins only after an intermediate checkpoint block is already solidified, so the costless simulation threat is mitigated (if C_0 is substantial).

This can be seen in the following illustration:

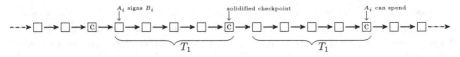

However, this checkpointing mechanism presents two significant problems:

1. New nodes who enter the decentralized network for the first time cannot tell whether the checkpoint blocks that they receive are trustworthy.
2. Due to propagation lag, adversarial stakeholders can collude by preparing an alternative branch of length $T_1 + 1$, and broadcast the competing forks at the same time, thus creating an irreversible split among the network nodes.

The first problem needs to be handled by utilizing a "Web of Trust" type of mechanism that is external to the cryptocurrency system. This means that participants who are unaware of the current state of the system should rely on reputable sources to fetch the blockchain data up to the latest checkpoint.

The second problem should also be resolved manually, meaning that participants who become aware of a network split can decide to instruct their node to switch to the other faction, e.g. if they see that they are in the minority. Note, however, that the second problem becomes increasingly unlikely for larger T_1 values. The exemplary parameters that we proposed in Sect. 2.2 imply that a fork of $T_1 + 1$ blocks represents more than one week of ledger history.

4   Conclusion

It is challenging to design sustainable decentralized cryptocurrency protocols that do not rely on depletion of physical scarce resources for their security maintenance. Our analysis argues that the security of existing such protocols is lacking. We offer novel constructions of pure *Proof of Stake* protocols that avoid depletion of physical scarce resources, and argue that our protocols offer better security than existing protocols. Future work could extend the scope of our analysis to broader strategy spaces.

References

1. Bahack, L., Courtois, N.: (2014). http://arxiv.org/abs/1402.1718
2. Ben-Or, M., Linial, N.: Collective coin flipping. In: Micali, S. (ed.) Randomness and Computation, pp. 91–115. Academic Press, New York (1990)
3. Bentov, I., Lee, C., Mizrahi, A., Rosenfeld, M.: Proof of activity. In: ACM SIG-METRICS Workshop - NetEcon (2014). http://eprint.iacr.org/2014/452
4. Boldyreva, A.: Efficient threshold signature, multisignature and blind signature schemes based on the gap-Diffie-Hellman-group signature scheme. In: PKC2003 (2003)
5. Eyal, I.: The miner's dilemma. In: 36th IEEE S&P (2015)
6. Eyal, I., Sirer, E.G.: Majority is not enough: bitcoin mining is vulnerable. In: Christin, N., Safavi-Naini, R. (eds.) FC 2014. LNCS, vol. 8437, pp. 431–449. Springer, Heidelberg (2014)
7. Garay, J., Kiayias, A., Leonardos, N.: The bitcoin backbone protocol: analysis and applications. In: Eurocrypt 2015 (2015)
8. Itakura, K., Nakamura, K.: A public key cryptosystem suitable for digital multisignatures. NEC Res. Dev. **71**, 1–8 (1983)
9. Kamp, J., Zuckerman, D.: Deterministic extractors for bit-fixing sources and exposure-resilient cryptography. In: SICOMP, vol. 36 (2007)
10. Kroll, J., Davey, I., Felten, E.: The economics of bitcoin mining, or bitcoin in the presence of adversaries. In: 12th WEIS (2013)
11. Lu, S., Ostrovsky, R., Sahai, A., Shacham, H., Waters, B.: Sequential aggregate signatures. J. Cryptology **26**(2), 340–373 (2013)
12. Nakamoto, S.: Bitcoin: a peer-to-peer electronic cash system. Bitcoin.org
13. Micali, S., Ohta K., Reyzin, L.: Accountable-subgroup multisignatures (extended abstract). In: Proceedings of CCS 2001, pp. 245–254. ACM Press (2001)
14. Poelstra, A.: (2014). https://download.wpsoftware.net/bitcoin/pos.pdf
15. Rosenfeld, M.: (2012). http://arxiv.org/abs/1402.2009
16. User "cunicula" (2012). https://bitcointalk.org/index.php?topic=122291
17. User "QuantumM..." (2011). https://bitcointalk.org/index.php?topic=27787

First Workshop on Secure Voting Systems, VOTING 2016

Coercion-Resistant Internet Voting with Everlasting Privacy

Philipp Locher[1,2]([✉]), Rolf Haenni[1], and Reto E. Koenig[1]

[1] Bern University of Applied Sciences, 2501 Biel, Switzerland
{philipp.locher,rolf.haenni,reto.koenig}@bfh.ch
[2] University of Fribourg, 1700 Fribourg, Switzerland
philipp.locher@unifr.ch

Abstract. The cryptographic voting protocol presented in this paper offers public verifiability, everlasting privacy, and coercion-resistance simultaneously. Voters are authenticated anonymously based on perfectly hiding commitments and zero-knowledge proofs. Their vote and participation secrecy is therefore protected independently of computational intractability assumptions or trusted authorities. Coercion-resistance is achieved based on a new mechanism for deniable vote updating. To evade coercion by submitting a final secret vote update, the voter needs not to remember the history of all precedent votes. The protocol uses two types of mix networks to guarantee that vote updating cannot be detected by the coercer. The input sizes and running times of the mix networks are quadratic with respect to the number of submitted ballots.

1 Introduction

Publishing the list of submitted ballots is a prerequisite for introducing public verifiability in electronic voting systems. Since the encrypted votes included in the ballots are protected by cryptographic techniques available today, there is no guarantee that the protection will withstand future advances in cryptanalysis and computational abilities. The secrecy of a vote submitted today is therefore not guaranteed to last forever. As a consequence, election organizers are often concerned about handing over the election data to everyone, even if this results in limiting the scope of public verifiability. Another serious concern for election organizers is the increased scalability of vote buying, bribery, or coercion attacks in an entirely digitalized environment. Providing a receipt to allow individual verifiability and not providing a receipt to disallow vote buying is a strong conflict in the design of electronic voting protocols.

1.1 Related Work

To the best of our knowledge, everlasting privacy and coercion-resistance have never been addressed together in a single cryptographic voting protocol. As each of them is a highly challenging problem on its own, offering them together seems to be nearly impossible. In the existing literature on everlasting privacy, the

© International Financial Cryptography Association 2016
J. Clark et al. (Eds.): FC 2016 Workshops, LNCS 9604, pp. 161–175, 2016.
DOI: 10.1007/978-3-662-53357-4_11

adversary is assumed to possess unlimited computational power and an infinite amount of time to break the privacy of the votes. Some of the proposed solutions are designed for the traditional setting, in which ballots are cast in a private polling booth, whereas other protocols offer everlasting privacy for Internet elections with the aid of trusted authorities. In each of these proposals, a subset of colluding authorities could potentially break the privacy of the votes. The first protocol not relying on trusted authorities has been proposed recently by Locher and Haenni (LH15) [8]. They use an efficient set membership proof and a proof of knowledge of the representation of a committed value to achieve everlasting privacy. Their protocol is a direct predecessor of the protocol presented in this paper.

In the literature on coercion-resistance, there are two complementary strategies for a voter to evade coercion. In the protocol of Juels et al. (JCJ05) [7], the voter under coercion presents a fake credential to the adversary. The system is designed in a way that ballots submitted with a fake credential are silently eliminated during tallying using a quadratic number of plaintext equivalence tests (PET). The adversary model of JCJ05 allows voters to escape from adversarial control for a short moment during the voting period, which they can use for submitting a ballot using their true credentials. The second principal strategy against coercion is to let voters update their votes arbitrarily many times. In some protocols implementing this strategy, voters need to remember the history of all precedent votes when submitting the final ballot, which implies that simulation attacks cannot be prevented. In a more recent protocol by Achenbach et al. (AKLM15) [1], voters can submit a final ballot without remembering any previous votes and such that no coercer can learn whether vote updating has taken place or not. To achieve what they call *deniable vote updating*, they need trusted authorities performing jointly a quadratic number of encrypted plaintext equivalence tests (EPET). The adversary model of AKLM15 allows voters to escape from adversarial control at the end of the voting period, which is a slightly stronger assumption than in JCJ05. On the other hand, voters under coercion can follow the adversary's instructions without lying or concealing something.

1.2   Contribution

The contribution of this paper is a new cryptographic protocol for remote electronic voting. For voters not observed by an adversary before or during vote casting, it provides everlasting privacy without relying on trusted authorities or computational intractability assumptions. This means that no one will ever be able to break the secrecy of the vote or the secrecy of the voter's participation. The protocol also offers adequate protection against vote buying, bribery, and coercion attacks by polynomially bounded adversaries. As far as we know, this protocol is the first to offer everlasting privacy and coercion-resistance simultaneously.

The core of the protocol is composed of a set membership proof, a proof of known representation of a committed value, and a new tallying process that guarantees that no adversary can learn if particular votes have been updated or not. The proposed mechanism is based on two types of mix networks, which are applied to a quadratic number of input encryptions. The shuffling destroys any link to the original list of submitted ballots, but at the same time preserves the information whether a given vote has been updated or not. The quadratic running time of the tallying procedure leads to a performance comparable to JCJ05 and AKLM15. Our approach is therefore not an efficient solution for large elections.

1.3 Paper Overview

We present our new protocol on two different levels of technical abstraction. In Sect. 2, we give a high-level overview of the approach by specifying the underlying adversary and trust model, and by discussing the resulting protocol properties. In Sect. 3, we introduce the cryptographic primitives, present the cryptographic details of the protocol, and provide a more precise discussion of the security properties. We summarize the findings of this paper in Sect. 4.

2 Coercion-Resistant Internet Voting with Everlasting Privacy

The approach presented in this paper is the first cryptographic voting protocol that offers verifiability, coercion-resistance, and everlasting privacy simultaneously. Three types of parties are involved in the protocol: an election administration, a group of trusted authorities, and the voters. They communicate over different communication channels. During registration, the protocol requires an authentic channel between voters and the election administration. Furthermore, a broadcast channel with memory—in the form of a robust append-only public bulletin board—is needed for collecting the election data. We assume that the election administration and the trusted authorities have their own designated areas on the bulletin board. Finally, for sending their votes to the bulletin board, voters need access to an anonymous channel. We assume that it is impossible to intercept and record the complete traffic over this channel during an election and storing the intercepted data for future use [2].

2.1 Adversary Model and Trust Assumptions

The general adversarial goals are to break the integrity or secrecy of the votes or to influence the election outcome via bribery or coercion. We consider active adversaries, which may interfere with the voting process at any point to reach their goals. To achieve coercion-resistance, we assume that a threshold number of authorities not colluding with the adversary is available for the tallying process. We also assume that no adversary can control the machines used during the voting process.[1]

---

[1] We are aware that requiring a secure platform is a strong and probably unrealistic assumption. We do not explicitly address this problem in this paper.

To discuss the aspect of everlasting privacy, we consider two types of adversaries with very different computational capabilities.

Present adversaries act before, during, or shortly after an election, i.e., within the cryptoperiod of the involved cryptographic keys. We assume present adversaries to be polynomially bounded and thus incapable of solving supposedly hard problems such as computing discrete logarithms in some large groups or breaking cryptographic primitives such as contemporary hash functions. Therefore, they cannot efficiently open computationally binding commitments or generate valid proof transcripts for zero-knowledge proofs without knowing the secret inputs. On the other hand, present adversaries may have the power and resources to bribe or coerce a large number of voters. A present adversary in our model is therefore equivalent to the adversary in JCJ05, except for the additional assumption that voters can escape adversarial control for submitting a final vote update. As discussed in AKLM15, this is a necessary pre-condition for offering coercion-resistance based on deniable vote updating.

Future adversaries may become active at any point in the future, i.e., strictly after the tallying phase of the election under attack. We assume that future adversaries cannot collude with present adversaries, for example by sharing information. On the other hand, we assume them to possess unlimited resources in terms of computational power and time. Clearly, contemporary cryptography will be completely useless in the presence of such an adversary, and any private keying material used in an election today will be revealed. However, the secrets hidden in perfectly hiding commitments or zero-knowledge proofs will never be revealed, even if they were generated today.

2.2 Protocol Overview

The protocol is a continuation of LH15. Trusted authorities are needed to guarantee fairness and to add coercion-resistance in form of deniable vote updating, but not for privacy. The same applies to computational intractability assumptions. They are only needed to prevent the creation of invalid ballots during vote casting and to allow voters to deny the submission of an updated vote, but not to protect privacy in the long run.

Like in LH15, the core of the protocol is a combination of a set membership proof and a proof of known representation of a committed value [3,5]. When casting a vote, the voter provides a zero-knowledge proof of knowledge of the representation of one of the registered public voter credentials. The same voter may submit multiple ballots, but the tallying procedure guarantees that only the last vote counts. In this way, precedent votes can be overridden without remembering their history. To guarantee that vote updating is deniable, we use two different types of mix networks to unlink the votes of a given voter from the voter's public credential. The main challenge in this step is to detect and exclude updated votes in a verifiable way without leaking any information to a potential coercer. The entire voting procedure consists of four consecutive steps (the first two steps are identical and the third step is very similar to LH15):

Registration. The voter creates a pair of private and public credentials and sends the public credential over an authentic channel to the election administration.

Election Preparation. The election administration publishes the list of public voter credentials—one for every registered voter—on the public bulletin board.

Vote Casting. The voter creates an electronic ballot and sends it over an anonymous channel to the public bulletin board. The ballot consists of the encrypted vote, a commitment to the public credential, a homomorphic encryption of an election credential, and the above-mentioned composition of zero-knowledge proofs. The voter's public credential and the election credential are derived from the same private credential.

Tallying. The trusted authorities verify the proofs included in the submitted ballots and eliminate ballots with invalid proofs. For each remaining ballot, the authorities compute a list of ciphertexts with the following property: whenever the ballot has been updated, at least one of its plaintexts is equal to 1. The construction of this list is similar to AKLM15, but to sort out updated ballots, we first shuffle the list in a verifiable mix network. The shuffle applies under encryption a one-way function to all plaintexts different from 1. In this way, the shuffled list is unlinked from the original list, but the above property that an encryption of 1 is an indicator for an updated ballot is preserved. By attaching the encrypted vote to the resulting shuffled list, we obtain an intermediate ballot containing all necessary information to conclude the tallying process. The list of all intermediate ballots is shuffled in a verifiable re-encryption mix network to unlink them from the original ballots on the bulletin board. For each output ballot of this shuffle, the trusted authorities need to decide about including the ballot in the final tally. For this, they start decrypting the ciphertexts until a plaintext equal to 1 is revealed. If this happens, the ballot is sorted out. The encrypted votes included in the remaining ballots are decrypted and counted. To enable public verification, all steps performed by a trusted authority must be accompanied by non-interactive zero-knowledge proofs.

This protocol provides everlasting privacy for the same reasons as its predecessor protocol LH15. All the identifying information contained in a ballot is either a perfectly hiding commitment or a zero-knowledge proof. To provide coercion-resistance, a relatively complex tallying phase is necessary to sort out updated votes in a verifiable way, but such that no coercer can learn if a ballot has been updated or not. Further aspects of coercion-resistance are discussed in the next subsection. Note that the tallying procedure requires two mix networks, which are both applied to a quadratic number of input encryptions. The performance of the tallying procedure is therefore comparable to AKLM15.

2.3   Discussion of Coercion-Resistance

To protect an electronic voting system from adversaries trying to bribe or coerce voters, receipt-freeness is a necessary precondition. Intuitively, a receipt consists of some auxiliary non-public information, which is sufficient for voters to prove towards a passive adversary how they voted. According to JCJ05, there are at least three additional coercive attacks, which receipt-freeness alone can not prevent. Voters could be forced to cast a random vote (randomization attack), to abstain from voting (forced-abstention attack), or to hand the private keying material over to the coercer (simulation attack).

Deniable vote updating as implemented in our protocol is an adequate counter-measure to coercion in general. Whatever a present adversary forces the voter into, the voter can extinguish the demands of the adversary by submitting secretly a final vote. Other than JCJ05, deniable vote updating is convincing by the fact that a voter can act exactly as demanded by the coercer without lying or pretending. In addition, as casting the last vote is independent of the history of votes submitted previously, the voter must not memorize any state. In other words, submitting a final vote will always erase any previous votes, even if they had been cast by the adversary. Erasing votes in this way remains undetected by the adversary, because the election credential added to the ballot is encrypted and obfuscated during the tallying phase. As a result, a present adversary will never succeed with a randomization, forced-abstention, or simulation attack.

A general problem of coercion-resistant systems such as JCJ, which are based the voter's ability to lie about some secret credential in the presence of the coercer, is the unintended use of a wrong credential. The resulting ballot will appear on the bulletin board and the voter can check its inclusion, but the vote will not be taken into account in the final tally. Since the system cannot respond with a warning in such a case, voters are unable to detect using a wrong credential. In a protocol based on deniable vote updating, the system can issue such a warning when votes are cast with a wrong credential. This is a remarkable difference when considering individual verifiability.

The everlasting privacy property of our protocol even prevents an additional coercive attack not discussed in JCJ05. A future adversary may try to coerce a voter by claiming to know how the voter has voted in the past and by threatening the voter with making it public (*"I know how you voted and I am going to tell everyone, unless..."*). In a protocol that offers everlasting privacy, this claim cannot be justified whatsoever.

3   Detailed Cryptographic Protocol

In this section, we present the cryptographic details of our new coercion-resistant protocol for electronic elections with everlasting privacy. We start with a short discussion of cryptographic preliminaries. Then we provide a detailed formal description of the protocol and analyse its security properties.

3.1   Cryptographic Preliminaries

Let $\mathcal{G}_p$ be a multiplicative cyclic group of prime order p, for which the DL assumption is believed to hold. Furthermore, let $\mathbb{G}_q \subset \mathbb{Z}_p^*$, be a large prime-order subgroup of the group of integers modulo p. Finally, suppose that independent generators $g_0, g_1 \in \mathcal{G}_p$ and $h, h_0, h_1, \ldots \in \mathbb{G}_q$ are publicly known. Independence with respect to generators of a cyclic group means that their relative discrete logarithms are not known to anyone.

Homomorphic Commitments and Encryptions. In our protocol, we use two instances of the perfectly hiding Pedersen commitment scheme, one over $\mathcal{G}_p$ and one over $\mathbb{G}_q$. We distinguish them by $\mathrm{com}_p(u, r) = g_0^r g_1^u$ for a commitment to $u \in \mathbb{Z}_p$ with randomization $r \in \mathbb{Z}_p$ and $\mathrm{com}_q(v, s) = h_0^s h_1^v$ for a commitment to $v \in \mathbb{Z}_q$ with randomization $s \in \mathbb{Z}_q$. In the case of $\mathbb{G}_q$, we write $\mathrm{com}_q(v_1, \ldots, v_n, s) = h_0^s h_1^{v_1} \cdots h_n^{v_n}$ for a commitment to n values $v_1, \ldots, v_n \in \mathbb{Z}_q$.

The protocol also requires an instance of an ElGamal encryption scheme over $\mathbb{G}_q$, where $x \in \mathbb{Z}_q$ is a shared private key and $y = h^x \in \mathbb{G}_q$ a public key. We write $E = \mathrm{enc}_y(m, r) = (h^r, my^r) \in \mathbb{G}_q \times \mathbb{G}_q$ for encrypting a message $m \in \mathbb{G}_q$ with randomization $r \in \mathbb{Z}_q$ and $m = \mathrm{dec}_x(E) = ba^{-x}$ for decrypting a ciphertext $E = (a, b)$ in a distributed way using the private key shares of x. We write $\mathbf{M} = \mathrm{dec}_x(\mathbf{E}) = (m_1, \ldots, m_n)$ for decrypting a list of ciphertexts $\mathbf{E} = (E_1, \ldots, E_n)$. To re-encrypt a ciphertext E with a new randomization $r' \in \mathbb{Z}_q$, we use the standard procedure $E' = \mathrm{reEnc}_y(E, r') = E \cdot \mathrm{enc}_y(1, r')$ of multiplying E with an encryption of 1. We write $\mathbf{E}' = \mathrm{reEnc}_y(\mathbf{E}, \mathbf{r}') = (E_1', \ldots, E_n')$ to re-encrypt a list of ciphertexts $\mathbf{E} = (E_1, \ldots, E_n)$ with new randomizations $\mathbf{r}' = (r_1', \ldots, r_n')$.

Zero-Knowledge Proofs. Our protocol relies strongly on various non-interactive zero-knowledge proofs of knowledge. A fundamental proof is the preimage proof $NIZKP[(a) : b = \phi(a)]$ for a one-way group homomorphism $\phi : X \to Y$, where $a = \phi^{-1}(b) \in X$ is the secret preimage of a public value $b \in Y$. Examples of such preimage proofs result from the above homomorphic commitment and encryption schemes, for example $NIZKP[(u, r) : C = \mathrm{com}_p(u, r)]$ for proving knowledge of the opening of a Pedersen commitment, $NIZKP[(m, r) : E = \mathrm{enc}_y(m, r)]$ for proving knowledge of the plaintext and randomization of an ElGamal ciphertext, or $NIZKP[(x) : \mathbf{M} = \mathrm{dec}_x(\mathbf{E}) \wedge y = h^x]$ for proving knowledge of the private key used in the decryption of a list of ciphertexts.

The most common construction of a non-interactive preimage proof is the Σ-protocol in combination with the Fiat-Shamir heuristic. Proofs constructed in this way are perfect zero-knowledge in the random oracle model. Their transcript consists of one or multiple commitments and one or multiple responses to a challenge obtained from querying the random oracle with the public inputs and the commitments. In practice, the random oracle is implemented with a cryptographic hash function. In the protocol description, we will write $\pi = NIZKP[\cdot]$ for the transcripts of non-interactive proofs.

Set Membership Proof. Let $U = \{u_1 \ldots, u_N\}$ be a finite set of values $u_i \in \mathbb{Z}_p$ and $C = \mathrm{com}_p(u, r)$ a commitment to an element $u \in U$. Both U and C are publicly known. With a *set membership proof*, denoted by

$$NIZKP[(u, r) : C = \mathrm{com}_p(u, r) \wedge u \in U],$$

the prover demonstrates knowledge of corresponding values $u \in U$ and $r \in \mathbb{Z}_p$. A general way of constructing a set membership proof is to demonstrate that $P(u) = 0$ for the polynomial $P(X) = \prod_{i=1}^{N}(X - u_i)$. This proof, denoted by

$$NIZKP[(u, r) : C = \mathrm{com}_p(u, r) \wedge P(u) = 0],$$

is a particular case of a *polynomial evaluation proof.* In a recent publication, Bayer and Groth proposed a polynomial evaluation proof with a logarithmic size, which is the current state-of-the-art [5].

Proof of Known Representation. In a cyclic group such as $\mathbb{G}_q$ with generators $h_1, \ldots, h_n$, a tuple $(v_1, \ldots, v_n) \in \mathbb{Z}_q^n$ is called *DL-representation* (or simply *representation*) of $u \in \mathbb{G}_q$, if $u = h_1^{v_1} \cdots h_n^{v_n}$ [6]. For such a value $u \in \mathbb{G}_q \subset \mathbb{Z}_p$, let $C = \mathrm{com}_p(u, r)$ and $D = \mathrm{com}_q(v_1, \ldots, v_n, s)$ be publicly known commitments. Following Au et al. [3], a proof of known *representation of a committed value* (or simply *representation proof*), denoted by

$$NIZKP[(u, r, v_1, \ldots, v_n, s) : C = \mathrm{com}_p(u, r) \wedge$$
$$D = \mathrm{com}_q(v_1, \ldots, v_n, s) \wedge u = h_1^{v_1} \cdots h_n^{v_n}],$$

demonstrates that the tuple of committed values in D is a DL-representation of the committed value in C.

Cryptographic Shuffle. The input of a cryptographic shuffle is a list $\mathbf{Z} = (z_1, \ldots, z_n)$ of input values $z_i \in Z$. The mixer applies a keyed one-way function $f : Z \times K \to Z$ to each input value z_i and permutes the results by picking a random permutation $\phi : [1, n] \to [1, n]$ from the set Φ_n of permutations of length n. The output of a cryptographic shuffle is therefore a list $\mathbf{Z}' = (z_1', \ldots, z_n')$ of values $z_j' = f(z_i, k_i)$ for indices $j = \phi(i)$ and keys $k_i \in K$. Additionally, the mixer proves the correctness of the shuffle using one of the existing techniques [4,9]. We denote the two steps of this procedure by

$$(\mathbf{Z}', \pi_{\mathbf{Z}}) = \mathrm{shuffle}_f^{\phi}(\mathbf{Z}, k_1, \ldots, k_n),$$

where $\pi_{\mathbf{Z}}$ is the transcript of the non-interactive zero-knowledge proof. To prevent that a single mixer must be fully trusted, the shuffling needs to be performed by multiple independent mixers in a mix network. The unlinkability between input and output is guaranteed as long as at least one permutation remains secret.

In our protocol, we need two instances of a cryptographic shuffle. In the first case, the input is a list $\mathbf{E} = (E_1, \ldots, E_n)$ of ElGamal ciphertexts $E_i \in \mathbb{G}_q \times \mathbb{G}_q$. For random values $\gamma_i \in_R \mathbb{Z}_q \backslash \{0\}$, the function $\exp(E_i, \gamma_i) = E_i^{\gamma_i}$ is applied to each input ciphertext E_i, which gives us $(\mathbf{E}', \pi_{\mathbf{E}}) = \text{shuffle}_{\text{exp}}^{\phi}(\mathbf{E}, \gamma_1, \ldots, \gamma_n)$.[2] In this particular shuffle, both the ciphertexts and the plaintexts are unlinked from their original values in $\mathbf{E}$. There is only one exception: an encryption of 1 remains an encryption of 1.

In the second case, the input list $\mathbf{EE} = (\mathbf{E}_1, \ldots, \mathbf{E}_n)$ contains n individual lists $\mathbf{E}_i = \{E_{i,1}, \ldots, E_{i,n}\}$ of ElGamal ciphertexts, i.e., $\mathbf{EE}$ contains a total of n^2 ciphertexts $E_{i,j} \in \mathbb{G}_q \times \mathbb{G}_q$. For random values $\mathbf{r}_i' = (r_{i,1}', \ldots, r_{i,n}') \in_R \mathbb{Z}_q^n$, the function $\text{reEnc}_y(\mathbf{E}_i, \mathbf{r}_i')$ is applied to each input list $\mathbf{E}_i$. In other words, $(\mathbf{EE}', \pi_{\mathbf{EE}}) = \text{shuffle}_{\text{reEnc}_y}^{\phi}(\mathbf{EE}, \mathbf{r}_1', \ldots, \mathbf{r}_n')$ re-encrypts all n^2 ciphertexts, but only the rows of the input $\mathbf{EE}$ are permuted, not the columns.

3.2 Protocol Description

As outlined in Sect. 2.2, the protocol consists of four consecutive phases. We will now present the details of each phase using the cryptographic primitives and formal notation introduced in the previous section. Summaries of all phases are included in corresponding figures at the end of each subsection. Note that the registration and election preparation phase are identical to the predecessor protocol in LH15, and vote casting is very similar. To achieve coercion-resistance, complexity has been added mainly to the tallying phase.

Registration. The first step of the protocol is the registration of voters before an election. To register, the voter picks a *private credential* $(\alpha, \beta) \in_R \mathbb{Z}_q \times \mathbb{Z}_q$ at random and computes the *public credential* $u = h_1^{\alpha} h_2^{\beta} \in \mathbb{G}_q$. Note that the private credential is a DL-representation of the public credential. Finally, the voter sends u over an authentic channel to the election administration (Fig. 1).

Registration (Voter):

1. Pick private credential $(\alpha, \beta) \in_R \mathbb{Z}_q \times \mathbb{Z}_q$.
2. Compute public credential $u = h_1^{\alpha} h_2^{\beta} \in \mathbb{G}_q$.
3. Send u over an authentic channel to the election administration.

Fig. 1. Summary of the registration phase.

Election Preparation. After the registration phase, the election administration defines the list $\mathbf{U} = ((V_1, u_1), \ldots, (V_N, u_N))$ based on the electoral roll. Each pair $(V_i, u_i) \in \mathbf{U}$ links a public credential u_i to the corresponding voter identity V_i. Next, the list $\mathbf{A} = (a_0, \ldots, a_N)$ of coefficients $a_i \in \mathbb{Z}_p$ of the polynomial $P(X) = \prod_{i=1}^{N}(X - u_i) \in \mathbb{Z}_p[X]$ is computed to allow voters the creation of

---
[2] Note that $\gamma_i \neq 0$ is a crucial pre-condition to avoid trivial output ciphertexts $(1,1)$. The verifier of $\pi_{\mathbf{E}}$ must therefore check $E_i \neq (1,1)$ for every $E_i \in \mathbf{E}$ and reject the proof if one of the checks fails.

the set membership proof during vote casting.[3] Finally, an independent *election generator* $\hat{h} \in \mathbb{G}_q$ is defined in some publicly reproducible way and $(\mathbf{U}, \mathbf{A}, \hat{h})$ is posted into the administration's designated area of the public bulletin board (Fig. 2).

Election Preparation (Election Administration):

1. Define $\mathbf{U} = ((V_1, u_1), \ldots, (V_N, u_N))$ based on the electoral roll.
2. Compute coefficients $\mathbf{A} = (a_0, \ldots, a_N)$ of $P(X) = \prod_{i=1}^{N}(X - u_i) \in \mathbb{Z}_p[X]$.
3. Define election generator $\hat{h} \in \mathbb{G}_q$.
4. Post $(\mathbf{U}, \mathbf{A}, \hat{h})$ into the designated area of the bulletin board.

Fig. 2. Summary of the election preparation phase.

Vote Casting. During the election, voters select their vote by choosing their preferred election options and encoding them by an element of the set $\mathbb{V} \subset \mathbb{G}_q$ of valid votes. We assume that the election options, their encoding in $\mathbb{V}$, and the public key y of the trusted authorities are publicly known.

To cast a vote, the voter computes a commitment $C = \text{com}_p(u, r)$ of the public credential and a commitment $D = \text{com}_q(\alpha, \beta, s)$ of the private credentials. Next, the voter computes an encryption $E = \text{enc}_y(\hat{h}^\beta, \rho)$ of the *election credential* $\hat{h}^\beta \in \mathbb{G}_q$ and an encryption $F = \text{enc}_y(v, \sigma)$ of the encoded vote $v \in \mathbb{V}$. Finally, the voter generates three non-interactive zero-knowledge proofs. The first proof,

$$\pi_1 = NIZKP[(u, r) : C = \text{com}_p(u, r) \wedge P(u) = 0],$$

is a set membership proof proving that C is indeed a commitment to the public credential of one of the eligible voters listed in $\mathbf{U}$. The second proof,

$$\pi_2 = NIZKP[(u, r, \alpha, \beta, s) : C = \text{com}_p(u, r) \wedge D = \text{com}_q(\alpha, \beta, s) \wedge u = h_1^\alpha h_2^\beta],$$

is a proof of known representation of the committed value in C. It prevents voters from taking someone else's credential from $\mathbf{U}$. Finally, the third proof,

$$\pi_3 = NIZKP[(\alpha, \beta, s, \rho, v, \sigma) : D = \text{com}_q(\alpha, \beta, s) \wedge E = \text{enc}_y(\hat{h}^\beta, \rho) \wedge F = \text{enc}_y(v, \sigma)],$$

demonstrates that D and E have been generated using the same value β and that the vote contained in F is known to the voter. The two commitments, the two ciphertexts, and the three proofs form the ballot $B = (C, D, E, F, \pi_1, \pi_2, \pi_3)$,

---

[3] As the computation of the coefficients is quite expensive ($\frac{1}{2}N^2$ multiplications in $\mathbb{Z}_p$), it is performed by the election administration, possibly already during the registration phase in an incremental way. Note that the coefficients can be re-computed and verified by anyone, and voters can efficiently verify the inclusion of their public credential u by checking $P(u) = 0$.

which is posted to the bulletin board over an anonymous channel. The voter may submit multiple such ballots during the election period. If multiple identical copies of the same ballot are posted to the bulletin board, we assume that only one of them is stored (Fig. 3).[4]

Vote Casting (Voter):

1. Select vote $v \in \mathbb{V}$.
2. Pick $r \in_R \mathbb{Z}_p$ and compute $C = \mathrm{com}_p(u, r) \in \mathcal{G}_p$.
3. Pick $s \in_R \mathbb{Z}_q$ and compute $D = \mathrm{com}_q(\alpha, \beta, s) \in \mathbb{G}_q$.
4. Pick $\rho \in_R \mathbb{Z}_q$ and compute $E = \mathrm{enc}_y(\hat{h}^\beta, \rho) \in \mathbb{G}_q \times \mathbb{G}_q$.
5. Pick $\sigma \in_R \mathbb{Z}_q$ and compute $F = \mathrm{enc}_y(v, \sigma) \in \mathbb{G}_q \times \mathbb{G}_q$.
6. Compute non-interactive proofs:

$$\pi_1 = NIZKP[(u, r) : C = \mathrm{com}_p(u, r) \wedge P(u) = 0],$$

$$\pi_2 = NIZKP[(u, r, \alpha, \beta, s) : C = \mathrm{com}_p(u, r) \wedge D = \mathrm{com}_q(\alpha, \beta, s) \wedge u = h_1^\alpha h_2^\beta],$$

$$\pi_3 = NIZKP[(\alpha, \beta, s, \rho, v, \sigma) : D = \mathrm{com}_q(\alpha, \beta, s) \wedge$$
$$E = \mathrm{enc}_y(\hat{h}^\beta, \rho) \wedge F = \mathrm{enc}_y(v, \sigma)].$$

7. Post $B = (C, D, E, F, \pi_1, \pi_2, \pi_3)$ to the bulletin board over an anonymous channel.

Fig. 3. Summary of the vote casting phase.

Tallying. At the end of the election period, the ballots submitted to the bulletin board need to be processed by the trusted authorities. We present this process by looking at the group of trusted authorities as a single entity performing the necessary shuffling and decryption tasks jointly. In reality, different trusted authorities will perform respective tasks using their own secret inputs and random values. The cryptographic shuffling is a serial and the distributed decryption (usually) a parallel process.

To initiate the tallying process, the trusted authority retrieves the list **B** of all ballots from the bulletin board. We assume that the ballots in **B** are ordered according to their submission. The authority verifies the non-interactive proofs π_1, π_2, π_3 for each ballot $(C, D, E, F, \pi_1, \pi_2, \pi_3) \in \mathbf{B}$, and ballots with invalid proofs are eliminated. From all ballots with valid proofs, the two ciphertexts (E, F) are selected. We denote the resulting ordered list of such pairs by $\mathbf{E} = ((E_1, F_1), \ldots, (E_n, F_n))$ and assume that $\mathbf{E}$ is ordered according to $\mathbf{B}$. This implies for all $j > i$ that (E_j, F_j) has been cast after (E_i, F_i). Furthermore, the validity of the proofs guarantees that each $(E_i, F_i) \in \mathbf{E}$ originates from a person

---

[4] The bulletin board could also accept multiple copies of the same ballot, which then need to be eliminated in the tallying phase. But this makes preventing replay and board flooding attacks more complicated.

in possession of valid private credentials. Finally, we know that two distinct pairs $(E_i, F_i), (E_j, F_j) \in \mathbf{E}$ belong to the same private credentials, whenever E_i and E_j contain the same plaintext.

In the next step, the trusted authority computes for each E_i a list $\mathbf{E}_i = (E_{i,1}, \ldots, \ldots, E_{i,n-1})$ of ciphertexts

$$E_{i,j} = \begin{cases} E_j & \text{for } j < i, \\ E_{j+1}/E_i & \text{for } j \geq i. \end{cases}$$

Note that $\mathbf{E}_i$ may contain one or multiple encryptions of 1, but only if some $E_j \in \{E_{i+1}, \ldots, E_n\}$ contain the same plaintext as E_i. If this is the case, then (E_i, F_i) has been updated and needs to drop out at some point. To determine the updated votes without decrypting $\mathbf{E}_i$, the authority first performs a cryptographic shuffle

$$(\mathbf{E}'_i, \pi_{\mathbf{E}_i}) = \text{shuffle}^{\phi_i}_{\exp}(\mathbf{E}_i, \gamma_{i,1}, \ldots, \gamma_{i,n-1})$$

on each $\mathbf{E}_i$, where $\phi_i \in_R \Phi_{n-1}$ is a random permutation and $\gamma_{i,j} \in_R \mathbb{Z}_q \backslash \{0\}$ are random exponents. The goal of this shuffle is to conceal any plaintext different from 1. Let $\mathbf{E}'_i = (E'_{i,1}, \ldots, E'_{i,n-1})$ be the result of this shuffle and $\mathbf{F}_i = (F_i, E'_{i,1}, \ldots, E'_{i,n-1})$ the extension of this list by inserting F_i at the front. For $\mathbf{FF} = (\mathbf{F}_1, \ldots, \mathbf{F}_n)$, the authority performs an additional cryptographic shuffle

$$(\mathbf{FF}', \pi_{\mathbf{FF}}) = \text{shuffle}^{\phi}_{\text{reEnc}_y}(\mathbf{FF}, \mathbf{r}'_1, \ldots, \mathbf{r}'_n),$$

for a random permutation $\phi \in_R \Phi_n$ and re-encryption randomizations $\mathbf{r}'_i = (r'_{i,1}, \ldots, r'_{i,n}) \in \mathbb{Z}_q^n$. The purpose of this shuffle is to remove the link to the original ballots. Let $\mathbf{FF}' = (\mathbf{F}'_1, \ldots, \mathbf{F}'_n)$ be the result of this shuffle and $\mathbf{F}'_i = (F'_i, E''_{i,1}, \ldots, E''_{i,n-1})$ a single entry of $\mathbf{FF}'$. To determine whether F'_i must be excluded from the final tally, the authority checks if $\text{dec}_x(E''_{i,j}) = 1$ holds for some $j \in [1, n-1]$. Let $U \subseteq [1, n]$ be the subset of indices i for which this is the case, and $V = [1, n-1] \backslash U$ the subset of indices for which this is not the case.[5] For every $i \in U$, the authority selects from $\mathbf{F}'_i = (F'_i, E''_{i,1}, \ldots, E''_{i,n-1})$ one of the encryptions $E''_{i,j}$ containing 1 as plaintext and computes a non-interactive proof

$$\tilde{\pi}_i = NIZKP[(x) : 1 = \text{dec}_x(E''_{i,j}) \wedge y = h^x].$$

For every $i \in V$, the authority computes $\mathbf{V}_i = \text{dec}_x(\mathbf{F}'_i)$ along with a non-interactive proof

$$\hat{\pi}_i = NIZKP[(x) : \mathbf{V}_i = \text{dec}_x(\mathbf{F}'_i) \wedge y = h^x].$$

The final tally is obtained by checking if the plaintext votes at the first position in every $\mathbf{V}_i$ are elements of $\mathbb{V}$ and by summing them up if this is the case. To complete the tallying process, the trusted authority posts

$$(\mathbf{E}, \{\mathbf{E}_i, \mathbf{E}'_i, \pi_{\mathbf{E}_i}\}_{i=1}^n, \mathbf{FF}, \mathbf{FF}', \pi_{\mathbf{FF}}, U, \{E''_{i,j}, \tilde{\pi}_i\}_{i \in U}, V, \{\mathbf{V}_i, \hat{\pi}_i\}_{i \in V})$$

to the designated area of the public bulletin board (Fig. 4).

---

[5] Think of U and V as the indices of the *updated* and *valid* votes, respectively.

Tallying (Trusted Authority):

1. Retrieve the list $\mathbf{B}$ of all ballots from the bulletin board.
2. For each $(C, D, E, F, \pi_1, \pi_2, \pi_3) \in \mathbf{B}$, verify π_1, π_2, π_3. Select the pairs (E, F) from ballots with valid proofs. Let $\mathbf{E} = ((E_1, F_1), ..., (E_n, F_n))$ denote the list of such pairs.
3. Compute $\mathbf{FF} = (\mathbf{F}_1, ..., \mathbf{F}_n)$ by applying to following steps to $1 \leq i \leq n$:
   (a) Compute $\mathbf{E}_i = (E_1, ..., E_{i-1}, E_{i+1}/E_i, ..., E_n/E_i)$.
   (b) Pick $\phi_i \in_R \Phi_{n-1}$ and $\gamma_{i,j} \in_R \mathbb{Z}_q \setminus \{0\}$.
   (c) Compute $(\mathbf{E}'_i, \pi_{\mathbf{E}_i}) = \text{shuffle}_{\exp}^{\phi_i}(\mathbf{E}_i, \gamma_{i,1}, ..., \gamma_{i,n-1})$.
   (d) For $\mathbf{E}'_i = (E'_{i,1}, ..., E'_{i,n-1})$, let $\mathbf{F}_i = (F_i, E'_{i,1}, ..., E'_{i,n-1})$.
4. Pick $\phi \in_R \Phi_e$ and $\mathbf{r}'_i = (r'_{i,1}, ..., r'_{i,n}) \in_R \mathbb{Z}_q^n$.
5. Compute $(\mathbf{FF}', \pi_{\mathbf{FF}}) = \text{shuffle}_{\text{reEnc}_y}^{\phi}(\mathbf{FF}, \mathbf{r}'_1, ..., \mathbf{r}'_n)$.
6. Let $U = \{i \in [1, n] : \exists j \in [1, n-1] \text{ s.t. } \text{dec}_x(E''_{i,j}) = 1\}$.
7. For every $i \in U$:
   (a) Select $E''_{i,j}$ from $\mathbf{F}'_i = (F'_i, E''_{i,1}, ..., E''_{i,n-1})$ such that $\text{dec}_x(E''_{i,j}) = 1$.
   (b) Compute $\tilde{\pi}_i = NIZKP[(x) : 1 = \text{dec}_x(E''_{i,j}) \wedge y = h^x]$.
8. For every $i \in V = [1, n] \setminus U$:
   (a) Compute $\mathbf{V}_i = \text{dec}_x(\mathbf{F}'_i)$.
   (b) Compute $\hat{\pi}_i = NIZKP[(x) : \mathbf{V}_i = \text{dec}_x(\mathbf{F}'_i) \wedge y = h^x]$.
9. Post $(\mathbf{E}, \{\mathbf{E}_i, \mathbf{E}'_i, \pi_{\mathbf{E}_i}\}_{i=1}^n, \mathbf{FF}, \mathbf{FF}', \pi_{\mathbf{FF}}, U, \{E''_{i,j}, \tilde{\pi}_i\}_{i \in U}, V, \{\mathbf{V}_i, \hat{\pi}_i\}_{i \in V})$ into the designated area of the bulletin board.

Fig. 4. Summary of the tallying phase with a single trusted authority.

3.3 Security Properties

We will now look at our protocol from the perspective of its security properties. We provide an informal discussion of how correctness, everlasting privacy, and coercion-resistance are achieved. Fairness is achieved in a trivial way by submitting votes encrypted.

Correctness. For a present adversary not colluding with any of the trusted authorities and not in possession of a private credential, there are two principle ways of creating a ballot that will be accepted in the final tally. First, the adversary may try to find (α', β') such that $u = h_1^{\alpha'} h_2^{\beta'}$ for some u in U, which is equivalent to solving the discrete logarithm problem. Second, the adversary may try to fake a proof transcript without knowing such a pair (α', β'), but this is prevented by the computational soundness of π_1, π_2, and π_3.

If the present adversary is an eligible voter in possession of a valid private credential, then using it for submitting more than one ballot is explicitly allowed by the protocol, but only the last ballot is considered in the final tally. The malicious voter could try to submit ballots with different election credentials, but the soundness of π_3 does not allow this. Without using the private credential, the voter is not more powerful than any other present adversary.

A present adversary colluding with one or several trusted authorities—or even the authorities themselves—may try to delete, modify, or add votes in the mixing or decryption steps of the protocol, but this is prevented by the computational soundness of $\pi_{\mathbf{E}_i}$, $\pi_{\mathbf{FF}}$, $\tilde{\pi}_i$, and $\hat{\pi}_i$. Their correctness can be verified by anyone.

Everlasting Privacy. A ballot posted over an anonymous channel to the bulletin board contains no information for identifying the voter. Clearly, the future adversary will be able to determine the private key x, use it to decrypt E_i into $\hat{h}^\beta$, and finally obtain β. As u can be regarded as a perfectly hiding commitment to β, a suitable value α' can be found for every credential u' in $\mathbf{U}$ such that $u' = h_1^{\alpha'} h_2^\beta$. Thus, knowing β and x does not link $E_i = \text{enc}_y(\hat{h}^\beta, \rho)$ to u. Since the proofs π_1, π_2, and π_3 are zero-knowledge and therefore of no additional help, even a future adversary is unable to break vote or participation secrecy.

Coercion-Resistance. A voter—either voluntarily or under coercion—may prove the authorship of a ballot by disclosing the randomizations used in the encryptions E_i and F_i. From this, the coercer learns the values $\hat{h}^\beta$ and v of a submitted ballot. To issue a conclusive receipt, the voter must also prove that the ballot is indeed included in the final tally, for example by proving that every subsequent ballot has been cast by somebody else. But this is impossible as the voter cannot prove *not* to know corresponding randomizations. Alternatively, the voter may try to show that $\{E_{i+1}, \ldots, E_n\}$ does not contain an encryption of $\hat{h}^\beta$ (or equivalently that $\mathbf{E}_i$ does not contain an encryption of 1) or to establish a link between $\mathbf{F}_i \in \mathbf{FF}$ and $\mathbf{F}'_{\phi(i)} \in \mathbf{FF}'$. Both tasks either require corrupting a majority of trusted authorities or solving the DDH or DL problem. Hence, the protocol is receipt-free under ordinary trust or computational intractability assumptions.

Attacks by an active coercer can be countered by the fact that voters cannot be urged to prove or disprove having cast a final vote in privacy (see reasoning above). A voter under a randomization attack will therefore follow the coercer's instructions and cast a random vote, but then the voter will submit a final vote in privacy and deny the vote update towards the coercer. For a voter under a forced-abstention attack, who will simply submit a final vote in privacy, everlasting participation secrecy is a perfect protection towards the coercer trying to check the voter's compliance. Finally, even if the private credentials α and β are handed over to the coercer in a simulation attack, the voter will always be able use the credentials for submitting a final vote in privacy and deny it towards the coercer. The coercer may try to check if vote updating using the same credentials has taken place, but this is impossible for the reasons explained above and because the commitments are perfectly hiding.

4   Conclusion

In this paper, we introduced the first cryptographic voting protocol offering everlasting privacy and coercion-resistance simultaneously. Everlasting privacy is realized with perfectly hiding commitments and zero-knowledge proofs of knowledge, and hence does not depend on trusted authorities or computational intractability assumptions. To achieve coercion-resistance, we propose a new deniable updating mechanism based on a combination of cryptographic mixing procedures. Computational intractability assumptions are obviously required for cryptographic mixing, but this is only problematical if the extent of a coercion attack exceeds the cryptoperiod of the chosen cryptographic setting. Attacks against vote or participation secrecy will always remain impossible.

The main drawback of our protocol is the quadratic running time of the tallying procedure. Compared to LH15, which requires $O(n \log N)$ exponentiations and $O(nN)$ multiplications in $\mathcal{G}_p$ to verify all submitted ballots, we require $O(n^2)$ additional exponentiations in $\mathbb{G}_q$. The performance is therefore similar to AKLM15, i.e., the applicability of our approach is restricted to relatively small electorates. Implementing our new protocol and analysing its performance to estimate the maximal possible electorate size is subject of further research.

Some problems remain unsolved in the current version of our protocol. An open issue is the problem of flooding the bulletin board with a very large number of valid ballots. This problem is a direct consequence of deniable vote updating. Another open issue is the problem of a malicious voting platform.

Acknowledgments. We thank the anonymous reviewers for their thorough reviews and appreciate their comments and suggestions. This research has been supported by the Swiss National Science Foundation (project No. 200021L_140650).

References

1. Achenbach, D., Kempka, C., Löwe, B., Müller-Quade, J.: Improved coercion-resistant electronic elections through deniable re-voting. USENIX J. Election Technol. Syst. (JETS) **2**, 26–45 (2015)
2. Arapinis, M., Cortier, V., Kremer, S., Ryan, M.: Practical everlasting privacy. In: Basin, D., Mitchell, J.C. (eds.) POST 2013 (ETAPS 2013). LNCS, vol. 7796, pp. 21–40. Springer, Heidelberg (2013)
3. Au, M.H., Susilo, W., Mu, Y.: Proof-of-knowledge of representation of committed value and its applications. In: Steinfeld, R., Hawkes, P. (eds.) ACISP 2010. LNCS, vol. 6168, pp. 352–369. Springer, Heidelberg (2010)
4. Bayer, S., Groth, J.: Efficient zero-knowledge argument for correctness of a shuffle. In: Pointcheval, D., Johansson, T. (eds.) EUROCRYPT 2012. LNCS, vol. 7237, pp. 263–280. Springer, Heidelberg (2012)
5. Bayer, S., Groth, J.: Zero-knowledge argument for polynomial evaluation with application to blacklists. In: Johansson, T., Nguyen, P.Q. (eds.) EUROCRYPT 2013. LNCS, vol. 7881, pp. 646–663. Springer, Heidelberg (2013)
6. Brands, S.: Rethinking Public Key Infrastructures and Digital Certificates: Building in Privacy. MIT Press, Cambridge (2000)
7. Juels, A., Catalano, D., Jakobsson, M.: Coercion-resistant electronic elections. In: 4th Workshop on Privacy in the Electronic Society, WPES 2005, pp. 61–70 (2005)
8. Locher, P., Haenni, R.: Verifiable internet elections with everlasting privacy and minimal trust. In: Haenni, R., Koenig, R.E., Wikström, D. (eds.) VoteID 2015. LNCS, vol. 9269, pp. 74–91. Springer, Heidelberg (2015)
9. Terelius, B., Wikström, D.: Proofs of restricted shuffles. In: Bernstein, D.J., Lange, T. (eds.) AFRICACRYPT 2010. LNCS, vol. 6055, pp. 100–113. Springer, Heidelberg (2010)

Selene: Voting with Transparent Verifiability and Coercion-Mitigation

Peter Y.A. Ryan[1]([⊠]), Peter B. Rønne[1,2], and Vincenzo Iovino[1]

[1] University of Luxembourg, Esch-sur-Alzette, Luxembourg
peter.ryan@uni.lu, vinciovino@gmail.com
[2] INRIA Nancy, Villers-làs-Nancy, France
peter.roenne@inria.fr

Abstract. End-to-end verifiable voting schemes typically involve voters handling an encrypted ballot in order to confirm that their vote is accurately included in the tally. While this may be technically valid, from a public acceptance standpoint it may be problematic: many voters may not really understand the purpose of the encrypted ballot and the various checks that they can perform. In this paper we take a different approach and revisit an old idea: to provide each voter with a private tracking number. Votes are posted on a bulletin board in the clear along with their associated tracking number. This is appealing in that it provides voters with a very simple, intuitive way to verify their vote, in the clear. However, there are obvious drawbacks: we must ensure that no two voters are assigned the same tracker and we need to keep the link between voters and trackers private.

We propose a scheme that addresses both of these problems: we ensure that voters get unique trackers and we close off coercion opportunities by ensuring that the voters only learn their tracking numbers after the votes have been posted. The resulting scheme provides receipt-freeness, and indeed a good level of coercion-resistance while also providing a more immediately understandable form of verifiability.

1 Introduction

The challenge with voting systems is to provide sufficient evidence to render the outcome beyond dispute while at the same time ensuring ballot secrecy and coercion resistance. Furthermore, the system has to be very easy to use and easily understandable. The response from the crypto community has been to develop the notion of End-to-End (E2E) Verifiability. A number of schemes have been proposed and some even implemented and deployed, for example, Prêt à Voter [25] Wombat [2] and Scantegrity II [26], Helios https://vote.heliosvoting.org/, Civitas [7], Pretty Good Democracy [24].

Typically these schemes involve the creation of an encrypted version of the vote at the time of casting. The voter gets to retain a copy of the encrypted vote which she can later confirm is correctly posted to a secure, append-only

© International Financial Cryptography Association 2016
J. Clark et al. (Eds.): FC 2016 Workshops, LNCS 9604, pp. 176–192, 2016.
DOI: 10.1007/978-3-662-53357-4_12

Web Bulletin Board (WBB). All the posted, encrypted ballots are then anonymously tabulated, either using mixes and decryption or exploiting homomorphic properties of the encryption to tabulate under encryption and then decrypt the result.

The assurance arguments are rather subtle though, and some people object to the use of crypto in voting on the grounds that the majority of the electorate will not really understand it and its role. Indeed, German Federal law, according to some interpretations, rules out the use of cryptography on the grounds that anyone should be able to understand the mechanisms without requiring any special knowledge. It is interesting therefore to explore the possibility of achieving some form of verifiability without the use of crypto. An early example of this is the article of Randell and Ryan [21] that uses scratch strips as an analogue of crypto. Another fine example is Rivest's ThreeBallot system [22].

Another approach is to have private ballot identifiers that allow voters to look up their vote in the clear on the WBB. Schneier in his book [27] for example suggests such an approach: voters are invited to invent their own random code and submit it with their vote. A slightly more sophisticated approach, in which the system and/or the voter's devices generates the numbers is presented in [1].

Introducing ballot identifiers has the appeal that it provides voters with a very simple, direct and easy-to-understand way to confirm that their vote is present and correct in the tally. There are however two significant drawbacks: care has to be taken to ensure that voters get distinct trackers and there is a danger of coercion. The first is an issue if, for example the system could identify two voters likely to vote the same way and assign them the same tracker. In this case it just posts one vote against this tracker and is free to stuff another vote of its own choice. The second danger is that a coercer requires the voter to hand over her tracker to allow him to check how she voted. Notice though that in this style of attack the coercer has a limited window of opportunity: he must request that the tracker be handed over before the results are published. It is this observation that we exploit to counter this threat: we arrange for the voters to learn their tracker numbers only after the vote/tracker number pairs have been posted to the WBB.

This paper presents a scheme that addresses both of these shortcomings by:

- Guaranteeing that voters get unique trackers.
- Arranging for voters to learn their tracker only after the votes and corresponding tracking numbers have been posted (in the clear).

We hope that by putting all the crypto under the bonnet, voters, election officials etc. may find such a scheme more acceptable that conventional E2E verifiable schemes that require voters to handle encrypted ballots. Here the voters just have to handle tracking numbers and votes in the clear. The scheme is also interesting in that it appears to shift the trust model for voter devices: in usual E2E schemes we need to worry about the voter's device encrypting the vote correctly. This typically necessitates complicating the protocol with *Benaloh challenges*, [3], or similar ballot assurance mechanisms. Now that voters get to check their vote in the clear, a misbehaving device can be detected more readily, resulting in a simpler voting ceremony.

A possible problem with the basic scheme, pointed out by Bill Roscoe, is that a coerced voter might by mis-chance choose the coercer's tracking number when she is deploying her coercion evasion strategy. Perhaps even more worrying is the possibility that the coercer will simply claim, falsely, that the tracker revealed by the voter is his and hence he "knows" that voter has not revealed her true tracker. This puts the voter in a very difficult situation. It seems that her best strategy is to stick to her guns and insist that she has revealed her true tracker. She does not know whether or not the coercer is telling the truth and indeed, ironically, the coercer does not have any means to prove to her that it is his tracker.

In large elections with a small number of candidates the odds of lighting on the coercer's tracker will typically be small (unless the coercer is backing a serious loser), but even the remote possibility may be worrying to some voters. If the coercer is not himself a voter the problem does not arise, but even here there may be an issue if many voters are being coerced. And, as remarked above, the coercer might claim, falsely, that the tracker is his.

It is not immediately obvious how to counter this danger, but in the full version [23] we present an enhancement to the basic scheme which counters this possibility, but where the tally is less transparent. An alternative version of the basic scheme which also counters the possibility of choosing the coercer's tracker is described in Sect. 8; however the cost is that coerced voters can no longer verify their cast vote.

The Selene scheme is in any case targeted at low coercion threat environments and so in such a context this problem could be regarded as minor. We suggest that, in some contexts, the benefits arising from the greater degree of transparency outweigh the rather remote threat. In any event, we show that the basic scheme still provides receipt-freeness.

It is worth noting that the constructions presented here could be thought of as a possible add-on to other schemes to provide a transparent form of verifiability. Indeed we could start with a simple, un-verifiable scheme that simply delivers (encrypted) votes to the server and render it verifiable by adding Selene constructs.

2   Background

Coercion can come in many flavours, from implicit, the coercer does not have to say anything, folk just know how they are expected to vote, to full-on: your personal coercer is on hand 24/7 to assist you in making the right voting choice. Making a voting system resistant to the latter form is extremely difficult, arguably impossible if the coercer really is observing the voter throughout the voting period. The Selene scheme is aimed at contexts where the coercion threat is closer to the former end of the spectrum: the coercer will issue some instructions and ask some awkward questions. Selene will mitigate such coercion attacks and at the same time allow the voters to directly verify that their vote is counted as intended.

3   Cryptographic Primitives

In this paper we will assume that the reader is familiar with signature schemes [13], threshold encryption [11], plaintext equivalence tests (PET), non-interactive zero-knowledge proofs of knowledge (NIZKPoK) [13] and verifiable shuffle protocols [20]. We further assume the existence of a secure Web Bullettin Board (WBB) [16]. We defer detailed descriptions of these to the the full version [23].

4   Related Work

E2E verifiable voting now has quite a long and rich literature, with many schemes having been proposed, both for in-person and remote, e.g. internet voting. Here we just mention some of the most closely related schemes. Note, Selene as presented here is intended for internet voting, but it would doubtless be straigforward to adapt it to in-person voting.

The most notable verifiable internet voting scheme is Adida's Helios, https:// vote.heliosvoting.org/. Helios is not receipt-free, but recently the Belenios RF scheme, [8], has been proposed to provide receipt freeness.

Juels et al. [17] proposed a formal definition of coercion resistance and a credential-based mechanism to achieve this. The Civitas system, [7], http:// www.cs.cornell.edu/projects/civitas/, implements this approach, with some enhancements.

The idea of voters having a private tracking number with which they can look up their vote in the clear on a bulletin board appears to go back the Schneier's "Applied Cryptography" book in which he suggests that voters choose a password to identify their vote. Much later the idea is revived for use in voting during ANR (Agence National de la Recherche) funding committee meetings. A scheme that has some similarities to Selene in that votes appear in the clear alongside identifying number, is Trivitas, [6]. Here, however, the clear-text votes appear on the bulletin board at an intermediate step, followed by further mixing and filtering. Hence the voters do not verify their vote directly in the tally. The goal is rather to allow voters to test the system by submitting dummy ballots.

5   The Set-Up Phase

The EA creates the threshold election key and keys share. Ideally this should be in a distributed, dealerless fashion [11]. We assume that any voter already has a PK/SK pair for an El Gamal encryption scheme and thus the PK of voter i has the form $\mathsf{pk}_i = g^{x_i}$, where x_i is her corresponding secret-key. When voters register for the election we assume that they, or more precisely their devices, create a fresh, ephemeral trapdoor key pair.

We now describe a distributed construction whose goal is to assign unique tracker numbers to the voters and inform them of their tracking numbers in a way that provides them with high confidence that it is correct but allowing them to deny it if coerced. We do this by generating trapdoor, Pedersen-style commitments to the tracking numbers. The tracking numbers could be rather sparse to be easily distinguishable, but can also be consecutive numbers $1, 2, \ldots$.

Distributed Generation of the Encrypted Tracker Numbers. The Election Authority publicly creates the tracking numbers n_i and computes g^{n_i} (to ensure that the resulting values fall in the appropriate subgroup) as well as the (trivial) ElGamal encryptions of the g^{n_i}: $\{g^{n_i}\}_{PK_T}$ and posts these terms to the WBB:

$$n_i, g^{n_i}, \{g^{n_i}\}_{\mathsf{pk}_T}$$

The (Mix) Tellers now put the last, encrypted terms through a sequence of verifiable, re-encryption mixes to yield:

$$\{g^{n_{\pi(i)}}\}'_{\mathsf{pk}_T}$$

These are now assigned to the voters' PKs

$$(\mathsf{pk}_i, \{g^{n_{\pi(i)}}\}'_{\mathsf{pk}_T})$$

Note that, thanks to the mixing, the assignment of these numbers to the voters is not known to any party, aside from a collusion of all the mix Tellers. Note also that as this is a verified mix, as long as all the input numbers are unique it is guaranteed that each voter will be assigned a unique (encrypted) number. We still need to ensure that the number revealed to each voter is the number assigned to them in the above construction; we will see this next.

5.1   Distributed Generation of the Tracker Number Commitments

Now, each Teller is required to produce n pairs of terms of the form:

$$(\{h_i^{r_{i,j}}\}_{\mathsf{pk}_T}, \{g^{r_{i,j}}\}_{\mathsf{pk}_T})$$

Here and in the following we have set $h_i := g^{x_i} = \mathsf{pk}_i$ for notational convenience.

We have to provide NIZKPoK proofs that these terms are well-formed, i.e. that the $r_{i,j}$ exponents in the two terms are indeed identical and known and that the Teller knows such value, we present these in the full version [23]. In addition we will have to assume that such proofs be non-malleable as we will explain later. Alternatively, one could also let the Tellers produce extra terms and perform a cut-and-choose audit.

Thus we now have a $n \times t$ array of such pairs, the columns corresponding to the Tellers and the rows to the voter ids. Now, for each voter, we form the product across the columns of the first elements to give:

$$\{h_i^{r_i}\}_{\mathsf{pk}_T} = \prod_{j=1}^{t}\{h_i^{r_{i,j}}\}_{\mathsf{pk}_T}$$

Where, due to the multiplicative homomorphic properties of ElGamal,

$$r_i := \sum_{j=1}^{t} r_{i,j}$$

Now we form the product of the $\{h_i^{r_i}\}_{\mathsf{pk}_T}$ and the $\{g^{n_{\pi(i)}}\}_{\mathsf{pk}_T}$:

$$\{h_i^{r_i} \cdot g^{n_{\pi(i)}}\}_{\mathsf{pk}_T} = \{h_i^{r_i}\}_{\mathsf{pk}_T} \cdot \{g^{n_{\pi(i)}}\}_{\mathsf{pk}_T}$$

This gives us the encryption under the Teller's PK of the trapdoor commitments to the tracking numbers: $(h_i^{r_i} \cdot g^{n_{\pi(i)}})$. We can now have a threshold set of Tellers perform verified, partial decryptions of these terms to reveal the commitments:

$$C_i := h_i^{r_i} \cdot g^{n_{\pi(i)}}$$

All of these steps are posted, along with NIZKPoK proofs and audits, to the WBB.

It seems that the Tellers cannot cheat in any effective way here aside from injecting invalid randoms which will result eventually in the voters being unable to open their commitment to a valid tracking number. But in any case, any such cheating will be detected by checks on the NIZKPoK proofs or random audits.

Now, for each voter there will be a tuple of terms posted to the WBB:

$$(\mathsf{pk}_i, \{g^{n_{\pi(i)}}\}_{\mathsf{pk}_T}, h_i^{r_i} \cdot g^{n_{\pi(i)}})$$

5.2   Voting

Voter V_i casts her vote in the form:

$$(\mathsf{Sign}_{\mathsf{V}_i}(\{\mathsf{Vote}_i\}_{\mathsf{pk}_T}), \Pi_i),$$

where the ballot is signed either with the voter's true PK, or with her pseudo-PK if this has been configured (see the full version [23]), and Π_i is a non-interactive proof of knowledge of the plaintext. The signature is to avoid ballot stuffing, see e.g. [9]. The proofs of knowledge are needed to ensure *ballot independence* [10, 12, 29], by preventing an attacker copying, re-encrypting a previously cast vote as his own.[1] Note that in conjunction with Selene such a copying attack

---

[1] As Bernhard *et al.* [5] showed, it is possible to tweak the so called Enc+PoK paradigm (where one adds a proof of knowledge to an ElGamal ciphertext) to achieve non-malleable encryption that is sufficient for ballot independence. Another possibility is to resort to threshold Cramer and Shoup [28]. Note that any change will be completely transparent in Selene where the vote cast system can be essentially arbitrary.

would be particularly virulent: the attacker copies the victim's vote and casts it as his own. When the votes and trackers are revealed he sees exactly how the victim voted.

It is important that the server check for duplication of encrypted votes. It is also advisable to post the votes only once voting is closed. The signatures and proofs are checked for validity and, if valid, the encrypted votes are now paired off with the PK (and encrypted tracking number) with which they were signed. Double votes are handled according to the policy in operation, e.g. only the last vote cast by V_i is retained. Thus we get a list of tuples on the WBB:

$$(\mathsf{pk}_i, \{g^{n_{\pi(i)}}\}_{\mathsf{pk}_T}, (h_i^{r_i} \cdot g^{n_{\pi(i)}}), \mathsf{Sign}_{V_i}(\{\mathsf{Vote}_i\}_{\mathsf{pk}_T}, \Pi_i))$$

5.3   Mixing and Decryption

Now, for each row on the WBB, the second and fourth terms of these tuples are extracted and the signature and proofs striped off the fourth term. This gives pairs of the form:

$$(\{g^{n_{\pi(i)}}\}_{\mathsf{pk}_T}, \{\mathsf{Vote}_i\}_{\mathsf{pk}_T})$$

These are now put through a verifiable, parallel shuffle, e.g. [20]. Once this is done, a threshold set of the Tellers perform a verifiable decryption of these shuffled pairs. All of these steps along with the proofs are posted to the WBB. Thus, finally we have a list of pairs: tracking number, vote:

$$(g^{n_{\pi(i)}}, \mathsf{Vote}_i)$$

from which the tracker/vote pair can immediately be derived: $(n_{\pi(i)}, \mathsf{Vote}_i)$.

5.4   Notification of Tracker Numbers

For the notification of tracking numbers we will think of the Pedersen commitments whose construction we described earlier as forming the β component, i.e. the $h^r \cdot m$, of an ElGamal encryption under the voter's PK, but with the α component, i.e. the g^r, kept hidden. Thus we think of an ElGamal encryption as being represented:

$$(\alpha, \beta) := (g^r, h^r \cdot m)$$

The goal then is to reveal the α term to the voter in a deniable fashion.

Once the trackers and votes have been made available on the WBB for a sufficient period for the voters to note any alternative trackers as may be required to parry any attempted coercion, the Tellers send the voter V_j their share of the $g^{r_{j,i}}$ over a private channel:

$$T_j \rightarrow V_i : g^{r_{j,i}}$$

Once V_i's device has received these from all the Tellers it combines them to form g^{r_i}, the α term which along with the β term of the commitment $h_i^{r_i} \cdot g^{n_{\pi(i)}}$ to give the ElGamal encryption of $g^{n_{\pi(i)}}$ w.r.t. the voter's PK h_i:

$$(g^{r_i}, h_i^{r_i} \cdot g^{n_{\pi(i)}})$$

The voter can now decrypt this in the usual fashion using her secret key x_i, thus revealing $g^{n_{\pi(i)}}$ and hence $n_{\pi(i)}$.

The advantage of this construction is that it is unnecessary to authenticate the message notifying the voter of the α term. Authenticating these terms naively would introduce coercion threats. Designated Verifier Signatures or similar would be a way to sidestep such coercion threats, but they would significantly complicate the ceremony.

The point is that an adversary, even if colluding with all the Tellers, can only construct an α term that opens up to a valid tracker different from the true tracker of the voter with negligible probability. Stated formally:

Theorem 1. *If the 1-DHI assumption [19] holds, then there exists no PPT algorithm $\mathcal{A}$ which takes as inputs a description of a DH-group $\mathcal{G}$ along with a generator g for it, a set T of tracker number of polynomial size, two values $C = g^n h^r$, $h = g^x \in \mathcal{G}$ and outputs with non-negligible probability a term α such that C/α^x is of the form $g^{n'}$ where $n' \neq n$ is a valid tracker, $n' \in T$. Further, this holds true even if the algorithm is given n and r.*

A deeper discussion and a proof of the theorem can be found in the full version [23].

By contrast, the voter, or more precisely her device, with knowledge of the trapdoor, can compute an alternative $g^{r_i'}$ term that will decrypt to an alternative, valid tracker of her choice. Suppose that she wants her commitment to decrypt to the tracker value $m^* := g^{n^*}$, she inputs this to her device along with the commitment value β_i and the device computes the fake α term α':

$$\alpha' = \left(\frac{\beta_i}{m^*}\right)^{x_i^{-1}}$$

Note also that for the privacy of the tracking numbers we do not really need to encrypt the g^{r_i} terms as the trackers are still protected by the encryption under the voter's PK. However, it is still important to send these terms to the voter over a private channel to ensure that they are deniable.

Another potential attack lies in the fact that a Teller could create his g^{r_j} term with knowledge of the g^{r_i}'s terms of the other Tellers so that the product of all r_i's be known to him. This would be possible if the NIZKPoK proofs be malleable and in fact this is the case if care is not taken when applying the Fiat-Shamir heuristic. In the full version [23] we discuss how it is possible to use standard techniques to make a NIZKPoK non-malleable. We stress that by assuming that the NIZKPoK is non-malleable, the aforementioned attack is nullified.

6   The Voter Experience

A goal of the design of this protocol is to make the voter experience as simple and intuitive as possible. We assume that the voters already possess public (signing) keys and will create trapdoor keys during a registration phase. First we describe the ceremony in the case that the voter does not experience any coercion. Then we describe the steps needed to counter a coercer.

6.1   The Core Ceremony

- The voter receives an invitation to vote along with a ballot.
- The voter inputs her choice and her device encrypts this under the Election PK and signs this. The device sends this to the Election Server.

After a suitable period the tracking number/vote pairs are anonymised and decrypted and displayed on the WBB. The voters receive an invite to visit the WBB, but will only be necessary at this stage if the voter is being been coerced.

- After a suitable delay, the voter receives a notification of the α term, which she inputs to her device to allow it to extract her tracking number. Once she has this she can visit the WBB and confirm that her vote appears correctly against this tracker.

The last step is optional, to enable to voter to check that her vote was correctly recorded and entered into the tally. She can skip this if she is not interested in performing such a check.

6.2   The Ceremony in the Event of Coercion

If the voter is being coerced she needs to take some additional, coercion evasion steps, shown in italics:

- The voter receives an invitation to vote along with a ballot.
- The voter inputs her choice and her device encrypts this under the Election PK and signs this. The device sends this to the Election Server.
- *Once the (tracker, vote) pairs are displayed on the WBB she visits the WBB and notes down a tracking number that appears against the vote demanded by the coercer.*
- *The voter inputs this fake tracking number into her device and it outputs a fake α' term that coupled with her commitment, the β term of the ElGamal encryption of her tracker, will decrypt to the fake tracker.*
- After a suitable delay, the voter receives a notification of her "true" α term, which she inputs to her device to allow it to extract her tracking number from the commitment.
- *If the coercer demands that she reveal her tracking number she "reveals" the fake one. If he further demands that she reveals the alpha notification value, she reveals the fake α' she computed earlier.*
- Once she has her tracker she can visit the WBB and confirm that her vote appears correctly against this tracker.

Of course, she should also notify the appropriate authorities that coercion was attempted.

6.3 Selene as an Add-On

It is, however, interesting to note that the constructions described above could in many cases be added to an existing scheme, one without any verification features or perhaps one having conventional E2E verification involving encrypted receipts. Indeed, in some cases it could even be retro-fitted to an election that had already taken place. Suppose that a Helios vote had been conducted and contested. The trapdoor commitments to the trackers could be generated and associated to the voters as described above and the mixes and decryptions performed afresh. For this to work, the base scheme must use encryption such that we can run a parallel shuffle with the corresponding encrypted trackers.

In the full version [23] we discuss more enhancements to the basic scheme such as the use of re-encryptable signatures [8].

7 Analysis

In this section we give a brief, informal analysis of the security properties of Selene. A full, formal security analysis is postponed for future research.

7.1 Verifiability and Verification

If we think of Selene as an add-on to a base scheme, the universal verifiability of Selene is at least as strong as the base vote casting. In Sect. 5.2 this is a Helios like scheme, but as mentioned in Sect. 6.3 it could also be a more general scheme. Such schemes most often provide tallied-as-stored security, i.e. that the vote is tallied as cast by the device of the voter.

However, Selene could also be added to a vote casting scheme without universal verifiability. Indeed, the strength of Selene is to provide additional individual direct verification that the vote is tallied as intended by the voter.

The security of the tracker construction relies on interested parties checking the proofs and calculations done on WBB as follows, but these are universally verifiable:

- Check that the trackers, n_i, written in plain on the WBB are indeed unique and their exponentiations g^{n_i} and the trivial encryptions thereof are correct (Sect. 5).
- Check the ZK proofs for the mix of the encrypted trackers (Sect. 5). This is to ensure both privacy and verifiability. We will elaborate on this in next subsection.
- Check the ZK proofs from the Tellers that the terms $\{h_i^{r_{i,j}}\}_{\mathsf{pk}_T}, \{g^{r_{i,j}}\}_{\mathsf{pk}_T}$ are well-formed. Further, it is checked that these are correctly multiplied together to give a commitment to the tracking number (Sect. 5.1). It can be shown (see the full version [23]) that an adversary with overwhelming probability cannot fake the α term, which the voter receives and uses together with the commitment to decrypt the tracker. This of course assumes that the voter's secret key $x_i = \log_g h_i$ is not known to the adversary. We will comment on this below.

– Check the proofs in the verifiable parallel shuffle of the voter/tracker pairs and their decryption (Sect. 5.3). As in a standard voting scheme using mixing for tallying this ensures that the tally is correct and in this case it further means that the tracker in the commitment is indeed the one shown next to the vote in the tally.

We conclude that if these checks are performed then a voter, who decrypts to a valid tracker, can be confident that this is the unique tracker assigned to her and the corresponding vote on the tally board is the vote stored encrypted on WBB.

More elaborate schemes also provide some security for the vote being stored as intended, even when the voter's device is malicious e.g. via Benaloh challenges [3] or by employing hardware tokens [15]. Selene, can however also provide verifiability in this respect. Checking the vote in the tally can reveal if a malicious device altered the intended vote. This requires that the voter checks her vote on an app or another device not controlled by the adversary. Further, the signature key used to cast the vote can also be different from the secret key x_i used to retrieve the tracker. In this case the device used to cast the vote does not even need to know x_i. This means that the adversary cannot calculate an alternative value for the α term and it will be more difficult to launch an attack. A voter can then even use the same device to receive the α term, then store it and then reveal the secret key to get the tracker. Later the voter can then check if it gives the same tracker on another device.

7.2 Ballot Privacy

The Selene scheme requires that the underlying ballot casting mechanism provides good privacy. Thus the encryption algorithm and its implementation used to encrypt the vote should ensure the secrecy of the vote. The first mix of the encrypted trackers means that only an adversary controlling all the mix servers would know the association of the tracking numbers to the voters, assuming that the proofs of the mixing have been checked. The posted commitments to the tracking numbers are perfectly hiding unless the adversary colludes with all the Tellers. Finally the parallel mix preserve ballot privacy for both the vote and the tracker just like in a standard vote scheme using tallying via mix nets. Finally, the α term, if this should come into the possession of an adversary, does not reveal the tracker since it just a part of an ElGamal encryption of the tracker.

7.3 Receipt-Freeness

In their seminal paper Benaloh and Tuinstra [4] defines receipt-free (which they call uncoercibility) informally as "no voter should be able to convince any other participant of the value of its vote".

If the vote casting scheme is receipt-free, e.g. by employing the model of BeleniosRF [8] for the vote casting, then Selene is receipt-free. Basically the extra information that the voter has in Selene is the unique tracking number. However, the voter can simply fake this (and importantly the corresponding α term) since the tally board is presented before the tracker retrieval. We do need to assume that he attacker cannot monitor the communication of the α terms to the voters. As mentioned before, it can happen that the voter chooses a fake tracker which coincide the tracker of the coercer, however, this does not constitute a proof of how she voted, it just undermines her claim to that tracker and associated vote.

To which extent this makes Selene vote buyer resistant is a subject of future research. The point is that even though the voter cannot prove her vote, she does have extra information, namely the tracker which is unique to her.

We also mention that Italian style (aka signature) attacks may be possible here when we are dealing with complex ballots. For some voting methods we may be able to counter this by splitting up the ballot into components and mixing separately.

7.4   Coercion: Threats and Mitigation

For Selene to be coercion resistant, we firstly need that this is true for the vote casting part. Some degree of coercion resistance can be obtained by combining BeleniosRF [8] with vote updating. Another possibility for partial coercion resistance is to use the scheme by Kulyk et al. [18] where each voter can cast several vote values and only the sum of these will count in the end. The total number of votes are hidden in a cloud of null votes which any participant can cast for the voter.

For Selene the extra tracker verification step however also opens up a coercion possibility: the coercer can demand to observe the receipt of the $g^{r_{j,i}}$. Of course the voter can always create a fake term $g^{r'_{j,i}}$ and pretend to the coercer that this is the term that was sent to her, see Sect. 5.4. Further, the terms are sent at randomized times and the coercer will thus have to intensively follow the voter. However, the possibility of receiving a wrong term while the coercer is present, might be discouraging for the voter. A possibility to circumvent this is to allow voters to secretly contact the voting authorities to request that only the fake $g^{r_{j,i}}$ term that the voter has calculated be communicated back to her. They are now safe from the coercion threat, but a coerced voter have lost the individual verifiability. This suggests a novel form of coercion resistance, distinct from the conventional one in which the voter gets to cast her intended vote and to verify it, or *coercion evidence*, [14], in which she gets to verify her vote but it might be nullified. Here she gets to cast her intended vote but if coerced may lose the possibility to verify it.

The coercion problem might escalate if the coercer is colluding (or pretends to be) with one of the Tellers. The voter then has to guess which $g^{r_{j,i}}$ to fake (this is incidentally also a problem in Civitas [7]). In the BeleniosRF construction there is a voting authority which is trusted for the receipt-freeness, and in this case we can circumvent this danger by letting this authority receive the $g^{r_{j,i}}$ terms and only forward the g^{r_i} to the voter.

True coercion-resistant vote schemes often work with credentials, e.g. Civitas [7]. The voter knows the true credential and can provide the coercer(s) with fake credential(s). Where Civitas is not directly compatible with Selene, one can imagine to combine its credential construction and the extra null votes of [18] to create a true coercion-resistant scheme compatible with the tracker construction. In this case the extra credentials can also be used to make the tracker retrieval coercion-resistant. A scheme could be as follows. After the tally board is created we allow a certain time for the voters to note the trackers, construct fake α-terms and contact the voting authorities privately with these terms. After this time the voter can log in to the voting system to get the α term, however the credential is also used in this process. The voting authority provide the true α term if the correct credential is used. If a fake credential is used, the system outputs the corresponding faked α-term which has been provided by the voter.

7.5 Dispute Resolution

Dispute resolution, the ability to determine the cheating or malfunctioning component or party when an error is reported, is quite hard to achieve, especially in the internet voting context. In Selene this appears to be tricky. If a voter claims that the vote corresponding to their tracker is not what they cast, it is hard to determine if it is the voter who is lying or mis-remembering, or the device or the system that cheated. But this is a problem with the tracking number approach anyway.

If a voter insists that the vote on the WBB is wrong, we could resolve this if the voter is prepared to sacrifice their ballot privacy by allowing threshold decryptions of their ballot for example. This has to be performed with great care and suitable controls, and presumably *in camera* to avoid introducing coercion opportunities. The use of voting codes may help here, but this necessitates mechanisms to distribute these to the voters in a secure fashion and complicates the scheme.

8   Alternative Selene Scheme

We will now briefly describe an alternative version of the scheme which dispels the chance of being caught lying about a faked tracker, but where the coerced voters loose their ability to verify their vote. The idea is that the voting authority adds $f \cdot c$ extra fake trackers, where f is a number greater than the expected number of coerced voters. These trackers are added in the clear before the mixing of the trackers and we thus in total have $v + f \cdot c$ trackers. All the trackers are sent through a first mixing giving the anonymised encrypted tracking numbers on the BB

$$\{g^{n_{\pi(a)}}\}'_{PK_T} , \quad a = 1, \ldots, v + f \cdot c$$

The first v trackers are used as in the basic Selene construction. The remaining $f \cdot c$ trackers are collected into f sets $\{g^{n'_{s,k}}\}'_{PK_T}$ where $s = 1, \ldots, f$ and

$k = 1, \ldots, c$. For each set, the c trackers are on the BB assigned to a vote for each candidate in a public fashion using trivial encryptions

$$(\{g^{n_{s,1}'}\}_{PK_T}, \{\mathsf{Cand}_1\}_{PK_T}), \ldots, (\{g^{n_{s,c}'}\}_{PK_T}, \{\mathsf{Cand}_c\}_{PK_T}).$$

In the final construction of the tally board on BB, the extra trackers are added to the ones which have gone through the basic Selene construction and are mixed along with these. This means that the resulting tally board contains f extra votes for each candidate corresponding to the $f \cdot c$ fake trackers. Due to the first and final mixing nobody at this stage knows which trackers are the fake ones.

After revealing the trackers, coerced voters can now contact the voting authority via an anonymous channel. The voting authority will then request a fake set of c trackers to be jointly decrypted by the Tellers, and it will send these trackers to the voter. Further it will instruct the Tellers not to inform the corresponding voter of the real α term. It will use a unique fake set for each coerced voter. The coerced voter can now use the unique tracker of choice to show to the coercer, and she can also compute the corresponding fake α term. The voter gets c trackers to sidestep an anonymity issue: if a voter asks for a fake tracker for a specific candidate, she probably did not vote for that candidate.

The coerced voter cannot get her real tracking number. The reason is that the coercer would then demand to see two unique tracking numbers for the candidate of his choice. This means that we have a new type of weak coercion-resistance where the un-coerced voters can verify, but coerced voters can cast the vote of their choice, but loose the ability to directly verify this vote. In the construction above each Teller is trusted for coercion-resistance, however, with a bit more elaborate construction this trust could be moved to the voting authority alone.

9   Conclusions

We present a new voting protocol, based on the idea of tracking numbers but with the twist that voters do not learn their number until after voting has finished and the tracker/vote pairs have been posted to the bulletin board. This counters the usual coercer attack on such tracking number systems: the coercer demands that the voter hand over her tracking number before the results are posted. We also provide a mix net construction that ensures that each voter gets a unique tracking number, preventing the attack of assigning the same tracker to voters likely to vote the same way. The construction ensures a high level of assurance that the voter receives the correct tracker while ensuring that this is deniable to a third party.

The resulting scheme provides a good level of verifiability and coercion resistance while at the same time providing a very direct and simple to understand mechanism for voter verification. The protocol is not crypto free, but the crypto is kept under the bonnet for ordinary voters, and in particular the voter verification step involves just tracking numbers and votes in the clear. Voters do not have to handle encrypted ballots as is the case for previous E2E verifiable schemes. A further advantage appears to be that we avoid the need to audit the ballots created by the voter's device. Typically this necessitates the introduction of some kind of cut-and-chose protocol into the voting ceremony, significantly complicating the voter experience. Now, because the voter gets to check her vote in the clear we can sidestep this complication, but at the cost of incurring dispute resolution issues.

For future research, it would be interesting to perform a usability experiment on the Selene protocol to gauge the user experience compared to other e-voting schemes. We also plan to investigate mechanisms to provide cleaner dispute resolution.

In is interesting to note that the Selene construction can be thought of as an add-on to an existing non-verifiable scheme, or indeed a conventional E2E verifiable scheme for which people want a greater degree of transparency in the verification. Indeed Selene could even be retrofitted to a cryptographic election that has been contested. Note further that an option is to run the basic Selene scheme, but if a significant level of coercion is reported before and during the vote casting period, the Selene II constructions (presented in the full version of the paper) could be dynamically added to the WBB give the higher degree of coercion resistance.

Acknowledgements. We would like to thank Sunoo Park, Bill Roscoe, Mark Ryan and Richard Stallman for interesting discussions and suggestions. Further, Vincenzo Iovino is supported by the National Research Fund, Luxembourg, and Peter B. Rønne is supported by the ANR/FNR project Sequoia ANR-14-CE28-0030-01.

References

1. Arnaud, M., Cortier, V., Wiedling, C.: Analysis of an electronic boardroom voting system. In: Heather, J., Schneider, S., Teague, V. (eds.) Vote-ID 2013. LNCS, vol. 7985, pp. 109–126. Springer, Heidelberg (2013)
2. Ben-Nun, J., Fahri, N., Llewellyn, M., Riva, B., Rosen, A., Ta-Shma, A., Wikström, D.: A new implementation of a dual (paper and cryptographic) voting system. In: 5th International Conference on Electronic Votin (eVOTE) (2012)
3. Benaloh, J.: Simple verifiable elections. In: Wallach, D.S., Rivest, R.L. (eds.) USENIX/ACCURATE Electronic Voting Technology Workshop, EVT 2006, Vancouver, BC, Canada, 1 August 2006. USENIX Association (2006)
4. Benaloh, J.C., Tuinstra, D.: Receipt-free secret-ballot elections (extended abstract). In: Leighton, F.T., Goodrich, M.T. (eds.) Proceedings of the Twenty-Sixth Annual ACM Symposium on Theory of Computing, 23–25 May 1994, Montréal, Québec, Canada, pp. 544–553. ACM (1994)
5. Bernhard, D., Pereira, O., Warinschi, B.: How not to prove yourself: pitfalls of the Fiat-Shamir heuristic and applications to Helios. In: Wang, X., Sako, K. (eds.) ASIACRYPT 2012. LNCS, vol. 7658, pp. 626–643. Springer, Heidelberg (2012)
6. Bursuc, S., Grewal, G.S., Ryan, M.D.: Trivitas: voters directly verifying votes. In: Kiayias, A., Lipmaa, H. (eds.) VoteID 2011. LNCS, vol. 7187, pp. 190–207. Springer, Heidelberg (2012)
7. Clarkson, M.R., Chong, S., Myers, A.C.: Civitas: a secure voting system. In: IEEE Symposium on Security and Privacy (2008)

8. Cortier, V., Fuchsbauer, G., Galindo, D.: Beleniosrf: a strongly receipt-free electronic voting scheme. IACR Cryptology ePrint Archive 2015:629 (2015)
9. Cortier, V., Galindo, D., Glondu, S., Izabachène, M.: Election verifiability for Helios under weaker trust assumptions. In: Kutyłowski, M., Vaidya, J. (eds.) ICAIS 2014, Part II. LNCS, vol. 8713, pp. 327–344. Springer, Heidelberg (2014)
10. Cortier, V., Smyth, B.: Attacking and fixing Helios: an analysis of ballot secrecy. In: Proceedings of the 24th IEEE Computer Security Foundations Symposium, CSF 2011, Cernay-la-Ville, France, pp. 297–311, 27–29 June 2011
11. Cramer, R., Gennaro, R., Schoenmakers, B.: A secure and optimally efficient multi-authority election scheme. In: Fumy, W. (ed.) EUROCRYPT 1997. LNCS, vol. 1233, pp. 103–118. Springer, Heidelberg (1997)
12. Gennaro, R.: Achieving independence efficiently and securely. In: Anderson, J.H. (ed.) 14th ACM Symposium Annual on Principles of Distributed Computing, pp. 130–136. Association for Computing Machinery, August 1995
13. Goldreich, O.: Foundations of Cryptography: Basic Applications, vol. 2. Cambridge University Press, Cambridge (2004)
14. Grewal, G.S., Ryan, M.D., Bursuc, S., Ryan, P.Y.A.: Caveat coercitor: coercion-evidence in electronic voting. In: 2013 IEEE Symposium on Security and Privacy, SP 2013, Berkeley, CA, USA, 19–22 May 2013, pp. 367–381. IEEE Computer Society (2013)
15. Grewal, G.S., Ryan, M.D., Chen, L., Clarkson, M.R.: Du-vote: remote electronic voting with untrusted computers. In: Fournet, C., Hicks, M.W., Viganò, L. (eds.) IEEE 28th Computer Security Foundations Symposium, CSF 2015, Verona, Italy, 13–17 July 2015, pp. 155–169. IEEE (2015)
16. Heather, J., Lundin, D.: The append-only web bulletin board. In: Degano, P., Guttman, J., Martinelli, F. (eds.) FAST 2008. LNCS, vol. 5491, pp. 242–256. Springer, Heidelberg (2009)
17. Juels, A., Catalano, D., Jakobsson, M.: Coercion-resistant electronic elections. In: Proceedings of the 2005 ACM Workshop on Privacy in the Electronic Society, WPES 2005, Alexandria, VA, USA, pp. 61–70, 7 November 2005
18. Kulyk, O., Teague, V., Volkamer, M.: Extending Helios towards private eligibility verifiability. In: Haenni, R., Koenig, R.E., Wikström, D. (eds.) VoteID 2015. LNCS, vol. 9269, pp. 57–73. Springer, Heidelberg (2015)
19. Pfitzmann, B., Sadeghi, A.-R.: Anonymous fingerprinting with direct non-repudiation. In: Okamoto, T. (ed.) ASIACRYPT 2000. LNCS, vol. 1976, pp. 401–414. Springer, Heidelberg (2000)
20. Ramchen, K., Teague, V.: Parallel shuffling and its application to prêt à voter. In: 2010 Electronic Voting Technology Workshop/Workshop on Trustworthy Elections, EVT/WOTE 2010, Washington, D.C., USA, 9–10 August 2010
21. Randell, B., Ryan, P.Y.A.: Voting technologies and trust. In: IEEE Symposium on Security and Privacy, pp. 50–56 (2006)
22. Rivest, R.L.: The ThreeBallot Voting System. https://people.csail.mit.edu/rivest/Rivest-TheThreeBallotVotingSystem.pdf
23. Ryan, P.Y.A., Rønne, P.B., Iovino, V.: Selene: voting with transparent verifiability and coercion-mitigation. IACR Cryptology ePrint Archive, 2015:1105 (2015)
24. Ryan, P.Y.A., Teague, V.: Pretty good democracy. In: Workshop on Security Protocols (2009)
25. Ryan, P.Y.A., Schneider, S.A.: Prêt à voter with re-encryption mixes. Technical report CS-TR-956, University of Newcastle (2006)
26. Scantegrity Team. Scantegrity. http://www.scantegrity.org/papers/whitepaper.pdf

27. Schneier, B.: Applied Cryptography - Protocols, Algorithms, and Source Code in C, 2nd edn. Wiley, Hoboken (1996)
28. Shoup, V., Gennaro, R.: Securing threshold cryptosystems against chosen ciphertext attack. In: Nyberg, K. (ed.) EUROCRYPT 1998. LNCS, vol. 1403, pp. 1–16. Springer, Heidelberg (1998)
29. Wikström, D.: Simplified submission of inputs to protocols. In: Ostrovsky, R., De Prisco, R., Visconti, I. (eds.) SCN 2008. LNCS, vol. 5229, pp. 293–308. Springer, Heidelberg (2008)

On the Possibility of Non-interactive E-Voting in the Public-Key Setting

Rosario Giustolisi[1], Vincenzo Iovino[2], and Peter B. Rønne[2,3]([✉])

[1] SICS Swedish ICT, Kista, Sweden
fgiustol@gmail.com
[2] University of Luxembourg, Luxembourg City, Luxembourg
vinciovino@gmail.com, peter.roenne@inria.fr
[3] INRIA Nancy, Villers-lès-nancy, France

Abstract. In 2010 Hao, Ryan and Zielinski proposed a simple decentralized e-voting protocol that only requires 2 rounds of communication. Thus, for k elections their protocol needs $2k$ rounds of communication. Observing that the first round of their protocol is aimed to establish the public-keys of the voters, we propose an extension of the protocol as a *non-interactive* e-voting scheme in the public-key setting (NIVS) in which the voters, after having published their public-keys, can use the corresponding secret-keys to participate in an arbitrary number of *one-round* elections.

We first construct a NIVS with a standard tally function where the number of votes for each candidate is counted.

Further, we present constructions for two alternative types of elections. Specifically in the first type (*dead or alive elections*) the tally shows if *at least one* voter cast a vote for the candidate. In the second one (*elections by unanimity*), the tally shows if *all* voters cast a vote for the candidate.

Our constructions are based on bilinear groups of prime order.

As definitional contribution we provide formal computational definitions for privacy and verifiability of NIVSs. We conclude by showing intriguing relations between our results, secure computation, electronic exams and conference management systems.

Keywords: E-voting · Bilinear maps · Secure computation · Electronic exams · Conference management systems

1 Introduction

Background. In 2010 Hao, Ryan and Zielinski [HRZ10] (see also [KSRH12]) designed a simple decentralized e-voting protocol that only needs 2 rounds of communication and is (publicly) verifiable. Their protocol for n participants can be summarized as follows. Let us assume that a trusted authority sets up a Diffie-Hellman [DH76] group $\mathbb{G}$ of prime order p with generator g. In the first round, each voter j chooses a secret element $x_j \leftarrow \mathbb{Z}_p$ and forwards g^{x_j} to the public

© International Financial Cryptography Association 2016
J. Clark et al. (Eds.): FC 2016 Workshops, LNCS 9604, pp. 193–208, 2016.
DOI: 10.1007/978-3-662-53357-4_13

bulletin-board. Now, each voter j computes the value $g^{y_j} \overset{\triangle}{=} g^{\sum_{k<j} x_k - \sum_{k>j} x_k}$ and in the second round sends her ballot $\mathsf{Blt}_j \overset{\triangle}{=} g^{v_j} g^{x_j y_j}$, where $v_j \in \{0, 1\}$ is her vote.

From the values Blt_j's the tally can be computed as the product, in fact it is easy to see that $\prod_{j \in [n]} g^{x_j y_j} = 1$ and thus $r \overset{\triangle}{=} \prod_{j \in [n]} \mathsf{Blt}_j = g^{\sum v_j}$.

Assuming that the result is small it can be computed by computing the discrete log of r in base g. The previous explanation is an oversimplification that skips some aspects, like zero-knowledge proofs for verifiability, that we will take into consideration later.

1.1   Multiple Non-interactive Elections in the PK Setting

The Public-Key Setting. The first round of the protocol outlined above can be viewed as the publication of the public-key (PK, henceforth) of the users. That is, we can imagine the element g^{x_j} as the PK of user j and x_j as her secret-key (SK, henceforth). After establishing these pairs of PKs/SKs the voter can cast her vote *non-interactively* (i.e., in a *single* round of interaction).

Note also that non-interactive e-voting is provable impossible to achieve without the PK setting because it clashes with any reasonable notion of privacy. In fact, if it was possible to compute the result of a YES/NO election from a tuple S of n ballots computed in a non-interactive way, then it would be possible to perform the following attack: discard the first $n - 1$ ballots in S and replace them with another tuple of ballots that all encode the vote for 0, and compute the tally to learn the vote of the n-th voter in S.

We thus raise the following question:

> In a PK setting, can we achieve a protocol that allows the voters to participate in an *unbounded* number of non-interactive elections? That is, after the users make public their PKs, while retaining the corresponding SKs, is it possible for them to engage in an unbounded number of *one-round* voting protocols?

The protocol of Hao *et al.* fails to satisfy this property. In fact, even if we consider the first round in their scheme as the establishment of the PKs/SKs and the voters make two non-interactive elections then the privacy is completely broken. The reason is that two ballots belonging to the same voter leak the difference of the votes.

We solve this issue by resorting to bilinear maps [BF01, Jou04]. Our new protocol extends the one of Hao *et al.* as follows. First of all, we will associate a unique identifier id $\in \{0, 1\}^{\lambda}$ to each election. These identifiers could be consecutive numbers, $1, 2, \ldots$ or some other unique identifiers announced for each election, e.g. containing the election date. That is, voters will associate an identifier id to their ballots and only ballots for the same identifier (i.e. for the same election) can be put together to compute the tally.

Let us assume a bilinear instance $\mathcal{I} \overset{\triangle}{=} (p, \mathbb{G}, \mathbb{G}_T, \mathbf{e})$ (see Sect. 2.2) in which $\mathbb{G}$ is a group of prime order p and $\mathbf{e}$ is a bilinear function mapping elements of

$\mathbb{G}$ to elements of $\mathbb{G}_T$ satisfying non-degeneracy and bilinearity, and let Hash be a hash function taking as input $\mathcal{I}$, an identifier of an election id and outputs elements of $\mathbb{G}$. In our analysis Hash will be modeled as a Random Oracle (RO, in short) model [BR93]. Our protocol in the PK setting is described next.

All voters randomly choose their secret-key $x_j \leftarrow \mathbb{Z}_p$ and publish their public-key $\mathsf{Pk}_j = g^{x_j}$. Each voter computes a random value $\mathsf{Hash}(\mathcal{I}, \mathsf{id}) \in \mathbb{G}$ to be used in the election associated with identifier id.

In election id each voter j will cast her vote[1] v_j as

$$\mathsf{Blt}_j \stackrel{\triangle}{=} \mathbf{e}(g^{y_j}, \mathsf{Hash}(\mathcal{I}, \mathsf{id}))^{x_j} \cdot \mathbf{e}(g^{v_j}, \mathsf{Hash}(\mathcal{I}, \mathsf{id})),$$

where g^{y_j} is computed from the PKs g^{x_j}'s exactly as in the Hao *et al.*'s protocol described above. As will be explained below, the ballot is cast with a proof of well-formedness.

If we define $g_{\mathsf{id}} \stackrel{\triangle}{=} \mathbf{e}(g, \mathsf{Hash}(\mathcal{I}, \mathsf{id}))$, the ballot can be written as $\mathsf{Blt}_j = g_{\mathsf{id}}^{v_j} g_{\mathsf{id}}^{x_j y_j}$ and the relation to Hao et al.'s approach becomes clear. In the target group of the bilinear map, we have constructed a hash function creating new generators for each election in such a way that the PK for any participant, in the new generator, can be calculated by any other participant, but the corresponding SKs stay unchanged and secret.

Privacy Game. This new model calls for new security definitions. We define the privacy for non-interactive e-voting schemes in the PK setting (NIVS, in short) by means of the following game.

The challenger computes a pair of PK/SK for each voter and feeds the adversary with the PKs. Then a random bit b is chosen and the adversary can adaptively make an unbounded number of queries to an oracle invoking it with two sets of votes, S_0 and S_1 with the same sum and receiving back the ballots computed with S_b by means of the SKs. At any point the adversary can output its guess b' and it wins the game iff $b' = b$.

A formal definition that also takes in account an adversary that corrupts a set of voters seeing their SKs, and allows for non-standard tally functions, is given in Sect. 2.1.

We will prove the following theorem.

Theorem 1. If the Bilinear Decision Diffie-Hellman Assumption [Boy08] defined in Sect. 2.2 holds, then in the RO model no non-uniform PPT adversary can break the privacy (see Definition 2) of the scheme of Sect. 3 with non-negligible probability.

The proof is given in Sect. 3.1. Note that the privacy definition does not capture e.g. vote copying attacks. In fact, it implicitly assumes a perfect synchronous broadcast channel. We postpone a stronger ballot privacy definition for future work.

---

[1] In the following the term $\mathbf{e}(g^{v_j}, \mathsf{Hash}(\mathcal{I}, \mathsf{id}))$ could be replaced without loss of generality by $\mathbf{e}(g^{v_j}, g)$.

Verifiability. As a further definitional contribution we provide a formal definition for verifiability. Verifiability for NIVSs is somewhat different from schemes
with trusted authorities. For example everybody, also third parties, can perform
the tally. Further we will think of being in a setting where the ballots and proofs
are cast using authenticated channels using the PK structure. Alternatively signatures can be added. This prevents attacks where an adversary votes on behalf
of another voter. Intuitively verifiability should then guarantee the ability of verifying that a voter cast a ballot according to the vote rules and that the tally has
ideal functionality. First of all, let us analyze how a well-formed ballot look like.

We expect that a well-formed ballot gives consistent results with other honestly computed ballots. That is, a ballot Blt should uniquely determine a vote v
that, along with any other set of valid ballots, results in a consistent computation.
Our definition of verifiability given in Sect. 2.1 is divided in two parts (that have
to hold together). The first part states that a ballot uniquely determines a vote
v such that for any other set of ballots corresponding to another vector of votes
v, the output of the algorithm that computes the tally will be equal either to
the output of the functionality with inputs v and v or to an error $\bot$.

The second part states that there exists an algorithm VerifyBallot whose aim
is to verify the well-formedness of a ballot Blt such that if the verification passes
for Blt then for any other set B of honestly computed ballots, the result of the
tally with respect to the set of ballots $B \cup \{Blt\}$ will not result in an error $\bot$.

In order to guarantee verifiability of the above sketched NIVS, like in Hao
et al., we add proofs of well-formedness of the ballot. Specifically we add a proof
that the vote in the ballot is 0 or 1 using the Cramer *et al.* technique adapted
to the bilinear setting. We discuss this in Sect. 2.3.

We stress that the proof of well-formedness of the ballot is sufficient to satisfy
our notion of verifiability. Unlike Hao *et al.* we do not add proofs of knowledge
to the public-keys as in our model we do not capture malleability or copying
attacks, however, it straightforward to add these proofs of knowledge.

We note that this protocol is not fair, e.g. the last to cast a ballot can compute
the result before casting her own vote. As explained in [KSRH12] this can be
mitigated by an extra commitment round. Also the protocol is not robust, i.e.
we cannot tally if someone fails to vote. This was also considered in [KSRH12]
and in this event it is enough to run an extra round for the remaining voters to
recover the tally result of the votes that has been cast.

Beyond YES/NO Elections. The drawback of the previous scheme is that
it only supports YES/NO elections. We can extend our scheme to support more
complex elections and multiple candidates but due to space constraints we defer
it to the full version [GIR15].

1.2   Relation to Secure Computation

Our results relate to secure computation [Yao82, Gol04] of specific functionalities. A recent result of Garg *et al.* [GGHR14] showed the first 2-rounds secure
computation protocol in the CRS model for any functionality.

However, even if we wish to use the protocol of Garg *et al.* to execute k secure evaluations of the functions described in this paper, we would need $2k$ rounds of communication. Instead, using our NIVSs we only need $k + 1$ rounds, one for establishing the PKs and one for each non-interactive secure function evaluation (of the functions supported by our schemes) in the PK setting.

Another related cryptographic notion is Input-Indistinguishable Computation proposed by Micali et al. [MPR06] that shares the indistinguishability-based flavor of NIVS but was implemented with more rounds than ours (though the main focus of the authors was on general functionalities and security under concurrent executions).

It seems that Multi-input Functional Encryption (MIFE, in short) [GGG+14] could be also used to obtain a form of a NIVS in the CRS model (setting the CRS to a token for the desired function). However, this is not straightforward since MIFE would have to be likely combined with signature schemes and, as the indistinguishability-security of MIFE only holds when the two challenge vectors of inputs are not 'splittable' under the functionality,[2] it would offer no security guarantee because in this case there exist many values splitting the challenge vectors.[3] A generalization of MIFE studied by Iovino and Żebrowski [IZ15] could be useful in this context.

It is an intriguing research direction to investigate the class of functionalities we can compute in our setting.

Applications to Secure Conference Management Systems and E-Exams. In the full version [GIR15] we also show relations and applications of our work to conference management systems and e-exams.

1.3 Our Results in a Nutshell

Our contributions can be summarized as follows.

- **A New Model.** We introduce the novel concept of non-interactive voting schemes in the PK setting that extends the two-rounds elections of Hao *et al.* In this model, n voters publish their public-keys retaining the corresponding secret-keys, and each voter using her secret-key can compute her ballot and send it to a public bulletin board. Then, the n ballots can be put together to compute the result of the election.

  Therefore, in this model k elections can be executed with $k + 1$ rounds of communications whereas using Hao *et al.*'s schemes would result in $2k$ rounds.

---

[2] For instance a value z splits two vectors (x_1, x_2) and (y_1, y_2) under a function f if $f(x_1, z) \neq f(y_1, z)$ or $f(z, x_2) \neq f(z, y_2)$. Two vectors are splittable if there exists a value z that splits them.

[3] Precisely, whereas it would be *difficult* to find an input that splits the two challenge vectors under the functionality (as it accounts to forge a signature), such splitting inputs *exist* and thus the security of MIFE is vacuous.

- **Formal Definitions.** In Sect. 2.1 we provide formal definitions for non-interactive voting schemes in the PK setting, in particular for privacy and verifiability, for which a formal treatment was missing.
- **Scheme for YES/NO Elections.** In Sect. 3 we present a non-interactive voting scheme in the PK setting for YES/NO elections (i.e., in which each voter can cast 0 or 1 and the tally computes the sum of all votes) that is provably secure from the Bilinear Decision Diffie-Hellman assumption.
- **Alternative Types of Elections.** In Sect. 1.1 we presented schemes for alternative types of (YES/NO) elections that could be of independent interest. In particular we can support a *dead or alive election* in which n voters can choose 1 candidate and the result shows for if *at least one* voter cast a vote for him. Another type of election we support is *election by unanimity*, in which the result shows if *all* voters cast a vote for the candidate.

  We implemented our NIVSs for YES/NO, dead or alive and unanimity elections using the pbc library [Lyn] and we tested them on a laptop equipped with an Intel Core i7 getting quite good performances.
- **Relation to Secure Computation.** In Sect. 1.2 we show relations between our results and secure computation.
- **Applications to Secure Electronic Exams and Conference Systems.** In Sect. 1.2 we show that our results have direct applications to secure electronic exams and conference management systems.

2   Definitions

Notation. A *negligible* function $\mathsf{negl}(k)$ is a function that is smaller than the inverse of any polynomial in k (from a certain point and on). We denote by $[n]$ the set of numbers $\{1, \ldots, n\}$, and we shorten *Probabilistic Polynomial-Time* as PPT. If g and A are elements of the same cyclic group, we denote by $\mathbf{dlog}_g A$ the discrete log of A in base g. If S is a finite set we denote by $a \leftarrow S$ the process of setting a equal to a uniformly chosen element of S.

2.1   Non-interactive Voting Scheme in the PK Setting

A non-interactive voting scheme in the PK setting (NIVS, in short) is associated with a natural number $n > 0$, the *number of voters*, a set D, the *domain of valid votes*, a set Σ, the *range of possible results*, and a *count function* $F : D^n \to \Sigma$. After that an authority sets-up the public parameters pp, each voter generates a pair of public- and secret-keys. By means of an algorithm Cast and of her own secret-key each voter can cast her vote $v \in D$ generating a ballot Blt and, using the public-keys of all voters, the tally can be publicly computed by means of an algorithm EvalTally. A single ballot can be verified to be the output of the Cast algorithm with input a valid vote $v \in D$ and with respect to a public-key of a voter by means of the algorithm VerifyBallot.

Definition 1 (Non-interactive Voting Scheme). A (n, D, Σ, F)-*non-interactive voting scheme in the PK setting* NIVS for number of voters n, domain of valid votes D, range of possible results Σ and count function F is a tuple.

NIVS $\stackrel{\triangle}{=}$ (Setup, KeyGen, Cast, VerifyBallot, EvalTally) of 5 PPT algorithms with the following syntax:

1. Setup(1^λ), on input the security parameter in unary, outputs *public* parameters pp.
2. KeyGen(pp), on input the public parameters pp outputs a *public-key* Pk and a *secret-key* Sk.
3. Cast(pp, j, id, Sk_j, $(Pk)_{i \in [n]-\{j\}}$, v), on input the public parameters pp, the secret-key Sk of voter j, the identifier id $\in \{0,1\}^\lambda$ of the election, the public keys $(Pk_i)_{i \in [v]-\{j\}}$ of the other voters, and a vote $v \in D$, outputs a *ballot* Blt;
4. VerifyBallot(pp, Pk, id, Blt), on input the public parameters pp, a public-key Pk of a voter, the identifier id $\in \{0,1\}^\lambda$ of the election and a ballot Blt, outputs a value in $\{\perp, OK\}$;
5. EvalTally(pp, $Pk_1, \ldots, Pk_n$, id, $Blt_1, \ldots, Blt_n$), on input the public parameters pp, the public-keys of all voters, the identifier id $\in \{0,1\}^\lambda$ of the election, and the ballots cast by all voter, outputs $y \in \Sigma \cup \{\perp\}$.

Correctness and Verifiability. In addition we require the following properties for a NIVS.

1. Correctness or self-tallying for NIVS. For all pp $\leftarrow$ Setup(1^λ), for all $(Pk_1, Sk_1), \ldots, (Pk_n, Sk_n)$ such that for all $i \in [n]$ $(Pk_i, Sk_i) \leftarrow$ KeyGen(pp), all $v_1, \ldots, v_n \in D$, for all identifiers id $\in \{0,1\}^\lambda$, for all $Blt_1, \ldots, Blt_n$ such that for all $i \in [n]$ $Blt_i \leftarrow$ Cast(pp, j, id, Sk, $(Pk)_{i \in [n]-\{j\}}$, v), we have that EvalTally(pp, $Pk_1, \ldots, Pk_n$, id, $Blt_1, \ldots, Blt_n$) = $F(v_1, \ldots, v_n)$.
2. Verifiability or dispute-freeness for NIVS. We present two versions of verifiability, one statistical and one computational.

   - Statistical verifiability for NIVS. To not overburden the presentation, we first present a simplified notion of verifiability against one malicious voter and then we will discuss how to extend it to withstand any number of malicious voters. The definition of statistical verifiability against one malicious voter consists of the following two conditions (that have to hold both).

   (1) For all except negligible fraction of pp $\leftarrow$ Setup(1^λ),[4] all $j \in [n]$, all Pk, all Blt, there exists a vote $v \in D$ such that: for all identifiers id $\in \{0,1\}^\lambda$, all except negligible fraction of $(Pk_i, Sk_i)_{i \in [n]-\{j\}}$ such

---

[4] In the sequel, we use the expression "all except negligible fraction of..." to mean that the statement holds for all except negligible fraction of the randomness values which the object is computed from. For instance, by "for all except negligible fraction of $(Pk_i, Sk_i)_{i \in [n]-\{j\}}$ such that for all $i \in [n] - \{j\}$ $(Pk_i, Sk_i) \leftarrow$ KeyGen(pp)..." we mean that for all except negligible fraction of the randomness values $r \in \{0,1\}^\lambda$, for $(Pk_i, Sk_i)_{i \in [n]-\{j\}}$ such that for all $i \in [n] - \{j\}$ $(Pk_i, Sk_i) \leftarrow$ KeyGen(pp; r)...

that for all $i \in [n] - \{j\}$ $(\mathsf{Pk}_i, \mathsf{Sk}_i) \leftarrow \mathsf{KeyGen}(\mathsf{pp})$, and all $v_i \in D$ with $i \in [n] - \{j\}$ and all except negligible fraction of $(\mathsf{Blt}_i)_{i \in [n] - \{j\}}$ satisfying $\mathsf{Blt}_i \leftarrow \mathsf{Cast}(\mathsf{pp}, i, \mathsf{id}, \mathsf{Sk}, (\mathsf{Pk})_{j \in [n] - \{i\}}, v_i)$, it holds that $\mathsf{EvalTally}(\mathsf{pp}, \mathsf{Pk}_1, \ldots, \mathsf{Pk}_{j-1}, \mathsf{Pk}, \mathsf{Pk}_{j+1}, \ldots, \mathsf{Pk}_n, \mathsf{id}, \mathsf{Blt}_1, \ldots, \mathsf{Blt}_{j-1}, \mathsf{Blt}, \mathsf{Blt}_{j+1}, \ldots, \mathsf{Blt}_n)$ outputs either $F(v_1, \ldots, v_{j-1}, v, v_{j+1}, \ldots, v_n)$ or $\bot$.

(2) In addition, we require the following to hold. For all except negligible fraction of $\mathsf{pp} \leftarrow \mathsf{Setup}(1^\lambda)$, for all $j \in [n]$, all Pk, all Blt, if $\mathsf{VerifyBallot}(\mathsf{pp}, \mathsf{Pk}, \mathsf{id}, \mathsf{Blt}) = \mathsf{OK}$ then: for all identifiers $\mathsf{id} \in \{0,1\}^\lambda$, all except negligible fraction of $(\mathsf{Pk}_i, \mathsf{Sk}_i)_{i \in [n] - \{j\}}$ such that for all $i \in [n] - \{j\}$ $(\mathsf{Pk}_i, \mathsf{Sk}_i) \leftarrow \mathsf{KeyGen}(\mathsf{pp})$, all $v_i \in D$ with $i \in [n] - \{j\}$, all except negligible fraction of $(\mathsf{Blt}_i)_{i \in [n] - \{j\}}$ such that for all $i \in [n] - \{j\}$ $\mathsf{Blt}_i \leftarrow \mathsf{Cast}(\mathsf{pp}, j, \mathsf{id}, \mathsf{Sk}, (\mathsf{Pk})_{i \in [n] - \{j\}}, v_i)$, it holds that $\mathsf{EvalTally}(\mathsf{pp}, \mathsf{Pk}_1, \ldots, \mathsf{Pk}_{j-1}, \mathsf{Pk}, \mathsf{Pk}_{j+1}, \ldots, \mathsf{Pk}_n, \mathsf{id}, \mathsf{Blt}_1, \ldots, \mathsf{Blt}_{j-1}, \mathsf{Blt}, \mathsf{Blt}_{j+1}, \ldots, \mathsf{Blt}_n) \neq \bot$.

As mentioned before, the above definition only takes in account a single malicious voter because we quantify over a single, possibly malicious, voter j, a single, possibly maliciously computed, PK Pk of voter j and a single, possibly maliciously computed, ballot Blt of voter j. By quantifying over all sets of up to n voters and changing it in the obvious way we get the actual definition.

Finally, we mention that for the RO model the above definition has to be adapted in the obvious way so as to hold in probability over the choices of the RO and giving the adversaries oracle access to the RO.

– Computational verifiability for NIVS. Computational verifiability for NIVS is identical to statistical verifiability for NIVS except that we quantify for all non-uniform PPT adversaries $\mathcal{A}$ and we require that both conditions (1) and (2) do not have to hold for all Pk and Blt but only for strings Pk and Blt output by $\mathcal{A}$ executed on input the security parameter λ and the public parameters pp.

Also here, as mentioned before, the actual definition has to quantify over multiple malicious voters.

Privacy. Now we formalize the notion of *privacy* (also called *maximal ballot privacy* in Hao *et al.*) in the style of indistinguishability-based security for encryption and related primitives. The privacy for a (n, D, Σ, F)-NIVS $\mathsf{NIVS} \overset{\triangle}{=} (\mathsf{Setup}, \mathsf{KeyGen}, \mathsf{Cast}, \mathsf{VerifyBallot}, \mathsf{EvalTally})$ is formalized by means of the following game $\mathsf{Priv}_{\mathcal{A}}^{n, D, \Sigma, F, \mathsf{NIVS}}$ between an adversary (with access to an oracle) $\mathcal{A} \overset{\triangle}{=} (\mathcal{A}_0, \mathcal{A}_1)$ and a *challenger* $\mathcal{C}$.

$\mathsf{Priv}_{\mathcal{A}}^{n,D,\Sigma,F,\mathsf{NIVS}}(1^\lambda)$

- Setup phase. $\mathcal{C}$ generates $\mathsf{pp} \leftarrow \mathsf{Setup}(1^\lambda)$, choose a random bit $b \leftarrow \{0,1\}$ and runs $\mathcal{A}_0$ on input pp;
- Corruption phase. $\mathcal{A}_0$, on input pp, outputs a set $S \subset [n]$ of indices of voters it wants to corrupt.
- Key Generation Phase. For all $i \in [n]$ the challenger generates n pairs of public- and secret-keys $(\mathsf{Pk}_i, \mathsf{Sk}_i) \leftarrow \mathsf{KeyGen}(\mathsf{pp})$, and runs $\mathcal{A}_1^{\mathsf{Vote}(\cdot)}$ on input $(\mathsf{Pk}_i, \mathsf{Sk}_i)_{i \in S}$ and $(\mathsf{Pk}_i)_{i \in [n]-S}$.
- Query phase. The adversary $\mathcal{A}_1$ has access to a stateful oracle Vote. The oracle Vote on input an identifier $\mathsf{id} \in \{0,1\}^\lambda$ and a pair of vectors $\boldsymbol{v}_0 \overset{\triangle}{=} (v_{0,1}, \ldots, v_{0,n})$ and $\boldsymbol{v}_1 \overset{\triangle}{=} (v_{1,1}, \ldots, v_{1,n})$ outputs the set of ballots $(\mathsf{Cast}(\mathsf{pp}, 1, \mathsf{id}, \mathsf{Sk}_1, (\mathsf{Pk}_i)_{i \in [n]-\{1\}}, v_{b,1}), \ldots, \mathsf{Cast}(\mathsf{pp}, n, \mathsf{id}, \mathsf{Sk}_n, (\mathsf{Pk}_i)_{i \in [n]-\{n\}}, v_{b,n})$.
- Output. At some point the adversary outputs its guess b'.
- Winning condition. The adversary wins the game if the following conditions hold:
  1. $b' = b$.
  2. $v_{0,i} = v_{1,i}$ for any $i \in S$.
  3. for any pair of vectors $(\boldsymbol{v}_0, \boldsymbol{v}_1)$ for which $\mathcal{A}$ asked a query to the oracle Vote it holds that: for any vector $\boldsymbol{v}$, $F(\boldsymbol{v}'_0) = F(\boldsymbol{v}'_1)$ where for $b = 0, 1$ $\boldsymbol{v}'_b$ is the vector equal to $\boldsymbol{v}$ in all indices in S and equal to $\boldsymbol{v}_b$ elsewhere.
  4. S has cardinality $< n$, $\boldsymbol{v}_0$ and $\boldsymbol{v}_1$ are vectors of n values in D and $\mathsf{id} \in \{0,1\}^\lambda$.

The advantage of adversary $\mathcal{A}$ in the above game is defined as

$$\mathsf{Adv}_{\mathcal{A}}^{\mathsf{NIVS},\mathsf{Priv}}(1^\lambda) \overset{\triangle}{=} |\mathrm{Prob}[\mathsf{Priv}_{\mathcal{A}}^{n,D\Sigma,F,\mathsf{NIVS}}(1^\lambda) = 1] - 1/2|$$

Definition 2. We say that NIVS for parameters (n, D, Σ, F) is *private* if all PPT adversaries $\mathcal{A} \overset{\triangle}{=} (\mathcal{A}_0, \mathcal{A}_1)$ have at most negligible advantage in the above game.

Remark 1. We make some remarks on the previous definitions.

- **Perfect Synchronous Broadcast Channel.** Our security definition implicitly assumes a synchronous broadcast channel and as such does not model e.g. malleability and copying attacks.
- **Parameterization.** A (n, D, Σ, F)-NIVS is fully specified only for the 4 parameters n, D, Σ and F, but often for simplicity we will drop the parameters and we will talk about a NIVS when it is clear from the context.
- **Supporting Multiple Functions.** It is possible to extend the definition of a (n, D, Σ, F)-NIVS by replacing the function F with a *set* of functions F so as to have a system that in each election can allow to evaluate the tally according to any function $f \in \mathsf{F}$. In this case, the setup algorithm has to take as additional input a finite description of the set and the other algorithms have to take as additional input a certain function $f \in \mathsf{F}$. The correctness, verifiability and privacy have to be changed accordingly. We point out that our NIVSs for YES/NO elections, for dead or alive elections and for elections by unanimity can be easily unified in a single NIVS for the set of the three corresponding functions.

- **Verifiability.** Note that the first part of the verifiability, let us say statistical, states that a ballot uniquely determines a single vote v that is compatible with any other correctly computed set of ballots. The second part guarantees that the VerifyBallot algorithm can discover whether a ballot is cast correctly. Thus, if the check is satisfies (i.e., with output OK), it means that for a given ballot Blt, any set of $n - 1$ correctly computed ballots, will give consistent results.

- **Constant or Polynomial Number of Voters.** The reader may have noticed that we leave unspecified the relation between the parameter n and the security parameter. In more cases, setting n to a constant is enough. However one could set n to be any polynomial in the security parameter.

- **Programmable RO.** Actually we will assume a definition of privacy identical to the one we formulated except that it is in the (programmable) RO model. In this case the adversary will have, in addition, oracle access to a function O drawn at random from the space of functions $\mathcal{O}$ that map $\{0,1\}^\lambda$ to some space Σ, but possibly modified by a PPT simulator in a polynomial (in λ) number of points. We skip the details of the formal definitions.

  In our schemes we assume that the adversary has access to more than one oracle, but using standard techniques this could be changed into a single oracle, but we refrain from doing it here since it complicates the description.

  We also require a definition of verifiability that holds in probability over the choices of the RO.

- **CRS vs Public-Coin Model.** The public parameters can be seen as a CRS, so one can wonder whether there is difference between the public-coin model and the CRS model. The difference is that in the CRS model the party that generates the public parameters is *not* trusted (though we mention that the trust could be distributed among a set of trusted parties in a threshold way), whereas in the standard model the security should hold even with respect to the party who generated the parameters.

  The above definition of privacy only takes in account the CRS model but can be changed to the standard model by allowing the adversary to see the random coins with which the public parameters are generated. We stress that our construction of Sect. 3 satisfies this stronger definition assuming a variant of BDDH (see Sect. 2.2).

2.2 Bilinear Maps

In this section we describe the bilinear setting with groups of prime order and the assumption that we will use to prove the privacy of the NIVSs presented in Sects. 3 and 1.1.

Prime Order Bilinear Groups. Prime order bilinear groups were first used in Cryptography by Boneh and Franklin [BF01], and Joux [Jou04]. We suppose the existence of an efficient group generator algorithm $\mathcal{G}$ which takes as input the security parameter λ and outputs a description $\mathcal{I} \triangleq (p, \mathbb{G}, \mathbb{G}_T, \mathbf{e})$ of a bilinear instance of prime order, where $\mathbb{G}$ and $\mathbb{G}_T$ are cyclic groups of prime order p, and $\mathbf{e}: \mathbb{G} \times \mathbb{G} \to \mathbb{G}_T$ is a map with the following properties:

1. (Bilinearity): $\forall\, g, h \in \mathbb{G}$ and $a, b \in \mathbb{Z}_p$ it holds that $\mathbf{e}(g^a, h^b) = \mathbf{e}(g, h)^{ab}$.
2. (Non-degeneracy): $\exists\, g \in \mathbb{G}$ such that $\mathbf{e}(g, g)$ has order p in $\mathbb{G}_T$.

Bilinear Decision Diffie-Hellman Assumption. More formally, we have the following definition. First pick a random bilinear instance $\mathcal{I} \triangleq (p, \mathbb{G}, \mathbb{G}_T, \mathbf{e}) \leftarrow \mathcal{G}(1^\lambda)$ and then pick $g \leftarrow \mathbb{G}, a, b, c, z \leftarrow \mathbb{Z}_p$, and set $D \triangleq (\mathcal{I}, g, g^a, g^b, g^c)$, $T_0 \triangleq \mathbf{e}(g, g)^{abc}$ and $T_1 \triangleq \mathbf{e}(g, g)^z$. We define the advantage of any $\mathcal{A}$ in breaking the BDDH Assumption (with respect to $\mathcal{G}$) to be

$$\mathsf{Adv}_{\mathsf{BDDH}}^{\mathcal{A}, \mathcal{G}}(\lambda) \triangleq |\mathrm{Prob}[\mathcal{A}(D, T_0) = 1] - \mathrm{Prob}[\mathcal{A}(D, T_1) = 1]|.$$

We say that Assumption BDDH holds for generator $\mathcal{G}$ if for all non-uniform PPT algorithms $\mathcal{A}$, $\mathsf{Adv}_{\mathsf{BDDH}}^{\mathcal{A}(\lambda), \mathcal{G}}$ is a negligible function of λ.

We mention that if we wish that our NIVS of Sect. 3 satisfy privacy in the public-coin model, we need to assume a stronger variant of the above definition in which the adversary also sees the random coins used to generate the bilinear instance.

2.3 NIZK in the RO

Let R be an efficiently computable binary relation. For pairs $(x, w) \in R$ we call x the statement and w the witness. Let L be the language consisting of statements in R.

Definition 3 (NIZK). A non-interactive zero-knowledge proof system (NIZK, in short), see [BFM88, FLS90], in the RO model, see [BR93, BFW15], for a relation R consists of the following PPT algorithms with access to an oracle O randomly drawn from a space $\mathcal{O}$ of functions with domain and co-domain $\{0, 1\}^\lambda$:

- $\mathsf{Prove}^{O(\cdot)}(x, w)$: takes as input a statement x and a witness w for x, and with oracle access to O produces a proof π.
- $\mathsf{Verify}^{O(\cdot)}(\mathsf{x}, \pi)$: takes in input a statement x and a proof π, and with oracle access to O outputs 1 if the proof is accepted and 0 otherwise.

We call NIZK a non-interactive zero-knowledge proof system for R if it has the properties described below.

- Perfect completeness. A proof system is complete if an honest prover with a valid witness can convince an honest verifier. Formally we have that for any $(x, w) \in R$

$$\Pr[O \leftarrow \mathcal{O}; \pi \leftarrow \mathsf{Prove}^{O(\cdot)}(x, w) : \mathsf{Verify}^{O(\cdot)}(\mathsf{x}, \pi) = 1] = 1.$$

- Soundness. A proof system is sound if it is infeasible to convince an honest verifier when the statement is false. For all non-uniform PPT adversaries $\mathcal{A}$ we have

$$\Pr[O \leftarrow \mathcal{O}; \ (x, \pi) \leftarrow \mathcal{A}^{\mathcal{O}}(1^{\lambda}) : \mathsf{Verify}^{O(\cdot)}(\mathsf{x}, \pi) = 1 \wedge \mathsf{x} \notin \mathsf{L}] = \mathsf{negl}(\lambda).$$

- (Adaptive Multi-theorem) Computational zero-knowledge [BFW15]. A proof system is computational zero-knowledge[5] in the RO model if the proofs do not reveal any information about the witnesses to a bounded adversary. We say a non-interactive proof NIZK is computational zero-knowledge if there exists a PPT *stateful* simulator $\mathsf{Sim} = (\mathsf{Sim}.\mathcal{RO}, \mathsf{Sim})$ that without access to the witness can simulate proofs having in addition the capability of programming the oracle O at any point, i.e., for any x and y it is able to set $O(x) \stackrel{\triangle}{=} y$. For all non-uniform PPT adversaries $\mathcal{A}$ with access to an oracle O, we have that the following quantity is negligible in λ:

$$|\Pr[O \leftarrow \mathcal{O} : \mathcal{A}^{O(\cdot), \mathsf{Prove}_2^{O(\cdot)}(\cdot, \cdot)}(1^{\lambda}) = 1] -$$
$$\Pr[O \leftarrow \mathcal{O} : \mathcal{A}^{\mathsf{Sim}.\mathcal{RO}^{O(\cdot)}, \mathsf{Sim}_2^{O(\cdot)}(\cdot, \cdot)}(1^{\lambda}) = 1]|,$$

where $\mathsf{Prove}_2^{O(\cdot)}(x, w) \stackrel{\triangle}{=} \mathsf{Prove}^{O(\cdot)}(x, w)$ for $(x, w) \in R$, $\mathsf{Sim}_2^{O(\cdot)}(x, w) \stackrel{\triangle}{=} \mathsf{Sim}^{O(\cdot)}(x)$ for $(x, w) \in R$, the latter oracles output $\perp$ for $(x, w) \notin R$ and $\mathsf{Sim}.\mathcal{RO}$ simulates the oracle O possibly modifying it at an arbitrary number of points.

NIZK in the RO for Encryption of 0 or 1. Recall that Hao *et al.* used a protocol of Cramer *et al.* [CDS94] to prove that their ballot correspond to a vote of either 0 or 1. To that aim they convert the terms of their protocol into the form of ElGamal encryptions by seeing the pair (g, g^{y_i}) terms as El Gamal PKs and thus seeing the pair $g^{x_i}, g^{y_i x_i} g^{v_i}$ as an El Gamal encryption with randomness x_i, public-key g^{y_i} and plaintext v_i. The Cramer *et al.*'s sigma protocol can prove that v_i is either 0 or 1 without revealing which. Using the Fiat-Shamir's heuristic [FS87] (see also [BFW15] for discussions about adaptiveness) it can be converted in a NIZK in the RO model.

In our work we need a NIZK in the RO for a relation identical as above except that g is an element of the target group of a bilinear group. Specifically the variable g above takes the form $g \stackrel{\triangle}{=} \mathbf{e}(g', \mathsf{Hash}(\mathcal{I}, s))$ where g' is an element of a bilinear group, $\mathcal{I}$ is a bilinear instance, s is some string and Hash is an hash function mapping the input to the base group.

It is straightforward to see that the protocol of Cramer *et al.* also work when g has this form. In fact the computational assumption on which the security of the sigma protocol of Cramer *et al.* depends, also holds when the underlying group is the target group of a bilinear group, and in particular when the generator of such

---

[5] Note that our definition of zero-knowledgeness is multi-theorem and adaptive like in [BFW15].

group has the above form. This is easy to verify assuming standard assumptions on bilinear maps, but in order not to overburden the presentation we skip the details.

Precisely our relation R_{wf} is the following.

Definition 4 (Relation R_{wf}). $R_{\mathsf{wf}}(x, w) \overset{\triangle}{=} 1$ if $x = (\mathcal{I}, g, A, B, C)$ consists of a bilinear instance $\mathcal{I} \overset{\triangle}{=} (p, \mathbb{G}, \mathbb{G}_T, \mathbf{e})$ and a triple of 3 elements of $\mathbb{G}_T$ and $w = (x, y, v)$ are such that $A = g^y, B = g^x, C = g^{xy}g^v$.

3 NIVS for YES/NO Elections

In this section we present our NIVS for YES/NO elections.

Definition 5 (NIVS for YES/NO Elections). Let O and O_2 be two random oracles (that in the implementation will be set to two secure hash functions, e.g., SHA3). Let $\mathcal{G}$ be a generator for a bilinear instance of prime order, let NIZK $=$ ($\mathsf{Prove}^O, \mathsf{Verify}^O$) be a NIZK in the RO for the relation R_{wf} of Definition 4. Let $n(\lambda)$ be the number of voters, $D \overset{\triangle}{=} \{0, 1\}$ be the domain of valid votes, $\Sigma \overset{\triangle}{=} [n]$ and F the sum function. Furthermore, we assume that the oracle O_2 takes as input a description of a bilinear instance $\mathcal{I} = (p, \mathbb{G}, \mathbb{G}_T, \mathbf{e})$ and maps strings from $\{0, 1\}^\lambda$ to G, and that oracle O maps strings from $\{0, 1\}^\lambda$ to $\{0, 1\}^{p(\star)}$ for some polynomial $p(\cdot)$ as needed by NIZK.

We define a (n, D, Σ, F)-NIVS
NIVS $=$ (Setup, KeyGen, Cast, VerifyBallot, EvalTally) in the RO model as follows.

- Setup(1^λ): on input the security parameter in unary, it outputs $\mathsf{pp} \overset{\triangle}{=} \mathcal{I}$ where $\mathcal{I} \overset{\triangle}{=} (p, \mathbb{G}, \mathbb{G}_T, \mathbf{e}) \leftarrow \mathcal{G}(1^\lambda)$.
- KeyGen(pp): on input the public parameters $\mathsf{pp} \overset{\triangle}{=} (g, p, \mathbb{G}, \mathbb{G}_T, \mathbf{e})$, the algorithm chooses a random $x \leftarrow \mathbb{Z}_p$ and outputs the pair ($\mathsf{Pk} \overset{\triangle}{=} g^x, \mathsf{Sk} \overset{\triangle}{=} x$).
- Cast($\mathsf{pp}, j, \mathsf{id}, \mathsf{Sk}, (\mathsf{Pk})_{i \in [n] - \{j\}}, v$), on input the public parameters pp, the secret-key $\mathsf{Sk} \overset{\triangle}{=} x$ of voter j, the identifier id of the election, the public keys $(\mathsf{Pk}_i)_{i \in [v] - \{j\}}$ of the other voters, and a vote $v \in D$, outputs a pair (Blt, π) where the *ballot* $\mathsf{Blt} \overset{\triangle}{=} \mathbf{e}(Y_j, O_2(\mathcal{I}, \mathsf{id}))^{\mathsf{Sk}} \cdot \mathbf{e}(g, O_2(\mathcal{I}, \mathsf{id}))^v$, where $Y_j \overset{\triangle}{=} \prod_{i<j} \mathsf{Pk}_i / \prod_{j>i} \mathsf{Pk}_i = g^{\sum_{i<j} x_i - \sum_{i>j} x_i}$ and π is the proof computed by NIZK.Prove^O with witness x_i and v of the fact that the ballot is well-formed and $v \in \{0, 1\}$.
- VerifyBallot($\mathsf{pp}, \mathsf{Pk}, \mathsf{id}, \mathsf{Blt}$), on input the public parameters pp, a public-key Pk of a voter, the identifier $\mathsf{id} \in \{0, 1\}^\lambda$ of the election and a ballot $\mathsf{Blt} \overset{\triangle}{=} (\mathsf{Blt}, \pi)$, outputs OK if NIZK.$\mathsf{Verify}^O(\mathsf{Blt}, \pi) = 1$ or $\perp$ otherwise.
- EvalTally($\mathsf{pp}, \mathsf{Pk}_1, \ldots, \mathsf{Pk}_n, \mathsf{id}, \mathsf{Blt}_1, \ldots, \mathsf{Blt}_n$), on input the public parameters pp, the public-keys of all voters, the identifier $\mathsf{id} \in \{0, 1\}^\lambda$ of the election, and the ballots cast by all voter, computes what follows.

It runs VerifyBallot on any ballot Blt_i, $i \in [n]$ and if for any ballot the verification fails, it outputs $\perp$. Otherwise it computes $R = \prod_{i \in [n]} \mathsf{Blt}_i$ and by brute force computes $r \overset{\triangle}{=} \mathbf{dlog}_{\mathbf{e}(g, O_2(\mathcal{I}, \mathsf{id}))} R$. Finally, the algorithm outputs r.

3.1   Properties and Security of the Scheme

Correctness. It is straightforward to verify that the scheme satisfy the correctness as, by construction of the y_i's it follows that $\sum x_i y_i = 0$.

Verifiability. The computational verifiability follows from the soundness of NIZK.

Privacy. Due to space constraints we defer the reduction of an adversary breaking the privacy of the scheme to an adversary breaking the BDDH assumption to the full version of this work [GIR15].

4   Future Directions

The most urgent problem to tackle is to add *robustness*, as defined by Hao *et al.*, without sacrificing non-interactiveness. In fact, if just a single voter does not cast her vote, the other voters cannot compute the result of the election. In our non-interactive case this problem is subtle as it seems to clash with privacy, and new definitions and techniques are needed. Another open problem is upgrade the privacy security and provide receipt-freeness. This could in turn be used to give an alternative solution to the problem of the anonymity difference between non-interactive elections and central elections for non-standard tally functions. Another intriguing open problem is to extend the class of the functions that we can support beyond e-voting. From the applied side we made a preliminary implementation (available on request) using the pbc library [Lyn] in linux and we expect to port it in Java [CI11]. It would be nice to implement our primitives in real-world applications, e.g., a conference revision system like [Hal] or a facebook app like in [BIPT11].

Acknowledgments. Vincenzo Iovino is supported by the Fonds National de la Recherche, Luxembourg, and Peter B. Rønne is supported by the ANR project Sequoia ANR-14-CE28-0030-01. We thank Yu Li for useful comments and Qiang Tang for pointing out a generalization of our definition of dispute-freeness.

References

[BF01] Boneh, D., Franklin, M.: Identity-based encryption from the weil pairing. In: Kilian, J. (ed.) CRYPTO 2001. LNCS, vol. 2139, pp. 213–229. Springer, Heidelberg (2001)

[BFM88] Blum, M., Feldman, P., Micali, S.: Non-interactive zero-knowledge and its applications (extended abstract). In: 20th Annual ACM Symposium on Theory of Computing, pp. 103–112. ACM Press (1988)

[BFW15] Bernhard, D., Fischlin, M., Warinschi, B.: Adaptive proofs of knowledge in the random oracle model. In: Katz, J. (ed.) PKC 2015. LNCS, vol. 9020, pp. 629–649. Springer, Heidelberg (2015)

[BIPT11] Braghin, S., Iovino, V., Persiano, G., Trombetta, A.: Secure and policy-private resource sharing in an online social network. In: PAS-SAT/SocialCom 2011, Privacy, Security, Risk and Trust (PASSAT), 2011 IEEE Third International Conference on and 2011 IEEE Third International Conference on Social Computing (SocialCom), Boston, MA, USA, 9–11 October 2011, pp. 872–875 (2011)

[Boy08] Boyen, X.: The uber-assumption family. In: Galbraith, S.D., Paterson, K.G. (eds.) Pairing 2008. LNCS, vol. 5209, pp. 39–56. Springer, Heidelberg (2008)

[BR93] Bellare, M., Rogaway, P.: Random oracles are practical: a paradigm for designing efficient protocols. In: Ashby, V. (ed.) ACM CCS 93: 1st Conference on Computer and Communications Security, pp. 62–73. ACM Press, November 1993

[CDS94] Cramer, R., Damgård, I.B., Schoenmakers, B.: Proof of partial knowledge and simplified design of witness hiding protocols. In: Desmedt, Y.G. (ed.) CRYPTO 1994. LNCS, vol. 839, pp. 174–187. Springer, Heidelberg (1994)

[CI11] De Caro, A., Iovino, V.: JPBC: Java pairing based cryptography. In: Proceedings of the 16th IEEE Symposium on Computers and Communications, ISCC 2011, Kerkyra, Corfu, Greece, June 28 - July 1, 2011, pp. 850–855 (2011)

[DH76] Diffie, W., Hellman, M.E.: New directions in cryptography. IEEE Trans. Inf. Theory 22(6), 644–654 (1976)

[FLS90] Feige, U., Lapidot, D., Shamir, A.: Multiple non-interactive zero knowledge proofs based on a single random string (extended abstract). In: 31st Annual Symposium on Foundations of Computer Science, pp. 308–317. IEEE Computer Society Press, October 1990

[FS87] Fiat, A., Shamir, A.: How to prove yourself: practical solutions to identification and signature problems. In: Odlyzko, A.M. (ed.) CRYPTO 1986. LNCS, vol. 263, pp. 186–194. Springer, Heidelberg (1987)

[GGG+14] Goldwasser, S., Gordon, S.D., Goyal, V., Jain, A., Katz, J., Liu, F.-H., Sahai, A., Shi, E., Zhou, H.-S.: Multi-input functional encryption. In: Nguyen, P.Q., Oswald, E. (eds.) EUROCRYPT 2014. LNCS, vol. 8441, pp. 578–602. Springer, Heidelberg (2014)

[GGHR14] Garg, S., Gentry, C., Halevi, S., Raykova, M.: Two-round secure MPC from indistinguishability obfuscation. In: Lindell, Y. (ed.) TCC 2014. LNCS, vol. 8349, pp. 74–94. Springer, Heidelberg (2014)

[GIR15] Giustolisi, R., Iovino, V., Rønne, P.B.: On the possibility of non-interactive e-voting in the public-key setting. Cryptology ePrint Archive, Report 2015/1119 (2015). http://eprint.iacr.org/

[Gol04] Goldreich, O.: Foundations of Cryptography: Basic Applications, vol. 2. Cambridge University Press, Cambridge (2004)

[Hal] Halevi, S.: Web submission and review softwares. http://people.csail.mit.edu/shaih/websubrev/

[HRZ10] Hao, F., Ryan, P.Y.A., Zielinski, P.: Anonymous voting by two-round public discussion. IET Inf. Secur. 4(2), 62–67 (2010)

[IZ15] Iovino, V., Żebroski, K.: Simulation-based secure functional encryption in the random oracle model. In: Lauter, K., Rodríguez-Henríquez, F. (eds.) LatinCrypt 2015. LNCS, vol. 9230, pp. 21–39. Springer, Heidelberg (2015)

[Jou04] Joux, A.: A one round protocol for tripartite Diffie-Hellman. J. Cryptol. 17(4), 263–276 (2004)

[KSRH12] Khader, D., Smyth, B., Ryan, P.Y.A., Hao, F.: A fair and robust voting system by broadcast. In: 5th International Conference on Electronic Voting 201, (EVOTE 2012), Co-organized by the Council of Europe, Gesellschaft für Informatik and E-Voting.CC, July 11–14, 2012, Castle Hofen, Bregenz, Austria, pp. 285–299 (2012)

[Lyn] Lynn, B.: Pairing-based cryptography library. https://crypto.stanford.edu/pbc/

[MPR06] Micali, S., Pass, R., Rosen, A.: Input-indistinguishable computation. In: 47th Annual Symposium on Foundations of Computer Science, pp. 367–378. IEEE Computer Society Press, October 2006

[Yao82] Yao, A.C.: Protocols for secure computations (extended abstract). In: 23rd Annual Symposium on Foundations of Computer Science, pp. 160–164. IEEE Computer Society Press, November 1982

Efficiency Comparison of Various Approaches in E-Voting Protocols

Oksana Kulyk[1($\boxtimes$)] and Melanie Volkamer[1,2]

[1] Technische Universität Darmstadt/CASED, Darmstadt, Germany
{oksana.kulyk,melanie.volkamer}@secuso.org
[2] Karlstad University, Karlstad, Sweden

Abstract. In order to ensure the security of remote Internet voting, the systems that are currently proposed make use of complex cryptographic techniques. Since these techniques are often computationally extensive, efficiency becomes an issue. Identifying the most efficient Internet voting system is a non-trivial task – in particular for someone who does not have a sufficient knowledge on the systems that currently exist, and on the cryptographic components that constitute those systems. Aside from these components, the efficiency of Internet voting also depends on various parameters, such as expected number of participating voters and ballot complexity. In this paper we propose a tool for evaluating the efficiency of different approaches for an input scenario, that could be of use to election organizers deciding how to implement the voting system.

1 Introduction

Both vote secrecy and verifiability of the result are the crucial requirements in Internet voting. For ensuring them, various cryptographic techniques have been proposed. The two common approaches to anonymise the votes are verifiable mix net and homomorphic tallying. Both these approaches, being versatile in use have been widely employed in the literature, and also implemented in systems used in practice [2,7,8]. Moreover, these approaches are interchangeable in some of the voting schemes: the Helios system, which used both mix net and homomorphic tallying approaches in its versions, is an example of such interchangeability. Thus, the choice of either mix net or homomorphic tallying approach does not have an impact on the security of the scheme. In such cases, the decision to use either one of them for ensuring vote secrecy has to be made by the election organizers. One of the important criteria is the efficiency of the resulting scheme.

In this paper we implement a prototype tool, that enables comparing the efficiency of both these approaches by estimating the theoretic performance of corresponding calculations. This tool is then supposed to support the election organizers to appropriately implement the voting system, by choosing the most efficient anonymisation approach.

We evaluate the efficiency of the anonymisation using different types of ballots: namely, different kinds of approval voting, divisive (weighted) voting and

© International Financial Cryptography Association 2016
J. Clark et al. (Eds.): FC 2016 Workshops, LNCS 9604, pp. 209–223, 2016.
DOI: 10.1007/978-3-662-53357-4_14

ranked voting. Each one of this type can be used either with the mix net approach, or homomorphic tallying with different kinds of validity proofs. We count the operations that require most performance and implement a prototype tool[1] that, using the formulas we provide, enables estimating the efficiency of different approaches given a specific election setting, thus helping to decide which of these approaches would be the most effective in this setting.

The paper is structured as follows. We outline the methodology that we use for estimating the efficiency in Sect. 2. We provide details on individual anonymisation approaches in Sect. 3. Finally, we describe the prototype tool we developed for evaluation in Sect. 4, and present the evaluation results of various election settings in Sect. 5.

2   Methodology

In this section we describe the methodology we used in order to estimate the time needed for the computations. First, we identify the appropriate election phases, which efficiency can differ depending on the anonymisation approach that is used. Then we describe the way to estimate the time for the computations during those phases.

2.1   Election Phases

The following election stages necessarily differ, depending on the anonymisation approach that is used:

Voting. The voter uses her private device in order to prepare and cast a vote over the internet. Depending on the anonymisation method, different proofs of well-formedness need to be computed, in order to prevent casting invalid ballots.

Validation. The voting system verifies the validity of each cast vote, by verifying the vote validity proofs that are appended to votes during the vote casting. The system can start validating the votes directly after they are being cast, and it needs to be fully completed before the tallying can start.

Tallying. After all the votes have been cast and verified, the result is being tallied. This includes performing the mixing in the case of mix net based approach, and finding the discrete logarithm in the case of homomorphic tallying. After the anonymisation, the results are being decrypted. The number of ciphertexts to be decrypted also depends on the type of the anonymisation. We assume, that both the tasks of mixing and of decrypting are performed by the same set of trustees.

---

[1] The tool will be made open-source following the publication.

2.2 Time Estimations

Let $\mathbb{G}_q$ be a cyclic group with order q, that is used for all the calculations in the election. In order to estimate the efficiency of different anonymisation approaches, we rely on the efficiency of performing one exponentiation in $\mathbb{G}_q$ on a computer that runs the election. This value depends on several factors: not just on the processor used, but also on the security parameters of the election, such as the bit size of underlying group elements and exponent order q, or on whether $\mathbb{G}_q$ is a subgroup of $\mathbb{Z}_p$ for a prime p, or an elliptical curve. Therefore, ideally it should be an input from the election organizers for each individual case.

This value, further denoted as $RExp$ is then used as a basis for estimating the efficiency of individual operations. For further optimising the estimations, we also consider the special kinds of exponentiations that might speed up the calculations, as well as the possibilities to precompute some of the values in advance.

Calculation Optimizations. Aside from calculating the exponentiations in a straight-forward way, one can apply other algorithms developed for calculating special kinds of exponentiations. These algorithms, outlined in [16], can perform computations in a more efficient way than computing each exponentiation separately. The special kinds of exponentiations that are relevant for this work are as follows:

Fixed-base exponentiations (FBExp). Computing multiple exponentiations $g^{e_1}, ..., g^{e_m}$ for a single base g.

Multi-exponentiations (MExp(m)). Computing the product of exponentiations $\prod_{i=1}^{m} g_i^{e_i}$.

In our calculations we assume, that the voting system can rely on precomputations, while the voting client does not. We further assume the exponent size of 256 bits, which is the recommended size for both integers and elliptical curves according to keylength.org. We then use following heuristics to determine the type of exponentiations used in calculations for optimal efficiency:

- the voting client uses multiexponentiations where available,
- the voting system uses fixed-base exponentiations where available,
- for multiexponentiations with large values of m, the product $\prod_{i=1}^{m} g_i^{e_i}$ is calculated in smaller batches[2] as $p_1 \cdot ... \cdot p_{\lceil m/7 \rceil}$ with $p_i = \prod_{j=7(i-1)+1}^{7i} g_j^{e_j}$.
- for fixed-base exponentiations, the representation of an exponent $e = \sum_{i=0}^{t-1} e_i \cdot b^i$ is used, with $b = 16$, $t = 64$, $e_i < b \forall i = 0, ..., t - 1$.

The time needed for both multiexponentiation and fixed-base exponentiation is then determined relatively to $RExp$, with $MExp(2) = 1.16 \cdot RExp$, $MExp(7) = 1.64 \cdot RExp$, $FBExp = 0.19 \cdot RExp$.

---

[2] We consider splitting the product in batches of size seven, due to its optimal performance.

Considerations About Pre-computations. A decision can be made by the election organizers, to perform some of the needed computations in advance, thus speeding up the computations during the election. As we assume, that no pre-computations can be done by the voter, the operations that can be pre-computed are as follows.

Special-kind of exponentiations. As already mentioned, special algorithms can be employed for performing some parts of calculations more efficiently. In particular, they can be of use when having to calculate a large number of exponentiations with common base, thus speeding up each new exponentiation with this base significantly.

Discrete logarithm. As in the homomorphic tallying approach, the calculation of a discrete logarithm is necessary given a set of values $g_1^{x_1}, ..., g_C^{x_C}$ with C as a total amount of resulting ciphertexts. Thus, for each g_i one could use a precomputed table of values (x, g_i^x) for all possible values of x.

Mix net matrix commitments. Given the mix net scheme in [20], a substantial part of the computations can be performed without the knowledge of ciphertexts that are about to be shuffled. We therefore assume, that the voting system performs precomputations that would allow to shuffle the votes from all eligible voters.

Parallelisation. The operations performed by a single entity that we consider can be parallelised, by distributing the calculations into different parts and combining the result. This is especially trivial for homomorphic tallying approaches, where the tasks of verifying the individual validity proofs or finding the discrete logarithm results can be easily distributed. For the mix net approach, the operations that are needed for either calculating a proof of shuffle or for verifying it can be parallelised as well with an appropriate implementation. For the sake of simplicity, we consider that either all of the operations are parallelised using the same number of processors, or none is.

3   Individual Calculations

In this section we provide the formulas that determine the estimated time needed for calculation of decryption of the final result, as well of specific anonymisation approaches.

3.1   Mix Net

One of the anonymization methods considered is a mix net scheme, whereby the input list is being shuffled by each one of the trustees in turn, so that the correspondences between the ciphertexts in the input and output lists are hidden. Each of the ciphertexts in the output list is being decrypted and added to the final tally according to the ballot rules.

As long as at least two nodes keep the correspondences between the shuffled lists secret, it is unfeasible to connect any ciphertext in the original list to its correspondence in the final resulting list. In order to provide robustness against faulty mix nodes, a reencryption mix net scheme is used, and for ensuring that the ciphertexts are shuffled correctly and not replaced by manipulated votes, the proof of shuffle is attached by each mix node. We chose to include the proof of shuffle suggested by [20, 22] due to it being to our knowledge the most efficient algorithm, the implementation and detailed specification of which is available for open usage [23]. For the mix net scheme, the efficiency of calculating the proof of shuffle for C ciphertexts in terms of exponentiations is $(C + 2)RExp + 2C \cdot MExp(2) + MExp(C + 1)$ for the offline phase (i.e. that can be precomputed), and $3MExp(C+1)+2C \cdot FBExp$ for the online phase. The efficiency of verifying such proof is $MExp(C) + RExp + MExp(C+2) + C \cdot MExp(3)$ exponentiations for the offline phase, and $MExp(C) + 3MExp(C + 2)$ for the online phase.

Note, that using the mix net based approach for anonymizing the votes does not place any restriction on the ballot type that is used; further, as long as individual vote can be encrypted in a single ElGamal ciphertext[3], the efficiency of the anonymization does not depend on ballot complexity.

3.2   Homomorphic Tallying

The second approach is to avoid decrypting individual votes, while aggregating them instead, and decrypting only the aggregated result. This is possible if homomorphic cryptosystem is used to encrypt the votes, which is usually exponential ElGamal. It follows, that the homomorphic tallying approach is suitable, whenever the final tallying result can be represented as the sum of individual votes. Furthermore, additional zero-knowledge proofs have to be implemented, that allow to check for vote validity upon vote casting prior to aggregating the votes, in order to exclude the possibility of overvoting or negative voting. Therefore, in this section we consider ways to prove the validity of votes cast according to different ballot types.

Let N be a number of voters, $C_1, ..., C_L$ available candidates. For each ballot type, we consider the valid representation of a single vote, and possible values of the election result. The first value is crucial in proving the validity of a single vote. The second is useful in calculating the final result: that is, more possible combinations of votes would mean that more calculations have to be made for calculating the discrete logarithm.

Given $v_1, ..., v_L$ as the number of votes given for each candidate by a single voter, there are various approaches to encode and encrypt this choice. As such, the proofs of validity suggested in [9], encode the votes such that a single ciphertext results for each voter. Proofs by Joachim [13] and the proofs used in Helios voting system [1,11], namely the v4 version, result in L ciphertext, whereby votes for each candidate are encoded separately; while the ciphertexts in Helios are encoded as g^{v_i} for the same generator g, proofs in [13] encode the votes as $g_i^{v_i}$ for

---

[3] We consider it to be realistic in most cases.

different generators. The number of ciphertexts is important for the efficiency of decryption and computations of the discrete logarithm at tallying.

Also note, that some of the methods proposed make use of a verifiable mix net scheme. Thus, we denote the time needed to prove the validity of shuffling C ciphertexts as $MixProve(C)$, and the time needed to verify such proof as $MixVerify(C)$. In our calculations we assume, due to considerations outlined earlier, that the scheme in [22] is used. However, the calculations are slightly different: first, there is no offline phase; second, due to the fact that the voting system has to verify a large amount of shuffles of the same ciphertexts. The resulting functions are $MixProve(C) = 4 \cdot MExp(C+1) + 2N \cdot FBExp + (C+2) \cdot RExp + 2C \cdot MExp(2)$, $MixVerify(C) = 2 \cdot MExp(C) + 3 \cdot RExp + MExp(C+1) + C \cdot MExp(2) + (4C+6) \cdot FBExp + RExp + 2 \cdot MExp(C+2)$.

Approval Voting $k_{min}...k_{max}$ of L. The most commonly used type of ballots can be grouped together as *Approval Voting*, whereby the voter is allowed to select at least k_{min}, at most k_{max} candidates. Thus, the single vote is conforming to the election rules, if it is of the form $\{v_1, ..., v_L : v_i \in \{0,1\}, \sum_{i=1}^{L} v_i \in [k_{min}, k_{max}]\}$; and the set of all possible election results is $\{v_1, ..., v_L : v_i \in [0, N], \sum_{i=1}^{L} v_i \in [N \cdot k_{min}, N \cdot k_{max}]\}$. Common elections that fall under this type are "Yes/No" elections (with $L = 1$, $k_{min} = 0$, $k_{max} = 1$, or 1 of L elections with $k_{min} = k_{max} = 1$. In Tables 1, 2 and 3 we summarize the proofs of validity of such ballots that exist in the literature, together with the number of resulting ciphertexts. Note, that together with proofs for the general case $k_{min}...k_{max}$ of L, a number of proofs tailored to special cases, such as $k_{min} = k_{max} = k$, or $k_{min} = 0$, $k_{max} = L$, has been developed.

Table 1. Homomorphic tallying approaches, approval voting: proof efficiency

Schema	Parameters	Proof
[11]	$k_{min}...k_{max}$ of L	$(2L+2) \cdot RExp + 2(k_{max} - k_{min} + 1 + L) \cdot MExp(2)$
[11]	$0...L$ of L	$2L \cdot MExp(2) + 2L \cdot RExp$
[13]	$k_{min}...k_{max}$ of L	$L \cdot RExp + MixProve(L + k_{max}) + L \cdot MExp(2) + MExp(L+1)$
[13]	k of L	$L \cdot RExp + MixProve(L + k) + L \cdot MExp(2) + MExp(L+1)$
[13]	$0...k_{max}$ of L	$L \cdot RExp + MixProve(L + k_{max}) + L \cdot MExp(2)$
[9]	k of L	$2 \cdot MExp(3k+2) + 2RExp + 1 + MExp(2)$
[9]	$0...L$ of L	$3RExp + MExp(L+2) + MExp(2)$

Divisive Voting (t, T) of L. The voter is allowed to distribute a total of T votes to L candidates, whereby each candidate can get up to t votes. This kind of elections is particularly relevant for shareholders elections, whereby each voter $i = 1, ..., N$ has a total of T_i votes to distribute, with T_i representing the amount of possessed shares. Without loss of generality, assume that $T_i = T \; \forall i = 1, ..., N$ is the same for all voters. A variant of this type of ballot $(t, 0...T)$ of L allows not to distribute all the T votes.

Table 2. Homomorphic tallying approaches, approval voting: verification efficiency

Schema	Parameters	Verification
[11]	$k_{min}...k_{max}$ of L	$(4L + 2 + 2k_{max} - 2k_{min}) \cdot (FBExp + RExp)$
[11]	$0...L$ of L	$4L(FBExp + RExp)$
[13]	$k_{min}...k_{max}$ of L	$MixVerify(L + k_{max}) + (4L + 4 + 2k_{max} - 2k_{min}) \cdot$ $FBExp + (2L + 4 + 2k_{max} - 2k_{min}) \cdot RExp$
[13]	k of L	$MixVerify(L + k) + (4L + 2) \cdot FBExp + (2L + 2) \cdot RExp$
[13]	$0...k_{max}$ of L	$MixVerify(L + k_{max}) + 3L \cdot FBExp + 2L \cdot RExp$
[9]	k of L	$(3k + 5) \cdot FBExp + 3 \cdot RExp$
[9]	$0...L$ of L	$(L + 5) \cdot FBExp + 3 \cdot RExp$

Table 3. Homomorphic tallying approaches, approval voting: ciphertexts for decryption and fixed-base precomputations

Schema	Parameters	Number of ciphertexts	Fixed-base precomputations
[11]	$k_{min}...k_{max}$ of L	L	128
[13]	$k_{min}...k_{max}$ of L	L	$64 \cdot (2L + k_{max} + 2)$
[9]	k of L	1	$128 + 64 \cdot (3k + 3)$
[9]	$0...L$ of L	1	$128 + 64 \cdot (3 + L)$

As such, according to the election rules, a single vote must lie in the set of $\{v_1, ..., v_L : v_i \in [0, t], \sum_{i=1}^{L} v_i = T\}$. The set of all the possible election results can be defined as $\{v_1, ..., v_L : v_i \in [0, Nt], \sum_{i=1}^{L} v_i = TN\}$.

The proof by Groth et al. supports only the variant of $t = T$. For $t \leq T$, a proof of validity was developed by Joachim et al. In the Helios implementation, it is only possible to conduct elections with $T = L \cdot t$, although supporting elections with $T < L \cdot t$ is possible with additional modifications[4]. The efficiency of individual proofs is summarized in Tables 4, 5 and 6.

Table 4. Homomorphic tallying approaches, divisive voting: proof efficiency

Schema	Parameters	Proof
[11]	(t, T) of L	$2Lt \cdot MExp(2) + (2L + 2) \cdot RExp$
[11]	$(t, 0...T)$ of L	$(2Lt + 2T) \cdot MExp(2) + (2L + 2) \cdot RExp$
[11]	$(t, 0...Lt)$ of L	$2Lt \cdot MExp(2) + 2L \cdot RExp$
[13]	$(t, 0...T)$ of L	$L \cdot RExp + MixProve(Lt + T) + L \cdot MExp(2)$
[9]	(T, T) of L	$MExp(L + 1) + MExp(5L + 1) + RExp + MExp(2)$

---

[4] Such modifications would require computing and verifying additional zero-knowledge proofs for all questions of the election, in order to verify, that the sum of all votes of the election does not exceed T.

Table 5. Homomorphic tallying approaches, divisive voting: verification efficiency

Schema	Parameters	Verification
[11]	(t, T) of L	$2 \cdot (FBExp + RExp) \cdot (Lt + L + 1)$
[11]	$(t, 0...T)$ of L	$2 \cdot (FBExp + RExp) \cdot (Lt + L + T + 1)$
[11]	$(t, 0...Lt)$ of L	$2L(t + 1)(FBExp + RExp)$
[13]	$(t, 0...T)$ of L	$MixVerify(Lt + T) + 3L \cdot FBExp + 2L \cdot RExp$
[9]	(T, T) of L	$(4 + 5L) \cdot FBExp + 3 \cdot RExp$

Table 6. Homomorphic tallying approaches, divisive voting: ciphertexts for decryption and fixed-base precomputations

Schema	Parameters	Number of ciphertexts	Fixed-base precomputations
[11]	(t, T) of L	L	128
[13]	$(t, 0...T)$ of L	L	$64(Lt + 2L + T + 3)$
[9]	(T, T) of L	1	$64(2 + 5L)$

Ranking k of L (Borda). In this ballot type, the voter is to assign the ranks 1 to k to k out of L candidates. The ranks from voters are summed up for each candidate to determine the election result.

Groths method offers only a solution for $k = L$. The proofs used in Helios system cannot guarantee the validity of the ballot: while one is able to proof that each individual vote lies in R, and the sum of all given votes equals $\sum_{i \in R} i$, in current implementation there is no way to guarantee that each candidates gets a unique rank.

A set of valid single votes therefore is defined as $\{(v_1, ..., v_L) : v_i \in 0 \cup R; \{v_i : v_i \neq 0\} = R\}$. The set of all possible election results is then $\{(v_1, ..., v_L) : v_i = \sum_{j=1}^{N} x_{ij}, x_{ij} \in 0 \cup R \ \forall x \in R : |(i, j) : x_{ij} = x| = N\}$. The efficiency of individual proofs is summarized in Tables 7, 8 and 9.

Table 7. Homomorphic tallying approaches, ranking voting: proof efficiency

Schema	Parameters	Proof
[13]	k of L	$k \cdot MixProve(L + 1) + MixProve(L) + (2L + 1) \cdot RExp + MExp(L + 1)$
[9]	L of L	$2 \cdot RExp + MExp(L + 1) + MExp(2)$

Table 8. Homomorphic tallying approaches, ranking voting: verification efficency

Schema	Parameters	Verification
[13]	k of L	$k \cdot MixVerify(L + 1) + MixVerify(L) + (3L + 2) \cdot FBExp + (2L + 2) \cdot RExp$
[9]	L of L	$(4 + L) \cdot FBExp + 3 \cdot RExp$

Table 9. Homomorphic tallying approaches, divisive voting: ciphertexts for decryption and fixed-base precomputations

Schema	Parameters	Number of ciphertexts	Fixed-base precomputations
[13]	k of L	$L(k+1)$	$64(2k+L+4)$
[9]	L of L	1	$64(2+L)$

3.3   Distributed Decryption

Regardless of the anonymisation approach that is used, the vote secrecy also heavily relies on the decryption process, that ensures that only the anonymised ciphertexts are being decrypted. For this purpose, verifiable distributed threshold secret sharing is employed, that enables decryption only if a threshold amount of trustees collaborate, while ensuring that no single entity is in posession of a secret key. A commonly used method is the threshold distributed ElGamal key generation followed by distributed verifiable decryption, as described in [18]. Depending on the anonymisation method in use, the number of ciphertexts to be decrypted varies, together with the efficiency of the decryption. For small number of ciphertexts ($C < 50$), the efficiency of the decryption phase can be estimated as $(C(t_r - 1) + 1) \cdot FBModExp + C(t_r - 1) \cdot MExp(2) + (2Ct_r + 1) \cdot RModExp$, requiring the precomputation of 64 exponentiations; for larger amounts of ciphertext, however, the optimal estimation would be $(2C(t_r - 1) + 1) \cdot FBModExp + C(t_r - 1) \cdot MExp(2) + (Ct_r + C + 1) \cdot RModExp$ with the precomputation of $64 \cdot (1 + t_r)$ exponentiations.

4   Prototype Evaluation Tool

In this section we describe the tool implemented for the efficiency evaluation, based upon the input of previous sections, and provide the efficiency evaluation of various election settings.

4.1   Relevant Parameters

We take a look at different parameters that influence the efficiency of the electronic voting, based upon the formulas we derived in Sect. 3. Depending on the anonymisation approach that is used, different kinds of parameters may or may not play a role in how long do the different stages of the election take.

Number of Voters. As one could expect, the main parameter that determines the efficiency of the election scheme, both for the mix net and homomorphic tallying approaches, is the number of voters that participate in the election. For the evaluation of precomputations that need to be done before the elections, the upper bound of participating voters is needed. For this, a total amount of eligible voters can be taken. For the efficiency estimation of the validation and tallying phases, the actual amount of participated voters is required, an expected value of which can be based i.e. on previous voter turnout.

In presence of multiple voting districts participating in a single election, several alternatives exist on how to implement the system. The first alternative would be to run the election in a centralized way, whereby all the votes are being stored, processed and tallied by a single central server, while the second way would be for the each voting district to run a separate instance of the voting system themselves. Depending on the chosen approach, one could estimate either the performance of centralized system or of a single district, by inputting the parameters for the corresponding voting system instance.

Number of Trustees. This parameter is most important for evaluating the efficiency of a mix net based approach, since the trustees have to act as mix nodes. Furthermore, number of trustees also has an effect on the efficiency of distributed decryption of the result. Given the assumption that more than half of T trustees have to be honest, we set the threshold value as $t_r = \lfloor T/2 \rfloor + 1$. In case of mix net based approach, given the fact that at least one honest mix node has to participate, we set the number of mix nodes as $t_m = T - t_r + 1$.

Number of Candidates and Other Ballot-Specific Parameters. The number of candidates or options is relevant for evaluating the efficiency of homomorphic tallying approach. It has an effect on the efficiency of proof of ballot validity, as well as on the total amount of possible election result - that is, on the complexity of calculating the discrete logarithm of the final result. Furthermore, number of candidates also influences the number of ciphertexts to be decrypted in some of the homomorphic tallying approaches. The same considerations hold for other ballot-specific parameters, as outlined in Sect. 3.2.

4.2   Software

A tool for comparing the schemes described above depending on input of the election parameters was implemented, using Java language. For the calculations we used the formulas for homomorphic tallying approaches mentioned in Sect. 3.2, mix net scheme from [20, 22], as mentioned in Sect. 3.1, and verifiable decryption scheme mentioned in Sect. 3.3. Upon entering the input (see Fig. 1), the tool computes the execution time needed for each one of the available schemes, as explained in Sect. 2. In our example calculations we consider the duration of $3ms$ for a single exponentiation, which roughly corresponds to the performance of a Macbook Pro Laptop using multiplicative group $\mathbb{G}_q \subset \mathbb{Z}_p$ of order q with p, q primes with bit lengths of 2048 and 256 respectively.

5   Evaluation of Example Settings

In this section we demonstrate the workings on the tool by selecting appropriate examples of the election settings, and showing how the efficiency of various approaches for this settings is estimated.

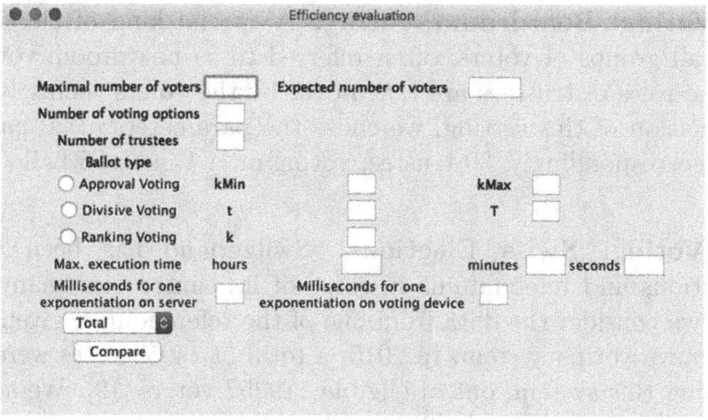

Fig. 1. Evaluation tool prototype interface

5.1 Description of Example Settings

We provide an example for the evaluation of an election setting, using the ballot types described in Sect. 3. Some of these settings are based on the public data from past elections[5], that were conducted using Internet voting. Others are are examples constructed by us for this evaluation specifically, which, however, might also be relevant for the elections, conducted in practice.

Approval Voting: Estonian Elections. During the 2011 parliamentary elections, a total of 140, 846 out of the registered 913, 346 voters chose to vote via electronic means. A total of 789 candidates registered, out of which the voters were supposed to make their choice [4,5]. The decryption key was distributed between 7 trustees. Thus, we evaluate an approval vote with "1 of 789" ballot.

Approval Voting: Norway Elections. We consider the local elections in Norway in 2011 [14]. As the actual election rules are rather complex, in our analysis we consider the distribution of seats between the parties, without paying attention to personalised votes. In 2011, a total of 167, 506 out of 27, 738 eligible voters have cast their vote electronically, and 21 parties participated. There were a total of 10 trustees.

Approval Voting: IACR Elections. The International Association for Cryptologic Research uses electronic voting for their internal elections. We consider the election of 2012 [12], where the voters had to cast their vote for any number of candidates out of registered 5. A total of 518 voters participated (out of 1530 eligible), and there were 3 trustees.

---

[5] Note, that the parameters in our examples may not correspond precisely to the real data.

Approval Voting: Boardroom Voting. A special kind of election setting involving small groups of voters, often referred to as boardroom voting, is the one where the roles of trustees are taken over by the voters themselves [10,15]. For the evaluation of this setting, we chose the parameters of 30 participating voters, and, correspondingly, 30 trustee, voting on a 1 out of 5 ballot.

Approval Voting: Swiss Elections. Switzerland has been conducting e-voting elections and referendums in some of its cantons for many years. As an example, we consider the data from one of the referendums, given votes cast using the Geneva voting system. In 2015, a total of 14052 votes were cast electronically using this system, out of eligible 119252 voters [19]. We assume 4 as the number of trustees, given the 2011 report [17].

Divisive Voting. As we are not aware of any real-world e-voting election that uses the divisive voting method, we had to construct an example by ourselves, partially using the data from traditional voting elections. Namely, we base our example election setting on the local Hesse elections [21], whereby the voters had to distribute 71 vote to 502 candidates, giving at most 3 votes to each candidate, and a total of 44385 out of 101666 eligible voters participated. We assume the participation of 3 trustees.

Ranking Voting. Similarly to the divisive voting ballot, we were unable to find data from a real-world election with this type of ballot. The closest example would be the elections in Australia, that also use the ranking voting ballot for their election, albeit using a different tallying method as opposed to Borda voting. We therefore use the parameters similar to the Victorian state elections [3,6] for our example: a total of 1121 participating voters, 7 trustees, and 40 candidates to be ranked.

5.2 Results and Discussion

The evaluation results for all the settings, showing the estimated performance for expected number of voters, are given in Table 10. For setting and each election stage, the approach most efficient during this stage is marked in bold.

As one can see from it, in many of the cases, with the exception of simple ballots like "yes/no" elections, or approval voting elections with relatively small number of available options, the mixnet approach outperforms all the approaches based on homomorphic tallying. This can be explained by the fact, that the efficiency of this approach does not depend on the ballot complexity. The large number of trustees, however, like in case of boardroom voting, has significantly larger effect on the mix net approach than on homomorphic tallying approaches. Furthermore, the precomputations have a significant effect on the overall efficiency of mix net approach, which tends to be higher, especially with a high total number of eligible voters.

Table 10. Evaluation results of different settings

Election	Election stage	Mixnet	HT: Helios	HT: Groth	HT: Joachim
Approval voting: Estonia	Precomputations	20.09 h	**2.061 s**	> 30 days	190.4 h
	Voting	**0.009 s**	14.97 s	0.024 s	21.4 s
	Validation	**14.08 m**	441.1 h	31.83 m	> 30 days
	Tallying	2.316 h	22.78 s	**0.039 s**	22.78 s
Approval voting: Norway	Precomputations	4.422 h	**0.6 s**	> 30 days	1.81 m
	Voting	**0.009 s**	0.411 s	0.024 s	0.603 s
	Validation	**2.774 m**	2.366 h	6.269 m	5.323 h
	Tallying	37.22 m	1.185 s	**0.06 s**	1.185 s
Approval voting: Switzerland	Precomputations	1.574 h	**0.495 s**	8.976 s	1.647 s
	Voting	**0.009 s**	0.018 s	0.021 s	0.057 s
	Validation	**1.405 m**	3.344 m	2.775 m	18.96 m
	Tallying	9.239 m	**0.03 s**	0.03 s	0.03 s
Approval voting: IACR	Precomputations	1.225 m	**0.387 s**	> 30 days	4.71 s
	Voting	**0.009 s**	0.096 s	0.024 s	0.216 s
	Validation	**3.108 s**	36.98 s	7.32 s	2.449 m
	Tallying	16.55 s	0.084 s	**0.021 s**	0.084 s
Approval voting: Boardroom	Precomputations	8.433 s	**0.384 s**	3.097 m	3.846 s
	Voting	**0.009 s**	0.108 s	0.021 s	0.156 s
	Validation	**0.174 s**	2.484 s	0.345 s	5.508 s
	Tallying	7.887 s	0.786 s	**0.159 s**	0.786 s
Divisive voting	Precomputations	1.342 h	**1.617 s**	-	16.98 m
	Voting	**0.009 s**	17.01 s	-	28.23 s
	Validation	**4.438 m**	183.1 h	-	474.9 h
	Tallying	23.54 m	**6.84 s**	-	6.84 s
Ranking voting	Precomputations	1.5 m	-	> 30 days	**38.59 s**
	Voting	**0.009 s**	-	0.045 s	33.86 s
	Validation	**6.726 s**	-	38.2 s	11.83 h
	Tallying	1.108 m	-	**0.039 s**	47.34 s

The homomorphic tallying approaches tend to be less efficient as ballot complexity increases. If the vote is encoded in a single ciphertext, the length of the exponent representing the election result strongly depends on both number of voters and candidates, while the proofs themselves remain relatively efficient, which is why this approach outperforms others in case of simple "yes/no" elections. In the homomorphic tallying approaches that require encoding the vote in multiple ciphertexts, while the exponent size remains relatively small even with the larger number of candidates and voters, the amount and the complexity of validity proofs to be constructed and verified per vote, becomes larger, thus making the election less efficient.

6   Conclusion

We have evaluated different approaches to anonymize the votes in different settings with regards to their efficiency. Namely, we focused on two anonymisation approaches common in use: mix net and homomorphic tallying with different ballot types. Furthermore, we have built a prototype of a tool that enables election organizers to perform such a comparison themselves with regards to their chosen setting, in order to choose the most efficient approach. As we found out, there is no single approach that is the most efficient in all the possible election settings. Therefore, an individual evaluation has to be done for each setting, which is what our tool is designed to assist in.

While efficiency is an important consideration in implementing e-votin systems, there are other criteria that can suggest using one approach over another. In particular, revealing individual votes, which is inavoidable in mixnet-based approach, can lead to privacy issues in certain settings, for example, in very small-scale elections, or if coercion and vote buying is an issue. Thus, in case both homomorphic tallying and mixnet-based approach is available for certain kind of elections, the organizers have to evaluate themselves the trade-off between efficiency and possible privacy concerns, while deciding for one or another approach. Identifying the scenarios, in which such privacy issues can arise, is the question of future work.

Acknowledgment. This project (HA project no. 435/14-25) is funded in the framework of Hessen ModellProjekte, financed with funds of LOEWE – Landes-Offensive zur Entwicklung Wissenschaftlich-ökonomischer Exzellenz, Förderlinie 3: KMU-Verbundvorhaben (State Offensive for the Development of Scientific and Economic Excellence).

References

1. Adida, B.: Helios: web-based open-audit voting. USENIX Security Symposium, vol. 17, pp. 335–348 (2008)
2. Adida, B., De Marneffe, O., Pereira, O., Quisquater, J.J., et al.: Electing a university president using open-audit voting: analysis of real-world use of Helios. EVT/WOTE 2009, pp. 10–10 (2009)
3. Burton, C., Culnane, C., Schneider, S.: Secure and verifiable electronic voting in practice: the use of vvote in the victorian state election. arXiv preprint http://arXiv.org/abs/1504.07098 (2015)

4. Committee, E.N.E.: Riigikogu elections 2011 - Riigikogu (parliament) elections - past elections - estonian national electoral committee. (2011). http://www.vvk.ee/past-elections/riigikogu-parliament-elections/riigikogu-elections-2011/. Accessed 2 Mar 2015
5. Committee, E.N.E.: Statistics - internet voting - voting methods in estonia - estonian national electoral committee (2015). http://www.vvk.ee/voting-methods-in-estonia/engindex/statistics. Accessed 2 Mar 2015
6. Culnane, C., Ryan, P.Y., Schneider, S., Teague, V.: Vvote: a verifiable voting system. arXiv preprint arXiv:1404.6822 (2014)
7. Dubuis, E., Fischli, S., Haenni, R., Hauser, S., Koenig, R.E., Locher, P., Ritter, J., von Bergen, P.: Verifizierbare internet-wahlen an schweizer hochschulen mit univote. In: GI-Jahrestagung, pp. 767–788. Citeseer (2013)
8. Gjøsteen, K.: The Norwegian internet voting protocol. In: Kiayias, A., Lipmaa, H. (eds.) VoteID 2011. LNCS, vol. 7187, pp. 1–18. Springer, Heidelberg (2012)
9. Groth, J.: Non-interactive zero-knowledge arguments for voting. In: Ioannidis, J., Keromytis, A.D., Yung, M. (eds.) ACNS 2005. LNCS, vol. 3531, pp. 467–482. Springer, Heidelberg (2005)
10. Hao, F., Ryan, P.Y., Zieliński, P.: Anonymous voting by two-round public discussion. IET Inf. Secur. 4(2), 62–67 (2010)
11. Helios: Helios v4 (2012). http://documentation.heliosvoting.org/verification-specs/helios-v4. Accessed 2 Mar 2015
12. IACR: IACR Election 2012 (2012). http://www.iacr.org/elections/2012/. Accessed 2 Mar 2015
13. Joaquim, R.: How to prove the validity of a complex ballot encryption to the voter and the public. J. Inf. Secur. Appl. 19(2), 130–142 (2014)
14. i Esteve, J.B., Goldsmith, B., Turner, J.: Norwegian E-vote Project - Speed and Efficiency of the Vote Counting Process (2012). https://www.regjeringen.no/globalassets/upload/krd/prosjekter/e-valg/evaluering/topic4_assessment.pdf. Accessed 2 Mar 2015
15. Kiayias, A., Yung, M.: Self-tallying elections and perfect ballot secrecy. In: Naccache, D., Paillier, P. (eds.) PKC 2002. LNCS, vol. 2274, pp. 141–158. Springer, Heidelberg (2002)
16. Menezes, A.J., Van Oorschot, P.C., Vanstone, S.A.: Handbook of Applied Cryptography. CRC Press, Boca Raton (1996)
17. Organization for Security, Co-operation in Europe,: Switzerland, Federal Elections, 23 October 2011: Final report (2015). http://www.osce.org/odihr/87417. Accessed 30 Oct 2015
18. Pedersen, T.P.: Distributed provers and verifiable secret sharing based on the discrete logarithm problem. DAIMI Rep. Ser. 21(388) (1992)
19. Bundeskanzlei, S.: Vote électronique - Versuchübersicht (2015). https://www.bk.admin.ch/themen/pore/evoting/08004/index.html?lang=de. Accessed 30 Oct 2015
20. Terelius, B., Wikström, D.: Proofs of restricted shuffles. In: Bernstein, D.J., Lange, T. (eds.) AFRICACRYPT 2010. LNCS, vol. 6055, pp. 100–113. Springer, Heidelberg (2010)
21. Volkamer, M., Budurushi, J., Demirel, D.: Vote casting device with VV-SV-PAT for elections with complicated ballot papers. In: 2011 International Workshop on Requirements Engineering for Electronic Voting Systems (REVOTE), pp. 1–8. IEEE (2011)
22. Wikström, D.: A commitment-consistent proof of a shuffle. In: Boyd, C., González Nieto, J. (eds.) ACISP 2009. LNCS, vol. 5594, pp. 407–421. Springer, Heidelberg (2009)
23. Wikström, D.: How to implement a stand-alone verifier for the verificatum mix-net (2011)

Remote Electronic Voting Can Be Efficient, Verifiable and Coercion-Resistant

Roberto Araújo[1], Amira Barki[2,3], Solenn Brunet[2,4(✉)], and Jacques Traoré[2]

[1] Faculdade de Computação, Universidade Federal do Pará, Rua Augusto Corrêa 01, Belém, PA 66075-110, Brazil
rsa@ufpa.br
[2] Orange Labs, Caen, France
{amira.barki,solenn.brunet,jacques.traore}@orange.com
[3] Sorbonne Universités, Université de Technologie de Compiègne (UTC), CNRS, UMR 7253 Heudiasyc, Compiègne, France
[4] Université de Rennes 1, Rennes, France

Abstract. The coercion issue in remote electronic voting has always been of particular interest. However, to date, all proposals addressing it either suffer from some shortcomings or are not efficient enough to be used in real world elections. To fill this gap, we propose a new coercion-resistant electronic voting scheme practical for real polls. Our scheme relies on credentials generated thanks to a recent algebraic Message Authentication Code (MAC) scheme due to Chase et al. To enable multiple elections and credentials revocation, we also design a novel sequential aggregate MAC scheme, that is of independent interest. Thanks to it, eligible voters' credentials can be efficiently updated.

1 Introduction

Internet voting offers a better voting experience since voters can cast their votes from their computers or even smartphones. By eliminating the need to visit polling places, it may attract more voters and thus increase voter turnout. In addition, it improves the efficiency for tallying authorities. These benefits motivated countries such as Estonia and Switzerland to adopt it in real world elections. However, it is still not widely spread. This is particularly due to many inherent concerns such as selective DDoS attacks on the election server, malware attacks on the voter client as well as risks entailed by the lack of private polling booths [14]. In this paper, we will mainly focus on the latter concern while assuming that votes will be cast-as-intended. Indeed, adversaries may leverage it to perform coercion or vote-selling attacks. Consequently, electronic voting schemes ought to address this issue that remained a challenge for many years.

To this end, Juels, Catalano and Jakobsson (JCJ) [10] introduced an essential property known as *coercion-resistance*. It considers the different actions that a coercer could undertake: constrain a voter to cast a given vote, force her to reveal her private vote information and subsequently vote on her behalf, or keep her from voting. They also proposed the first coercion-resistant scheme based

J. Clark et al. (Eds.): FC 2016 Workshops, LNCS 9604, pp. 224–232, 2016.
DOI: 10.1007/978-3-662-53357-4_15

on anonymous credentials. To be able to vote, an eligible voter is beforehand provided with a valid credential. Under coercion, she can use a fake credential instead of her valid one. Thereby, she deceives any adversary about her true vote intention as a coercer is unable to distinguish the fake credential from the valid one. Unfortunately, JCJ's scheme was inefficient for large scale voting scenarios as, for N ballots, the complexity of the tallying is in $O(N^2)$.

Related Work. To enhance JCJ's voting system, other coercion-resistant schemes were then proposed[1]. AFT [1] was the first proposal to achieve linear time complexity. Nevertheless, it does not support multiple elections. Indeed, at each new election, the voter has to visit the registration place in order to obtain her credential associated to the new poll. To address this drawback, AT [2] proposed a scheme that allows credentials revocation and multiple elections. To issue a new credential, it requires the registration authorities to jointly generate a BBS [3] group signature. Unfortunately, up to now, there is no practical solution to compute such a signature in a distributed manner, which makes AT impractical for real polls. They also proposed a generic technique to identify valid (but illegitimate) voting credentials that a majority of colluding registrars could compute. Although such an event is unlikely, their generic technique also applies to our scheme. Finally, Clark and Hengartner [7] and Spycher et al. [13] proposed two different approaches to tackle the coercion-resistance issue. However, both schemes do not really have linear time complexity. They truly achieve it only if the level of anonymity is lowered. More specifically, a voter's ballot is indistinguishable from a small set of ballots and not from all the received ones.

Contribution. To tackle all these shortcomings, we propose a novel efficient coercion-resistant voting scheme, with linear time complexity, that is suitable and practical for real polls. Our scheme relies on credentials generated based on the recent Algebraic MAC scheme due to Chase et al. [6]. We prove that although a part of our credentials are made publicly known, a coercer is unable to distinguish a valid credential from a fake one. Furthermore, our scheme allows talliers to check credentials validity while being encrypted. To also enable multiple elections and credentials revocation, we propose a new sequential aggregate signature scheme, which is of independent interest. Using it, eligible voters' credentials can be efficiently updated thereby allowing them to vote in new elections. Credentials of voters who are no longer eligible to vote can be revoked as well. Thanks to our improvements, coercion-resistance is obtained almost for free as our scheme is just slightly slower than non coercion-resistant classical mix-net based voting schemes.

---

[1] Due to lack of space, we only mention the most promising coercion-resistant proposals.

2   Preliminaries

In this section, we first introduce our main notation and required conventional cryptographic primitives. Then, we detail building blocks including our new sequential aggregate signature scheme necessary to update voters' credentials.

2.1   Classical Tools

Notation. The notation $x \in_R X$ states that x is chosen uniformly at random from the set X. Besides, $\vec{x}$ and B_i respectively denote the vector $(x_0, x_1, \ldots, x_n)$ and the ith element of the tuple $B = \langle a, b, \ldots, z \rangle$.

Computational Assumptions. The decisional Diffie-Hellman assumption, known as DDH, is defined as follows: given a cyclic group $\mathbb{G} = <h>$ of prime order p, it is hard, given $(h; h^a; h^b; h^c) \in \mathbb{G}^4$, to decide whether $c \overset{?}{=} ab$.

ElGamal Encryption. The ElGamal cryptosystem is an asymmetric encryption scheme with multiplicative homomorphic property. Let $\mathbb{G}$ be a cyclic group with safe prime order p. The public key pk is defined as $pk = (g, h = g^{sk})$ where g is a generator of $\mathbb{G}$ and $sk \in_R \mathbb{Z}_p^*$ is the corresponding private key. The ElGamal encryption of a message $m \in \mathbb{G}$ using pk is denoted by $E_{pk}[m]$ and equal to $C = (c_1, c_2)$ where $c_1 = g^r$, $c_2 = mh^r$ and $r \in_R \mathbb{Z}_p^*$. The plaintext is then recovered as $m = c_2/c_1^{sk}$. Its multiplicative homomorphic property states that given two ciphertexts $C_1 = (c_1, c_2)$ and $C_2 = (c_1', c_2')$ of the messages m_1 and m_2 respectively, one can efficiently compute the ciphertext of the product $m_1 m_2$ of the two original messages as $C'' = (c_1'' = c_1 c_1', c_2'' = c_2 c_2')$.

Non-interactive Zero-Knowledge Proofs of Knowledge (NIZKPK). Non Interactive Zero-Knowledge Proofs of Knowledge enable a prover $\mathcal{P}$ to convince a verifier $\mathcal{V}$ that she knows some secrets satisfying a given statement without revealing anything else about them. Following the usual notation introduced by Camenisch and Stadler [5], they are denoted by $\pi = \text{PoK}\{\alpha, \beta : \text{ statements about } \alpha, \beta\}$ where Greek letters correspond to the knowledge of $\mathcal{P}$.

2.2   Algebraic MACs

Message Authentication Codes (MACs) are cryptographic primitives that rely on pseudorandom functions to provide authentication for messages. In these protocols, MAC construction and verification are performed using the same key. Unlike usual constructions, algebraic MACs are based on group operations.

In what follows, we describe the algebraic MAC_{GGM} scheme due to Chase et al. [6]. It is a generalization of the algebraic MAC algorithm proposed by Dodis et al. [8] and is proven unforgeable against chosen message and verification attack (UF-CMVA) in the generic group model.

Setup(1^k). Define a secure cyclic group $\mathbb{G}$ with prime order p of k-bits as well as g and h, two of its generators such that $\log_g h$ is unknown. It outputs $params = (\mathbb{G}, p, g, h)$.

Keygen($params$). Generate a secret key $sk = \vec{x} \in_R \mathbb{Z}_p^{n+1^*}$. Optionally, compute the parameters $(X_1 = h^{x_1}, X_2 = h^{x_2}, \ldots, X_n = h^{x_n})$ denoted by $iparams$ and $C_{x_0} = g^{x_0} h^{\tilde{x}_0}$, a commitment to x_0 where $\tilde{x}_0 \in_R \mathbb{Z}_p^*$.

MAC($sk, \vec{m}$). Given a message $\vec{m} \in_R \mathbb{Z}_p^n$, choose $u \in_R \mathbb{G}\setminus\{1\}$ and compute the tag $\sigma = (u, u')$ where $u' = u^{x_0 + m_1 x_1 + m_2 x_2 + \ldots + m_n x_n}$.

Verify($sk, \vec{m}, \sigma$). Check the correctness of σ i.e. $u \neq 1$ and $u^{x_0 + m_1 x_1 + \ldots + m_n x_n} \stackrel{?}{=} u'$.

We show in the following lemma that it is hard for an adversary to decide whether a given triplet $(s', u, u' = u^{x_0 + s x_1})$ is a valid MAC on s or not.

Lemma 1. *Under the DDH assumption, it is unfeasible to decide whether* $s' \stackrel{?}{=} s \bmod p$ *from* s', $C_{x_0} = g^{x_0} h^x$, $X_1 = h^{x_1}$, $u = h^b$, $u' = u^{x_0 + s x_1}$ *where* $s, s', x, x_0, x_1, b \in_R \mathbb{Z}_p^*$ *and* $g, h \in_R \mathbb{G}$ *two generators.*

Proof. Suppose that we have an oracle deciding whether $s' \stackrel{?}{=} s \bmod p$ given s', $X_1 = h^{x_1}$, $C_{x_0} = g^{x_0} h^x$, $u = h^b$, $u' = u^{x_0 + s x_1}$, for $s, s', x, x_0, x_1, b \in_R \mathbb{Z}_p^*$ and $g, h \in_R \mathbb{G}$ two generators. Then, we show how to decide whether $c \stackrel{?}{=} x_1 b \bmod p$ given $h, \alpha = h^{x_1}, \beta = h^b$ and $\gamma = h^c$ for $x_1, b, c \in_R \mathbb{Z}_p^*$, hence contradicting the DDH assumption.

The reduction is as follows. Set $C_{x_0} = g^{x_0} h^x$ for $x_0, x \in_R \mathbb{Z}_p^*$, choose $s' \in_R \mathbb{Z}_p^*$ and give $s', C_{x_0}, X_1 = \alpha, u = \beta, u' = u^{x_0} \gamma^{s'}$ to the oracle. We have two cases:

Case 1. If $c = x_1 b \bmod p$ then $u' = u^{x_0 + s' x_1}$.

Case 2. If $c \neq x_1 b \bmod p$ then $c = x_1 b (1 + c')$ for some $c' \neq 0 \bmod p$ (since $x_1 \neq 0$ and $b \neq 0$) and $u' = u^{x_0 + s x_1}$ with $s = s'(1 + c') \neq s'$ (since $s' \neq 0$).

Therefore, given $s', C_{x_0}, X_1 = \alpha, u = \beta, u'$, the oracle will tell whether $s' \stackrel{?}{=} s$ from which we decide whether $c \stackrel{?}{=} x_1 b$.

In the particular case where $s = 0$, even a computationally unbounded adversary will not be able to figure out whether $u' \stackrel{?}{=} u^{x_0}$. This is due to the fact that the Pedersen's commitment $C_{x_0} = g^{x_0} h^x$ perfectly hides the value x_0.

2.3 Our Sequential Aggregate MAC Scheme

An aggregate signature scheme [4] is a variant of a digital signature scheme that additionally supports aggregation. Indeed, it allows to aggregate n signatures on n distinct messages from n signers into a single compact signature. Along with the n messages, the resulting signature will convince the verifier that the n messages were signed by the n signers. A sequential aggregate signature scheme [11] is a particular type of aggregate signature schemes. Indeed, the final signature is created sequentially with each signer signing the aggregate signature in turn. Based on the MAC$_{GGM}$ due to Chase et al., we design a new sequential aggregate signature (MAC) scheme which supports n signers with n different messages. In the case of two signers S_1 and S_2, it works as follows:

Setup(1^k). Create the system public parameters $param = (\mathbb{G}, p, g, h)$ as defined in Sect. 2.2.

KeyGeneration($params$). Generate the secret key $sk_1 = (x_0, x_1)$ of the first signer S_1 and $sk_2 = x_2$ of the second signer S_2. The corresponding public parameters are respectively $C_{x_0} = g^{x_0} h^x$ where $x \in_R \mathbb{Z}_p^*$, $X_1 = h^{x_1}$ and $X_2 = h^{x_2}$.

Signing($params, S_1(sk_1, m_1), S_2(sk_2, m_2)$). Produce an aggregate signature on messages m_1 and m_2 sequentially by S_1 and S_2. First, S_1 generates the signature $\sigma_1 = (u, u')$ on the message m_1 where $u' = u^{x_0 + m_1 x_1}$. Then, S_2 can generate $\sigma_2 = (w = u^t, w' = (u' u^{m_2 x_2})^t)$ a sequential aggregate signature on both m_1 and m_2 where $t \in_R \mathbb{Z}_p$.

Verification($params, \sigma_2, m_1, m_2, sk$). Verify that σ_2 is the aggregate of the signatures of S_1 on m_1 and S_2 on m_2 i.e. $u \neq 1$ and $w' \stackrel{?}{=} w^{x_0 + m_1 x_1 + m_2 x_2}$.

Theorem 1. *Our sequential aggregate signature scheme is* existentially unforgeable under chosen message attacks *(EUF-CMA) under the assumption that* MAC$_{GGM}$ *is UF-CMVA.*

Proof. Owing to space limitations, the proofs will be detailed in an extended version. It is, however, worth mentioning that the EUF-CMA proof is similar to the one provided in [12].

We will subsequently use it in our voting scheme to update voter's credentials thereby enabling multiple elections and credentials revocation. m_2 and x_2 will be respectively set to the new election identifier and the associated secret key.

3   A MAC Based Coercion Resistant Voting Scheme

In this section, we first provide an overview of our coercion-resistant voting scheme then, detail it while explaining how it enables multiple elections and credentials revocation.

3.1   An Overview of the Scheme

Our coercion-resistant voting scheme consists of five main phases. During the *setup* phase, key material as well as election parameters are cooperatively generated by a set of authorities. The public parameters are then published on a Web Bulletin Board (WBB). To be able to vote, an eligible voter must register through a *registration* phase. After proving her identity, she receives a unique and valid credential that depends on a secret s only known by the voter. The credential is issued by the registration authorities and made publicly available. Later, during *voting* phase, the voter uses her credential and the secret s to generate a ballot that she sends via an anonymous channel. It contains her credential randomized, the ciphertext of her vote as well as a set of NIZKPs proving the validity of the ballot. If the voter is under coercion, she can cast a fake ballot using an invalid secret s' without the adversary being able to distinguish it from a valid one. Before tallying votes, a *pre-verification* phase is carried out to remove both erroneous ballots and duplicate votes. Once done, the tallying authorities may perform the *tallying* phase. To do so, they first send the remaining ballots to a verifiable mix net and then anonymously identify the valid votes, *i.e.* votes published with valid credentials. Finally, they cooperatively decrypt the associated ciphertexts to recover votes and publish results on the WBB.

3.2 Our Novel Coercion-Resistant Voting Scheme

Our voting scheme, which assumes a bulletin board communication model, involves as participants a set of registration authorities known as *registrars*, a set of tallying authorities called *talliers*, and a set of *voters*. For security reasons, the roles of both registrars and talliers are distributed among a large group of authorities. We describe our proposal as follows:

Setup Phase. Let O be the set of eligible options (candidates) and $v \in O$ a vote for a candidate. Let $\mathbb{G}$ be a cyclic group with a prime order p and $o \in \mathbb{G}$ be a public generator selected for this election. The talliers share the threshold ElGamal key pair $(T, \widehat{T})$. As for the registrars, they jointly select and share a secret key $sk = (x_0, x_1) \in_R \mathbb{Z}_p^{2*}$ associated to the public values $(C_{x_0}, X_1 = h^{x_1})$ where $C_{x_0} = g^{x_0} h^x$ such that $x \in_R \mathbb{Z}_p^*$. This key is also shared among talliers.

Registration Phase. Once her eligibility proved, the voter obtains a unique and valid voting credential σ. Indeed, by cooperatively choosing $s \in_R \mathbb{Z}_p$ and $u \in_R \mathbb{G}\backslash\{1\}$, the registrars jointly compute $\sigma = (u, u')$ where $u' = u^{x_0 + s x_1}$. It is then provided, through an untappable channel, to the voter along with the secret value s and a Designated Verifiable Proof[2] [9] that σ is a valid credential on s. Concurrently, the credential σ is stored in the database DB, which contains all the valid credentials, while s is kept as a secret only known by the voter. Thereby, in case of coercion, the voter would deceive the coercer by revealing her credential with a fake value s' without the coercer noticing it. Indeed, under the DDH assumption, the coercer cannot decide whether s' is valid with respect to the voter's credential σ or not (see Lemma 1). The generic technique proposed in [2] can be subsequently used to detect any vote cast with a valid but illegitimate credential computed by a set of malicious colluding registrars.

Voting Phase (First Election). To vote in a first election, the voter first randomizes the received credential σ to generate $\sigma_r = (u^r, u'^r) = (w, w')$ where

---

[2] The DVP proof can only convince the corresponding voter and nobody else. So, it is useless in case of coercion and even for vote-selling.

$r \in_R \mathbb{Z}_p$. Then, she chooses her candidate $v \in O$ and casts her vote that consists of the ballot $B = \langle E_T[v], w, w', E_T[w^s], o^s, P \rangle$ where P is a set of NIZKPs ensuring that the ballot is well formed. In particular, P includes both $\pi_1 = PoK\{\alpha : B_4 = E_T[w^\alpha] \wedge B_5 = o^\alpha\}$ related to the knowledge of s and $\pi_2 = PoK\{\beta : B_1 = E_T[\beta] \wedge \beta \in O\}$ proving that v belongs to the set O.

Pre-verification Phase. This phase aims to verify votes posted on the WBB. Talliers should perform it before the tallying phase detailed later on. It is worth mentioning that, during this phase, ballots with invalid credentials are not yet discarded. Hereinafter, we describe the four steps of this phase.

1. *Verifying proofs.* For each posted ballot, the proofs P are verified to remove ballots with invalid proofs.
2. *Removing duplicates.* By comparing all o^s values, duplicates votes (*i.e.* ballots published using the same secret s) are removed. The policy, in this case, could be to keep the last one.
3. *Reconstruction of the credential.* For each ballot, the ElGamal ciphertext $E_T[w]$ of w is cooperatively computed. Using ElGamal homomorphic property, the ciphertexts $E_T[w^{x_0}]$ and $E_T[(w^s)^{x_1}]$ are jointly obtained thanks to the shared secret values x_0 and x_1 as well as $E_T[w]$ and $E_T[w^s]$. Thereby, the talliers can compute $E_T[w^{x_0+sx_1}] = E_T[w^{x_0}] \cdot E_T[w^{sx_1}]$. By dividing the ciphertext second component by w', they obtain $C = E_T[w^{x_0+sx_1}]/w'$. If the credential $\sigma_r = (w, w')$ is valid, C should be equal to $E_T[1]$, a ciphertext of 1.
4. *PET pre-test.* In this last step, a Plaintext Equivalence Test (PET) is performed on credentials. To this end, C is cooperatively raised to a random value $\alpha \in_R \mathbb{Z}_p$. For a valid credential σ, $D = C^\alpha$ should be equal to $E_T[1^\alpha] = E_T[1]$. Note that D is still kept encrypted to prevent any information leakage especially in case of coercion.

Tallying Phase. To compute election results, the talliers perform three steps:

1. *Mixing tuples.* The tuples $\langle D, E_T[v] \rangle$ that succeeded all pre-verifications are sent to a verifiable mix net. The output is then published on the WBB.
2. *Identifying valid votes.* For each tuple, the ciphertext D is jointly decrypted. If the plaintext is equal to 1, the credential σ_r and the associated ballot are considered as valid. Otherwise, the ballot is said invalid and is thus discarded.
3. *Decrypting and counting votes.* Finally, for each valid ballot, $E_T[v]$ is cooperatively decrypted in order to count the votes. The obtained results are then published on the WBB.

Theorem 2. *Our voting scheme satisfies the* eligibility[3] *requirement under the assumption that* MAC$_{GGM}$ *is UF-CMVA secure and the* coercion-resistance[4] *requirement, in the random oracle model, under the DDH assumption.*

---

[3] The eligibility requirement informally states that only eligible voters can cast the votes and that every voter can cast only one vote.
[4] As defined by JCJ [10]: A voter can deceive the coercer about her true vote intention by making him believe that she behaved as instructed while it is not the case.

Proof (sketch). Owing to space limitations, the proofs will be detailed in an extended version. Intuitively, eligibility follows from the unforgeability of the $\mathsf{MAC_{GGM}}$ and the removal of duplicates in step 2. Therefore, only one vote per credential (valid or fake) will be processed during the tallying phase. Coercion-resistance follows from the fact that a coercer cannot decide, under the DDH assumption, whether a credential is valid or not (see Lemma 1) or trace a ballot during the tallying phase (owing to the use of Mix-nets and PET that are secure under the DDH assumption).

Universal Verifiability: We would also like to stress that every step of the tallying phase is publicly verifiable. Thus, anyone can check that the election outcome corresponds to the ballots published on the WBB (Universal Verifiability) and in particular, that only invalid ballots containing invalid credentials have been discarded.

For every new election or in the case where some voters are no longer eligible, the authorities should be able to update eligible voters' credentials without requiring them to register again. To this end, we design the following scheme that relies on our sequential aggregate signature scheme introduced in Sect. 2.3.

Multiple Elections and Credentials Revocation. For every new election, the registrars generate both a specific election identifier and a new pair of keys. For the ith election, this pair is defined as $(x_i, X_i = h^{x_i})$ where $x_i \in_R \mathbb{Z}_p$ is shared among registrars and talliers. Hereinafter, we detail the case of a second election identified by e_I and where the new key pair is $(x_2, X_2 = h^{x_2})$.

For each initial credential $\sigma = (u, u') \in DB$ belonging to an eligible voter, the registrars jointly select a random value $t \in_R \mathbb{Z}_p$, compute $\sigma_2 = (u^t, (u'u^{e_I x_2})^t) = (w, w' = w^{x_0 + sx_1 + e_I x_2})$ and update DB. Then, the new database is published to enable eligible voters to learn their new credential. These changes are irrelevant except for the pre-verification phase whose third step requires these modifications:

- *Reconstruction of the credential.* First, the talliers cooperatively encrypt w to get $E_T[w]$. Then, as previously and thanks to ElGamal homomorphic property, they jointly compute the three ciphertexts: $E_T[w^{x_0}]$, $E_T[w^{sx_1}]$ and $E_T[w^{e_I x_2}]$ using e_I, $E_T[w]$ and $E_T[w^s]$ as well as their shared secret keys x_0, x_1 and x_2. Thereby, the talliers can compute $E_T[w^{x_0}] \cdot E_T[w^{sx_1}] \cdot E_T[w^{e_I x_2}] = E_T[w^{x_0 + sx_1 + e_I x_2}]$. By dividing the ciphertext second component by w', they obtain $C = E_T[w^{x_0 + sx_1 + e_I x_2}]/w'$. If the associated credential is valid, C should be equal to $E_T[1]$, a ciphertext of 1.

4   Conclusion

We proposed a new efficient coercion-resistant voting scheme that enables credentials revocation as well as multiple elections without requiring voters to visit the registration place again. This is achieved through the design of a new sequential aggregate MAC scheme based on Chase et al. Algebraic MAC scheme.

References

1. Araújo, R., Foulle, S., Traoré, J.: A practical and secure coercion-resistant scheme for remote elections. In: Chaum, D., Kutylowski, M., Rivest, R.L., Ryan, P.Y.A. (eds.) Frontiers of Electronic Voting, pp. 330–342. Schloss Dagstuhl, Germany (2007)

2. Araújo, R., Traoré, J.: A practical coercion resistant voting scheme revisited. In: Heather, J., Schneider, S., Teague, V. (eds.) Vote-ID 2013. LNCS, vol. 7985, pp. 193–209. Springer, Heidelberg (2013)

3. Boneh, D., Boyen, X., Shacham, H.: Short group signatures. In: Franklin, M. (ed.) CRYPTO 2004. LNCS, vol. 3152, pp. 41–55. Springer, Heidelberg (2004)

4. Boneh, D., Gentry, C., Lynn, B., Shacham, H.: Aggregate and verifiably encrypted signatures from bilinear maps. In: Biham, E. (ed.) EUROCRYPT 2003. LNCS, vol. 2656, pp. 416–432. Springer, Heidelberg (2003)

5. Camenisch, J., Stadler, M.: Proof systems for general statements about discrete logarithms. Technical report (1997)

6. Chase, M., Meiklejohn, S., Zaverucha, G.: Algebraic MACs and keyed-verification anonymous credentials. In: Proceedings of the 2014 ACM SIGSAC CCS, CCS 2014, pp. 1205–1216. ACM, New York (2014)

7. Clark, J., Hengartner, U.: Selections: internet voting with over-the-shoulder coercion-resistance. In: Danezis, G. (ed.) FC 2011. LNCS, vol. 7035, pp. 47–61. Springer, Heidelberg (2012)

8. Dodis, Y., Kiltz, E., Pietrzak, K., Wichs, D.: Message authentication, revisited. In: Pointcheval, D., Johansson, T. (eds.) EUROCRYPT 2012. LNCS, vol. 7237, pp. 355–374. Springer, Heidelberg (2012)

9. Jakobsson, M., Sako, K., Impagliazzo, R.: Designated verifier proofs and their applications. In: Maurer, U.M. (ed.) EUROCRYPT 1996. LNCS, vol. 1070, pp. 143–154. Springer, Heidelberg (1996)

10. Juels, A., Catalano, D., Jakobsson, M.: Coercion-resistant electronic elections. In: Atluri, V., di Vimercati, S.D.C., Dingledine, R. (eds.) WPES, pp. 61–70. ACM, New York (2005)

11. Lysyanskaya, A., Micali, S., Reyzin, L., Shacham, H.: Sequential aggregate signatures from trapdoor permutations. In: Cachin, C., Camenisch, J.L. (eds.) EURO-CRYPT 2004. LNCS, vol. 3027, pp. 74–90. Springer, Heidelberg (2004)

12. Pointcheval, D., Sanders, O.: Short randomizable signatures. Cryptology ePrint Archive, Report 2015/525 (2015)

13. Spycher, O., Koenig, R.E., Haenni, R., Schläpfer, M.: A new approach towards coercion-resistant remote e-voting in linear time. FC **2011**, 182–189 (2011)

14. US Vote Foundation: end-to-end verifiable internet voting. In: The Future of Voting, Expert Statement (2015). https://www.usvotefoundation.org/sites/default/files/E2EVIV_expert_statements.pdf

Universal Cast-as-Intended Verifiability

Alex Escala[1], Sandra Guasch[2]([⊠]), Javier Herranz[1], and Paz Morillo[1]

[1] Universitat Politècnica de Catalunya, Barcelona, Spain
{alex.escala,javier.herranz,paz.morillo}@upc.edu
[2] Scytl Secure Electronic Voting, Barcelona, Spain
sandra.guasch@scytl.com

Abstract. In electronic voting, we say that a protocol has cast-as-intended verifiability if the contents of each encrypted vote can be audited in order to ensure that they match the voter's selections. It is traditionally thought that this verification can only be performed by the voter who casts the vote, since only she knows the content of her vote. In this work, we show that this is not the case: we present the first cast-as-intended verification mechanism which is universally verifiable, i.e., the first protocol in which anyone (the voter herself or another party) can check that the contents of an encrypted vote match the voter's selections. To achieve this goal, we assume the existence of a trusted registrar. We formally define universal cast-as-intended verifiability and we show that our protocol satisfies such property, while also satisfying ballot privacy. We give a general construction of the protocol and an efficient instantiation which is provably secure in the random oracle model. We also present a voting system which can be implemented on top of the voting protocol, which is intended to present a more intuitive process to the voter.

1 Introduction

Traditionally, verifiability properties of electronic voting are divided in two categories, depending on the entities who can make use of them. Individual verifiability involves auditing the processes of vote creation and vote storage by the voter. Universal verifiability consists on auditing that only votes from eligible voters are stored in the ballot box, and that all stored votes are properly tallied, which can be performed by everyone. Systems providing both types of verifiability are known as *end-to-end verifiable* systems [3].

One of the individual verifiability properties is vote casting assurance [3], also known as cast-as-intended verification, which is focused on the audit of the vote creation process. This property is only meaningful when the vote is cast using a voting device, therefore excluding voting systems where selections are done on a physical ballot. Another property is recorded-as-cast verification, aimed at auditing the correct reception and storage of the vote in a remote voting server.

In this paper, we focus on cast-as-intended verification, which we present here using a simplified electronic voting scenario. In this simplified voting system, the voter uses a voting device in order to select her choices. After she confirms her vote, the voting device encrypts the selections using a public key encryption scheme. The encrypted vote is then stored in a (local or remote) ballot box.

© International Financial Cryptography Association 2016
J. Clark et al. (Eds.): FC 2016 Workshops, LNCS 9604, pp. 233–250, 2016.
DOI: 10.1007/978-3-662-53357-4_16

When the voting period finishes, the votes in the ballot box are decrypted in order to obtain the election results. By encrypting the vote at the voting device, the secrecy of the vote is ensured during its transmission and storage in the ballot box, until the time of decrypting and tallying the votes.

Naturally, neither the voter or any other entity is able to check if the content of the encrypted vote that is cast really matches what the voter selected. This implies that a malicious voting device would be able to encrypt other options than those selected by the voter. Cast-as-intended verification mechanisms provide the system with means to audit the content of the encrypted vote in order to detect this kind of attacks.

Traditionally, the electronic voting community has considered that the cast-as-intended verification can only be performed by the voter who cast the vote, given that she made her selections in secret. However, leaving the responsibility of this verification to the voter may not be effective at all. On the one hand, we might think of systems which make the cast-as-intended verification mandatory in order to cast a vote. The problem is that current cast-as-intended verification systems present important drawbacks: verification mechanisms are usually not very usable and in most cases voters have to engage in highly interactive protocols and/or be able to perform complex computations. Therefore, mandatory cast-as-intended verification would disenfranchise less skilled voters. On the other hand, we could allow the cast-as-intended verification to be an optional step which the voter can do before casting the vote. This does not solve the problem though, as targeted attacks against non-skilled voters, who will probably not use the verification system, can succeed undetectably.

Our goal is to propose an alternative paradigm which solves the above-mentioned problem, by allowing any party (not only the voter) to publicly verify that an encrypted cast vote really matches the selection of a voter. We refer to this property as universal cast-as-intended verifiability.

1.1   Our Contributions

In this paper, we present a universal cast-as-intended verification protocol, i.e., a protocol where cast-as-intended verification is not restricted to the voter anymore. This allows to deploy mechanisms for auditing all the cast votes in an extensive form, and ensure no tampering attacks happen. Once the voter has cast a ballot, our protocol does not require her to take any further step to verify that her cast ballot corresponds to her chosen candidates.

This is a change of paradigm with respect to current voting protocols, as in our new protocol the verification of the content of the encrypted votes does not rely on the willingness or skills of the voters. Indeed, it can now rely on third parties (e.g. election auditors) without compromising voters' privacy.

The main idea of our protocol is the following: a voter registers to vote with a registrar, who generates a pair of public-secret values for each voting option in the election. The secret values are sent to the voter, while the public ones are published, linked to the voting options they are related to. We need to assume that the registrar is trusted and follows these instructions correctly.

During the voting phase, the voter provides her selected voting options and a subset of the secret values she received during registration to the voting device. The voting device then encrypts the voter's selections and creates a non-interactive zero-knowledge proof of knowledge (NIZKPK), which will be valid only in the case the voting device encrypted what the voter selected.

Thanks to the zero-knowledge property of the proofs, they can be publicly verified while maintaining the voter's privacy. Therefore, we can say that the system provides *universal cast as intended verifiability*.

1.2 Related Work

Helios [1] is a well-known electronic voting protocol which has been used in several real-world binding elections. Both Helios and our new voting protocol are ballot private (even though the ballot privacy definition needs to be adapted for considering voter-private information) and non-receipt free. However, our new protocol has universal cast-as-intended verifiability, whereas Helios only considers individual cast-as-intended verifiability.

At a first glance one would say that our voting protocol is similar to any Code Voting protocol [7]: in both systems voters introduce codes in their voting devices. However, there are important differences between our voting protocol and any Code Voting protocol. Unlike Code Voting systems, privacy of our voting protocol does not depend on the secrecy of the voting codes. In addition, not only our voting protocol is (universally) cast-as-intended verifiable but it can be extended to be end-to-end verifiable by using known techniques such as a Bulletin Board [16] and a verifiable Mix-Net [22]. As far as we know, the only end-to-end verifiable Code Voting protocols (with individual cast-as-intended verifiability) are VeryVote [18], in which verifiability is achieved at the cost of making the scheme non-private to the voting server, and Pretty Good Democracy [21], in which verifiability implies knowledge and use of the election private key by a set of trustees during the voting phase. Finally, note that our voting protocol does not attempt to solve the secure platform problem [15] and, in particular, it can be implemented with a user-friendly point and click voting interface (even though voters still need to introduce voting codes).

Other systems which provide cast-as-intended verifiability while trying to reduce the participation of the voter in the process, such as Scratch & Vote [2], MarkPledge [19], Chaum's *Secret-Ballot Receipts* [8] and *Prêt à voter* [20] are focused on poll-site voting systems, and require specific hardware and procedures, such as optical scanners or DREs with printers, which are not available to remote voters.

Finally, the Eperio cryptographic election verification protocol [13] can be considered a precursor of universal cast-as-intended verifiability. In this protocol, voters might delegate their individual verifiability, without any privacy loss, by giving a copy of their voting receipt to any other party. However, Eperio is designed to be used in traditional elections in which only the tallying process is done electronically.

1.3   Structure of the Paper

We give the syntax of a voting system which enables such universal cast-as-intended property in Sects. 2.1 and 2.2 we informally state the security assumptions we make, and provide a definition for universal cast-as-intended verifiability. The building blocks of our protocol are presented in Sect. 3. In Sect. 4 we give a generic construction of our new protocol. We provide the results of our security analysis (included in the full version of this paper) in Sect. 5. In addition, we give an efficient instantiation of our new protocol which is provably secure in the random oracle model in Sect. 6. In Sect. 7 we present an implementation of our new voting protocol which might lead to the design of usable voting systems. Finally, we detail some lines of future research in Sect. 8.

2   Electronic Voting Definitions

2.1   Syntactical Definition

We now give the syntax of a voting scheme, which we will later use to present our protocol. This definition is based on single-pass voting schemes, as defined in [5]. These kind of schemes are characterized by the fact that voters interact with the system only by submitting their ballots. Voters may have credentials in order to be able to cast such ballots, but how voters get them is outside the scope of this scheme.

As defined in [5], a voting scheme has the following participants: the *Election Authorities* are in charge of setting up the election, computing the tally and publishing the results; the *Voters* participate in the election by choosing their preferred options; and the *Bulletin Board Manager* receives, processes and publishes the ballots received, as well as other public information.

In addition, we also consider the following participants: the *Registrars* are responsible for providing to the voters that chose them all the information they need to vote, in particular the information that will provide the UCIV property. We also explicitly consider the *Voting Device* as a participant. As opposed to *Voters*, who only choose their preferred voting options, the *Voting Device* is in charge of casting a ballot given those voting options. This distinction is important when introducing the concept of universal cast-as-intended verifiability.

We assume that non-cryptographic election specifications such as the set of voting options V or the set of voters are fixed in advance by the *Election Authorities*. Further we assume a counting function $\rho : (V \cup \{\bot\})^* \to R$ is given, where V is the set of voting options, $\bot$ denotes an invalid vote and R is the set of results.

For sake of simplicity, we will assume that there is only one Election Authority and one Registrar. Detailed trust assumptions for Election Authorities and Registrars are further discussed in Sect. 2.2.

The voting scheme is characterized by the following algorithms:

- Setup(1^λ) is a protocol executed by the Election Authority. On input a security parameter 1^λ, it generates and outputs an election public/private key pair (epk, esk). In addition, it defines the space of secret Universal Cast-As-Intended Verification (UCIV from now on) information SVI, the space of voting option-dependent secret UCIV information $\widetilde{SVI}$, the space of public UCIV information PVI and a family of functions $\sigma. : SVI \rightarrow \widetilde{SVI}$ such that, for each voting option $v \in V$ the function σ_v maps the secret UCIV information to some voting option-dependant secret UCIV information (*The function σ_v will need to be evaluated by the voter, so it should be a relatively simple one. In our scheme the function will consist on selecting some elements from a given set*).

- Register(vid, V, epk) is run by the Registrar. It takes as input a voter identity vid, the set of voting options V and the election public key epk. It outputs the secret UCIV information $s_{uciv}^{vid} \in SVI$ and the public UCIV information $p_{uciv}^{vid} \in PVI$.

- Vote($vid, v, \sigma_v(s_{uciv}^{vid}), p_{uciv}^{vid}, epk$) is a probabilistic protocol run by voting devices. It receives as input the voter identity vid, a voting option $v \in V$, the function σ_v evaluated on the secret UCIV information $s_{uciv}^{vid} \in SVI$, the public UCIV information $p_{uciv}^{vid} \in PVI$, the election public key epk and outputs a ballot b.

- ProcessBallot(BB, b, vid) is run by the bulletin board manager. It receives as input a bulletin board BB, a ballot b and a voter identity vid and outputs either success (1) or reject (0).

- Tally(BB, esk) is run by the Election Authority. It takes as input a bulletin board BB and the election secret key esk and outputs a result $r \in R$ and a correct tabulation proof Π.

Finally, the scheme is executed as follows:

Configuration Phase: in this phase, the Election Authority runs the Setup algorithm. The Election Authority publishes the election public key epk on the bulletin board BB and keeps the election secret key esk.

Registration Phase: in this phase, a voter registers to vote in the election. The Registrar runs the Register algorithm, provides the secret UCIV information s_{uciv}^{vid} to the voter, and publishes the public UCIV information p_{uciv}^{vid} in the bulletin board.

Voting Phase: in this phase each registered voter vid can vote. To vote, the voter chooses a voting option v, evaluates $\sigma_v(s_{uciv}^{vid})$ and provides $(vid, v, \sigma_v(s_{uciv}^{vid}))$ to the voting device. The voting device takes the election public key epk and the public UCIV information p_{uciv}^{vid} from the bulletin board and runs the Vote algorithm, producing a ballot b. The ballot b and the voter's identity vid are then sent to the bulletin board. Upon reception of the ballot, the bulletin board manager executes the ProcessBallot algorithm. In case the output is 1, the ballot is published in the bulletin board, otherwise the ballot is discarded and the voter is notified accordingly.

Counting Phase: in the counting phase the Election Authority runs the Tally algorithm using the election private key *esk* and the information in the bulletin board, including the ballots. The output of the Tally algorithm is published on the bulletin board.

A voting system as defined above is correct if, when the four phases are run with all the participants behaving correctly, the result r output by the Tally algorithm is equal to the evaluation of the counting function ρ on the voting options corresponding to the ballots cast by the voters.

2.2 Security Definitions

In this section we give the security definitions of privacy and universal cast-as-intended. We will not define recorded-as-cast verifiability nor counted-as-recorded verifiability, since these properties are out of the scope of this paper. Similarly, we focus on the notions of privacy provided by existing schemes such as [1], and leave the consideration of stronger notions of vote privacy, such as receipt freeness or coercion resistance, for a future work.

Assumptions on Voting Devices, Election Authorities and Registrars. When considering voting devices, we distinguish between privacy and integrity. In order to guarantee privacy, we assume that the voting device behaves properly by correctly encrypting the voter's choice and not leaking any information. This is a common assumption in electronic voting schemes where the voter can use a point and click interface to make her choices, such as Helios [1]. On the other hand, we do not trust the voting device at all when it comes to integrity, since we assume it could try to change the voters' choice prior to encryption. In the same way, the verifiability of the scheme does not rely on the voting device being honest.

We will assume that there is only one election authority, which is trusted for privacy. Secret sharing and multi-party computation techniques can be easily deployed, as done in [11], to overcome this limitation so that privacy is guaranteed as long as a subset of the election authorities are trusted. The electoral authorities do not need to be trusted for our new verifiability property. Indeed, in the UCIV security definition we assume that the election private key is leaked to the adversary.

In addition, we will also assume that any common reference strings are generated by a single, trusted authority. This is a strong assumption, which can be solved by using the multi-string model defined by Groth and Ostrovsky in [17]. In this model, several parties provide their common reference strings and security relies on assuming that a threshold of such parties are honest. We consider that directly using the multi-string model would make our paper utterly complex and, on the other hand, it would not add much value to the paper. Moreover, when we instantiate our scheme with protocols with ROM-based security, no common reference string is needed at all.

We also assume that there is only one registrar, who is trusted to produce the UCIV information correctly and keep it secret, so that the secret UCIV information is not leaked to the adversary. This assumption is common in other protocols for the information generated by the registrars for providing individual verifiability properties, such as [21] or [2]. There are several well-known techniques that can be used to weaken these assumptions. One is to randomly audit a set of outputs produced by the registrar in order to ensure the UCIV information is produced correctly. This audit involves the publication of the secret UCIV information, and therefore an audited set of UCIV information should not be used by a voter to cast her vote. Another one is to consider a set of registrars and use multi-party computation techniques in order to guarantee the privacy of the UCIV information, as far as a subset of the registrars are honest. The printer which may be in charge of putting the shares of secret UCIV information together and providing them to the voter is then trusted not to reveal this information, as in [21]. Finally, another approach is to allow each voter to choose which registrars she registers with: she might register with only one registrar or with all of them. These extensions will be detailed in the full version of the paper.

Ballot Privacy. Intuitively, a voting system has ballot privacy if an adversary with access to the bulletin board is not able to guess what voting options the voters chose. We adopt the formalization given in [4], where they give a definition correcting the flaws of previous definitions.

Ballot privacy is defined using two experiments between an adversary A and a challenger C. The goal of the adversary is to disinguish between the two experiments. In both experiments, we let the adversary corrupt voters and submit ballots on their behalf. In addition, for each honest voter the adversary can also specify two votes to be used for casting her ballot. The votes which will be used to cast the honest voters' ballots will depend on which experiment is taking place. The goal of the adversary is to distinguish between both experiments i.e., to distinguish which votes were used to cast the honest voters' ballots. As revealing the "true" tally would easily allow the adversary to distinguish between the experiments, the same tally is always shown to the adversary, regardless of which vote was used to cast honest voters' ballots.

For compactness, we present the two experiments as a single experiment depending on a bit β. The experiments are parametrized by the set of voting options V and an algorithm SimProof(BB, r) such that, given a bulletin board and a result simulates a proof of correct tabulation.

1. **Setup Phase.** The challenger sets up two empty bulletin boards L and R. It runs the Setup(1^λ) protocol to obtain the election public key epk and the election private key esk. It then posts epk on both bulletin boards. The adversary is given read access to either L if $\beta = 0$ or R if $\beta = 1$. In addition, C initializes an empty list ID.
2. **Registration Phase.** The adversary may make one type of query.

- **Register**(*vid*) query. The adversary provides a voter identity such that (*vid*) $\notin$ *ID*. The challenger runs Register on inputs (*vid*, *V*, *epk*) to generate the partial public UCIV information p_{uciv}^{vid} and the partial secret UCIV information s_{uciv}^{vid}. *C* provides both p_{uciv}^{vid} and s_{uciv}^{vid} to *A* and p_{uciv}^{vid} is published on both bulletin boards. The identity *vid* is added to *ID*.

3. **Voting Phase.** The adversary may make two types of queries.
    - **Vote**(*vid*, v_L, v_R) queries. The adversary provides a voter identity *vid* such that *vid* $\in$ *ID* and two votes v_L, v_R $\in$ *V*. The challenger runs Vote(*vid*, v_L, $\sigma_{v_L}(s_{uciv}^{vid})$, p_{uciv}^{vid}, *epk*) which outputs b_L and Vote(*vid*, v_R, $\sigma_{v_R}(s_{uciv}^{vid})$, p_{uciv}^{vid}, *epk*) which outputs b_R. *C* then obtains new versions of the boards *L* and *R* by running ProcessBallot(*L*, b_L, *vid*) and ProcessBallot(*R*, b_R, *vid*) and updating the boards accordingly.
    - **Ballot**(*b*, *vid*) queries. These are queries made on behalf of corrupt voters. Here the adversary provides a ballot *b* and an identity *vid* such that *vid* $\in$ *ID*. The challenger runs ProcessBallot(*L*, *b*, *vid*) and if the process accepts it also runs ProcessBallot(*R*, *b*, *vid*) and updates the boards accordingly.

4. **Tallying Phase.** The challenger evaluates Tally(*L*, *esk*) obtaining the result *r* and the proof of correct tabulation *Π*. If $\beta = 0$, the challenger posts (*r*, *Π*) on the bulletin board *L*. If $\beta = 1$, the challenger runs SimProof(*R*, *r*) obtaining a simulated proof *Π'* and posts (*r*, *Π'*) on the bulletin board *R*.

5. **Output.** The adversary *A* outputs a bit $\alpha^{A,V}$.

We say that a voting protocol as defined in Sect. 2.1 provides ballot privacy if there exists an algorithm SimProof such that for any probabilistic polynomial time (p.p.t.) adversary *A* and any set of voting options *V*, the following advantage is negligible in the security parameter λ.

$$\mathbf{Adv}_V^{\mathbf{priv}}(A) := |\Pr[\alpha^{A,V} = 1|\beta = 1] - \Pr[\alpha^{A,V} = 1|\beta = 0]|$$

We want to remark that in case of honest voters the ballots are properly encrypted. In other words, this implies that the voting devices used to cast those ballots use *good* randomness and do not leak information about the randomness used. In addition, the ballot privacy does *not* rely on the adversary not having access to the secret UCIV information.

Universal Cast-as-Intended Verifiability: Intuitively, a voting system satisfies the cast-as-intended property if a corrupt voting device is not able to cast a ballot for a voting option different to the one chosen by the voter. This should hold as long as the voter is honest. If the voter is malicious no guarantees can be given besides the fact that the ballot must correspond to at most one voting option (i.e., it could also correspond to an invalid voting option which will not be counted). We define cast-as-intended on a per-ballot basis, not considering the tallying phase inside the definition.

In this definition, we use an extractor algorithm Extract which is defined as follows: for any (*epk*, *esk*) in the image of Setup, for any voter identity *vid*, for any correctly generated public and secret UCIV information $p_{uciv}^{vid}, s_{uciv}^{vid}$ and for any $v \in V$, it is satisfied that $\mathsf{Extract}(\mathsf{Vote}(vid, v, \sigma_v(s_{uciv}^{vid}), p_{uciv}^{vid}, epk), esk) = v$.

Universal cast-as-intended verifiability is defined as an experiment between an adversary A and a challenger C. In this experiment, the adversary may corrupt registrars, voters or voting devices. The goal of the adversary is to cast ballots in behalf of a non-corrupt voter so that the ballot does not extract to the voting option chosen by the voter. The *extract* is one with which the voting scheme is strongly consistent, which according to [4] states that the tally of a bulletin board must correspond to the result of applying a counting function to the *contents* of the ballots in the bulletin board. The experiment is parametrized by the set of voting options V and an algorithm $\mathsf{Extract}(b, esk)$ such that, given a ballot and the election private key returns a vote or $\bot$ denoting an invalid vote.

1. **Setup Phase.** The challenger sets up an empty bulletin board BB and runs the $\mathsf{Setup}(1^\lambda)$ protocol to obtain the election public key epk and the election private key esk, posts epk on the board and gives (epk, esk) to the adversary. The adversary is given read access to BB. In addition, C initializes three empty lists ID_R, ID_P, ID_F. For convenience, we define $ID = ID_P \cup ID_F$.
2. **Registration Phase.** The adversary may make one type of query.
   - **Register**(vid) query. The adversary provides a voter identity such that $(vid) \notin ID_R$. The challenger runs $\mathsf{Register}(vid, V, epk)$ to generate the public UCIV information p_{uciv}^{vid} and the secret UCIV information s_{uciv}^{vid}. C provides p_{uciv}^{vid} to A, publishes p_{uciv}^{vid} on the bulletin board and adds vid to ID_R.
3. **Voting Phase.** The adversary may make two types of queries.
   - **CorruptVotingDevice**(vid, v_{vid}) queries. The adversary provides a voter identity $vid \notin ID$ such that $vid \in ID_R$ and a voting option v_{vid} corresponding to such identity. Then, C provides $\sigma_{v_{vid}}(s_{uciv}^{vid})$ to A. The challenger adds vid to ID_P.
   - **CorruptVoter**(vid) queries. The adversary provides a voter identity $vid \notin ID$ such that $vid \in ID_R$. Then, C provides s_{uciv}^{vid} to A. The challenger adds vid to ID_F.
4. **Output.** The adversary submits a pair (b^*, vid^*). The output of the experiment is a bit δ^V, which is defined as 1 if (i) $vid^* \in ID_P$, (ii) $\mathsf{ProcessBallot}(BB, b^*, vid^*) = 1$ and (iii) $\mathsf{Extract}(b^*, esk) \neq v_{vid^*}$, where v_{vid^*} is the voting option submitted by the adversary in the CorruptVotingDevice query for vid^*. δ^V, is defined as 0 in any other case.

We say that a voting protocol as defined in Sect. 2.1 has universal cast-as-intended verifiability with respect to a counting function ρ if there exists an algorithm $\mathsf{Extract}$ such that the following two conditions hold:

(i) for all sets of voting options V the voting protocol is strongly consistent with respect to $\rho, \mathsf{Extract}$.
(ii) for any probabilistic polynomial time (p.p.t.) adversary A and any set of voting options V, the following advantage is negligible as a function of λ.

$$\mathbf{Adv}_V^{\mathbf{uciv}}(A) := \Pr[\delta^V = 1]$$

We want to remark that the universal cast-as-intended verifiability property does not rely on the secrecy of the private election key.

3 Building Blocks

ENCRYPTION SCHEME. An encryption scheme consists of three probabilistic polynomial time (PPT) algorithms: KGen, Enc_{pk} and Dec_{sk}. On input a security parameter 1^k, the KGen algorithm outputs a public key pk and a secret key sk, and implicitly defines a message space M_{sp}, a ciphertext space C_{sp} and a randomness space R_{sp}. The Enc_{pk} algorithm takes as input a message $M \in M_{sp}$ and uses the public key pk to output a ciphertext $C \in C_{sp}$. The Dec_{sk} algorithm takes as input a ciphertext $C \in C_{sp}$ and uses the secret key sk to output a message $M \in M_{sp}$, or halts outputting $\perp$.

We use the notion of NM-CPA security [5] for the encryption scheme.

ONE-WAY FUNCTIONS. Roughly speaking, a one-way function is a function which is easy to compute but very difficult to invert. More formally, a function $F : X \rightarrow Y$ between two finite sets is said to be one-way if the following two properties are satisfied, where $k = \log |X|$: (i) For each $x \in X$, the value $F(x)$ can be computed in time polynomial in k; (ii) For any algorithm A running in time polynomial in k, and for $x \in X$ chosen with the uniform distribution, the probability that A, on input $F(x)$, outputs x is negligible.

NON-INTERACTIVE ZERO-KNOWLEDGE PROOFS OF KNOWLEDGE. Namely, a NIZKPK for the relation R is composed by three PPT algorithms ($\mathsf{GenCRS}, \mathsf{Prove}, \mathsf{Verify}$): GenCRS takes as input a security parameter 1^k and outputs a common reference string crs. Prove takes as input the common reference string crs, a statement x and a witness w such that $(x, w) \in R$ and outputs a proof π. Verify takes as input the common reference string crs, a statement x and a proof π and outputs 1 if it accepts the proof or 0 if it rejects it.

A NIZKPK must satisfy the following three properties (see for instance [12,23]): completeness, knowledge soundness and zero-knowledge, which implies *witness indistinguishability* [14].

4 Core Voting Protocol

4.1 Overview

In this section we present our new voting protocol. We will not take into account usability issues from a voter's point of view; we will take care of these issues on the voting systems proposed in Sect. 7. We think that by splitting the core protocol from the voting systems built on top of it the reader can get a clearer picture of our solution.

Our protocol is a mix-net based voting protocol, although the ideas can be also applied to the setting of homomorphic tallying schemes. In mix-net based protocols, the voters encrypt their votes (we will assume that each selection is encrypted individually), then all the ciphertexts submitted by the voters are shuffled and re-encrypted in several nodes and then the shuffled ciphertexts are decrypted. We will work with a simplified scheme where votes are only shuffled and decrypted once.

The goal of our work is to provide a protocol which provides ballot privacy and universal cast-as-intended verifiability. Other requirements of voting schemes such as the assurance of the authorship of the vote (an eligible voter), recorded-as-cast verifiability and counted-as-recorded verifiability are not considered in this work, since other measures can be built around the protocol in order to fulfill them. For instance, digital signatures, public bulletin boards or verifiable mix-nets could be used to satisfy the mentioned properties respectively.

The main idea of the core protocol is the following: during the registration phase, a voter registers to vote. The registrar generates a secret value for each voting option of the election, and provides them to the voter. A one-way function will be applied to each secret value and the resulting images will be made public (maintaining the relation with the voting options).

Once the voter has selected her voting options by using a voting device, she will provide a subset of the secret values (previously unknown) to the voting device. Then the voting device will encrypt the voting options, and will create a non-interactive zero-knowledge proof of knowledge (NIZKPK). By carefully choosing which secret values the voter discloses, the voting device will only be able to create a valid NIZKPK if it really encrypted the voter's selections.

The NIZKPK used in the protocol can be publicly verified, since the voter's privacy is maintained in such case due to the zero-knowledge property of the proofs. Therefore, the system provides *universal cast as intended verifiability* since the proofs can be universally verified, and this validation is successful only in the case the voting device encrypted the voter's selections.

A sketch on how this NIZKPK works is the following: In the voting phase, the voter will provide the secret values whose images are associated to the voting options she did not choose to the voting device; this idea is reminiscent of the Bingo voting scheme [6]. The voting device will then create, for each possible voting option, a NIZKPK of the statement "either this voting option is encrypted in the ciphertext *or* I know the pre-image of the public value which corresponds to it". Without further information, the voting device will be able to create all the proofs as long as it encrypted the voter's selected voting option.

The proofs also guarantee that, as long as the voter behaved honestly, the encrypted vote contains a valid voting option. This might be useful to discern whether a malformed vote was intentionally created by a malicious voter or by a malicious voting device (used by a honest voter). Note that, as we are giving a mix-net based protocol, if both the voter and the voting device are malicious and submit a vote containing a non-valid option, this vote will be anyway discarded once the votes have been mixed and decrypted, prior to being added to the count. Therefore, this is not an attack against the system.

4.2   2-cnf-Proof of Knowledge

In Sect. 3 we defined an encryption scheme $(\mathsf{KGen}, \mathsf{Enc}_{pk}, Dec)$ with an associated message space M_{sp}, ciphertext space C_{sp} and randomness space R_{sp}. Consider the relation $R_{enc} = \{((C, M); r) | M \in M_{sp}, C \in C_{sp}, r \in R_{sp}, C = \mathsf{Enc}_{pk}(M; r)\}$ which consists of the tuples of ciphertexts, messages and randomness such that the ciphertext is an encryption of the message using the specified randomness. Note that, in this relation, the statement is the pair ciphertext - message, while the witness is the randomness.

Also consider that we have a one-way function F with an associated input space X and output space Y. Consider the relation $R_{ow} = \{(y; x) | x \in X, y \in Y, y = F(x)\}$ which consists of the pairs of values such that the first value is the image of the second one under the one-way function F. In this case, the image value (i.e., the first element, y) is the statement while the pre-image (i.e., the second element, x) is the witness.

The relation for which we will make the NIZKPK is the following one:

$$R_{2\text{-}cnf} = \{((C, (M_1, \ldots, M_n), (y_1, \ldots, y_n)); (r, (x_1, \ldots, x_n))) |$$
$$(((C, M_1); r) \in R_{enc} \lor (x_1, y_1) \in R_{ow}) \land$$
$$(((C, M_2); r) \in R_{enc} \lor (x_2, y_2) \in R_{ow}) \land$$
$$\cdots \qquad\qquad\qquad \land$$
$$(((C, M_n); r) \in R_{enc} \lor (x_n, y_n) \in R_{ow})\}$$

This way of presenting the relation $R_{2\text{-}cnf}$ allows us to analyze it easily: the relation takes a statement which is a ciphertext, a set of messages and a set of image values, and a witness, which is some randomness and a set of pre-images. The tuple of statement and witness belongs to the language iff every predicate in the AND clause is satisfied. This is, we require that for every $i \in \{1, \ldots, n\}$ the predicate $(((C, M_i); r) \in R_{enc} \lor (x_i, y_i) \in R_{ow})$ is satisfied. This predicate perfectly captures the intuition given above: either the ciphertext encrypts the message M_i or a pre-image of y_i is known. The description of the language $R_{2\text{-}cnf}$ will also allow us to generate a NIZKPK from the composition of simpler NIZKPKs for the relations R_{enc} and R_{ow}. In Sect. 6 we present efficient NIZKPK systems for this $R_{2\text{-}cnf}$ relation.

4.3   Detailed Protocol

Our protocol implements a voting scheme where the counting function ρ is the multiset function as defined in [4]. This function returns a random permutation of its input, filtering invalid votes. This is the case for all mix-net based protocols.

Here we describe the protocol for single-mark ballots. An extension for multiple-mark ballots is provided in the full version.

The protocol uses as building blocks an encryption scheme $(\mathsf{KGen}, \mathsf{Enc}_{pk}, \mathsf{Dec}_{sk})$, a one-way function F and a NIZKPK $(\mathsf{GenCRS}, \mathsf{Prove}, \mathsf{Verify})$ for the relation $R_{2\text{-}cnf}$ defined in Sect. 4.2.

In our protocol, the secret UCIV information for a voter is a set of pre-images $(x_1^{vid}, \ldots, x_n^{vid})$ of F, one for each element in V (the set of voting options), and the public UCIV information is $(y_1^{vid}, \ldots, y_n^{vid}) = (F(x_1^{vid}), \ldots, F(x_1^{vid}))$, the images of each element of the secret UCIV information. Each pair (x_i^{vid}, y_i^{vid}) is related to the corresponding voting option v_i, and the relation between y_i^{vid} and v_i is public.

The function σ_{v_i} has as input the set of all pre-images $(x_1^{vid}, \ldots, x_n^{vid})$ and outputs the the the same values except for x_i^{vid}. Note that this implicitly defines $SVI, \widetilde{SVI}, PVI$. As all this information is only determined by F, there is no need to consider the specification of $SVI, \widetilde{SVI}, PVI, \sigma$ as part of the Setup algorithm.

The protocol consists of the following algorithms:

Setup(1^λ): the algorithm first runs GenCRS to generate the common reference string crs. The algorithm also runs KGen to generate a pair of public/private encryption keys (pk, sk). This implicitly defines the message space M_{sp}. For the sake of simplicity, we will assume that $V \subset M_{sp}$ so that no specific encoding is needed. The election public key epk is defined as $epk = (\mathsf{crs}, pk)$ and the election secret key is defined as $esk = sk$.

Register(vid, V, epk): the algorithm generates the secret UCIV information s_{uciv}^{vid} for that voter by generating, for each voting option $v_i \in V$, a random value $x_i^{vid} \in X$. The public UCIV information p_{uciv}^{vid} is generated by computing the image $y_i^{vid} = F(x_i^{vid})$ for each voting option.

Vote($vid, v, \sigma_v(s_{uciv}^{vid}), p_{uciv}^{vid}, epk$): the algorithm parses epk as (crs, pk). It then parses $\sigma_v(s_{uciv}^{vid})$ as $\{\{x_i^{vid}\}_{i \text{ s.t. } v_i \neq v}\}$ and p_{uciv}^{vid} as $\{(y_1^{vid}, \ldots, y_n^{vid})\}$. It then runs the Enc$_{pk}$ algorithm using fresh randomness $r \in R_{sp}$, producing a ciphertext $C = \mathsf{Enc}_{pk}(v, r)$. Then, by using the witness $w = (r, (\xi_1^{vid}, \ldots, \xi^{vid}))$, where ξ_k^{vid} with $k = j$ such that $v_j = v$ is the empty string ε and it is x_k^{vid} otherwise, the algorithm computes a NIZKPK for the relation $R_{2\text{-}cnf}$ as $\pi = \mathsf{Prove}(\mathsf{crs}, C, y_1^{vid}, \ldots, y_n^{vid}, w)$. The resulting ballot b is defined by the pair (C, π).

ProcessBallot(BB, b, vid): upon reception of a ballot b, which can be parsed as $b = (C, \pi)$, it is checked if in the bulletin board there is another pair (id, b') (i.e., with the same id), or another ballot $b' = (C', \pi')$ such that $C = C'$. If any of such case is found, the algorithm stops and returns 0. Otherwise, p_{uciv}^{vid} is recovered from the bulletin board and parsed as $\{(y_1^{vid}, \ldots, y_n^{vid})\}$. Then, Verify($\mathsf{crs}, C, y_1^{vid}, \ldots, y_n^{vid}, \pi$) is run, where crs is also recovered from the bulletin board. The output of Verify is returned as the output of ProcessBallot.

Tally(BB, esk): at the end of the election, ProcessBallot(BB, b, vid) is run for all pairs (b, vid) appearing in the bulletin board. Then, each individual ballot b is decrypted $\tilde{v} = \mathsf{Dec}_{sk}(C, sk)$ and ρ is applied to the resulting decryptions $\{\tilde{v}\}$. The output of ρ is defined as the result and the proof of correct tabulation is defined to be the empty string ε.

5   Security of the Protocol

Here we provide the results of our security analysis for ballot privacy and universal cast-as-intended verifiability. The security proofs will be available in the full version of the paper.

Theorem 1. *Let* $(\mathsf{KGen}, \mathsf{Enc}_{pk}, \mathsf{Dec}_{sk})$ *be a NM-CPA secure encryption scheme and let* $(\mathsf{GenCRS}, \mathsf{Prove}, \mathsf{Verify})$ *be a NIZKPK for the relation* $R_{2\text{-}cnf}$ *defined in Sect. 4.2. Then, the protocol defined in Sect. 4.3 satisfies the ballot privacy property.*

Theorem 2. *Let* F *be a one-way function and let* $(\mathsf{GenCRS}, \mathsf{Prove}, \mathsf{Verify})$ *be a NIZKPK. Let the number of voting options be polynomial in the security parameter. Then, the protocol defined in Sect. 4.3 satisfies the universal cast-as-intended property.*

6   A Possible Instantiation

The instantiation of our protocol that we propose is quite efficient and its security holds in the ROM. It works over a fixed cyclic group $G = \langle g \rangle$ of prime order q. It uses a modified version of ElGamal with a Schnorr proof (Signed ElGamal [24]), which is NM-CPA secure in the ROM; the encryption of a message $m \in G$ becomes $C = (g^r, pk^r \cdot m, h, z)$, where $r, s \in Z_q$ are randomly chosen, $h = H(g^r, g^s, pk^r \cdot m)$ for some suitable hash function H (included in the common reference string) and $z = r + sh \mod q$.

The exponentiation function defined as $F(x) = g^x$, given an $x \in Z_q$, with the same cyclic group and generator used for the encryption scheme, is used for the one-way function.

Finally the NIZKPK for the relation $R_{2\text{-}cnf}$ is constructed by combining existing techniques. On the one hand, a σ-protocol for proving knowledge of a discrete logarithm [24] (also known as a Schnorr protocol) and a σ-protocol for proving equality of two discrete logarithms [9] (also known as a Chaum-Pedersen protocol). On the other hand, as shown in [10], given a σ-protocol for a relation R_1 and another σ-protocol for a relation R_2 one can construct both a σ-protocol for the relation R_{or} defined as $(x, w) \in R_{or}$ iff $(x, w) \in R_1$ or $(x, w) \in R_2$ and a σ-protocol for the relation R_{and} defined as $(x, w) \in R_{and}$ iff $(x, w) \in R_1$ and $(x, w) \in R_2$.

Focusing on the election scheme for single-mark ballots, with n candidates, a ballot in this specific instantiation of our scheme will have the form (C, π), where $C = (c_1, c_2, c_3, c_4) = (g^r, pk^r \cdot v, h, z)$, if the chosen option is $v = v_j$, and the non-interactive zero-knowledge proof of knowledge $\pi = (h, \{h_1^{(i)}, s_1^{(i)}, s_2^{(i)}\}_{1 \le i \le n})$ for the relation $R_{2\text{-}cnf}$ can be computed by combining the Fiat-Shamir heuristic and the afore-mentioned techniques, as detailed below (for simplicity, we denote $x_i = x_i^{vid}$ and $y_i = y_i^{vid}$, for each $i = 1, \dots, n$):

1. For $i = 1, \dots, n$, $i \ne j$, choose $s_1^{(i)}, h_1^{(i)} \in Z_q$ at random. Define the values $c_1^{(i)} = g^{s_1^{(i)}} \cdot c_1^{-h_1^{(i)}}$ and $c_2^{(i)} = pk^{s_1^{(i)}} \cdot (c_2/v_i)^{-h_1^{(i)}}$.
2. For index j, choose $s_2^{(j)}, h_2^{(j)} \in Z_q$ at random, and define the value $R^{(j)} = g^{s_2^{(j)}} \cdot y_j^{-h_2^{(j)}}$.
3. For $i = 1, \dots, n$, $i \ne j$, choose $\alpha^{(i)} \in Z_q$ at random and compute $R^{(i)} = g^{\alpha^{(i)}}$.

4. For index j, choose $\beta^{(j)} \in Z_q$ and $z^{(j)} \in G$, at random, and compute $c_1^{(j)} = g^{\beta^{(j)}}$ and $c_2^{(j)} = pk^{\beta^{(j)}}$.

5. Compute the hash function $h = H(c_1, c_2, c_3, c_4, \{c_1^{(i)}, c_2^{(i)}, R^{(i)}\}_{1 \leq i \leq n}) \in Z_q$.

6. For $i = 1, \ldots, n$, $i \neq j$, compute $h_2^{(i)} = h - h_1^{(i)} \mod q$. For index j, compute $h_1^{(j)} = h - h_2^{(j)} \mod q$.

7. For $i = 1, \ldots, n$, $i \neq j$, compute $s_2^{(i)} = \alpha^{(i)} + x_i h_2^{(i)} \mod q$.

8. For index j, compute $s_1^{(j)} = \beta^{(j)} + r h_1^{(j)} \mod q$.

To verify the correctness of the proof π, one has to compute first, for each $i = 1, \ldots, n$, the values $h_2^{(i)} = h - h_1^{(i)} \mod q$, $c_1^{(i)} = g^{s_1^{(i)}} \cdot c_1^{-h_1^{(i)}}$, $c_2^{(i)} = pk^{s_1^{(i)}} \cdot (c_2/v_i)^{-h_1^{(i)}}$ and $R^{(i)} = g^{s_2^{(i)}} \cdot y_i^{-h_2^{(i)}}$. After that, the proof is accepted if and only if $h = H(c_1, c_2, c_3, c_4, \{c_1^{(i)}, c_2^{(i)}, R^{(i)}\}_{1 \leq i \leq n})$.

Efficiency Comparison to Helios. Each element in Z_q and each element in G can be represented with λ bits, where λ is the length in bits of the prime number q (that is, the security parameter of the scheme). Therefore, the size of each ballot (C, π) in this instantiation is $(3n+5)\lambda$ bits: 4λ bits for C and $(3n+1)\lambda$ bits for π. The number of modular exponentiations that must be computed to generate such a ballot is $3n + 4$.

We can compare these costs with the costs of the basic version of Helios for the case of a single-mark election, with n candidates. Let us remember that a ballot in Helios consists of n ElGamal encryptions $C_1, \ldots, C_n$ of 0 or 1, one encryption for each of the n candidates (the voter encrypts 1 only for the chosen option, and 0 everywhere else), along with a non-interactive zero-knowledge proof of knowledge π of the fact that each ciphertext encrypts 0 or 1, and the product of all the ciphertexts (which is an encryption of the sum of the n plaintenxts, by the homomorphic properties of ElGamal) also encrypts 0 or 1. The size of each ballot in Helios is $(5n + 4)\lambda$ bits: $2n\lambda$ bits for the n ElGamal ciphertexts, and $(3(n + 1) + 1)\lambda$ bits for π. The number of modular exponentiations required to generate a ballot in Helios is $6n$.

The instantiation that we have just presented is more efficient than the basic version of Helios, for single-mark elections, in terms of the size of the ballots and the computational cost to generate them, while adding a new property (universal cast-as-intended verifiability). This efficiency comparison shows that our new protocol has ballots of a reasonable size and that ballot creation is efficient enough to be used in a real election.

7   Towards Designing Usable UCIV Systems

The protocol presented in Sect. 4 requires the voter to provide one secret value per each of the voting options that she did not choose to the voting device. This may require a considerable effort, since the number of voting options available in an election may be quite large, even if the voter can only make one selection (as in single-marking ballot elections). In addition, these values will be fairly big, for instance 256 bits if elliptic curves are used. Finally, providing secrets for the non-selected options is counter-intuitive (note that it is just inverse to what is required in code-voting schemes, for example), since the voter usually expects to enter information related to what she selects. Clearly, requiring the voter to introduce such information is not very user-friendly.

We present now a voting system built on top of our new voting protocol which provides a more intuitive approach for the voter introducing the codes. We provide this example as a first step towards an implementation in a real scenario: usability tests should be done to assess the real usability of this system.

The voting system that we propose uses high-capacity barcodes such as QR codes. These QR codes will contain the secret values the voter has to enter in the voting device. A paper sheet with printed QR codes provides means for storage for those secrets, as well as a channel which can not be eavesdropped by the voting device. The security of the channel depends on the method for delivering the QR sheets to the voters, for example in sealed envelopes sent by postal mail.

The QR contents can be organized in a way such that the voter is only required to scan the QR codes corresponding to the options she selects in order to retrieve the secrets corresponding to the other voting options.

For each voter, a QR paper sheet will be created as follows. First, one QR code will be assigned to each voting option. Let n be the total number of voting options and let ℓ be the number of voting options which the voter can select. Then, each secret value x_i^{vid} (which corresponds to the voting option v_i) will be divided into $n - 1$ shares using a threshold secret sharing scheme [25] with threshold ℓ. This will result in shares $x_{i,k}^{vid}$ for $k \in \{1, \ldots, n\} \backslash i$, this is, $n - 1$ shares, each one assigned to each voting option different from v_i. Then, the QR code assigned to the option v_i will be created containing all the shares $x_{j,i}^{vid}$ for $j \in \{1, \ldots, n\} \backslash i$, this is, the i-th share of each secret value except for x_i^{vid}.

It follows that, given the information of ℓ QRs codes (assigned to ℓ voting options), only the secret values for the voting options not assigned to those QR codes can be reconstructed from the shares inside the QR codes. Scrath surfaces or stickers can be used in order to enforce that only the designated QR codes are scanned by the voting device's camera.

Note that the maximum capacity of a QR code is around 23 thousand bits, which should be more than enough, since each QR code will contain $n - 1$ secret values of size 256 bits each (if using elliptic curves).

This system can be used either in remote or in poll-site/kiosk-based electronic voting schemes. The QR sheets may be distributed to the voters by postal mail or by hand, depending on the scenario.

8   Future Work

We have proposed in this work a generic way to achieve the new notion of universal cast-as-intended verifiability. It would be interesting, and even necessary, to investigate if this new property can be achieved by other means, for instance by modifying existing voting protocols. In particular, the systems Scratch & Vote [2] and Pretty Good Democracy [21] seem very good candidates; taking into account that commitments (or encryptions) are particular cases of one-way functions, our intuition is that a modification of Scratch & Vote or of Pretty Good Democracy would lead to schemes that could be thought as a particular instantiation of our generic construction. The formalization of this intuition, as well as the comparison with the implementation proposed in this work, is left as future work.

Another interesting line of research is to improve the efficiency of the voting protocol. In particular, the size of ballots scales badly with the number of voting options and the number of choices a voter can make. This is in contrast with typical (non-UCIV) mix-net protocols, where the size of ballots increases at most linearly with the number of choices a voter can make.

Although in this work we focused on the notions of privacy provided by existing schemes such as [1], we consider for future works to design a protocol with universal cast-as-intended verifiability, together with stronger notions of privacy such as receipt-freeness or coercion-resistance. Another challenge to solve is to design a voting protocol such that the voting device does not learn the identity of the voter even in front of dishonest registrars.

Finally, we consider there is work to do in the usability field. Although we have proposed a solution for making the voting process more intuitive for the voter, there is still a long way to walk to have a usable voting scheme. Feedback from usability tests and user experience designers may be used in order to find out the best approaches to follow.

Acknowledgements. Authors want to thank the Program Committe of the 1st Workshop on Advances in Secure Electronic Voting for their valuable comments, in particular for pointing out that some notion of UCIV may be achieved by adapting existing schemes such as Scratch & Vote or Pretty Good Democracy.

The work of the third and fourth authors is partially supported by project MTM 2013-41426-R of Spanish Ministry MINECO.

References

1. Adida, B.: Helios: web-based open-audit voting. In: van Oorschot, P.C. (ed.) USENIX Security Symposium, pp. 335–348. USENIX Association, Berkeley (2008)
2. Adida, B., Rivest, R.L.: Scratch and vote: self-contained paper-based cryptographic voting. In: Juels, A., Winslett, M. (eds.) ACM Workshop on Privacy in the Electronic Society, WPES 2006, pp. 29–40. ACM (2006)
3. Benaloh, J.: Simple verifiable elections. In: Electronic Voting Technology Workshop, EVT 2006, p. 5. USENIX Association, Berkeley (2006)
4. Bernhard, D., Cortier, V., Galindo, D., Pereira, O., Warinschi, B.: SoK: a comprehensive analysis of game-based ballot privacy definitions. In: IEEE Symposium on Security and Privacy, SP 2015, pp. 499–516. IEEE Computer Society (2015)
5. Bernhard, D., Pereira, O., Warinschi, B.: IACR Cryptology ePrint Archive
6. Bohli, J.-M., Müller-Quade, J., Röhrich, S.: Bingo voting: secure and coercion-free voting using a trusted random number generator. In: Alkassar, A., Volkamer, M. (eds.) VOTE-ID 2007. LNCS, vol. 4896, pp. 111–124. Springer, Heidelberg (2007)

7. Chaum, D.: Physical and digital secret ballot systems, WO Patent App. PCT/US2001/002,883, 2 August 2001
8. Chaum, D.: Secret-ballot receipts: true voter-verifiable elections. IEEE Secur. Privac. **2**(1), 38–47 (2004)
9. Chaum, D., Pedersen, T.P.: Wallet databases with observers. In: Brickell, E.F. (ed.) CRYPTO 1992. LNCS, vol. 740, pp. 89–105. Springer, Heidelberg (1993)
10. Cramer, R., Damgård, I.B., Schoenmakers, B.: Proof of partial knowledge and simplified design of witness hiding protocols. In: Desmedt, Y.G. (ed.) CRYPTO 1994. LNCS, vol. 839, pp. 174–187. Springer, Heidelberg (1994)
11. Cramer, R., Gennaro, R., Schoenmakers, B.: A secure and optimally efficient multi-authority election scheme. In: Fumy, W. (ed.) EUROCRYPT 1997. LNCS, vol. 1233, pp. 103–118. Springer, Heidelberg (1997)
12. Damgård, I.B.: Commitment schemes and zero-knowledge protocols. In: Damgård, I.B. (ed.) EEF School 1998. LNCS, vol. 1561, pp. 63–86. Springer, Heidelberg (1999)
13. Essex, A., Clark, J., Hengartner, U., Adams, C.: Eperio: mitigating technical complexity in cryptographic election verification. IACR Cryptology ePrint Archive 2012, 178 (2012)
14. Feige, U., Shamir, A.: Witness indistinguishable and witness hiding protocols. In: 22nd Annual ACM Symposium on Theory of Computing, STOC 1990, pp. 416–426. ACM Press (1990)
15. Gerck, E., Neff, C.A., Rivest, R.L., Rubin, A.D., Yung, M.: The business of electronic voting. In: Syverson, P.F. (ed.) FC 2001. LNCS, vol. 2339, pp. 234–259. Springer, Heidelberg (2002)
16. Gharadaghy, R., Volkamer, M.: Verifiability in electronic voting - explanations for non security experts. In: Krimmer, R., Grimm, R. (eds.) Electronic Voting. LNI, vol. 167, pp. 151–162. GI (2010)
17. Groth, J., Ostrovsky, R.: Cryptography in the multi-string model. J. Cryptol. **27**(3), 506–543 (2014)
18. Joaquim, R., Ribeiro, C., Ferreira, P.: VeryVote: a voter verifiable code voting system. In: Ryan, P.Y.A., Schoenmakers, B. (eds.) VOTE-ID 2009. LNCS, vol. 5767, pp. 106–121. Springer, Heidelberg (2009)
19. Neff, C.A.: Practical high certainty intent verification for encrypted votes (2004)
20. Ryan, P.Y.A., Bismark, D., Heather, J., Schneider, S., Xia, Z.: Prêt à voter: a voter-verifiable voting system. IEEE Trans. Inf. Forensics Secur. **4**(4), 662–673 (2009)
21. Ryan, P.Y.A., Teague, V.: Pretty good democracy. In: Christianson, B., Malcolm, J.A., Matyáš, V., Roe, M. (eds.) Security Protocols 2009. LNCS, vol. 7028, pp. 111–130. Springer, Heidelberg (2013)
22. Sako, K., Kilian, J.: Receipt-free mix-type voting scheme. In: Guillou, L.C., Quisquater, J.-J. (eds.) EUROCRYPT 1995. LNCS, vol. 921, pp. 393–403. Springer, Heidelberg (1995)
23. Santis, A.D., Persiano, G.: Zero-knowledge proofs of knowledge without interaction (extended abstract). In: FOCS, pp. 427–436. IEEE Computer Society (1992)
24. Schnorr, C.-P., Jakobsson, M.: Security of signed elgamal encryption. In: Okamoto, T. (ed.) ASIACRYPT 2000. LNCS, vol. 1976, pp. 73–89. Springer, Heidelberg (2000)
25. Shamir, A.: How to share a secret. Commun. ACM **22**(11), 612–613 (1979)

4th Workshop on Encrypted Computing and Applied Homomorphic Cryptography, WAHC 2016

Hiding Access Patterns in Range Queries Using Private Information Retrieval and ORAM

Gamze Tillem[⊠], Ömer Mert Candan, Erkay Savaş, and Kamer Kaya

Sabancı University, İstanbul, Turkey
{gtillem,mcandan,erkays,kaya}@sabanciuniv.edu

Abstract. We study the problem of privacy preserving range search that provides data, query, and response confidentiality to the users for range queries. We propose two methods based on Private Information Retrieval (PIR) and Oblivious RAM (ORAM) techniques. For PIR-based queries, Lipmaa's computationally-private information retrieval (CPIR) scheme is employed. For the ORAM-based method, Stefanov et al.'s Path ORAM scheme is adapted to enable privacy preserving range search. Our analyses show that from the computational point of view, the ORAM-based method performs much better due to cheap server operations. However, CPIR utilizes the bandwidth better especially for large databases, its security definitions are more formal, and it is more flexible for various settings with multiple clients and/or bandwidth limitations. In this work, to make CPIR a practical alternative for large databases, we improve its performance via shared memory OpenMP and distributed memory OpenMP-MPI parallelization with a scalable data/task partitioning.

Keywords: Privacy preserving range queries · Private information retrieval · Oblivious RAM · Data privacy · Parallel computing

1 Introduction

While outsourcing the data storage to cloud is beneficial for data owners to reduce the associated costs, ensuring a secure and private access to it becomes the next big challenge. The threat is that a curious data-holder may try to retrieve information from the stored data or the results of the queries sent by the data owner. Therefore, several approaches have been proposed in the literature to securely search over outsourced data for a specific item or for multiple items in a range. Existing approaches for range queries on encrypted data include encryption techniques that preserve the order of plaintext values [1], use of predicate functions based on cryptographic properties [2], utilizing special data structures [10], and using a bucketization method [5] based on data partitioning.

Regardless of the approach used, a privacy preserving range query scheme needs, in general, to deal with three security issues: providing data confidentiality, providing query confidentiality, and preventing the disclosure of the query

© International Financial Cryptography Association 2016
J. Clark et al. (Eds.): FC 2016 Workshops, LNCS 9604, pp. 253–270, 2016.
DOI: 10.1007/978-3-662-53357-4_17

access patterns. Data confidentiality is guaranteed by encryption in existing privacy preserving range query methods. The confidentiality of a query is provided by its transformation into a secure representative. But, almost none of the existing methods aims to hide the query access patterns, since the solution of the problem requires the use of computationally expensive schemes such as Private Information Retrieval or Oblivious RAM. Nonetheless, recent advances in the literature such as the fast Path ORAM method of Stefanov et al. [7], yield almost practical schemes to enable hiding query access patterns. Similarly, certain acceleration techniques for PIR yield significant performance improvements [6,9].

The main contribution of this work is to explore the feasibility of hiding access patterns in secure and private range queries. We introduce two techniques; one based on CPIR [6], and the other on Path ORAM [7] and compare them in terms of communication and computation costs. For the CPIR-based scheme, we devise novel parallelization approaches in both shared and distributed memory settings. Although the CPIR-based scheme is computationally less efficient than the Path ORAM-based one, as our analyses show, a practical, parallel CPIR-based implementation is an important contribution since Path ORAM has a significant bandwidth usage and it is not as flexible as CPIR for various settings such as one with multiple clients.

The outline of the paper is as follows: Section 2 gives the background. In Sect. 3, multi-dimensional privacy preserving range query methods using PIR and Path ORAM are explained in detail. The security of proposed methods are explained in Sect. 4. Section 5 provides a complexity analysis of the two approaches in terms of their communication and computational complexities. Experimental results to compare these two approaches are given in Sect. 6. Section 7 concludes the paper.

2   Background

Our work is based on three main concepts: Lipmaa's BddCPIR model [6], Stefanov's Path ORAM model [7], and Hore's bucketization model [5]. Here we explain these concepts.

2.1   Privacy Preserving Range Queries Using Bucketization

In bucketization, a secure index tag for each data item is generated using a predefined rule and the data items are partitioned to a bucket depending on this tag [4]. The data buckets are stored in encrypted form in the database and a query is first translated into the corresponding bucket ids (by the client). Then, the data items with the matching bucket ids are retrieved from the database. If the server knows the matching bucket ids and has some information on some of the items, the privacy of the query can be disrupted. To obfuscate the retrieved data range and increase the security level, false positives are used within each bucket. However, the existence of false positives creates a performance overhead.

Hore et al. [5] proposed an algorithm which aims to generate optimized buckets in terms of performance and security; it starts with a greedy multi-partitioning phase which initially puts all the items in a single bucket and iteratively partitions an existing bucket into two until a desired number of buckets are obtained. At each iteration, a compactness function is used to decide the bucket to be partitioned. This approach reduces the number of false positives within a bucket; then a second algorithm, known as *controlled diffusion* [5], is applied on the buckets to redistribute bucket contents based on a pre-defined degradation factor and thus, calibrates the number of false positives within each bucket for an acceptable security level.

The methods introduced in this paper do not solely depend on a controlled diffusion mechanism since the server cannot uniquely identify the retrieved buckets. Especially for the CPIR-based approach, the retrieved bucket can be an arbitrary one in the database from the server's point of view.

2.2 Lipmaa's BddCPIR Protocol for PIR

The BddCPIR scheme [6] employs the Damgård-Jurik cryptosystem [3] which is based on the hardness of the decisional composite residuosity problem. To improve the efficiency in terms of communication and computation, the scheme employes binary decision diagrams.

Damgård-Jurik Cryptosystem. While the setting of the homomorphic Damgård-Jurik (DJ) cryptosystem is similar to that of RSA which also employs two sufficiently large primes p and q to work with a composite modulus $N = pq$; the security of the scheme is based on the hardness of decisional composite residuosity rather than integer factorization. The key property of DJ cryptosystem is a positive integer s which provides block-length adjustment capability for the encryptions in different levels of Lipmaa's BddCPIR. The DJ scheme is summarized in Fig. 1.

Key generation:
  - Choose large primes p and q, and set $N = pq$.
  - Choose $g \in Z^*_{N^{s+1}}$ s.t. $g = (1 + N)^j x \bmod N^{s+1}$ with j is a known relative prime of N and $x \in H$, where H is isomorphic to Z^*_N
  - Compute $\lambda = lcm(p - 1, q - 1)$, and choose d s.t. $d \equiv 1 \bmod N^s$ and $d \equiv 0 \bmod \lambda$.
  - Public parameters: (N, g)
  - Private parameters: d
Encryption:
  - $E(m, r) = g^m r^{N^s} \bmod N^{s+1}$, where plaintext is $m \in Z_N$ and $r \in Z^*_{N^{s+1}}$ is a random integer.
Decryption:
  - Compute $c^d \bmod N^{s+1}$ and using the algorithm proposed in [3] find m.
Additive homomorphic properties:
  - $E(m_1)E(m_2) = E(m_1 + m_2)$
  - $E(m)^c = E(mc)$

Fig. 1. Damgård-Jurik cryptosystem

Binary Decision Diagram (Bdd). Bdds can be considered as binary trees. The internal nodes of a binary tree are represented as $R_{i,j}$, where i is the level of the node in the tree and j is the location of the node in the current level. The leaf nodes of the binary tree hold the data items. Each leaf node is represented as f_x such that x is an m-bit string that represents the route taken from the root to f_x for a tree with height $m+1$. Figure 2 demonstrates an example of Bdd with 4 child nodes where 0 and 1 are used for the left and right child, respectively.

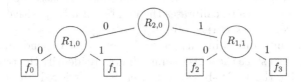

Fig. 2. An illustration of a toy Bdd which contains 4 files.

(2,1)-CPIR Protocol. The client inputs either 0 or 1 to retrieve one of the 2 files (f_0 or f_1) stored in the server without leaking information. The flow of the protocol is as follows:

- Client generates public and private keys (pk, sk). She then chooses an $x \in \{0,1\}$, computes the encrypted selection bit $c = E_{pk}(x)$, and sends pk and c to the server.
- Server computes $R = E_{pk}(f_0)c^{f_1-f_0}$ and sends R to the client.
- Client decrypts R with his private key sk to find f_x.

From (2,1)-CPIR to (n,1)-CPIR. The 1-out-of-2 CPIR protocol can be extended to 1-out-of-n using a Bdd. The extended protocol starts with the leaf nodes of the tree and iteratively merges siblings until the root is reached. For each merge, an R value is calculated. The final result for the tree root is then sent to the client. In $(n, 1)$-CPIR, the client needs to send m selection bits as $x = (x_0, x_1, \ldots, x_{m-1})$ to denote the path. Furthermore, the result should be decrypted m times to retrieve the requested file. Figure 3 illustrates $(n, 1)$-CPIR protocol for a 4-file case based on the binary tree in Fig. 2.

Client:
  - Encrypt the selection bits $c_0 = E(x_0)$ and $c_1 = E(x_1)$ and send them to the server.

Server:
  - For the lowest level of the tree compute:
    $R_{1,0} = E(f_0)c_0^{f_1-f_0}$
    $R_{1,1} = E(f_2)c_0^{f_3-f_2}$
  - For the next level repeat the computations; this time use $R_{i,j}$ instead of the files and the encrypted selection bits of the current level:
    $R_{2,0} = E(R_0)c_1^{R_1-R_0}$.
  - Send $R_{2,0}$ to the client.

Client:
  - Apply double decryption to $R_{2,0}$ to retrieve the selected file.

Fig. 3. An example of $(n, 1)$-CPIR for a database of 4 files

2.3 Path ORAM

Path ORAM [7] is a simple Oblivious RAM protocol used to prevent the leakage of access patterns to the outsourced data. In each access a full path of data is retrieved by client and it is written back to database after shuffling and re-encryption. The details of the protocol are as follows:

- **The server** stores the data in a binary tree structure. Each node of the tree is called a bucket. In each bucket, Z blocks of data are stored. If a bucket has less than Z blocks, dummy blocks are added. At the beginning, all buckets are initialized with some dummy values.
- **The client** maintains a local stash, a small and private storage, to perform shuffling and re-encryption operations on the accessed data path. She also maintains a position map that gives the current location of a data item. At the beginning of the protocol, the stash is empty and the position map assigns data items into some random buckets.
- **Access protocol for read and write operations:** To read/write data, the client reads a path containing the block from the server. She remaps the position of each block to a random position in the path. For writes, she also updates the value of data in the block and add values from the stash to the path. She then writes the path back to the tree.

3 Privacy Preserving Range Query Using PIR and ORAM

We introduce two new approaches for privacy preserving range queries. First approach is an implementation of PIR protocol on an existing range query scheme, [5]. In the second one, we apply Path ORAM method for privacy preserving range queries.

3.1 CPIR for Privacy Preserving Range Queries

Setup. In the setup phase, the data is partitioned into buckets with greedy multi-partitioning [5]. The total number of buckets and size of each bucket is set as a power of 2 to utilize a tree structure in the BddCPIR model. The bucket sizes are equal; some dummy values are inserted into buckets if necessary.

Once the buckets are generated, the next step is to send them to the server; here we assume that the data items in buckets are encrypted, therefore, data confidentiality is guaranteed. The server stores the buckets within tree leaves such that a leaf node corresponds to one part of each bucket. If the bucket size is equal to DJ block size, i.e., if a bucket's items can be stored within a single file, there is only one tree. When buckets are larger, multiple (structurally equivalent) trees are used to store the buckets in a way that the leaves with the same binary representation (location) in each tree is a part of the same bucket. Hence the number of trees is proportional to the bucket size and the size of the tree(s) is determined by the number of buckets.

Query. To perform a range query, the client finds the bucket(s) that have the items within the requested data range using a query translation operation. Based on these bucket ids, she prepares the selection bits to retrieve the related content from the server. Although different bits are required for multiple buckets, for a single bucket, she does not need to compute a different set of selection bits for each tree, since, for a given selection-bit set, the corresponding nodes in the trees map to the same bucket.

Response. Based on the selection bits sent by the client, the server performs BddCPIR on each tree to retrieve the corresponding bucket. Since the performance of the PIR scheme is crucial for efficiently retrieving the buckets, instead of Lipmaa's BddCPIR scheme, an enhanced version of it, e.g., [9], is used in our implementation. In the new CPIR scheme, the performance of the PIR operations are enhanced by the following changes:

- Instead of the binary trees, octal and hexadecimal trees are used to reduce the depth of the tree which yields a significant improvement on the performance.
- A shared-memory non-trivial parallel algorithm for CPIR operations is introduced to improve the performance further.

Parallel CPIR. To utilize the parallelism in the best way in the new CPIR scheme, we used a (sub)tree-based data distribution and an adaptive query processing algorithm. When there are more trees than the number of server nodes, the trees are equally distributed to the nodes. Otherwise, when there are more than one node per tree, a tree's subtrees are equally distributed to the corresponding nodes. Here, the number of nodes per tree is used to decide the height of the subtrees. An example distribution with 2 trees and 8 server nodes is given in Fig. 4. With 4 nodes, the subtree roots would be in the first level.

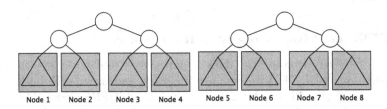

Fig. 4. A data distribution example for 2 (binary) trees and 8 nodes.

After each (sub)tree is processed, if it is possible the results are combined on a different node to achieve a better parallelism. For example, to combine the results in the first level, in Fig. 4, the $(k+1)^{th}$ node sends its data to the kth node for $k = 1, 3, 5, 7$. To combine the results in the root level, the $(k+2)^{th}$ node sends its data to the kth node for $k = 1, 5$. That is for each subtree division, a master node is selected to combine the partial results due to this division, to utilize the nodes as much as possible and obtain a scalable solution.

Within a single node, we use a hybrid, coarse/fine-grain query processing algorithm which adapts itself to the number of trees and cores; when the number of trees per node exceeds the number of available cores in the node, coarse-grain parallelism is employed on the tree level, i.e., each (sub)tree is processed in parallel, but the CPIR operation within a (sub)tree is performed serially. On the other hand, when the number of (sub)trees is less than the number of cores, the cores are distributed to the (sub)trees and each CPIR operation within a (sub)tree is performed in a fine-grain fashion in addition to the coarse-grain parallelism obtained in the (sub)tree level.

3.2 Path ORAM for Privacy Preserving Range Queries

Implementation of Path ORAM for privacy preserving range queries is rather straightforward compared to the CPIR model. The method does not require any change on the server side. The server is only responsible for sending the path that contains the requested data and writing the path back to the tree without any additional computations. Similarly, the client side operations do not require any fundamental changes.

In the setup phase of the method, the binary tree structure on the server is filled with dummy values. To place the data items into binary tree, the client performs repetitive write operations using the access protocol. The properties of a data item are same with CPIR method. That is each item has several attributes and based on the total size of the item, it is encrypted with AES using a suitable block size. After each retrieval operation, the data is re-encrypted. To enable different ciphertext values for the same data item, some random value is padded to a plaintext for each encryption operation.

For range queries, an extra query processing operation is employed in addition to the original scheme [7]; when a client wants to search for a range, the query processor finds the buckets which store the requested items. Since the query range might be mapped to several buckets, the client may need to perform more than one read operation to retrieve the items.

4   Analysis of Security in Privacy Preserving Range Queries

The proposed approaches assume an honest but curious server model where client is the owner of the database. As mentioned in Sect. 1, a privacy preserving range query scheme needs to ensure three security conditions, data, query and access pattern confidentiality. Data confidentiality is provided by encrypted storage of data under AES encryption. Query confidentiality is handled by sending bucket ids in CPIR based method and the id of sink node in Path ORAM based method instead of original query range. Finally, leakage of access patterns is prevented by utilizing the security definitions of CPIR and Path ORAM. In the rest of this section these security definitions are briefly explained.

4.1   Security Analysis of CPIR

According to Lipmaa [6], a CPIR protocol achieves client security when it is difficult for a probabilistic polynomial time server to distinguish between two queries $Q(x_0)$ and $Q(x_1)$ where x_0 and x_1 are client's selection bits.

Accordingly, to reveal the access pattern, a curious server needs to differentiate the value of selection bits for the target data. In Lipmaa's CPIR setting, DJ cryptosystem, which is based on Decisional Composite Residuosity assumption, is utilized for cryptographic operations. The cryptosystem satisfies ciphertext indistinguishability by operating randomized algorithms. Thus, differentiating an encrypted selection bit from a random bit string and determining its value is difficult for the server.

4.2   Security Analysis of Path ORAM

Stefanov [7] defines security of Path ORAM based on the indistinguishability of access patterns $A(y)$ and $A(z)$ of any two data request vectors y and z of same length, considering the failure of scheme with a negligible probability.

The security can be proved by observing the indistinguishability property on position of data and on encrypted data path. Assume the position of a data item, which is stored in private stash, is discovered by server. However, since in each access the data item is mapped to a new random position and since the new position and former position are statistically independent from each other, server cannot differentiate addresses [7]. On the other hand, in each access operation the data path is re-encrypted and encryption is randomized by padding. Thus, encrypted data paths become computationally indistinguishable from a random bit sequence for curious server.

5   A Quantitative Analysis of Path ORAM and CPIR

The volume of exchanged data is an important issue for the efficiency of the range query algorithms. Hence, a detailed inspection of bandwidth requirements is required for a fair comparison of the schemes.

5.1   Communication Complexity Analysis

CPIR. There are two data transfer phases; the first one is sending the encrypted selection bits to the server. The size of a single selection bit on the sth level of the tree is $(s+1)|N|$ where $|N|$ is the size of the modulus N [9]. Hence, at the lowest level, the size of one encrypted selection bit is $2|N|$. At the root level, the bit size is $\lceil \log_k n + 1 \rceil |N|$ where n is the number of items in the database and k is the branching factor of the tree which is 8 and 16 (i.e., octal and hexadecimal) in our implementation. The proposed model requires 7 selection bits in octal trees and 15 selection bits in hexadecimal trees for each tree level. Thus, for one bucket request, we can find the cost of the client-to-server communication in terms of the number of bits as $(k - 1) \times (2 + 3 + \cdots + (\log_k n + 1)) \times |N|$, where $k = 8$ and $k = 16$ for octal and hexadecimal trees, respectively. Although there can be multiple trees, sending the selection bits only for a single tree and employing them on all the trees is sufficient.

The second data transfer is the response of the server to the client. For a single bucket request and with a single tree, the number of bits transferred in this phase is $(\log_k n + 1)|N|$. Unlike the client-to-server communication, the volume of the server-to-client communication for CPIR is determined by the number of trees, since in each tree there are data items for the requested bucket. Therefore, the cost needs to be multiplied by the number of trees to compute the total bandwidth usage.

Path ORAM. To read the path of the requested bucket from the database, the server sends $Z \log T$ blocks to the client where Z is the number of blocks within each bucket, T is the number of buckets and $\log T$ is the length of the path containing the retrieved node. And to write the accessed path back to tree, the client sends $Z \log T$ blocks of data back to the server. Therefore, the total number of blocks sent/received for Path ORAM is $2Z \log T$. In our experiments, Z is fixed to 4 as in the original Path ORAM method [7], and each data item is considered as a tuple with 5 integer attributes (including the primary key), i.e., 160 bits. However, the data needs to be stored in encrypted form; thus, a 160 bit plaintext value is mapped to a 256-bit ciphertext block of AES.

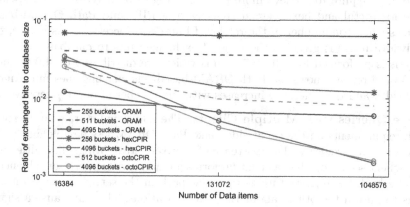

Fig. 5. The ratio of exchanged bits to the database size for the CPIR- and Path ORAM-based range query schemes with different database sizes.

The bandwidth usage in case of a single bucket request for the CPIR- and Path ORAM-based range query schemes are presented on Fig. 5. The y-axis in the figure shows the ratio of the number of exchanged bits to database size (in log scale), whereas the x-axis shows the number of data items in the database. As the figure shows, with the same number of buckets, the CPIR-based approach is superior in terms of bandwidth usage and Path ORAM-based scheme consumes much more bandwidth to get a single bucket especially for large databases which is the case for many applications today.

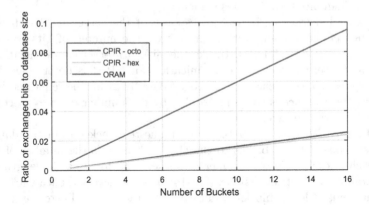

Fig. 6. The bandwidth usage for the CPIR- and Path ORAM-based schemes to retrieve multiple buckets (x axis) for 1,048,576 items distributed into 4,096 buckets.

Although the above analysis assumes single bucket retrieval, querying for a range may require to retrieve more than one. Figure 6 analyzes the bandwidth usage for (octal and hexadecimal tree based) CPIR- and Path ORAM-based schemes when the number of the retrieved buckets is increasing. As before, the bandwidth usage is given as the ratio of exchanged bits to database size. The analysis is performed for 1,048,576 items which are distributed on 4,096 buckets. As the results show, the Path ORAM-based scheme consumes much more bandwidth and the difference increases with the number of buckets retrieved.

Range Queries with Multiple Clients. The additional storage and private stash requirements on the client side make Path ORAM less flexible and inefficient for many scenarios. The existence of a private stash brings difficulties in a multi-client scenario; when a client performs a read or write operation, she needs to write back the retrieved items to a new path in the server. In addition, she needs to inform the others about these new locations. This can cause a significant amount of computational overhead and bandwidth consumption for each additional client using the database. Thus, the scalability of such a system is questionable. On the other hand, for a multi-client CPIR-based implementation individual client accesses are seamless, and hence, the scheme is not affected by the number of clients.

To visualize the bandwidth usage in multi-client scenario, a simulation is conducted for 100,000 (single bucket) queries using several number of clients as shown in Fig. 7. In the simulation, two different approaches are applied for Path ORAM to update the locations in client's local. The first one is a push-based approach which requires to push the updated locations to the other clients in each query operation. The second approach is a pull-based approach in which a client needs to perform a comparison with other clients for the most recent value of the position information. Figure 7 shows that CPIR-based method is superior in communication for both approaches, since it does not require any additional bandwidth usage in a multi-client scenario. Additionally, a pull-based Path ORAM method provides better results than a push-based method due to the possibility of communicating with fewer number of clients in each query operation.

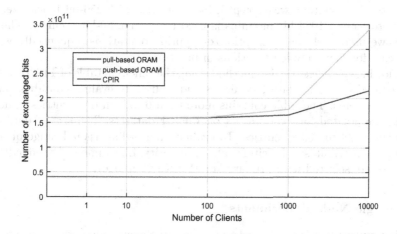

Fig. 7. The bandwidth usage in multiple client scenario for CPIR, pull-based Path ORAM and push-based Path ORAM method

5.2 Computational Complexity Analysis

Path ORAM is an efficient method for retrieving encrypted data; the server only returns the requested path to the client and does nothing else. Therefore, there is no computational burden on the server. On the other hand, for a single data access, the client side gets $\mathcal{O}(\log K)$ blocks, where K is the number of total blocks outsourced to the server. The client needs to decrypt, shuffle, and re-encrypt these blocks for each data access.

Lipmaa's CPIR requires $\mathcal{O}(n)$ computation on the server and $\mathcal{O}(\log^2 n)$ computation on the client. Furthermore, since each bucket may be partitioned into several trees, the server's cost may increase by a constant factor. Hence, a CPIR-based range query scheme is slower than a Path ORAM-based one. However, as we will show in the next section, CPIR can still be a very practical approach for privacy preserving range queries with a tuned tree structure and parallelization.

6 Experiments

We implement the CPIR- and Path ORAM-based privacy preserving range query schemes in C++ using gcc 4.9.2. GNU Multiple Precision Arithmetic Library for large integer arithmetic. OpenMP is used for parallelizing the client- and server-side operations and MPI is employed for server operations in the distributed setting. The single node experiments are performed at a machine running on 64 bit CentOS 6.5 with two Intel Xeon E7-4870 v2 clocked at 2.30 GHz each having 15 cores. The distributed, multi-node experiments are conducted on a cluster with 32 computational nodes connected with 20 Gbps InfiniBand, each with dual Intel Xeon E5520 Quad-core CPUs (with 8MB of L3 cache per processor), 48 GB of main memory, and 64 bit CentOS 6.

To store a data item, we encrypt it by using AES with 256-bit block size. For DJ cryptosystem, 1024-bit modulus is used to provide 80-bit security. The DJ library we used performs encryption/decryption operations sequentially which is the case for many implementations in practice.

Following the bucketization method of [5], the Lineitem table of TPCH benchmark is used [8] as the dataset which is widely used to evaluate database management systems. The table contains more than 6 million data entries, random subsets are created for experiments on smaller datasets. The size of data sets varies from 128 to 16,384 entries. To evaluate multi-dimensional range queries, four integer attributes of Lineitem table –Quantity, Linenumber, ExtendedPrice and Tax– are selected with primary key PartKey-SuppKey.

6.1 Single-Node Experiments

The first experiment is conducted to compare the client-side performance of our CPIR- and Path ORAM-based implementations. For the CPIR-based scheme, we measure the query times of single bucket retrieval for octal and hexadecimal trees and present them in Tables 1 and 2, respectively. In the tables, n is the number of data items distributed among a number of buckets which is given in the second column. For the encryption stages, the tree structure and the

Table 1. Client-side timings for the CPIR-based method with octal trees (ms)

		Encryption					Decryption				
		Number of threads					Number of threads				
n	No. buckets	1	2	4	8	16	1	2	4	8	16
128	8	15	9	4	2	2	9	4	2	2	2
	64	76	41	22	11	8	7	7	7	7	7
1,024	8	15	9	4	2	2	68	34	17	9	4
	64	76	41	22	11	9	27	13	7	7	7
	512	227	128	65	32	30	14	14	14	14	14
16,384	8	15	9	4	2	2	1099	549	274	138	69
	64	76	41	22	11	9	424	213	106	53	27
	512	227	128	65	32	30	113	56	28	14	14
	4,096	512	281	144	73	62	25	25	25	25	25

Table 2. Client-side timings for the CPIR-based method with hexadecimal trees (ms)

| | | Encryption | | | | | Decryption | | | | |
| | | Number of threads | | | | | Number of threads | | | | |
n	No. buckets	1	2	4	8	16	1	2	4	8	16
128	16	32	17	9	4	2	4	2	2	2	2
1,024	16	32	17	9	4	2	34	17	9	4	2
	256	163	85	44	22	11	7	7	7	7	7
16,384	16	32	17	9	4	2	549	274	137	69	34
	256	163	85	44	22	11	106	53	27	13	7
	4,096	487	258	130	65	32	17	17	17	17	17

number of buckets are important parameters to understand the speedup results. As described in Sect. 5.1, for the octal case, 7 selection bits are encrypted for each tree level except the one containing the root and there are 2, 3, 4, and 5 levels (including the root level) for 8, 64, 512, and 4096 buckets, respectively. For the hexadecimal case, there are 2, 3, and 4 levels for 16, 256, and 4096 buckets, respectively, and the client encrypts 15 bits per level. As the tables show, for the encryption stage with $n = 16,384$ items, we obtained 7.5–8.3 speedup for the octal case and 14.8–16 speedup for the hexadecimal case with 16 threads.

Since the encryption complexity of DJ is quadratic with respect to the input size, which increases as we move to the upper levels in the tree, the encryption tasks for different tree levels do not have the same computational complexity. We aim to distribute a level's tasks to the threads as even as possible to have a better load balance; starting from the most expensive level (the first one), we order the bit encryption tasks according to their levels and assign one task to a thread at a time by tuning the OpenMP scheduling policy. This approach works well for the hexadecimal case for which 15 encryption tasks exist for each level. On the other hand, as Table 1 shows, the speedups for the octal case is not satisfactory with 16 threads since there are only 7 bits to be encrypted at each level and most of the threads cannot get a task from the most expensive level. However with 8 threads, the speedup values for the octal case are between 6.9–7.5 which shows that the load balancing scheme works well as expected when there is enough number of tasks per thread. In the future work, we are planning to parallelize each encryption task and use a hybrid load-balancing approach to have better speedups for the octal case.

For the decryption stage, the main limitation on our parallelization strategy is the number of trees used in the CPIR-based scheme. For each tree, the server returns a ciphertext to the client and we performed the decryption operations on the ciphertexts independently with a single thread per decryption. Hence, when the number of threads exceeds the number of ciphertexts, some cores remain idle. This is why the decryption time do not decrease for some cases when the number of threads increases. On the other hand, we obtain linear scaling for all the cases which is expected since the decryption tasks use the same DJ modulus and have the same complexity. For example, for the octal case (Table 1) with $n = 16,384$ items and 512 buckets, the scheme puts 32 items to each bucket. Considering that each 256-bit block can store only 4 data items, the CPIR-based scheme uses 8 trees. For this case, we obtain 8.1 speedup both with 8 and 16 threads.

Overall, as the table shows, the hexadecimal implementation is advantageous for large datasets. The better performance of hexadecimal tree is a result of the less number of levels and hence less complexity of the encryption/decryption operations. For example, for 16,384 items and 4,096 buckets, the octal and hexadecimal tree implementations require a tree with 5 and 4 levels, respectively. Hence, the client-side encrypts 28 and 45 selection bits, respectively. Although the number of bits is more for the hexadecimal case, the costs of client-side encryptions are similar (512 and 487 ms). Furthermore, the load will be better distributed to the threads in our simple hexadecimal implementation since the variance between the task sizes is much less. As a result, with 16 threads, the encryption operations cost 2 times more for the octal case than the hexadecimal case (62 and 32 ms). For the client-side decryption with the same number of data items and buckets, both implementations use a single tree, i.e., a single ciphertext is returned, but the cost in the octal case is more due to a taller tree (25 and 17 ms).

To make the Path ORAM-based operations comparable with those of the CPIR-based scheme, we use the same bucket sizes in our analysis. The average processing time of the client-side computations in the Path ORAM-based scheme is usually around 1ms for 128, 1024, and 16384 items. Only for 16,384 items and 7–15 buckets, the client spends 6ms for the query preparation. The AES encryption and decryption operations comprise the majority of computation in Path ORAM, whereas the exponentiations performed during the encryption of the selection bits and the decryption of query responses are the main burden on the CPIR-based scheme. As our comparison shows, the Path ORAM-based scheme performs better than the CPIR-based scheme. However, both schemes can be considered as practical considering the core numbers in today's CPUs.

We also measure the cost of the server-side operations for the CPIR-based scheme (Path ORAM-based scheme does not require any server computation). Table 3 shows the server-side cost to retrieve one bucket with octal and hexadecimal trees, respectively. When multiple CPIR trees are employed, the server can process the query on these trees independently. Hence, when the number of threads is smaller than the number of trees, a coarse-grain parallelization can be applied on the tree level. For such cases, the system scales linearly; for example, with an octal tree structure, $n = 16,384$ data items and 512 buckets, the server uses 8 trees as explained above. As Table 3 shows, with 8 threads, i.e., one tree per thread, our implementation obtains 7.9 speedup (the server response time reduces to 748 ms from 5,940 ms). On the other hand, when the number of threads exceeds the number of trees, the parallelization is not straightforward; one can simply apply a fine-grain parallelism and use all the threads

Table 3. Server-side timings for the CPIR-based method (in ms)

n	No. buckets	Number of threads				
		1	2	4	8	16
128	8	28	14	7	7	7
128	64	85	56	42	35	35
1,024	8	227	114	57	29	15
1,024	64	338	170	85	53	41
1,024	512	743	405	236	152	124
16,384	8	3,641	1,827	914	454	230
16,384	64	5,410	2,712	1,358	680	341
16,384	512	5,940	2,976	1,488	748	407
16,384	4,096	6,067	3,103	1,614	873	537

n	No. buckets	Number of threads				
		1	2	4	8	16
128	16	17	9	9	9	9
1,024	16	139	72	36	19	11
1,024	256	172	102	67	50	43
16,384	16	2,245	1,128	574	296	156
16,384	256	2,760	1,386	702	353	183
16,384	4,096	2,823	1,441	757	418	247

to process a single tree in parallel and repeat the same for all the trees. However, since there exist relatively less number of expensive tasks in the upper levels of a tree, the tree structure can limit the scalability of the fine-grain approach. To alleviate this, we applied a hybrid scheme where all the trees are processed at the same time and in parallel with the same number of threads; for the octal setting with 16,384 data items, 512 buckets, and 16 threads, 2 threads are assigned to each tree. With this hybrid strategy, we obtained 14.6 speedup (407 ms) with 16 threads, where a pure fine-grain strategy per tree only yields a 6 speedup (991 ms).

To analyze the octal and hexadecimal case more clearly, we measured the number of data items the client-side can request and the server-side can provide in a second (DiPS) with various parameters and different number of cores. Figure 8 shows the DiPS values for the server side; a small number of large buckets requires

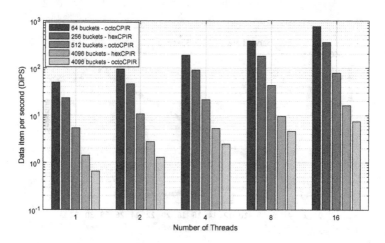

Fig. 8. The number of data items the server-side can provide in a second (DiPS) with various parameters and different number of cores

less computation per data item, and a hexadecimal tree structure is better than an octal structure when the same number of buckets have been employed. Thanks to parallelization, with large buckets which are preferable by the queries with large result sets, the server can provide more than 700 data items per second with 16 threads. On the other hand, for the same DiPS value, the client only needs 2 cores (we omit the chart due to space limitations). Hence, as in practice, the client-side requires less computation power compared to the server-side to use the proposed CPIR-based range query scheme at its limit.

6.2   Multi-node Experiments

For multi-node experiments, we used a database of size $n = 16,777,216$ and a hexadecimal tree with depth 5. Figure 9 shows the query processing times and the speedups for this experiment with various number of server nodes. Similar to the single-node experiments, a leaf in the tree can store 4 data items. Since there are 16 items per bucket, there are 4 trees in total. Hence, up to 4 server nodes, simply partitioning the trees to the nodes is enough for a balanced load distribution. To use more server nodes, the trees are decomposed into their subtrees; a single division generates 16 subtrees since we are using hexadecimal trees. For each division, a master node is selected to combine the partial results for the corresponding subtree division. The final results for each tree are then sent to the server's entry node which is also responsible for receiving the query from the client and distributing it to the other processing nodes. The overall communication in the server is negligible; with 32 server nodes, the intra-server communication is around 1 % of the overall query response time. The query response time is reduced from 615 s to 20.5 s yielding a 30× speedup over a single node (8 core) execution.

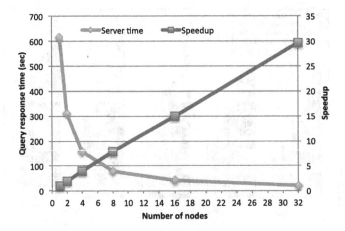

Fig. 9. Server computation cost on different number of nodes each having 8 cores. A hexadecimal tree with depth 5 is used to store $16^6 = 16,777,216$ items for each experiment. The numbers are averages of 5 experiments for each setting.

7   Conclusion

We proposed two methods for privacy preserving range queries using PIR and ORAM techniques. While most of the existing privacy preserving range query schemes do not deal with hiding query access patterns, our methods aim to prevent the disclosure of access patterns in addition to provide data and query confidentiality. For Private Information Retrieval, we adopted an improved version of Lipmaa's BddCPIR and applied it on an existing range query scheme [5]. For ORAM, we adapted Stefanov et al.'s [7] Path ORAM. Our analyses show that the Path ORAM-based scheme is much more efficient than the CPIR-based one in terms of computation. However, it is not as flexible as the CPIR-based scheme, and considering its high bandwidth usage, the CPIR-based scheme can be more suitable in practice for various cases such as one with multiple clients and slow communication. Furthermore, the computation cost of the CPIR-based scheme can be reduced with parallelization on a distributed- and shared-memory server and client, respectively, which is a very common setting in practice.

Acknowledgments. Erkay Savaş was supported by TÜBİTAK under Grant Number 113E537. Gamze Tillem was supported by TÜBİTAK under BİDEB 2211 program. Kamer Kaya was supported by TÜBİTAK BİDEB 2232 program under grant number 115C018. The authors would like to thank Cengiz Örencik for his valuable comments on the paper.

References

1. Boldyreva, A., Chenette, N., Lee, Y., O'Neill, A.: Order-preserving symmetric encryption. In: Joux, A. (ed.) EUROCRYPT 2009. LNCS, vol. 5479, pp. 224–241. Springer, Heidelberg (2009). http://dx.doi.org/10.1007/978-3-642-01001-9_13
2. Boneh, D., Waters, B.: Conjunctive, subset, and range queries on encrypted data. In: Vadhan, S.P. (ed.) TCC 2007. LNCS, vol. 4392, pp. 535–554. Springer, Heidelberg (2007). http://dl.acm.org/citation.cfm?id=1760749.1760788
3. Damgård, I., Jurik, M.: A generalisation, a simplification and some applications of Paillier's probabilistic public-key system. In: Kim, K. (ed.) PKC 2001. LNCS, vol. 1992, pp. 119–136. Springer, Heidelberg (2001). http://dl.acm.org/citation.cfm?id=648118.746742
4. Hacıgümüş, H., Iyer, B., Li, C., Mehrotra, S.: Executing SQL over encrypted data in the database-service-provider model. In: Proceedings of 2002 ACM SIGMOD International Conference on Management of Data, SIGMOD 2002, Madison, Wisconsin, 3–6 June 2002, pp. 216–227. ACM (2002). http://doi.acm.org/10.1145/564691.564717
5. Hore, B., Mehrotra, S., Canım, M., Kantarcıoğlu, M.: Secure multidimensional range queries over outsourced data. VLDB J. **21**(3), 333–358 (2012). http://dx.doi.org/10.1007/s00778-011-0245-7
6. Lipmaa, H.: First CPIR protocol with data-dependent computation. In: Lee, D., Hong, S. (eds.) ICISC 2009. LNCS, vol. 5984, pp. 193–210. Springer, Heidelberg (2010). http://dl.acm.org/citation.cfm?id=1883749.1883769

7. Stefanov, E., van Dijk, M., Shi, E., Fletcher, C., Ren, L., Yu, X., Devadas, S.: Path ORAM: an extremely simple oblivious RAM protocol. In: Proceedings of 2013 ACM SIGSAC Conference on Computer and Communications Security, CCS 2013, Berlin, Germany, 4–8 November 2013. pp. 299–310. ACM (2013). http://doi.acm.org/10.1145/2508859.2516660
8. TPC-H: Decision Support Benchmark. http://www.tpc.org/tpch
9. Ünal, E., Savaş, E.: On acceleration and scalability of number theoretic private information retrieval. IEEE Trans. Parallel Distrib. Syst. **27**(6), 1727–1741 (2016). doi:10.1109/TPDS.2015.2456021
10. Capitani, D., di Vimercati, S., Foresti, S., Paraboschi, S., Pelosi, G., Samarati, P.: Efficient and private access to outsourced data. In: Proceedings of 2011 31st International Conference on Distributed Computing Systems, ICDCS 2011, pp. 710–719 (2011). http://dx.doi.org/10.1109/ICDCS.2011.37

Optimizing MPC for Robust and Scalable Integer and Floating-Point Arithmetic

Liisi Kerik[1], Peeter Laud[1(✉)], and Jaak Randmets[1,2]

[1] Cybernetica AS, Tartu, Estonia
[2] University of Tartu, Tartu, Estonia
{liisi.kerik,peeter.laud,jaak.randmets}@cyber.ee

Abstract. Secure multiparty computation (SMC) is a rapidly maturing field, but its number of practical applications so far has been small. Most existing applications have been run on small data volumes with the exception of a recent study processing tens of millions of education and tax records. For practical usability, SMC frameworks must be able to work with large collections of data and perform reliably under such conditions. In this work we demonstrate that with the help of our recently developed tools and some optimizations, the SHAREMIND secure computation framework is capable of executing tens of millions integer operations or hundreds of thousands floating-point operations per second. We also demonstrate robustness in handling a billion integer inputs and a million floating-point inputs in parallel. Such capabilities are absolutely necessary for real world deployments.

Keywords: Secure Multiparty Computation · Floating-point operations · Protocol design

1 Introduction

Secure multiparty computation (SMC) [19] allows a group of mutually distrusting entities to perform computations on data private to various members of the group, without others learning anything about that data or about the intermediate values in the computation. Theory-wise, the field is quite mature; there exist several techniques to achieve privacy and correctness of any computation [15,16,19,21,28], and the asymptotic overheads of these techniques are known. In practical terms, the search for best implementations and deployment strategies for performing computations on real-world scale is still ongoing. There exist several SMC platforms [4,9,13,17,20,29,31,35] and independent implementations of SMC protocols for complex computational tasks [11,25] looking for the right trade-offs.

SHAREMIND [9,10] is one of the most mature SMC platforms and the base of some of the largest SMC deployments until now. With the help of SHARE-MIND, we have performed statistical analyses over tens of millions of records [22, Chap. 6], and searched for anomalies in a set of 100 million records [5]. SHARE-MIND achieves the versatility and scalability through a simple security model

© International Financial Cryptography Association 2016
J. Clark et al. (Eds.): FC 2016 Workshops, LNCS 9604, pp. 271–287, 2016.
DOI: 10.1007/978-3-662-53357-4_18

(enabling efficient protocols) and a large set of composable protocols for primitive operations, which can be used as building blocks for large applications. The total number of implemented primitive protocols for integer, fixed- and floating-point operations for arguments of various sizes is significantly over 100. While historically the protocols have been implemented in C++, with more complex protocols invoking simpler ones in hierarchic manner, recently we have introduced a domain-specific language (the Protocol DSL) for specifying them [27]. The Protocol DSL brings at least two benefits. First, it allows tighter composition of protocols, enabling subprotocols with data dependencies to run in parallel without any additional effort from the developer of the protocol set. Second, it allows the developer to try out different implementation options for complex protocols with an effort that is orders of magnitude smaller compared to using C++.

In this paper, we report on our optimizations for the protocols in SHAREMIND's protocol set, enabled by the Protocol DSL. Many of the improved protocols are used for operations on private floating-point numbers. Our reported optimizations may be useful for other SMC platforms and protocol sets providing private floating-point numbers, as several of our optimizations are not that dependent on particular details of SHAREMIND. In addition to optimizations of private floating-point operations, we also show how the protocol construction toolchain, central to which is the Protocol DSL, allowed us to implement a major architectural change of all protocols with relatively little effort. This provides additional validation of the choices made in [27].

This paper has the following structure. In Sect. 2 we give an overview of SHAREMIND and the protocols it uses, as well as the related work on privacy-preserving floating-point operations. In Sect. 3 we describe our improvements to various floating-point protocols, both generic changes and modifications of specific protocols, as well as the constructions of protocols for new operations. In Sect. 4 we describe another optimization that applies to all protocols in the main protocol set of SHAREMIND. We show that the optimizations in this and previous section improve the performance of protocols for various operations. In Sect. 5 we give a more thorough description on how we have measured the performance of the protocols of SHAREMIND. We provide precise running times of certain protocols, thereby making clear the current state of the art. Finally, we conclude in Sect. 6.

2   Background

In a SHAREMIND deployment, the involved parties are divided into three classes which may overlap: the *input parties* provide inputs to the private computation, the *computation parties* execute the SMC protocols for performing operations with private data, and *result parties* learn the result(s) of the computation [6]. While the architecture of SHAREMIND supports the use of several SMC protocol sets [8], the main set in use is based on additively sharing the private values among three computing parties [10]. The sharing can be over any finite ring and there are protocols to convert between different rings. Hence the input parties secret share their inputs among computation parties, and the result parties recombine the shares of outputs they receive from computation parties. The computation parties follow the description of the private functionality specified in the SECREC language [8], invoking the SMC protocols in specified order.

Sharemind's protocol set provides security against one passively corrupted party. Its security and privacy guarantees are composable, allowing the security of complex protocols to be deduced from the security of its component protocols [7]. The development of secure protocols is also greatly assisted by a protocol privacy checker [32] for the Protocol DSL [27].

Typically, rings $\mathbb{Z}_{2^n}$ are used in SHAREMIND applications and supported by the Protocol DSL. In the following, we let $[\![x]\!]$ denote the value x which has been secret-shared among the computing parties, and $[\![x]\!]_i$ denotes the i-th party's share.

For private numeric computations (e.g. for the satellite collision analysis [23]), SHAREMIND features a set of protocols for working with secret-shared fixed-point and floating-point numbers [23,26]. In this protocol set, a floating-point number x is represented as $x = (-1)^s \cdot f \cdot 2^e$, where $s \in \{0,1\}$ is the sign bit, $f \in \mathbb{Z}_{2^m}$ the significand, and $e \in \mathbb{Z}_{2^n}$ the exponent. The representation with $(m,n) = (32,8)$ [resp. $(m,n) = (64,11)$] is called $single\ precision$ [resp. $double\ precision$]. For a private value, each part is separately secret-shared among the computing parties. The same representation (plus an indication whether the number is 0) is used also by Aliasgari et al. [3] who have built a private floating-point protocol set implementing arithmetic operations and a number of elementary functions on top of Shamir's threshold secret sharing [34]. In a different line of work, protocols for private floating-point operations have been built atop garbled circuits or the GMW protocol set [18,30] with various optimizations.

Internally, many of our floating-point protocols call protocols for computations on private $fixed\text{-}point$ numbers. In our protocols, a fixed-point number x is represented as an integer $x \cdot 2^M$ for a suitable M. Several sets of SMC protocols for fixed-point computations (including both arithmetic operations and elementary functions) have been proposed [14,26]. Our Protocol DSL has allowed us to experiment with the details of these protocols and propose more efficient implementations.

3   Improvements in Protocol Design

In our floating-point protocols, we use the following operations as primitive building blocks:

- Zero-extension of secret shared integers denoted with `Extend`$([\![u]\!], n)$ where $[\![u]\!] \in \mathbb{Z}_{2^m}$. This operation converts a private integer from $\mathbb{Z}_{2^m}$ to $\mathbb{Z}_{2^{n+m}}$ without changing its value.
- Dropping some least-significant bits of a secret shared integer, denoted with `Cut`$([\![u]\!], n)$ where $[\![u]\!] \in \mathbb{Z}_{2^m}$ and $n \le m$. The cut operation removes n least

significant bits of $[\![u]\!]$ and results in an $(m-n)$-bit integer. It computes $\lfloor u/2^n \rfloor$ more efficiently than division or shift-right operation.

- Multiplication of integer with an array of integers $\mathtt{MultArr}([\![u]\!], \{[\![v_i]\!]\}_{i=1}^k)$, where $[\![u]\!] \in \mathbb{Z}_{2^n}$ and $[\![v_i]\!] \in \mathbb{Z}_{2^n}$ for every $i \in \{1, \dots, k\}$. The operation results in an array $\{[\![w_i]\!]\}_{i=1}^k \in \mathbb{Z}_{2^n}^k$ where $w_i = u \cdot v_i$. The implementation is straightforward based on regular integer multiplication protocol. Efficiency is improved by sending the shares of u only once instead of k times.

We do not describe the implementations of those operations here. However, all of them are relatively straightforward to implement using the tools provided in [10].

Algorithm 1. Protocol $\mathtt{PowArr}$ for integer powers of a fixed-point number.

Data: $[\![\widetilde{x}]\!], k, n, n'$

Result: Computes the powers of a secret fixed-point number. Takes in a secret fixed-point number $[\![\widetilde{x}]\!]$ with 0 bits before and n bits after the radix point. Outputs a secret fixed-point array $\{[\![\widetilde{x^i}]\!]\}_{i=1}^k$ with $n' + n$ bits before and n bits after the radix point.

1 **if** $k = 0$ **then**
2 $\quad$ **return** $\{\}$
3 **else**
4 $\quad$ $l \leftarrow \lceil \log_2 k \rceil$
5 $\quad$ $[\![\widetilde{x^1}]\!] \leftarrow \mathtt{Extend}([\![\widetilde{x}]\!], n' + (l+1)n)$
6 $\quad$ **for** $i \leftarrow 0$ **to** $l - 1$ **do**
7 $\quad\quad$ $\{[\![\widetilde{x^j}]\!]\}_{j=2^i+1}^{2^{i+1}} \leftarrow \mathtt{MultArr}([\![\widetilde{x^{2^i}}]\!], \{[\![\widetilde{x^j}]\!]\}_{j=1}^{2^i})$
8 $\quad\quad$ **for** $j \leftarrow 1$ **to** 2^{i+1} **do in parallel**
9 $\quad\quad\quad$ $[\![\widetilde{x^j}]\!] \leftarrow \mathtt{Cut}([\![\widetilde{x^j}]\!], n)$
10 $\quad\quad$ **end**
11 $\quad$ **end**
12 $\quad$ **return** $\{[\![\widetilde{x^i}]\!]\}_{i=1}^k$
13 **end**

3.1 Efficient Polynomial Evaluation

Most of our floating-point functions are implemented using polynomial approximation. For example, when computing the square root of $2^e \cdot f$ we approximate the square root of fixed-point f with a polynomial and return $2^{e/2} \cdot \sqrt{f}$ [26, Algorithm 5]. Fast and precise fixed-point polynomial evaluation is important to ensure the speed and accuracy of floating-point operations. Recall that fixed-point addition is just regular integer addition. Multiplication requires extending both inputs to larger integers, integer multiplication and dropping the lowest bits.

We have significantly improved upon the fixed-point polynomial evaluation presented in [26, Algorithm 1]. Improved protocol for polynomial evaluation is presented in Algorithm 2 and a helper function for evaluating integer powers of a fixed-point number is presented in Algorithm 1. First, polynomial coefficients are now represented in two's complement form as opposed to using sign bits. This means we do not need to pick different multiplication results depending on the sign bits. Second, we have improved the efficiency of fixed-point multiplications which are used to evaluate the polynomial. The algorithm in [26] uses ordinary fixed-point multiplications throughout. Fixed-point multiplication requires extending the operands beforehand, multiplying, and then cutting off the lowest bits. This approach is costly, and we would like to avoid extending the operands before each multiplication. So, we extend the argument of the polynomial only once, in the beginning, by a sufficient number of bits to allow for all subsequent cuts. This approach is analogous to the one used in [27, Algorithm 8] for computing the product of several fixed-point numbers. Third, we have made the last round of polynomial evaluation more efficient; while in [26, Algorithm 1] the powers of the argument are multiplied by the corresponding coefficients, the lowest bits of the results are cut off, and then they are added up to find the value of the polynomial, we first perform the summation and *then* cut off the lowest bits of the sum, thus replacing k cut operations with 1. In addition to efficiency this shortcut slightly improves precision as it results in smaller rounding error of the end result.

Algorithm 2. Fixed-point polynomial evaluation protocol.

Data: $[\![\widetilde{x}]\!], \{\widetilde{c}_i\}_{i=0}^k, n, n'$

Result: Computes a public polynomial on a secret fixed-point number. Takes in a secret fixed-point number $[\![\widetilde{x}]\!]$ with 0 bits before and n bits after the radix point and public fixed-point coefficients $\{\widetilde{c}_i\}_{i=0}^k$ with $n' + n$ bits before and n bits after the radix point (the highest n bits are empty). Outputs a secret fixed-point number $[\![\widetilde{y}]\!]$ with 0 bits before and n bits after the radix point that is the value of the polynomial at x.

1   $\{[\![\widetilde{x^i}]\!]\}_{i=1}^k \leftarrow \texttt{PowArr}([\![\widetilde{x}]\!], k, n, n')$
2   $[\![\widetilde{z_0}]\!] \leftarrow \texttt{Share}(\widetilde{c_0})$
3   **for** $i \leftarrow 1$ **to** k **do in parallel**
4 | $[\![\widetilde{z_i}]\!] \leftarrow \widetilde{c}_i \cdot [\![\widetilde{x^i}]\!]$
5   **end**
6   **for** $i \leftarrow 0$ **to** k **do in parallel**
7 | $[\![\widetilde{z_i'}]\!] \leftarrow \texttt{Trunc}([\![\widetilde{z_i}]\!], n')$
8   **end**
9   $[\![\widetilde{y}]\!] \leftarrow \texttt{Cut}(\texttt{Sum}(\{[\![\widetilde{z_i'}]\!]\}_{i=0}^k), n)$
10 **return** $[\![\widetilde{y}]\!]$

Our polynomial evaluation algorithm is in a way less general than [26, Algorithm 1] as both the argument and the result have to be in range $[0, 1)$. However, this approach is sufficient for all the floating-point functions that we have implemented. In fact, this striction offers an advantage as it ensures that the powers of x do not overflow. Note that we do not place any restrictions on the size of the *coefficients*, while [26, Algorithm 1] requires the coefficients to fit into the same fixed-point format as the argument and the result. In [26, Algorithm 5], when computing the square root of a fixed-point number in range $[0.5, 1)$, the argument has to be shifted right in order to achieve a fixed-point format with enough bits before radix point to fit in the coefficients; our approach allows for coefficients that are larger than the argument, and therefore, no precision is lost through shifting out the lowest bits of the argument.

We, similarly to [26], approximate functions by interpolating through Chebyshev nodes [12, p. 521]. We have implemented two adjustments which result in better approximations.

First, sometimes we want the result to be in a certain range. For example, we assume that the result of 2^{x-1} where $x \in [0, 1)$ ought to be in range $[0.5, 1)$. However, approximation errors might cause results outside the range and overflows. In [26] this problem was solved by the so-called *correction* protocol which normalizes the result into the correct range. We get a suitable result directly, with no need for the correction step. If we interpolate function $f(x)$ in range (a, b) and we need $f(a)$ to be rounded upwards and $f(b)$ to be rounded downwards we pick a small positive constant ϵ and interpolate function $f(x) + \epsilon \cdot (a + b - 2x)/(b - a)$ instead. The small linear term ensures that approximation errors are in the right direction. If we want to round $f(a)$ downwards and $f(b)$ upwards then ϵ has to be negative. Should need arise to achieve errors in the same direction on both ends a small quadratic term added to the function can achieve this result.

Second, large coefficients pose a problem: due to the particularities of fixed-point polynomial evaluation they can result in large approximation errors and make the algorithm too imprecise for practical use in some cases. For example, interpolating $\mathrm{erf}(8x)$ in range $[0.125, 0.25)$ with 17 nodes results in coefficients that are larger than 2^{30} and therefore need 31 bits before radix point; when evaluating this polynomial, the rounding errors inherent to fixed-point computations result in an extremely imprecise approximation. We can improve the situation by noting that the first three bits of the input are always the same (001) and shifting the input 3 bits to the left, which amounts to multiplying it by 8 and subtracting 1. The initial range $[0.125, 0.25)$ is mapped into $[0, 1)$ and the new function that has to be interpolated is $\mathrm{erf}(x + 1)$. Interpolation with 17 nodes yields coefficients which are less than 1 and therefore require 0 bits before radix point and thus, precision is improved, and in this example the length of most variables in polynomial computation is reduced by almost 4 bytes. This approach of shifting out the known highest bit(s) of the argument and modifying the function for interpolation has improved the efficiency and precision of square root, logarithm, and error function.

As a result of aforementioned changes, evaluating a polynomial of degree 16 on a 64-bit fixed-point number takes 57 rounds and 7.5 KB of communication, while with the old algorithm, it takes 89 rounds and 27 KB of communication.

3.2   Additional Improvements to Floating-Point Protocols

In addition to improvements made to polynomial evaluation that benefit most floating-point functions, we have also modified other protocols from [26], namely inverse, square root, exponent function, and error function.

The new inverse protocol has been presented in [27, Algorithm 8]. We have found that correction of fixed-point inverse approximation results is not necessary as with this method 0.5^{-1} is always rounded down and 1^{-1} is always rounded up.

Computation of exponent function begins by separating the input x into whole part and fractional part. In [26, Algorithm 6] the whole part $\lfloor x \rfloor$ is computed in integer format and converted to floating-point format. The fractional part $\{x\}$ is computed through floating-point subtraction: $\{x\} = x - \lfloor x \rfloor$. Then $\{x\}$ has to be converted to fixed-point format in order to approximate 2^x. Instead of combining costly integer to floating-point conversion and floating-point subtraction, we have designed a special separation protocol which efficiently separates a floating-point number into whole and fractional part (in integer and fixed-point format, respectively) by obliviously choosing between all possible results.

Another optimization we have devised for exponent function is an improvement to the computation of polynomials on $\{x\}$ and $1-\{x\}$. Instead of computing the powers of $1-\{x\}$ in ordinary manner we use the powers of $\{x\}$ and binomial coefficients. This employs only fast, local operations - multiplication by a public integer and addition. (For why we need to compute the value of a polynomial on both $\{x\}$ and $1-\{x\}$ see [26, Algorithm 6].)

When $2^{\{x\}}$ has been found and converted to floating-point format, the end result is computed as $2^{\lfloor x \rfloor} \cdot 2^{\{x\}}$. In [26, Algorithm 6] this is achieved through floating-point multiplication. We have found a more efficient approach: since $2^{\{x\}}$ is a floating-point number we can just add $\lfloor x \rfloor$ to the exponent (which allows us to avoid an integer to floating-point conversion and a floating-point multiplication).

Finally, we have added a new feature to exponent function. When 2^x becomes so small it cannot be represented accurately, we round the result down to zero.

In [26, Algorithm 7] $\text{erf}(x)$ is approximated by $2x/\sqrt{\pi}$ if $x < \epsilon$ and 1 if $x \geqslant 4$. The interval $[\epsilon, 4)$ is divided into 4 pieces and in each one the function is approximated with a different polynomial. In our implementation, double-precision $\text{erf}(x)$ is approximated by 1 if $x \geqslant 8$. The interval $[\epsilon, 8)$ is divided into 8 pieces; in first six the function is approximated with polynomials and in last two with constants. We compute several different polynomials (4 in single-precision case and 6 in double-precision case) on the same number and perform oblivious choices in the end. We can optimise this calculation by computing the powers of the argument only once as they are the same for all polynomials. But the main improvement in performance comes from restructuring the algorithm to compute only the correct value of $\text{erf}(x)$ instead of computing several different values and obliviously choosing between them in the end. In [26, Algorithm 7] several possible shift rights of the significand are computed (essentially giving us several possible results of the floating-point to fixed-point conversion). On all of them, error function is computed, and finally, the correct result is picked obliviously. We have reversed the order of the last two steps: first, we obliviously pick the correct shift right of the significand (essentially performing a floating-point to fixed-point conversion) and *then* we compute the error function on the single correct value.

Our improvements have increased precision compared to [26]. The maximum relative error of inverse is $2.69 \cdot 10^{-9}$ for single precision and $7.10 \cdot 10^{-19}$ for double precision (compared to $1.3 \cdot 10^{-4}$ and $1.3 \cdot 10^{-8}$ in [26]). For square root our errors are respectively $4.92 \cdot 10^{-9}$ and $1.30 \cdot 10^{-15}$ (compared to $5.1 \cdot 10^{-6}$ and $4.1 \cdot 10^{-11}$ in [26]). In a few cases we have achieved better accuracy guarantees than what IEEE 754 single- and double-precision floating-point numbers allow. This is possible because we are using slightly longer fractional parts.

3.3   New Floating-Point Protocols

In addition to improving the floating-point protocols published in [23, 26, 27] we have also designed a few new ones, namely logarithm, sine, floor and ceiling. Here we shall present a short explanation of logarithm and sine.

In order to compute the binary logarithm of a floating-point number we note that $\log_2(2^e \cdot f) = e + \log_2 f$. As f is in range $[0.5, 1)$ its binary logarithm is in range $[-1, 0)$. However, in order to easily convert it to a floating-point number, we would like to get a result in range $[0.5, 1)$. Therefore, we transform the expression above as follows: $e + \log_2 f = (e - 2) + 2(\log_4 f + 1)$. If f is in range $[0.5, 1)$ then the value of $\log_4 f + 1$ is in range $[0.5, 1)$. This is the function that we approximate with a fixed-point polynomial. For double precision, we split the interval into two equal parts and use two different polynomials. Finally, $e - 2$ is converted to floating-point format and the end result is computed through floating-point addition. Near 1 we use second degree Taylor polynomial $\log_2 x \approx \log_4 e \cdot (x - 1)(3 - x)$ to achieve better precision. In order to convert binary logarithm to natural logarithm we use the conversion $\ln x = \ln 2 \cdot \log_2 x$.

The algorithm for computing the sine is relatively straightforward as we can use to our advantage all kinds of symmetry inherent to the function. First, we divide the argument by 2π and find the fractional part in fixed-point format, thus reducing the computation to two full turns (from -2π to 2π). We note that $\sin(-x) = -\sin x$, $\sin(x + \pi) = -\sin x$, and $\sin(\pi/2 - x) = \sin(\pi/2 + x)$. Thus, we have reduced the computation to one quarter-turn (from 0 to $\pi/2$). Then we use fixed-point polynomial approximation and convert the end result to floating-point format. When the argument is near zero we use the approximation $\sin x \approx x$ to achieve better precision.

4   Optimization Techniques

The Protocol DSL has allowed us to easily apply certain optimizations across the entire suite of protocols employed in SHAREMIND. They are described in the following. The optimizations are specific to the "main" protocol set [10] of SHAREMIND based on additive secret sharing over finite rings, using three computing parties.

4.1 Shared Random Number Generators

To ensure that a party's view in a protocol could be generated from only its inputs, we commonly use the *resharing* protocol, to ensure independence from other parties' inputs and outputs. For example, usually every input of a protocol is explicitly reshared. The resharing protocol takes a private value $[\![u]\!] \in R$ and returns a $[\![v]\!] \in R$ such that $u = v$ and all shares $[\![v]\!]_i$ are uniformly distributed and independent of the shares $[\![u]\!]_j$. The protocol is implemented as follows: each party $\mathcal{P}_i$ generates a random value $r_i \leftarrow R$ and sends it to the next computing party $\mathcal{P}_{n(i)}$, adds the generated value r_i to the input share $[\![u]\!]_i$, and subtracts the random number $r_{p(i)}$ received from the previous computing party $\mathcal{P}_{p(i)}$. The shares of the output $[\![v]\!]$ of the protocol are $([\![u]\!]_1 + r_1 - r_3, [\![u]\!]_2 + r_2 - r_1, [\![u]\!]_3 + r_3 - r_2)$. We see that $v = [\![v]\!]_1 + [\![v]\!]_2 + [\![v]\!]_3 = [\![u]\!]_1 + [\![u]\!]_2 + [\![u]\!]_3 = u$.

We can spot a common pattern that occurs in resharing (and in some other primitive protocols): a party generates a random number and sends it to some other party. This pattern can be optimized by letting both parties generate the same random number using a common random number generator (RNG). Analysis of our protocols shows that network communication can be reduced by 30 % to 60 % using this technique (exactly 60 % in the case of integer multiplication protocol). This optimization is not new and has previously been used in [24]. Our toolchain around the Protocol DSL allows this optimization to be automatically introduced, with no changes to the specification of the protocols. The optimization itself is straightforward on our intermediate representation: we detect randomness nodes that are sent to one other computing party, and transform them to instead take use of shared randomness nodes.

We have manually implemented this optimization for the multiplication protocol (for which the Protocol DSL has not been used) and compared the performance to the unoptimized version to validate the effectiveness of this modification. Multiplication protocol has been chosen because of its simplicity, efficiency, ubiquity in application, and because it is one of the least computation heavy protocols. The comparison was performed using the methodology described in Sect. 5 and the results are displayed in Table 1. We see a slowdown of at most 15 % on small input lengths (up to one hundred elements), but for large inputs we see a universal speedup that reaches up to 60 %. The performance of 64-bit multiplication has been universally improved. The slowdown on small inputs can be explained by a slight increase in computation overhead (critical path became longer due to invoking the shared RNG in the end of the protocol) and the speedup can be explained by the decrease in network communication. In fact, network communication is reduced by exactly 60 %.

Table 1. Speedups of shared RNG (SRNG) and symmetric multiplication protocols over the regular multiplication. The speedups have been measured from 1 element inputs to 10^8 element input vectors.

Bit-width	SRNG					Symmetric					SRNG and Symmetric				
	10^0	10^2	10^4	10^6	10^8	10^0	10^2	10^4	10^6	10^8	10^0	10^2	10^4	10^6	10^8
64	1.03	1.03	1.48	1.44	1.61	1.08	1.09	1.13	1.08	1.04	1.10	1.12	1.67	1.55	1.68
32	0.95	0.98	1.34	1.45	1.30	1.09	1.08	1.14	1.02	1.08	1.04	1.06	1.53	1.48	1.41
16	0.85	0.90	1.14	1.36	1.41	1.18	1.12	1.17	1.02	1.02	1.00	1.01	1.34	1.39	1.43
8	0.96	0.96	1.03	1.11	1.01	1.04	1.03	0.91	1.03	1.07	0.99	0.98	0.95	1.14	1.08

4.2 Symmetric Protocols

Multiplication protocol in additive schemes is commonly presented as Algorithm 3 such as in [10, 27]. The given protocol is perfectly reasonable when the SRNG optimization is not used: the resharing sub-protocol sends the network messages in one direction and the multiplication protocol itself in the other. As a result the communication channels are under similar workload. However, using the SRNG optimization results in a protocol that sends network messages only over one of the two network channels. We propose a small modification in the form of Algorithm 4 as an alternative multiplication protocol that uses the network in a balanced manner. The correctness and security of the algorithm can be shown the same way as it was shown for the multiplication protocol in [10].

Algorithm 3. Multiplication protocol.

Data: Shared values $[\![u]\!], [\![v]\!] \in R$
Result: Shared value $[\![w]\!] \in R$ such that $uv = w$.
1 $[\![u]\!] \leftarrow \mathtt{Reshare}([\![u]\!])$
2 $[\![v]\!] \leftarrow \mathtt{Reshare}([\![v]\!])$
3 All parties $\mathcal{P}_i$ perform the following:
4   Send $[\![u]\!]_i$ and $[\![v]\!]_i$ to $\mathcal{P}_{\mathsf{n}(i)}$
5   Receive $[\![u]\!]_{\mathsf{p}(i)}$ and $[\![v]\!]_{\mathsf{p}(i)}$ from $\mathcal{P}_{\mathsf{p}(i)}$
6      $[\![w]\!]_i \leftarrow [\![u]\!]_i \cdot [\![v]\!]_i + [\![u]\!]_{\mathsf{p}(i)} \cdot [\![v]\!]_i + [\![u]\!]_i \cdot [\![v]\!]_{\mathsf{p}(i)}$
7 $[\![w]\!] \leftarrow \mathtt{Reshare}([\![w]\!])$
8 **return** $[\![w]\!]$

The symmetric protocol provides a small performance gain over the SRNG optimized protocol. The comparison against our legacy multiplication protocol (see Table 1) shows better results and disappearance of the slowdown present with only the SRNG optimization. Only the 8-bit multiplication experiences a small slowdown in a few cases. We predict that the speedups will be greater in a setting where network latency is worse or the available bandwidth is smaller because in these cases the network will become the dominant bottleneck. This claim is supported by the evidence that the speedups improve as the protocols need to send more data over the network (larger bit-widths or larger input vectors).

Algorithm 4. Symmetric multiplication protocol.

Data: Shared values $[\![u]\!], [\![v]\!] \in R$
Result: Shared value $[\![w]\!] \in R$ such that $uv = w$.

1 $[\![u]\!] \leftarrow \texttt{Reshare}([\![u]\!])$
2 $[\![v]\!] \leftarrow \texttt{Reshare}([\![v]\!])$
3 All parties $\mathcal{P}_i$ perform the following:
4   Send $[\![u]\!]_i$ to $\mathcal{P}_{\mathsf{n}(i)}$ and $[\![v]\!]_i$ to $\mathcal{P}_{\mathsf{p}(i)}$
5   Receive $[\![u]\!]_{\mathsf{p}(i)}$ from $\mathcal{P}_{\mathsf{p}(i)}$ and $[\![v]\!]_{\mathsf{n}(i)}$ from $\mathcal{P}_{\mathsf{n}(i)}$
6     $[\![w]\!]_i \leftarrow [\![u]\!]_i \cdot [\![v]\!]_i + [\![u]\!]_{\mathsf{p}(i)} \cdot [\![v]\!]_i + [\![u]\!]_{\mathsf{p}(i)} \cdot [\![v]\!]_{\mathsf{n}(i)}$
7 $[\![w]\!] \leftarrow \texttt{Reshare}([\![w]\!])$
8 **return** $[\![w]\!]$

This modification can be applied to many other protocols, but a few of the protocols are inherently asymmetric (such as squaring a value, or finding the bitwise conjunction of a single bit with a 64-bit integer). For all asymmetric protocols we can implement two versions that are unbalanced in different directions, and pick versions of them such that overall the communication is roughly balanced (we do not expose this facility to the end user). This optimization has been applied manually as the set of primitive protocols is manageable and the protocol DSL enables such changes easily. We have not explored the possibility of automatically performing communication balancing.

4.3 Speedup over Previous Results

We have applied the systematic optimizations presented in this section to all our protocols and compared the results against operations without those optimizations. In addition to the optimizations mentioned previously we have also eliminated many resharing calls (this optimization does not reduce network communication) as allowed by [7] and verified the security of resulting protocols using our privacy analyser [32]. Table 2 shows comparison results for floating-point addition, multiplication and square root. These protocols provide a rough idea of how the optimizations fare across all protocols.

Table 2. Speedup of optimized floating-point protocols.

Operation	Precision	Speedup on given input length						
		10^0	10^1	10^2	10^3	10^4	10^5	10^6
$[\![x]\!] + [\![y]\!]$	Single	1.04	1.13	1.48	1.94	1.73	1.71	1.73
	Double	0.97	1.03	1.38	1.67	1.61	1.69	1.77
$[\![x]\!] \times [\![y]\!]$	Single	0.91	0.92	1.04	1.42	1.60	1.45	1.57
	Double	1.03	1.08	1.28	1.81	1.82	1.80	1.79
$\sqrt{[\![x]\!]}$	Single	0.91	0.98	1.33	1.82	1.73	1.66	1.64
	Double	1.06	1.22	1.71	1.86	1.85	1.85	1.87

Table 2 shows an almost universal improvement in performance. In a few cases single-precision floating-point operations perform slightly worse (less than 10 %) but only on small input sizes. In the case of inputs of length 100 and more we see significant speedups across the board. In a few cases speedups reach over 80 %.

5   Large-Scale Performance Evaluation

Benchmarking was performed on a dedicated cluster of three computers connected with 10 Gbps Ethernet. Each computer was equipped with 128GB DDR4 memory, two 8-core Intel Xeon (E5-2640 v3) processors and was running Debian 8.2 Jessie (15th Sep 2015). Both memory overcommit and swap were disabled. During benchmarking only the necessary system processes and some low overhead services (such as SSH and monitoring) were enabled.

A single run-time measurement was computed by taking the running times of each of the computing parties and finding the maximum of those. This is necessary as a protocol may terminate faster for some participants and the maximum reflects the time it takes for the result of the operation to become available to all. The average running time was estimated by computing the mean of all the measurements. On every input length we performed at least 5 repetitions (10 for integer operations) and, to reduce variance, significantly more on small input lengths (up to 10000 repetitions). Measurements were performed in a randomized order because we found that running the tests sequentially in an increasing size of inputs gave significantly better performance results. Sequential order results in a steady increase of network load which is predictable for the networking layer but is not a very realistic scenario for all SMC applications.

Performance results for floating-point operations are presented in Table 3. We have measured addition, multiplication, comparison, reciprocal, square root, exponentiation, natural logarithm, sine, and error function from 1 element input to one million element input vectors. All the results have been presented in operations per millisecond (thousands of operations per second). Looking at the table, it is clear that performance scales very well with vectorization: only a few hundred scalar operations can be executed per second but by computing on many inputs in parallel we can perform hundreds of thousands of operations per second.

We have also thoroughly measured the performance of integer and fixed-point multiplication operations (Table 4). The fixed-point operations, especially addition and multiplication, have turned out to be useful tools in implementing efficient higher-level applications. As the respective floating-point operations are rather slow, the computations relying heavily on them may become impractical (for example, floating-point addition [23, Algorithm 4] requires private shifts which makes it a costly operation). While not a universal solution, efficient signed fixed-point operations alleviate the problem in many cases.

We have also evaluated private integer multiplication to establish a baseline, against which to compare more complex protocols when choosing the operations to be used in a larger application. We have limited the performance evaluation of multiplication to 10^9 element input vectors. This is due to memory limitations:

Table 3. Performance (in operations per millisecond) of optimized floating-point operations. Combing all manual and automatic optimizations presented in this work. Variables x and y denote floating-point numbers.

Operation	Precision	OP/ms on given input length						
		10^0	10^1	10^2	10^3	10^4	10^5	10^6
$[\![x]\!] + [\![y]\!]$	Single	0.32	3.0	20.4	54.3	60.6	52.8	53.1
	Double	0.27	2.4	12.9	24.5	22.9	23.9	25.3
$[\![x]\!] \times [\![y]\!]$	Single	0.52	4.8	36.1	140	231	172	185
	Double	0.54	4.8	32.2	111	131	107	106
$[\![x]\!] < [\![y]\!]$	Single	1.14	10.5	78.8	210	237	199	209
	Double	0.97	9.0	62.3	133	120	111	118
$[\![x]\!]^{-1}$	Single	0.30	2.7	18.1	48.7	52.4	45.5	49.4
	Double	0.23	1.9	9.0	16.8	16.9	17.6	18.6
$\sqrt{[\![x]\!]}$	Single	0.26	2.4	16.4	44.8	48.7	45.1	44.1
	Double	0.21	1.7	6.5	10.4	9.4	11.2	11.2
$\exp [\![x]\!]$	Single	0.18	1.7	11.4	28.8	33.1	30.4	29.2
	Double	0.16	1.3	5.4	9.1	8.8	9.5	9.9
$\ln [\![x]\!]$	Single	0.14	1.2	6.8	12.3	12.0	11.2	11.1
	Double	0.12	1.0	3.3	4.2	4.0	4.4	4.6
$\sin [\![x]\!]$	Single	0.14	1.2	6.3	9.4	8.4	8.8	9.3
	Double	0.12	0.9	2.7	2.8	2.8	3.3	3.4
$\mathrm{erf} [\![x]\!]$	Single	0.23	2.0	12.1	24.2	24.1	23.5	23.7
	Double	0.18	1.3	4.2	5.9	5.5	6.7	6.8

Table 4. Performance of optimized integer and signed fixed-point multiplication. Numbers are provided in operations per second with suffix K denoting thousands and M denoting millions.

Type	10^0	10^1	10^2	10^3	10^4	10^5	10^6	10^7	10^8	10^9
uint8	7.4K	71.6K	703.5K	5.8M	24.1M	38.9M	40.1M	28.0M	37.9M	41.5M
uint16	7.0K	68.4K	663.4K	5.4M	22.0M	34.0M	29.5M	29.3M	35.0M	37.1M
uint32	6.6K	65.7K	629.7K	5.0M	17.1M	22.4M	18.8M	20.7M	22.1M	21.4M
uint64	6.4K	63.5K	586.9K	4.3M	11.2M	12.1M	10.5M	12.1M	13.7M	13.3M
fix32	640	6.0K	51.2K	270.8K	435.4K	344.1K	361.1K	369.4K	351.6K	
fix64	680	6.2K	46.6K	187.3K	226.2K	184.3K	186.0K	187.6K	179.0K	

a single 10^{10} element vector of 64-bit integers takes roughly 80 gigabytes of RAM (it would be possible to only allocate a single vector and use that as both input and output, but this would compute square and not product). Capability to handle arrays of 10^9 elements with ease demonstrates the robustness of our platform.

We have compared the performance of arithmetic operations and square root against previous works. Unfortunately it was not possible to provide comparison in an identical setups as both previous works we compare against have the performance measures on a 1 Gbps Ethernet connection over LAN (opposed to our 10 Gbps connection over LAN). However, we found that we never came close to saturating a 1 Gbps of the connection. Performance in [33] was measured on cluster of three nodes each equipped with 48 GB of RAM and 12-core 3 GHz Intel CPUs supporting AES-NI and HyperThreading. Performance in [18] was measured on two desktop computers each equipped with a 3.5 GHz Intel Core i7 CPU and 16 GB of RAM (the number of cores was unspecified).

In the case of additive 3-party secret sharing the best results so far have been obtained in [33]. In the case of scalar operations our results show 132 fold speedup for addition, 67 fold speedup for multiplication and 618 fold speedup for square root. The speedups also remain good for 10^4 element input vectors: 16, 14 and 416 fold respectively. Additionally [33] reports the performance of garbled circuit based on IEEE 754 floating-point numbers. Compared to those we provide 13, 20 and 27 fold speedups in the case of scalars and 102, 364 and 495 fold speedups in the case of 10^4 element input vectors.

While garbled circuit approach is not directly comparable to secret sharing we also compare our results against [18] which provides, to our knowledge, as of now, the best performance for 2-party garbled circuit approach. For scalar operations we are, at worst, 80 % slower, and in case of 10^4 element input vectors at worst 50 % slower, and at best 4.6 times faster. This is considering only online time. When offline time is also taken into account we report similar performance for scalar operations and significant speedups for vectorized ones (over 40 fold). These comparisons are against the better of GMW (vector operations) and Yao (scalar operations).

6   Conclusions

We have demonstrated the current state of the art in the performance of SMC protocols for numeric computations. Our results show that with careful design and the right set of tools, significant performance improvements are still possible. But currently, as Table 4 shows, the performance of SMC operations on modern but reasonably-spec'd hardware is comparable to a computer with a 80386 processor.

References

1. 2013 ACM SIGSAC Conference on Computer and Communications Security, CCS 2013, Berlin, Germany, 4–8 November 2013. ACM (2013)
2. Proceedings of the 22nd ACM SIGSAC Conference on Computer and Communications Security, Denver, CO, USA, 12–16 October 2015. ACM (2015)

3. Aliasgari, M., Blanton, M., Zhang, Y., Steele, A.: Secure computation on floating point numbers. In: 20th Annual Network and Distributed System Security Symposium, NDSS 2013, San Diego, California, USA, 24–27 February 2013. The Internet Society (2013)
4. Ben-David, A., Nisan, N., Pinkas, B.: FairplayMP: a system for secure multi-party computation. In: CCS 2008: Proceedings of the 15th ACM Conference on Computer and Communications Security, pp. 257–266. ACM (2008)
5. Bogdanov, D., Jõemets, M., Siim, S., Vaht, M.: A short paper on how the national tax office evaluated a tax fraud detection system based on secure multi-party computation. In: Proceedings of 19th International Conference on Financial Cryptography and Data Security. LNCS, vol. 8975, pp. 227–234. Springer, Heidelberg (2015)
6. Bogdanov, D., Kamm, L., Laur, S., Pruulmann-Vengerfeldt, P., Talviste, R., Willemson, J.: Privacy-preserving statistical data analysis on federated databases. In: Preneel, B., Ikonomou, D. (eds.) APF 2014. LNCS, vol. 8450, pp. 30–55. Springer, Heidelberg (2014)
7. Bogdanov, D., Laud, P., Laur, S., Pullonen, P.: From input private to universally composable secure multi-party computation primitives. In: IEEE 27th Computer Security Foundations Symposium, CSF 2014, pp. 184–198. IEEE, July 2014
8. Bogdanov, D., Laud, P., Randmets, J.: Domain-polymorphic programming of privacy-preserving applications. In: Proceedings of the Ninth Workshop on Programming Languages and Analysis for Security, PLAS@ECOOP 2014, Uppsala, Sweden, 29 July 2014, p. 53. ACM (2014)
9. Bogdanov, D., Laur, S., Willemson, J.: Sharemind: a framework for fast privacy-preserving computations. In: Jajodia, S., Lopez, J. (eds.) ESORICS 2008. LNCS, vol. 5283, pp. 192–206. Springer, Heidelberg (2008)
10. Bogdanov, D., Niitsoo, M., Toft, T., Willemson, J.: High-performance secure multi-party computation for data mining applications. Int. J. Inf. Secur. 11(6), 403–418 (2012)
11. Bogetoft, P., et al.: Secure multiparty computation goes live. In: Dingledine, R., Golle, P. (eds.) FC 2009. LNCS, vol. 5628, pp. 325–343. Springer, Heidelberg (2009)
12. Burden, R.L., Faires, J.D.: Numerical Analysis, 9th edn. Brooks/Cole, Boston (2011)
13. Burkhart, M., Strasser, M., Many, D., Dimitropoulos, X.: SEPIA: privacy-preserving aggregation of multi-domain network events and statistics. In: USENIX Security Symposium, pp. 223–239. Washington, DC, USA (2010)
14. Catrina, O., Saxena, A.: Secure computation with fixed-point numbers. In: Sion, R. (ed.) FC 2010. LNCS, vol. 6052, pp. 35–50. Springer, Heidelberg (2010)
15. Cramer, R., Damgård, I.B., Maurer, U.M.: General secure multi-party computation from any linear secret-sharing scheme. In: Preneel, B. (ed.) EUROCRYPT 2000. LNCS, vol. 1807, pp. 316–334. Springer, Heidelberg (2000)
16. Cramer, R., Damgård, I.B., Nielsen, J.B.: Multiparty computation from threshold homomorphic encryption. In: Pfitzmann, B. (ed.) EUROCRYPT 2001. LNCS, vol. 2045, pp. 280–299. Springer, Heidelberg (2001)
17. Damgård, I., Geisler, M., Krøigaard, M., Nielsen, J.B.: Asynchronous multiparty computation: theory and implementation. In: Jarecki, S., Tsudik, G. (eds.) PKC 2009. LNCS, vol. 5443, pp. 160–179. Springer, Heidelberg (2009)
18. Demmler, D., Dessouky, G., Koushanfar, F., Sadeghi, A., Schneider, T., Zeitouni, S.: Automated synthesis of optimized circuits for secure computation. In: Proceedings of the 22nd ACM SIGSAC Conference on Computer and Communications Security, Denver, CO, USA, 12–6 October 2015 [2], pp. 1504–1517 (2015)

19. Goldreich, O., Micali, S., Wigderson, A.: How to play any mental game or a completeness theorem for protocols with honest majority. In: STOC, pp. 218–229. ACM (1987)

20. Henecka, W., Kögl, S., Sadeghi, A.R., Schneider, T., Wehrenberg, I.: TASTY: tool for automating secure two-party computations. In: Proceedings of the 17th ACM Conference on Computer and Communications Security, CCS 2010, pp. 451–462. ACM (2010)

21. Ishai, Y., Paskin, A.: Evaluating branching programs on encrypted data. In: Vadhan, S.P. (ed.) TCC 2007. LNCS, vol. 4392, pp. 575–594. Springer, Heidelberg (2007)

22. Kamm, L.: Privacy-preserving statistical analysis using secure multi-party computation. Ph.D. thesis, University of Tartu (2015)

23. Kamm, L., Willemson, J.: Secure floating point arithmetic and private satellite collision analysis. Int. J. Inf. Secur. **14**(6), 531–548 (2015)

24. Keller, M., Scholl, P., Smart, N.P.: An architecture for practical actively secure MPC with dishonest majority. In: 2013 ACM SIGSAC Conference on Computer and Communications Security, CCS 2013, Berlin, Germany, 4–8 November 2013 [1], pp. 549–560 (2013)

25. Kerschbaum, F., Schröpfer, A., Zilli, A., Pibernik, R., Catrina, O., de Hoogh, S., Schoenmakers, B., Cimato, S., Damiani, E.: Secure collaborative supply-chain management. IEEE Comput. **44**(9), 38–43 (2011)

26. Krips, T., Willemson, J.: Hybrid model of fixed and floating point numbers in secure multiparty computations. In: Chow, S.S.M., Camenisch, J., Hui, L.C.K., Yiu, S.M. (eds.) ISC 2014. LNCS, vol. 8783, pp. 179–197. Springer, Heidelberg (2014)

27. Laud, P., Randmets, J.: A domain-specific language for low-level secure multiparty computation protocols. In: Proceedings of the 22nd ACM SIGSAC Conference on Computer and Communications Security, Denver, CO, USA, 12–16 October 2015 [2], pp. 1492–1503 (2015)

28. Lindell, Y., Pinkas, B.: A proof of security of Yao's protocol for two-party computation. J. Cryptology **22**(2), 161–188 (2009)

29. Liu, C., Huang, Y., Shi, E., Katz, J., Hicks, M.W.: Automating efficient ram-model secure computation. In: 2014 IEEE Symposium on Security and Privacy, SP 2014, Berkeley, CA, USA, 18–21 May 2014, pp. 623–638. IEEE Computer Society (2014)

30. Liu, Y.C., Chiang, Y.T., Hsu, T.S., Liau, C.J., Wang, D.W.: Floating point arithmetic protocols for constructing secure data analysis application. Procedia Comput. Sci. **22**, 152–161 (2013). 17th International Conference in Knowledge Based and Intelligent Information and Engineering Systems - KES2013

31. Malka, L.: VMCrypt: modular software architecture for scalable secure computation. In: Proceedings of the 18th ACM Conference on Computer and Communications Security, CCS 2011, Chicago, Illinois, USA, 17–21 October 2011, pp. 715–724. ACM (2011)

32. Pettai, M., Laud, P.: Automatic proofs of privacy of secure multi-party computation protocols against active adversaries. In: 2015 IEEE 28th Computer Security Foundations Symposium (CSF 2015) (2015)

33. Pullonen, P., Siim, S.: Combining secret sharing and garbled circuits for efficient private IEEE 754 floating-point computations. In: Brenner, M., Christin, N., Johnson, B., Rohloff, K. (eds.) FC 2015 Workshops. LNCS, vol. 8976, pp. 172–183. Springer, Heidelberg (2015)

34. Shamir, A.: How to share a secret. Commun. ACM **22**(11), 612–613 (1979)

35. Zhang, Y., Steele, A., Blanton, M.: PICCO: a general-purpose compiler for private distributed computation. In: 2013 ACM SIGSAC Conference on Computer and Communications Security, CCS 2013, Berlin, Germany, 4–8 November 2013 [1], pp. 813–826

On-the-fly Homomorphic Batching/Unbatching

Yarkın Doröz$^{(\boxtimes)}$, Gizem S. Çetin, and Berk Sunar

Worcester Polytechnic Institute, Worcester, USA
{ydoroz,gscetin,sunar}@wpi.edu

Abstract. We introduce a homomorphic batching technique that can be used to pack multiple ciphertext messages into one ciphertext for parallel processing. One is able to use the method to batch or unbatch messages homomorphically to further improve the flexibility of encrypted domain evaluations. In particular, we show various approaches to implement Number Theoretic Transform (NTT) homomorphically in Fast Fourier Transform (FFT) speed. Also, we present the limitations that we encounter in application of these methods. We implement homomorphic batching in various settings and present concrete performance figures. Finally, we present an implementation of a homomorphic NTT method in which we process each element in an independent ciphertext. The advantage of this method is we are able to batch independent homomorphic NTT evaluations and achieve better amortized time.

Keywords: Homomorphic encryption · Homomorphic batching · Homomorphic number theoretic transform

1 Introduction

Fully Homomorphic Encryption (FHE) is an encryption method that allows to perform arbitrary circuit or function evaluations on encrypted data without the need for decryption of the ciphertexts. The first FHE scheme was a lattice-based construction introduced by Gentry [12] in 2009. In 2010, Gentry and Halevi [15] simplified the construction and completed the first practical FHE implementation. Even with the optimizations the FHE scheme lacked in performance, since a crucial operation called recryption had to be performed after each bit AND operation which was taking 30 seconds. After the first FHE implementation various schemes [3–5,9,13,14] have emerged with different optimization techniques on fully or somewhat homomorphic encryption (SHE). In [26] batching and SIMD operations were introduced to pack multiple messages into a ciphertext and thereby allow for parallel homomorphic evaluations. Other operations such as bootstrapping [12], relinearization [23], modulus reduction [3,5], key switching [3] and flattening [17] are used as key and noise management techniques permitting the evaluation of deeper circuits with similar parameter sizes.

In [3] Brakerski, Gentry and Vaikuntanathan implemented a leveled FHE scheme that is capable of evaluating polynomial-size circuits by using noise management techniques. Their scheme is based on the Learning With Errors (LWE)

© International Financial Cryptography Association 2016
J. Clark et al. (Eds.): FC 2016 Workshops, LNCS 9604, pp. 288–301, 2016.
DOI: 10.1007/978-3-662-53357-4_19

problem. Later, the BGV scheme was implemented as a software library HElib [19] using C++. The library was used to re-implement the homomorphic evaluation of an earlier AES circuit [16] by Gentry, Halevi and Smart. They achieved an amortized time of 2 seconds for 120 blocks of AES implementation. Later, [2] presented a new tensor product technique that reduces the noise from quadratic to linear growth. The technique is applicable to LWE schemes, i.e. BGV style schemes. Later, López-Alt, Tromer and Vaikuntanathan (LTV) [23] proposed an FHE scheme based on a variant of NTRU [27] that has multi key support. Doröz, Hu and Sunar implemented the proposed LTV scheme and using it evaluated a custom AES circuit and a level optimized Prince block cipher circuit [10,11] homomorphically. These implementations were later accelerated using a GPU by Dai et. al. [7,8]. With GPU support, amortized timings of homomorphic Prince and AES evaluations reduced to 24 msec and 7.3 sec respectively. Recently, a new *approximate eigenvector* FHE scheme with reduction to LWE was proposed by Gentry, Shai and Waters (GSW) [17]. The approximate eigenvector, eigenvalue pairs are used in the construction and they introduce a new noise management technique called flattening. GSW is asymptotically faster due to the use of standard matrix operations in order to apply homomorphic addition and multiplications. With flattening the need for costly relinearization operations and any association storage of massive evaluation keys is eliminated.

Applications. The increasing number of new FHE schemes proposed along with a variety of optimizations, motivated researchers to conduct experiments on their practicality in applications. For example, Lagendijk et al. [20] give details on applicability of homomorphic encryption and multi-party computation for signal processing operations. These signal processing operations include but are not limited to linear filters, correlation evaluations, thresholding, signal transformations, inner product calculations and dimension reduction.

In [24], Lauter et al. focus on simple statistical operations that can be used in real-life cloud services for medical or financial applications such as finding the mean, the standard deviation and the logistical regression. Since these functions do not have high multiplicative depth, they are not necessarily required to be implemented using an FHE scheme, but an SHE construction is sufficient. In the same work, they also implement the SHE scheme of Brakerski and Vaikuntanathan [4] using Magma algebra program. The same reference discussed how to pack multiple message bits into a ciphertext. As noted, even though it is possible to pack multiple ciphertexts into a single ciphertext, there are some problems. First of all, they state that there is no known technique to unpack the messages in the encrypted form, so they cannot retrieve the messages within a packed ciphertext. Secondly, arithmetic operations become limited, i.e. we cannot perform multiplication without destroying the messages in the ciphertext.

Later, in [21] Lauter et al. investigate another homomorphic application: genomic data computation algorithms. They measure the performance of algorithms such as Pearson Goodness-of-Fit test, the D' and r^2-measures of linkage disequilibrium, the Estimation Maximization algorithm for haplotyping, and the Cochran-Armitage Test for Trend. Another homomorphic encryption application on medical data is performed in [1] by Bos et al. The technique is applied on medical data to perform private predictive analysis on the probability of cardio-vascular disease.

There are many other homomorphic applications from various fields that are implemented by various groups of researchers. A machine learning algorithm, i.e. Linear Means Classifier and Fisher's Linear Discriminant Classifier on the Wisconsin Breast Cancer Data set, is implemented in [18] by Graepel et al. Another application is dynamic programming that is presented by Cheon et al. [6]. They implemented algorithms such as Hamming distance, edit distance, and the Smith-Waterman algorithm on genomic data.

2   Motivation

The recent progress in fully homomorphic encryption schemes motivated researchers to investigate applications of FHE schemes as solutions to real life privacy concerning problems. In these applications, researchers face difficulties to evaluate some of the basic primitive operations homomorphically. The lack of these homomorphic primitive operations limits the applications or forces proto-col changes, e.g. by moving some of the more difficult operations to the client side. In this work, we focus on two different problems. The first one is a remark-ably important, yet still open problem of homomorphic unbatching of a single ciphertext that contains batched messages. The second one is the homomorphic evaluation of the NTT operation over multiple ciphertexts. The details are as follows:

- **Homomorphic Unbatching.** This problem was explicitly posed by Lauter et al. in [24]: How can we unpack information belonging to numerous clients packed at the beginning of a homomorphic evaluation session into a single ciphertext for efficiency. The authors mention that if there was a method for *homomorphic unbatching*, a server might easily batch messages of different clients on a single ciphertext, process the ciphertext and later it can homomor-phically unbatch the individual results to different ciphertexts to be delivered to the respective clients. Basically, this method helps to significantly improve the computational performance on servers by compressing the different cipher-text messages from users into a single ciphertext for parallel processing. In addition it gives the option to separate these results into different ciphertexts so that the result is only send to the owner of the data. Here we show a way to achieve homomorphic unbatching by using the NTT homomorphically. We focus on ways to implement the homomorphic NTT and show the difficulties of achieving FFT speed to this end.
- **Homomorphic NTT.** In this case, we implement the homomorphic NTT using a different method and we succeed to achieve FFT speed, and with this method our goal is to compute convolutions, instead of unbatching. This operation can be used for many NTT/FFT applications, such as filtering, large integer and polynomial multiplications, Chebyshev approximation and efficient matrix-vector multiplications in the FHE setting.

Our Contribution. In this work we present an array of solutions to improve the versatility of homomorphic NTT, specifically:

- We tackle the problem of computing the Number Theoretical Transform homomorphically over the domain defined by the message space. It turns out that noise growth is a significant issue and FFT speed evaluation is difficult to achieve without homomorphic modular reduction. We work out a solution and provide concrete performance figures.
- Empowered by homomorphic NTT we define homomorphic batching/unbatching which allows us to move the coefficients of encrypted message polynomials into message slots and vice versa. Using homomorphic batching one may **unpack** message polynomials, i.e. extract coefficients from encrypted message polynomials; and more broadly change the processing domain on-the-fly while evaluation proceeds.
- From a security perspective, homomorphic batching/unbatching allows us to prevent information leakage through partial evaluation results that accumulate in batched messages. This is of utmost concern in multi-user settings where multiple streams of information are bundled together and processed simultaneously.
- We implement homomorphic NTT using another method in which we encrypt the elements of the NTT in different ciphertexts and perform levels of NTT computations on these ciphertexts. In the end we achieve the elements of NTT result in different ciphertexts. This way we are able to achieve the FFT speed, batch independent NTT operations for parallel processing and achieve amortized time. However we are unable to compute batch/unbatch homomorphically.
- Also, we give run-time complexity analysis on both of the proposed homomorphic NTT methods.
- Finally we note that homomorphic NTT is of independent interest to numerous applications, e.g. filtering in digital signal processing, spectral decomposition and analysis, etc.

3   FHE Background

In this work, we use customized leveled FHE implementation proposed by Doröz, Hu and Sunar (DHS) [10]. The library is written in C++ and it uses NTL software with GMP support. The library supports the leveled multi-key FHE scheme implementation proposed in 2012 by López-Alt, Tromer and Vaikuntanathan (LTV) [23]. It is based on a variant of Stehlé and Steinfeld's [27] NTRU encryption with new operation called relinearization and existing operation modulus switching to control noise. Although the scheme can support multi-keys (users), the implemented library focuses on the single-key (user) scenario.

The LTV scheme uses the following primitives; there is a polynomial ring $R_q = \mathbb{Z}_q[x]/\langle x^N + 1 \rangle$ with N being the polynomial degree and q being the prime modulus. The message space is defined using a prime modulus p. In the scheme, polynomials are sampled using a truncated discrete Gaussian distribution χ. These are B-bounded polynomials, i.e. each coefficient of the polynomial is selected between $[-B, B]$. The scheme consists of the following primitive functions: KeyGen, Encrypt, Decrypt and Eval. The primitive Eval consist of a multiplication operation which is later followed by a relinearization and a modulus switch operation. The relinearization and modulus switch operations are used to correct the corrupted encryption mask and reduce the noise caused by the multiplication, respectively. Here we describe the primitive functions of the LTV scheme:

KeyGen. In the scheme modulus q is a decreasing sequence of prime numbers for each level: $q_0 > q_1 > q_2 \cdots > q_d$. We select the prime modulus q_i, according to the noise size at i^{th} level. We sample two polynomials $g^{(i)} \leftarrow \chi$ and $u^{(i)} \leftarrow \chi$ to compute the secret keys $f^{(i)} = pu^{(i)} + 1$ and the public key $h^{(i)} = pg^{(i)}f^{-(i)}$ for each level. We compute the evaluation keys as $\zeta_\rho^{(i)}(x) = h^{(i)}s_\rho^{(i)} + pe_\rho^{(i)} + 2^\rho f^{2(i-1)}$ where $\{s_\rho^{(i)}, e_\rho^{(i)}\} \leftarrow \chi$ and $\rho \in [0, \lfloor \log(q_i) \rfloor]$ for each level i.

Encrypt. We encrypt a message $b \in \mathbb{Z}_p$ (or it can be a message polynomial $b(x) \in \mathbb{Z}_p[x]$) by evaluating $c^{(i)} = h^{(i)}s^{(i)} + pe^{(i)} + b$ by sampling $\{s^{(i)}, e^{(i)}\} \in \chi$ for i^{th} level.

Decrypt. The decryption for i^{th} level is simply achieved by evaluating: $m = c^{(i)}f^{(i)} \pmod{p}$.

Eval. The multiplication and summation of the ciphertexts corresponds to multiplication and addition of messages in the ring $\mathbb{Z}_p[x]$. These operations increase the noise level of the ciphertexts and multiplication explicitly outweighs addition in terms of noise growth. The scheme uses two significant operations to control the noise; relinearization and modulus switching. We summarize these two operations as follows:

- **Modulus Switching.** This operation is a way of reducing the existing noise in the ciphertexts. Basically, we perform $\tilde{c}^{(i)}(x) = \lfloor \frac{q_i}{q_{i-1}} \tilde{c}^{(i-1)}(x) \rceil_p$ on each coefficient of the ciphertxt. We achieve following two things; a reduction in the noise by $\log(q_i/q_{i-1})$ bits and a new field $\mathbb{Z}_{q_i}$ for modular arithmetic. The ceil/floor operation $\lfloor \cdot \rceil_p$ refers to rounding to match the parity for modular p. An advantage of the scheme is that its performance is increased as we switch levels due to a smaller modulus q_i.
- **Relinearization.** This operations is necessary after each multiplication operation in order to prevent the noise growth and the increase of inverse powers of secret keys $f^{(i)}$. Simply we are switching square power of secret key $f^{-2(i-1)}$ for level $i-1$ with the new secret key $f^{(-i)}$ of level i. We evaluate the relinearization operation by computing: $\tilde{c}^{(i)}(x) = \sum_\rho \zeta_\rho^{(i)}(x)\tilde{c}_\rho^{(i-1)}(x)$. In the equation $\tilde{c}_\rho^{(i-1)}(x)$ are binary polynomials that forms $\tilde{c}^{(i-1)}(x) = \sum_\rho 2^\rho \tilde{c}_\rho^{(i-1)}(x)$.

Specializations. In DHS library [10], the decreasing modulus sequence is selected as a power of a fixed prime, i.e. $q_i = \sigma^{k-i}$. Here the prime σ is equal to the noise cutting size for each level and k is the circuit depth plus one. This special ring structure is used to promote the evaluation keys to the next level using modulo reduction when needed, i.e. $\zeta_\rho^{(i)}(x) = \zeta_\rho^{(0)}(x) \bmod q_i$. This reduces the key size significantly, as we only need to store the first level evaluation keys.

4   NTT Background

In this section, we will briefly go over Fourier Transform (FT) and its finite version, Discrete Fourier Transform (DFT) which is more widely used in practical applications. Then, we will talk about NTT which is a variant of DFT.

4.1   Fourier Transform

Fourier Transform is a signal transformation method that is used in many mathematical and scientific applications such as filtering, time domain and frequency domain conversions, large integer multiplications and sine/cosine wave transformations. For practical applications, DFT, the finite version of the FT, is used. If we have a sequence of N complex numbers $x_0, \cdots, x_{N-1}$ in one domain, applying DFT will give us a new sequence of N complex numbers $X_0, \cdots, X_{N-1}$ in another domain and these values can be computed by simply evaluating:

$$X_k = \sum_{j=0}^{N-1} x_j e^{-2\pi i k \frac{j}{N}}, \qquad \forall k \in [0, N-1] .$$

This linear transformation can be represented using a transformation matrix. We can define the same operation as a multiplication of our input vector $\overrightarrow{x} = [x_0, \ldots, x_{N-1}]$ with a special transformation matrix $\mathbf{W}$, i.e. $\overrightarrow{X} = \mathbf{W} \cdot \overrightarrow{x}$. We have the output vector $\overrightarrow{X} = [X_0, \ldots, X_{N-1}]$ of length N. The transformation matrix $\mathbf{W}$ has the structure of a Vandermonde matrix with entries $\alpha_{k,j} = \left(\alpha^k\right)^j$ where $\alpha = e^{\frac{-2\pi i}{N}}$ and can be visualized as follows:

$$\begin{bmatrix} \alpha^0 & \alpha^0 & \alpha^0 & \cdots & \alpha^0 & \alpha^0 \\ \alpha^0 & \alpha^1 & \alpha^2 & \cdots & \alpha^{N-2} & \alpha^{N-1} \\ \alpha^{2 \cdot 0} & \alpha^{2 \cdot 1} & \alpha^{2 \cdot 2} & \cdots & \alpha^{2 \cdot (N-2)} & \alpha^{2 \cdot (N-1)} \\ \vdots & \vdots & \vdots & \ddots & \vdots & \vdots \\ \alpha^{(N-2) \cdot 0} & \alpha^{(N-2) \cdot 1} & \alpha^{(N-2) \cdot 2} & \cdots & \alpha^{(N-2) \cdot (N-2)} & \alpha^{(N-2) \cdot (N-1)} \\ \alpha^{(N-1) \cdot 0} & \alpha^{(N-1) \cdot 1} & \alpha^{(N-1) \cdot 2} & \cdots & \alpha^{(N-1) \cdot (N-2)} & \alpha^{(N-1) \cdot (N-1)} \end{bmatrix}$$

In a naïve implementation the time complexity of the DFT becomes $\mathcal{O}(N^2)$. However, by using a Fast Fourier Transform (FFT) algorithm namely Cooley-Tukey method, we can reduce the cost of the evaluation to $\mathcal{O}(N \log(N) \log \log(N))$. The Cooley-Tukey algorithm is based on re-expressing the DFT equation into summation of two sub-DFT equations:

$$X_k = \sum_{j=0}^{N-1} x_j e^{-i2\pi k \frac{j}{N}} = \underbrace{\sum_{m=0}^{N/2-1} x_{2m} e^{-i2\pi k \frac{m}{N/2}}}_{Even} + \underbrace{e^{\frac{-2\pi ik}{N}} \sum_{m=0}^{N/2-1} x_{2m+1} e^{-i2\pi k \frac{m}{N/2}}}_{Odd}$$

As shown on the equation above, summation on the left calculates the DFT of the even indices and the summation on the right calculates the DFT of the odd indices. These odd/even DFT summations can also be re-expressed as summation of sub -odd and -even indicies. This procedure can be applied recursively until the DFT size is small enough to be evaluated fast enough. Later, the FFT can be calculated by reconstructing the calculated sub-DFT's by going into upper levels in the recursive function.

4.2   Number Theoretic Transform

Number Theoretic Transform is a specialization of DFT over the ring $\mathbb{Z}/p\mathbb{Z}$ by replacing $e^{-i2\pi k \frac{j}{N}}$ with a primitive N^{th} root of unity ω. One of the most common usage of the method is to evaluate large integer or polynomial multiplications. It prevents the errors that might be caused by the floating point arithmetic of FFT and provides precise arithmetic evaluations. We can compute the NTT by simply evaluating:

$$X_k = \sum_{j=0}^{N-1} x_j \omega^{k \cdot j} \pmod{p},$$

where $\vec{x}$ is again the input vector, p is the prime modulus and $k \in [0, N-1]$. The inverse-NTT of the evaluated vector $\vec{X}$ is computed using the same equation by replacing ω with $\omega^{-1} \pmod{p}$:

$$x_k = \sum_{j=0}^{N-1} X_j \omega^{-k \cdot j} \pmod{p}.$$

Thus the transformation matrix $\mathbf{W}$ and the inverse transformation matrix $\mathbf{W}^{-1}$ becomes:

$$\begin{bmatrix} 1 & 1 & \cdots & 1 \\ 1 & \omega & \cdots & \omega^{N-1} \\ \vdots & \vdots & \ddots & \vdots \\ 1 & \omega^{N-1} & \cdots & \omega^{(N-1)\cdot(N-1)} \end{bmatrix} \quad \text{and} \quad \begin{bmatrix} 1 & 1 & \cdots & 1 \\ 1 & \omega^{-1} & \cdots & \omega^{-(N-1)} \\ \vdots & \vdots & \ddots & \vdots \\ 1 & \omega^{-(N-1)} & \cdots & \omega^{-(N-1)\cdot(N-1)} \end{bmatrix}$$

respectively. Using the Cooley-Tukey approach that is explained in the previous section, the NTT conversion can achieve a runtime of $\mathcal{O}(N \log(N) \log \log(N))$.

5   Homomorphic NTT

In this section we give two methods to perform homomorphic NTT and discuss their advantages and disadvantages. In the first method we show that we are able to homomorphically batch/unbatch messages on a single ciphertext, but also show that it has limitations to achieve FFT speed. In the second method we show that we can overcome the problem and achieve FFT speed, but we need use N ciphertexts for input and output.

5.1 Homomorphic Batching/Unbatching

Batching is a powerful data encoding technique that is used for processing independent data in parallel. It, when used in homomorphic computing, yields great versatility in the computations and greatly improves performance. Although batching is important in homomorphic computing, existing implementations used batching only to process independent data in parallel. Therefore, these implementations perform batching only before the encryption and after the decryption of the messages as follows. First many independent data is embedded into *message slots*. The message slot contents are then *encoded* into a polynomial representation with the help of the (inverse) Chinese Remainder Theorem (CRT). The encoded message polynomial is then encrypted. Once batched messages are encrytped, then they are processed in independent homomorphic evaluation paths, i.e. evaluation of many AES encryption(by batching) using single polynomial ciphertext. Once the evaluations are completed, the output message polynomial is decrypted and the message slot contents are retrieved using the CRT residue computation.

Here, we want to extend the capabilities of homomorphic encryption by implementing a batching technique homomorphically so that we are able to batch any data on-the-fly. In order to do that, we need a transformation that is capable to bring the message slot contents into the coefficients in the polynomial representation and back while all data is maintained in encrypted form. This homomorphic arithmetic actually is the equivalent of evaluating a CRT and its inverse homomorphically. We define this as homomorphic batching as follows.

Definition 1 (Homomorphic Batching). *The isomorphism* $\mathbb{Z}_p[x]/(\Phi(x)) \cong \mathbb{Z}_p[x]/(x-\zeta) \times \mathbb{Z}_p[x]/(x-\zeta^2) \times \cdots \times \mathbb{Z}_p[x]/(x-\zeta^{N-1})$ *where* $\Phi(x) = \prod(x-\zeta^i)$ *denotes the characteristic polynomial in* $\mathbb{Z}_p$ *of degree* $N-1$ *and* ζ *denotes a primitive* N^{th} *root of unity in* $\mathbb{Z}_p$. *We refer to the homomorphic evaluation of the isomorphism and its inverse as homomorphic unbatching and batching, respectively.*

From a computational perspective, the encoding/decoding operations both amount to the evaluation of a linear transformation on the message slot/polynomial coefficients, respectively. For instance, the message polynomial $m(x)$ is decoded as $\bar{m} = \langle m(\zeta), m(\zeta^2), \ldots, m(\zeta^{N-1})\rangle$. The encoding function may be computed, for example, using Lagrange interpolation. Computations may be expressed as linear transformations as:

$$\mathsf{Decode}(m(x)) = \bar{m} = \mathbf{W}\vec{m} \quad \text{and} \quad \mathsf{Encode}(\bar{m}) = \vec{m} = \mathbf{W}^{-1}\bar{m},$$

which $[\mathbf{W}]_{ij} = \zeta^{ij} \in \mathbb{Z}_p$ and $\vec{m}$ is a vector that holds the coefficients of $m(x)$. The operation appears simple enough since modulo p operations is the natural domain of the homomorphic evaluations and since all we need to compute is constant multiplications by powers of ζ. Typically, when batching in cleartext we compute the encoding and decoding operation with the aid of an Nth root of unity $\zeta \in \mathbb{Z}_p$ via a number theoretical transform (NTT) to gain *FFT speed*, i.e. $\mathcal{O}(N \log(N))$ encoding/decoding performance. However, using cyclotomic polynomials to batch messages bring limitations for us to directly evaluate NTT and achieve *FFT speed*.

Limitations. The batched messages in a polynomial presents independent computation paths. However, when we compute it's linear transformation we need to sum the scaled message slot contents. Thus we need a means to move the message slot contents. We achieve this by using $\Phi(x) = \prod_{i \in [N-1]}(x - \zeta^{b^i})$ where b is a primitive element of $\mathbb{Z}_N^*$ and later by evaluating $m(x^b)$, we rotate the message slot contents. The side-effect of this shift operation on a ciphertext is that the key is altered during the evaluation process:

$$c(x^b) = pg(x^b)s(x^b)f^{-1}(x^b) + pe(x^b) + m(x^b)$$

The ciphertext will still decrypt correctly since $g(x^b)$, $s(x^b)$ and $e(x^b)$ will have small norm. However, to decrypt the ciphertext the key needs to be updated to $f(x^b)$. To restore the original key we may use *key switching*: L.KeySwitch$(c(x^b), \theta)$ where $\theta = \{$L.Encrypt$(w^\tau f(x^b)_\tau)$ for $\tau \in [\log q]\}$. With this approach we can rotate the message slot contents an arbitrary i positions by evaluating the ciphertext polynomial as $c(x^{b^i})$ and then by applying a key switching operation with $f(x^{b^i})$.

Here the problem lies with the selection of cyclotomic polynomial $\Phi(x)$ as the modulus. It gives a decoding matrix $\mathbf{W}$ as:

$$
\begin{bmatrix}
\alpha^0 & \alpha^1 & \alpha^2 & \cdots & \alpha^{N-2} & \alpha^{N-1} \\
\alpha^{2 \cdot 0} & \alpha^{2 \cdot 1} & \alpha^{2 \cdot 2} & \cdots & \alpha^{2 \cdot (N-2)} & \alpha^{2 \cdot (N-1)} \\
\vdots & \vdots & \vdots & \ddots & \vdots & \vdots \\
\alpha^{(N-2) \cdot 0} & \alpha^{(N-2) \cdot 1} & \alpha^{(N-2) \cdot 2} & \cdots & \alpha^{(N-2) \cdot (N-2)} & \alpha^{(N-2) \cdot (N-1)} \\
\alpha^{(N-1) \cdot 0} & \alpha^{(N-1) \cdot 1} & \alpha^{(N-1) \cdot 2} & \cdots & \alpha^{(N-1) \cdot (N-2)} & \alpha^{(N-1) \cdot (N-1)}
\end{bmatrix}
$$

and an encoding matrix $\mathbf{W}^{-1}$ (mod p). The formed matrices $\mathbf{W}$ and $\mathbf{W}^{-1}$ of $\Phi(x)$ are not Vandermonde matrices, therefore we are unable to apply Cooley-Tukey's algorithm. Since we cannot apply the even-odd splitting trick, we are unable to apply fast NTT.

We can solve $\mathbf{W}$ and $\mathbf{W}^{-1}$ not being Vandermonde matrices by switching the cyclotomic polynomial $\Phi(x)$ with $x^N - 1$ which has the following form:

$$x^N - 1 = (x - 1) \cdot \Phi(x) = \prod_{i=0}^{i=N-1} (x - \zeta^i),$$

where N is power of 2. This converts the batching operation to be applicable using Vandermonde matrix multiplication which is suitable for fast NTT using Cooley-Tukey. Although the scheme is suitable for fast NTT, we are not able to rotate the messages as in cyclotomic polynomials. The message in the first slot, i.e. in $(x - \zeta^0)$, never rotates in function $f(x^{b^i})$ for any i.

Homomorphic Batch/Unbatch. With the issues addressed above, we are able to compute homomorphic unbatching by the following equation:

$$\mathsf{L.Unbatch}(c) = \sum_{s \in N} c^{(s)} \cdot \mathsf{Encode}\left((\mathbf{W}^{\mathrm{rot}})^\top[\mathsf{s}]\right).$$

Here $c^{(s)}$ represents the rotated versions of the ciphertext (and message) coefficients by s positions. $\mathbf{W}^{\mathrm{rot}}$ is the transformation matrix where each row index i is rotated by i. The symbol $\top$ represents the transpose of the matrix and $[\mathsf{s}]$ is used for the row index s of the matrix. In case of batching we only replace $\mathbf{W}$ with $\mathbf{W}^{-1}$. The all operation requires only one level of circuit depth for evaluation.

Packing/Unpacking. Packing and unpacking messages in homomorphic encryption is useful for processing the information in parallel by batching/unbatching multi-user information. In multi-user scenarios where we have many users that provides input for a process, we can pack the informations to efficiently process. In word message space we can input N user information into the same chipertext that will provide N times speedup for information processing. In [24] Lauter et al. show how to pack the messages from multiple ciphertexts into one ciphertext. They mention that they cannot present a technique to unpack messages which restricts their computations. After a packing operation the polynomial multiplications rounds and deforms the information because of the polynomial modulus. Our main motivation here was to transfer the message slot contents into the polynomial coefficients and back. However, we achieve unpacking, which is regarded as difficult to achieve, with the aid of homomorphic batching. We may unpack the kth coefficient $c^{(k)} = \mathsf{L.Encrypt}(m_k x^k)$ and $c = \left(\sum_{i \in [N]} m_i x^i\right)$ with the following steps:

- Push coefficients into the message slots $\tilde{c} = \mathsf{L.Unbatch}(c) \in \mathcal{R}$,
- Filter desired coefficient(s) by multiplying with constant cleartext mask $\mu_k(x) = \mathsf{NTT}^{-1}(I_k)$,
- Push message slot contents back into coefficients by homomorphic batching $c^{(k)} = \mathsf{L.Batch}(c\mu_k(x)) \in \mathcal{R}$.

The packing/unpacking operation enables to do *privatization* in the homomorphic encryption. We may easily batch the information for parallel processing and later send the result informations for filtering the results for each users in multi-user scenarios. This prevents the information leaks while returning the results to the users, since we are able to eliminate the results of other users from the ciphertext.

5.2   Homomorphic NTT Using Parallel Batching

There is an alternative and straightforward way to implement homomorphic NTT that is not limited by the issues given in the previous section. We can encrypt each message to be used in the NTT separately: $c_i = hs_i + pe_i + m_i$. Then, we can compute the fast NTT using the Cooley-Tukey algorithm as:

$$C_k = \sum_{j=0}^{N-1} c_j \zeta^{jk} = \underbrace{\sum_{j=0}^{N/2-1} c_{2j} \zeta^{2jk}}_{Even} + \underbrace{\zeta^{jk} \sum_{j=0}^{N/2-1} c_{2j+1} \zeta^{2jk}}_{Odd}$$

where ζ is a primitive N^{th} root of unity modulo p. Since each message is in an independent ciphertext, we can easily divide them into even and odd indicies. This way we can easily compute the fast NTT of the input. However there are two main issues with the scheme that limits the operation:

- The modulo p reduction does not take place until the very end of the decryption step, i.e. L.Decrypt$(c) = \lceil cf \rceil_q \pmod{p}$.
  Therefore, intermediate results will accumulate powers of ζ, which likely will cause a wraparound and decryption failure. One alternative is to aggressively apply noise reduction, e.g. modulus switching, even for the constant multiplications. However, this will increase the evaluation levels significantly. For instance, even a moderate $N = 2^{13}$ would add 13 evaluation levels. To overcome noise accumulation we abandon FFT style evaluation and instead only multiply with precomputed $\mathbf{W}, \mathbf{W^{-1}} \in \mathbb{Z}_p^{(N-1) \times (N-1)}$.
- The number of ciphertexts increase to the number of NTT elements, i.e. N in our case, from a single ciphertext. This increases the ciphertext input size by N times and it is equal to $N^2 \log q$. More than the computational complexity, it increases the I/O transactions of the scheme significantly. Although we have N ciphertexts at the end, we can simply batch them by evaluating:

$$\sum_{i=0}^{i=N-1} C_k \cdot x^i.$$

This solves the issue of having many ciphertexts. However, we are unable to unbatch the values in the equation which limits further processing. We can access the values individually only after a decryption operation.

Although we are not able to batch the dependent elements in a fast NTT operation, we are able to batch N independent fast NTT operations. Basically, we are able to use the empty message slots to evaluate N parallel fast NTT operations. This way we are able to achieve an amortized time that is N times better than the total runtime.

6   Complexity Analysis

Here we discuss the complexity of the two proposed algorithms. In homomorphic batching we need to compute N multiplications of ciphertext with a polynomial formed by the row values of $\mathbf{W}$. Using a large polynomial multiplication algorithm, such as Schönhage-Strassen algorithm, we achieve a run-time complexity of $\mathcal{O}(N \log N \log \log N)$. Furthermore, we have to perform key-switching operations to the ciphertexts to correct the public keys that are corrupted in rotation operation. This is a similar operation to the relinearization, so we can apply the time complexity of relinearization in [10] for key-switching as well. We have N key-switching operations with run-time complexity of $\mathcal{O}(\log{(q)}N \log N \log \log N)$. In total the algorithm has a run-time complexity of $\mathcal{O}(\log{(q)}N^2 \log N \log \log N)$.

In the second algorithm, i.e. homomorphic NTT using parallel batching, we have $\log N$ stages of NTT operations. Each stage N multiplications of a constant with a ciphertext which makes N^2 coefficient multiplications per stage. In total the algorithm has run-time of $\mathcal{O}(N^2 \log N)$.

An important thing to note is that the complexity analysis takes into account only the number of coefficient multiplications. It does not include the run-time complexity of the coefficient multiplications. In the first case we have small and fix size coefficients which gives an advantage in real time applications against the second method. The second method has larger coefficients because of the leveled implementation. Thus it takes longer time to process the second method even though the run-time complexity of the method is smaller in terms of number of coefficient multiplications.

7 Implementation Results

We implemented the algorithms using a leveled LTV scheme using Shoup's NTL library version 9.0 [25] compiled with the GMP 5.1.3 package. For parameter selection we utilized the two Hermite factor analysis using the formula in [22], i.e. $1.8/\log \delta - 110$. The security level of the experiments varies on the settings, but each setting has at least 100-bit security.

In the homomorphic NTT using homomorphic batching we use special cyclotomic polynomial $\Phi_m(x)$, where we set m as a prime number to have $\Phi_m(x) = x^0 + x^1 + x^2 + \cdots + x^N$, to perform faster modular reduction. The results are summarized in Table 1. In the algorithm we have one constant polynomial multiplication and N additions, so our prime modulus q does not grow too large. The values of N are chosen to be close to as powers of two, i.e. 2048, 4096, 8192. The message slots are used for the same NTT operation so there is no amortized time.

Table 1. Timings for homomorphic batching/unbatching operation.

N	$\log q$	Security (in bits)	Total time (in minutes)
2080	64	140	2.5
4252	64	400	10.7
8782	64	943	43

In the second case, we compute homomorphic NTT by using parallel batching. We choose the polynomial degree $N = 16384$ and modulus bitsize $\log q = 512$ which are slightly higher values compared to the first algorithm. The reason behind this is that we need to handle the noise in stages, so the modulus q grows significantly. Our implementation achieves a runtime of 108 minutes. Since we are able to batch N independent homomorphic NTT computation, we achieve 0.4 second of amortized time.

8 Conclusion

To improve the versatility of homomorphic encryption applications, we tackled another challenging problem, i.e. the problem of moving data in encrypted form from the message slots into the message polynomial coefficients and back. We called this operation homomorphic batching/unbatching. Via homomorphic batching one can extract coefficients and achieve unpacking operations easily. In addition, the batching operation enabled via a homomorphic NTT operation, which will be of interest for numerous signal processing applications.

References

1. Bos, J.W., Lauter, K., Naehrig, M.: Private predictive analysis on encrypted medical data. Technical report MSR-TR-2013-81 (2013). http://research.microsoft.com/apps/pubs/default.aspx?id=200652
2. Brakerski, Z.: Fully homomorphic encryption without modulus switching from classical gapSVP. IACR Cryptology ePrint Archive 2012/78 (2012)
3. Brakerski, Z., Gentry, C., Vaikuntanathan, V.: (Leveled) fully homomorphic encryption without bootstrapping. In: Proceedings of the 3rd Innovations inTheoretical Computer Science Conference, pp. 309–325. ACM (2012)
4. Brakerski, Z., Vaikuntanathan, V.: Fully homomorphic encryption from ring-LWE and security for key dependent messages. In: Rogaway, P. (ed.) CRYPTO 2011. LNCS, vol. 6841, pp. 505–524. Springer, Heidelberg (2011)
5. Brakerski, Z., Vaikuntanathan, V.: Efficient fully homomorphic encryption from (standard) LWE. SIAM J. Comput. 43(2), 831–871 (2014)
6. Cheon Jung, H., Miran, K., Kristin, L.: Secure DNA-sequence analysis on encrypted DNA nucleotides (2014). http://media.eurekalert.org/aaasnewsroom/MCM/FIL_000000001439/EncryptedSW.pdf
7. Dai, W., Doröz, Y., Sunar, B.: Accelerating NTRU based homomorphic encryption using GPUs. In: 2014 IEEE High Performance Extreme Computing Conference (HPEC), pp. 1–6 (2014)
8. Dai, W., Sunar, B.: cuHE: a homomorphic encryption accelerator library. In: Pasalic, E., et al. (eds.) BalkanCryptSec 2015. LNCS, vol. 9540, pp. 169–186. Springer, Heidelberg (2016). doi:10.1007/978-3-319-29172-7_11
9. van Dijk, M., Gentry, C., Halevi, S., Vaikuntanathan, V.: Fully homomorphic encryption over the integers. In: Gilbert, H. (ed.) EUROCRYPT 2010. LNCS, vol. 6110, pp. 24–43. Springer, Heidelberg (2010)
10. Doröz, Y., Hu, Y., Sunar, B.: Homomorphic AES evaluation using the modified LTV scheme. Des. Codes Cryptogr. 80, 1–26 (2015)

11. Doröz, Y., Shahverdi, A., Eisenbarth, T., Sunar, B.: Toward practical homomorphic evaluation of block ciphers using prince. In: Böhme, R., Brenner, M., Moore, T., Smith, M. (eds.) FC 2014 Workshops. LNCS, vol. 8438, pp. 208–220. Springer, Heidelberg (2014)
12. Gentry, C.: A Fully Homomorphic Encryption Scheme. Ph.D. thesis, Stanford University (2009)
13. Gentry, C.: Fully homomorphic encryption using ideal lattices In: Proceedings of the Forty-First Annual ACM Symposium on Theory of Computing, STOC 2009, pp. 169–178. ACM (2009)
14. Gentry, C., Halevi, S.: Fully homomorphic encryption without squashing using depth-3 arithmetic circuits. IACR Cryptology ePrint Archive 2011/279 (2011)
15. Gentry, C., Halevi, S.: Implementing Gentry's fully-homomorphic encryption scheme. In: Paterson, K.G. (ed.) EUROCRYPT 2011. LNCS, vol. 6632, pp. 129–148. Springer, Heidelberg (2011)
16. Gentry, C., Halevi, S., Smart, N.P.: Homomorphic evaluation of the AES circuit. IACR Cryptology ePrint Archive 2012 (2012)
17. Dai, W., Sunar, B.: cuHE: a homomorphic encryption accelerator library. In: Pasalic, E., et al. (eds.) BalkanCryptSec 2015. LNCS, vol. 9540, pp. 169–186. Springer, Heidelberg (2016). doi:10.1007/978-3-319-29172-7_11
18. Graepel, T., Lauter, K., Naehrig, M.: ML confidential: machine learning on encrypted data. In: Lee, M.-K., Kwon, D., Kwon, T. (eds.) ICISC 2012. LNCS, vol. 7839, pp. 1–21. Springer, Heidelberg (2013)
19. Halevi, S., Shoup, V.: HElib, homomorphic encryption library. Internet Source (2012)
20. Lagendijk, R., Erkin, Z., Barni, M.: Encrypted signal processing for privacy protection: conveying the utility of homomorphic encryption and multiparty computation. IEEE Signal Process. Mag. **30**(1), 82–105 (2013)
21. Lauter, K., López-Alt, A., Naehrig, M.: Private computation on encrypted genomic data. In: Aranha, D.F., Menezes, A. (eds.) LATINCRYPT 2014. LNCS, vol. 8895, pp. 3–27. Springer, Heidelberg (2015)
22. Lindner, R., Peikert, C.: Better key sizes (and attacks) for LWE-based encryption. In: Kiayias, A. (ed.) CT-RSA 2011. LNCS, vol. 6558, pp. 319–339. Springer, Heidelberg (2011)
23. López-Alt, A., Tromer, E., Vaikuntanathan, V.: On-the-flymultiparty computation on the cloud via multikey fully homomorphic encryption. In: Proceedings of the Forty-Fourth Annual ACM Symposium on Theory of Computing STOC 2012, pp. 1219–1234. ACM (2012)
24. Naehrig, M., Lauter, K., Vaikuntanathan, V.: Can homomorphic encryption bepractical? In: Proceedings of the 3rd ACM Workshop on Cloud ComputingSecurity Workshop, CCSW 2011, pp. 113–124. ACM (2011)
25. Shoup, V.: NTL: A library for doing number theory (2001). http://www.shoup.net/ntl/
26. Smart, N.P., Vercauteren, F.: Fully homomorphic SIMD operations. Des. Codes Cryptogr. **71**(1), 57–81 (2014)
27. Stehlé, D., Steinfeld, R.: Making NTRU as secure as worst-case problems over ideal lattices. In: Paterson, K.G. (ed.) EUROCRYPT 2011. LNCS, vol. 6632, pp. 27–47. Springer, Heidelberg (2011)

Using Intel Software Guard Extensions for Efficient Two-Party Secure Function Evaluation

Debayan Gupta[1], Benjamin Mood[2], Joan Feigenbaum[1(✉)], Kevin Butler[2], and Patrick Traynor[2]

[1] Yale University, New Haven, CT 06520, USA
{debayan.gupta,joan.feigenbaum}@yale.edu
[2] University of Florida, Gainesville, FL 32611, USA
bmood@ufl.edu, {butler,traynor}@cise.ufl.edu

Abstract. Recent developments have made two-party secure function evaluation (2P-SFE) vastly more efficient. However, because they make extensive use of cryptographic operations, these protocols remain too slow for practical use by most applications. The introduction of Intel's Software Guard Extensions (SGX), which provide an environment for the isolated execution of code and handling of data, offers an opportunity to overcome such performance concerns. In this paper, we explore the challenges of using SGX to achieve security guarantees similar to those found in traditional 2P-SFE systems. After demonstrating a number of critical concerns, we develop two protocols for secure computation in the semi-honest model on this platform: one in which both parties are SGX-enabled and a second in which only one party has direct access to this hardware. We then show how these protocols can be made secure in the malicious model. We conclude that implementing 2P-SFE on SGX-enabled devices can render it practical for a wide range of applications.

1 Introduction

Secure Function Evaluation (SFE) is a powerful way to protect sensitive data. Made possible by a range of cryptographic primitives, SFE allows multiple parties to compute the output of a function without revealing the potentially sensitive inputs of any individual party. In this paper, we focus on the case of two-party secure function evaluation (2P-SFE). While both the performance of and the security provided by these underlying primitives have improved dramatically over the past decade [8,16,24,26,28,32,43], the expense of using 2P-SFE remains too high for most practical applications.

An emerging hardware primitive may help to reduce the cost of such computation substantially. Intel's Software Guard Extensions (SGX) [1,25] provide a module within upcoming chipsets that allow for the creation of secure containers called "enclaves." These hardware-enforced sandboxes allow for code and data to be executed without the influence of code running in the traditional registers of the processor. In addition, an SGX system can use hardware-based attestation

© International Financial Cryptography Association 2016
J. Clark et al. (Eds.): FC 2016 Workshops, LNCS 9604, pp. 302–318, 2016.
DOI: 10.1007/978-3-662-53357-4_20

to prove that an enclave performs the operations as claimed. While not necessarily appropriate for all scenarios, this set of capabilities may help to support the use of fast and strong 2P-SFE in a wide range of practical applications.

In this paper, we perform the first analysis of SGX as a platform on which to implement 2P-SFE. Beginning with a tutorial example, we show why the naive execution of functions within SGX fails to provide the strong properties necessary to prevent significant leakage. From this observation, we then make the following contributions:

- We show how to augment an SGX system to provide stronger guarantees against leakage and provide a protocol that enables two SGX systems to perform 2P-SFE more efficiently than a pure garbled-circuits implementation. We refer to this approach as *SGX-supported 2P-SFE*. We then provide a protocol for securely outsourcing the SGX-supported 2P-SFE computation from a resource constrained device (*i.e.*, one without an SGX module) to an SGX-compliant device (*i.e.*, another device that has an SGX module). This allows us to take advantage of a remote SGX hardware unit without requiring universal deployment.
- We show how to modify 2P-SFE protocols secure against semi-honest adversaries so that, when run on augmented SGX machines, they are secure against malicious adversaries.
- We describe a number of novel use cases for SGX with our augmentations.

The rest of the paper is organized as follows: Sect. 2 provides background on 2P-SFE and SGX. Section 3 explains problems that arise in straightforward attempts to use SGX for 2P-SFE. Section 4 describes how to augment SGX so that it can be used to implement 2P-SFE, a secure-outsourcing protocol for non-SGX machines, and how 2P-SFE and SGX can be used efficiently in conjunction to provide better security. Section 5 discusses previous work on secure-execution environments, and Sect. 6 provides conclusions and open questions.

2 Technical Background

We begin with a brief overview of garbled-circuit 2P-SFE and SGX. We use this as a point of departure for our investigation of SGX-based protocols for 2P-SFE and why they are harder to design than one might imagine at first glance.

2.1 Garbled Circuits for Two-Party, Secure Function Evaluation

In a garbled-circuit protocol, two parties with private inputs jointly compute a function represented as a Boolean circuit. Both parties receive outputs – the scenario described in Sect. 1, which has a single output y for both parties, is a special case; in general, the protocol may deliver different outputs to each party. First, a compiler [32,37] is used to convert the function into a Boolean circuit. One of the parties, the *generator*, encrypts, or *garbles* the Boolean circuit.

He then sends it to the *evaluator*, who evaluates the garbled circuit without learning any information about the generator's inputs, intermediate values (*i.e.*, those computed by non-output gates of the circuit), or the generator's output. Finally, the evaluator sends the generator's (encrypted) output back to him.

Each gate in a Boolean circuit can be evaluated using its truth table to get the output corresponding to the input values. Likewise, a garbled circuit is made up of many garbled gates, and each gate is evaluated in turn. A garbled gate's output entry in the truth table is encrypted under a unique combination of the two inputs: $TT_{i,j} = Enc(X_i, Y_j) \oplus Out_{i,j}$, where $TT_{i,j}$ is the truth-table entry created by the ith value of wire X and the jth value of wire Y, and $Out_{i,j}$ is the corresponding unencrypted output value. The truth-table entries are permuted so that the position of the (only) decryptable entry does not leak the underlying Boolean value. Once the evaluator receives the garbled gates and the input values, she finds the correct garbled output by trying to decrypt each truth-table entry or by using the point-and-permute optimization [32].

There are two basic types of adversaries in the garbled-circuit literature: semi-honest and malicious adversaries; each captures a basic threat model. (There exist others, such as the covert model, but we do not discuss them here.) Semi-honest adversaries faithfully follow the protocol but attempt to gain information by observing all transmitted messages. Malicious adversaries, on the other hand, may behave in any arbitrarily manner in an attempt to gain information about another party's input or output, to corrupt the computation (*i.e.*, to cause incorrect outputs), or to block the protocol execution from completing.

To achieve security against malicious adversaries, the computation must be performed N times in order to prevent the generator from creating an incorrect circuit. The security parameter N sets the upper bound on an adversary's successfully cheating at $\frac{1}{2^N}$. There must be mechanisms to ensure that the same inputs are used each time and a way to ensure the evaluator does not corrupt the generator's output. These are solved problems in the garbled-circuit literature.

2P-SFE and garbled circuits were introduced in the seminal paper of Yao [50], and the area has since been studied extensively by the cryptography community. One very notable achievement was the creation of the first general-purpose 2P-SFE platform, Fairplay [32]. Today, many 2P-SFE platforms exist [8,16,24,26, 28,31,36,43], and their performance is improving. Such platforms have been used for scenarios as varied as those of farmers conducting beet-root auctions [7], inter-domain routing [23], governments reporting aggregated salary data [6], and database policy compliance [14]. For a detailed explanation of many essential garbled-circuit techniques, see Kreuter *et al.* [28] and Perry *et al.* [40].

2.2   Intel's Software Guard Extensions Module

The Software Guard extensions (SGX) module allows parts of programs to be executed inside of separate segments of the CPU called *enclaves*. This is a general-purpose module (unlike, say, a DRM module). SGX provides a hardware-based guarantee that the programs and memory inside an enclave cannot be read or modified from outside of the enclave (including by a program in a different enclave). In particular, neither `root` nor any other type of special-access program can read or modify the memory inside an enclave. Technically, the data inside of an enclave are still within the same registers and cache as other programs; however, SGX processors provide functionality to prevent unauthorized access.

An adversary should not be able to determine what is accessed inside of the enclave or what is written back to RAM when the cache is full. Therefore, any data in the enclave that must be written back to main memory is encrypted and signed so that it cannot be read or modified by another program. Modifications of code, data, or stack outside an enclave cannot interfere with the operation of the enclave except in one way: If something needed by a program in the enclave is simply unavailable or has been corrupted, then the program may have to abort.

Comprehensive overviews of SGX can be found in Intel's whitepapers [1,25]. Design of systems and protocols that make extensive use of SGX is covered by, e.g., Baumann et al. [5] and Schuster et al. [42].

2.3 Towards Using Secure Hardware for Garbled-Circuit Protocols

Both garbled circuits and SGX are designed for scenarios in which parties have private input data for a computation in which they want to receive the result of the computation while no one else learns either the input or the result. Therefore, it is natural to consider using SGX-enabled machines to execute a garbled-circuit protocol. The reason that it is not straightforward to do so is that garbled circuits and SGX use different techniques to protect private inputs.

In garbled-circuit protocols (and SFE more generally), cryptographic guarantees are used to ensure the privacy of the data. In SGX, users rely on secure hardware to guarantee data privacy. SGX provides security against malicious adversaries as long as one trusts Intel's setup process. In the SFE world, this is comparable to having a trusted setup, on top of which one runs one's protocol (here, part of the "setup" occurs at the Intel factory when the hardware and private key are created). The security properties of the exact model used by SGX are described in Intel's whitepapers [1,25].

3   Why Simple "Solutions" Do Not Quite Work

The security guarantees provided by SGX do not immediately translate into being able to perform 2P-SFE protocols in general or even garbled-circuit protocols in particular. Simple solutions that use unmodified SGX primitives may leak information or, in some cases, undermine the security of other code running under SGX. In this section, we explain how that can happen.

3.1   A Simple 2P-SFE Protocol Implemented with SGX

Below, we describe a naive, straw-man protocol for performing SGX-supported 2P-SFE. There exist numerous ways of doing this, but almost all of them suffer from a number of problems that we discuss in the next subsection.

Setup: We start with the standard 2P-SFE setup – two mutually distrustful parties with private inputs who wish to jointly compute a function and produce private results. In this scenario, both parties have SGX-enabled machines and have agreed to run a specific program. The two parties are as follows: the *evaluator*, who will use his SGX module to evaluate the program, and the *sender*, who will check the agreed-upon program and then send her input. In the following, a superscripted "+" denotes a public key, while a superscripted "−" denotes a private key that does not leave the SGX enclave.

Protocol

1. The sender ensures the evaluator will evaluate the correct program, $prog_{sgx}$, by checking the signed measurement, $Ecv^{eval}_{measure}$, from the evaluator's enclave. $Ecv^{eval}_{measure}$ is signed by the evaluator enclave's private key $Ecv^{-}_{key_{eval}}$.
2. The sender encrypts her input, $input_{sender}$, under the evaluator enclave's public key, $Ecv^{+}_{key_{eval}}$, and sends it to the evaluator.
3. The sender's encrypted input, $Enc(input_{sender})$ is decrypted inside of the evaluator's enclave using $Ecv^{-}_{key_{eval}}$.
4. The evaluator enters his own input, $input_{eval}$ into the enclave.
5. The enclave puts $input_{sender}$ and $input_{eval}$ into the SGX program, $prog_{sgx}$. It then executes $prog_{sgx}$ and encrypts the sender's output, $output_{sender}$, under the sender enclave's public key, $Ecv^{+}_{key_{send}}$.
6. The evaluator's enclave releases the evaluator's output to him and sends the sender's encrypted output, $Enc(output_{sender})$, to the sender.
7. The sender decrypts $Enc(output_{sender})$ using $Ecv^{-}_{key_{send}}$.

3.2 Problems with Simple SGX-Supported 2P-SFE

Side Channels

1. **Runtime:** 2P-SFE protocols are not directly vulnerable to timing attacks. This is achieved by ensuring all program paths take equal time, at the cost of efficiency. In SGX-supported 2P-SFE, if a secret value x determines the number of times, for instance, a loop is executed, the timing could easily narrow the range of x. Principally, an attacker could execute the same program offline with many different iterations of the same loop inside of the enclave to see how long several different numbers of iterations take. This may provide a lot of information if each iteration of the loop is easily identifiable, *e.g.*, if each iteration takes a second to execute.

2. **RAM Access:** Data access is not hidden in SGX-supported 2P-SFE, which can potentially leak significant amounts of data. For example, consider a simple database-style query using a binary search, where one side, the client, sends a private query to check whether a given value exists within the database. The enclave on the server reads in the plaintext records and matches them, one by one, to the queried value. In such a scenario, the data access alone is enough to leak information about the queried value. (If the query matches, we have the value itself, and, if not, we know that the value lies

within a certain range.) There exist some methods to add hardware-level cryptographic support to FPGAs [45], but not for RAM. The best ways to make RAM secure are still Oblivious RAM and similar techniques [19].

3. **RAM Timing:** A timing attack could reveal a lot of information about the item being queried in the binary search. If the item is located on the first jump, we know that it's the value in the middle, etc.

Cryptography vs Memory Out of Bounds. Garbled circuits rely on cryptography for data privacy; information leakage is not an issue, because we have proofs of correctness and security. While it is theoretically possible to "leak" data by simply outputting it in the predefined program, such a blatant problem is easy to notice. SGX, if used improperly, might leak information if memory goes out of bounds; this is one of the most common bugs in everyday programming [42] and can have catastrophic consequences [13,48]. Unfortunately, in SGX, such an error would not only break the security of the program (and enclave) in question but would also affect the security of SGX as a whole, because users might be able to access or modify data that they should not be able to see.

Trusting SGX vs Trusting Cryptography. SGX requires the users to trust that the evaluator of the program has not broken into the enclave to watch the memory and that the supply chain was not disrupted with insecure parts. These might not be acceptable assumptions for nation states or large companies. In contrast, 2P-SFE protocols provide cryptographic guarantees. They prove themselves equivalent to the "ideal model," which uses a trusted third party. SGX uses the trusted platform model, which is weaker than the trusted third party model and allows side-channel and information flow attacks.

SGX requires us to have trust in hardware and standard cryptographic primitives (which are used by SGX to protect data), while a 2P-SFE protocol needs only the latter. Moving the "trust" from software to hardware presents additional problems – the authors are unaware of any techniques that could be used to sign and verify hardware. Given recent reports of nation states' actively infiltrating hardware vendors at massive scales for bulk data collection, this is a major problem. Ultimately, the trust in SGX boils down to trust in hardware suppliers and whether or not the hardware can be opened and the CPU read.

4   Using SGX for 2P-SFE Computations

Having outlined the capabilities and limitations of SGX-supported 2P-SFE, we now present our solutions to the problems faced when trying to use SGX for 2P-SFE protocols. Throughout this section, because of space limitations, we present only short, intuitive sketches of correctness and security proofs; complete proofs will appear in a future, expanded version of the paper.

4.1   Using SGX for 2P-SFE: Problems and Solutions

Our solution is to augment the SGX programs to prevent (or reduce) data leakage in SGX for 2P-SFE computations. These augmentations are described below.

Timing Side Channel: We must ensure that all code paths take approximately the same amount of time. There are many such obfuscation-based palliative mechanisms, as well as general mitigation strategies [33]. However, these problems are more complex in some scenarios – e.g., when a secret variable determines how many times a loop executes. In this case, the time the program takes can reveal information about the value of the secret variable. It is possible to prevent any secret values from being revealed by having a fixed loop bound, but this may not always be preferable. We can limit the amount of information leaked when executing a loop by including N extra loop iterations, where N is a pseudo-random number based on secret information from both parties. Using this technique, neither party learns the number of iterations executed.

Memory Side Channel: We must ensure that all memory that can be touched by the SGX program is touched exactly once at the beginning of the program. Once the SGX program touches a piece of plaintext memory, the memory should not be read again unless the read is not dependent on secret information. If the read is dependent on secret information, the evaluator may be able to learn something about the secret [17,38]. However, if we need too much data and some are encrypted and stored outside of the enclave, there might be a correlation between when a block of memory is read and when a block of encrypted memory is sent back to RAM; for example, if a binary-search program that runs inside an enclave reads one element at a time, mere observation yields the secret query (within a range, if it is missing). In order to prevent this problem, we must ensure that a *mix* operation is performed to remove any correlation between plaintext memory and encrypted memory; e.g., this would occur if the memory were placed outside of the enclave in the same order as it was entered. Such mix operations, which continuously shuffle and re-encrypt data as they are accessed, already exist and are widely used to implement Oblivious RAM [19,46].

Array Out of Bounds: To mitigate the risk of arrays out of bounds in SGX, we apply safe memory-access techniques to ensure that memory does not go out of bounds. SGX programs can use bound-checking data structures or memory-safe languages [42]. Although such techniques slow down the execution time of the application, both of the aforementioned methods would still be significantly faster than executing the programs in a 2P-SFE protocol.

Cost of a 2P-SFE Protocol vs SGX: In Table 1, we note the expected cost of normal 2P-SFE using garbled circuits and SGX-supported 2P-SFE. We examine the costs of setup, input, the operation itself, data access, and memory access. As shown in the table, the primary reason for the expected improvement in the speed of SGX-supported 2P-SFE over a garbled-circuit protocol is the amount of cryptography required for each operation and data access in 2P-SFE (which is free in SGX). However, unlike garbled-circuit protocols, SGX encounters a cost to push memory out of the cache to RAM (*Non-Cache Access*).

Table 1. Cost (in terms of cryptography) for operations in 2P-SFE and SGX-supported 2P-SFE. "-" means there is no cryptography required. N is length of input. C is length of the circuit/program. K is the bit-security parameter. S is the stat parameter (number of circuits in 2P-SFE). ^{a} - per gate for 2P-SFE and per processor instruction for SGX-supported 2P-SFE. ^{b} - the cost of saving and loading a value to or from main memory for SGX. $^+$ - assumes we attained a symmetric key during the setup phase and used it to encrypt the input.

	2P-SFE$_{Semi}$		2P-SFE$_{Malicious}$		SGX	
	Sym	Asym	Sym	Asym	Sym	Asym
Setup	-	-	-	-	$O(1)$	$O(1)$
Input	$O(N)$	$O(K)$	$O(N*S)$	$O(K*S)$	$O(N)^+$	-
Per operation^a	$O(1)$	-	$O(S)$	-	-	-
Data (array) access	$O(N)$	-	$O(N*S)$	-	-	-
Non-cache access^b	-	-	-	-	$O(1)$	-

4.2 Half and Half

With the techniques above, 2P-SFE protocols and SGX can be used together in scenarios in which parties trust each other enough to want to cooperate in the first place but not enough to release private data or blindly trust the other parties not to cheat [29]. However, when different groups of parties want to perform a secure computation together, a user may trust one group over another; the different guarantees and characteristics of SGX-supported 2P-SFE and current 2P-SFE protocols mean that it might make sense to use one technique for a certain group but not another. We now consider how to perform a secure computation using current 2P-SFE protocols for one part of the evaluation and SGX-supported 2P-SFE for another part.

We start with two companies, A and B (as shown in Fig. 1), that want to perform a secure computation involving nodes both inside and outside their private networks. Parts of the computation are done inside of each company,

Fig. 1. Half and Half. In this usage, we convert SGX-supported 2P-SFE values to standard 2P-SFE values and back in order to take advantage of the speed of the combined form when the trust model is acceptable and still allow for a stronger model when the trust model of SGX-supported 2P-SFE is not acceptable (say, the user does not trust Intel when using a public network).

while others require A and B to cooperate. Thus, companies could use the trust model of SGX when within their own networks and 2P-SFE when they want cryptographic guarantees instead of assuming that the hardware remains secure.

To perform such hierarchical or "mixed" SGX computations, users need to know how to convert a value from a 2P-SFE protocol to an SGX-supported 2P-SFE value and vice-versa. Once we know how to perform these transformations, we can run "mixtures" of 2P-SFE protocols and SGX. For simplicity, we deal with the semi-honest setting, although we note there are ways to do the same conversions in the malicious setting. For the purposes of this short protocol, the evaluator is the evaluator in both 2P-SFE and SGX-supported 2P-SFE. The generator is the generator for 2P-SFE and the sender in SGX-supported 2P-SFE.

Before we briefly describe the conversion process, we describe garbled circuits in more detail. During the evaluation of the garbled circuit, each wire holds an encrypted value. The generator knows the possible encrypted values (that is, which values represent 0 and 1) but does not know which value is actually on the wire (the value the evaluator has). The evaluator knows the encrypted value on each wire value but does not know what any value represents.

Conversion from Garbled Circuit to SGX:

1. For each garbled wire w_i we will convert to an SGX value, the evaluator has w_i^r (the encrypted result), and the generator has w_i^0 and w_i^1 (the encrypted values that represent 0 and 1).
2. The generator enters w_i^0 and w_i^1 into $prog_{sgx}$ (the SGX program) as input.
3. The evaluator enters in w_i^r into $prog_{sgx}$ as her input.
4. $prog_{sgx}$ calculates whether w_i^r is w_i^0 or w_i^1 and sets the corresponding input, b_i, to match w_i^r.
5. $prog_{sgx}$ uses each b_i as input.

Conversion from SGX to Garbled Circuit:

1. For each bit b_i that will be converted into a garbled value w_i, the generator creates both possible garbled values, w_i^0 and w_i^1, that will represent the two possible values of b and enters them into $prog_{sgx}$.
2. $prog_{sgx}$, based on whether b_i is a 0 or 1, selects either w_i^0 or w_i^1 to be w_i^r.
3. Each w_i^r is sent to the evaluator to be used as input to the garbled circuit.
4. The generator uses his values, w_i^0 and w_i^1, in the creation of the garbled circuit to ensure w_i^r will map to a value.

Security: In order for either the generator or the evaluator to learn additional information, it has to (1) possess either w_i^0 or w_i^1 and possess w_i^r, or (2) see b_i outside of the enclave. Since b_i only exists inside of the enclave, it will not be seen by either the generator or evaluator. The generator only ever sees w_i^0 and w_i^1 and never sees w_i^r. Likewise, the evaluator only sees w_i^r and never sees w_i^0 or w_i^1. Thus, neither party will learn any additional information.

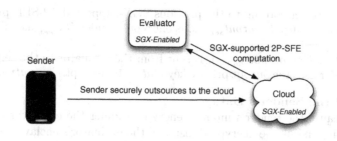

Fig. 2. Outsourcing. Shows the different parties in our outsourcing protocol.

4.3   Outsourcing

For devices that do not have an SGX module (or are slow), it would be useful to have the ability to securely outsource computation to a more powerful or better equipped system. There have already been a number of works addressing this situation in 2P-SFE [9–12, 35]. In this section, we examine how we can outsource from a constrained device (that does not possess an SGX module) when we want to perform SGX-supported 2P-SFE.

In our setup, seen in Fig. 2, the sender does not have an SGX unit and is outsourcing to a server, the cloud, that has an SGX unit. Any outsourcing protocol must guarantee that (1) the party we are outsourcing to (the cloud) cannot cheat, and (2) the party that performs the SGX execution (the other party in the original SGX-supported 2P-SFE computation, the evaluator) cannot cheat.

We assume that we are trying to protect the input and output of the sender; we also assume that the cloud and evaluator do not collude, *i.e.*, they are not working together to corrupt the sender's output or input. As before, superscripted "+" and "−" signs denote public and private keys, respectively.

Protocol

1. The cloud and evaluator perform the standard SGX setup to initialize their SGX units and confirm that they are running the desired program.
2. Both parties pass enclave public keys, $Ecv^{+}_{key_{cloud}}$ and $Ecv^{+}_{key_{eval}}$ to the sender and authenticate by using MRSIGNER [1, 25].
3. Both the evaluator and cloud enclaves send to the sender their enclave measurements, $Ecv^{cloud}_{measure}$ and $Ecv^{eval}_{measure}$.
4. The sender checks that $Ecv^{cloud}_{measure}$ and $Ecv^{eval}_{measure}$ are correct.
5. The sender encrypts its input, $input_{sender}$, and a public key for its output, Out^{+}_{key}, under $Ecv^{+}_{key_{eval}}$ to create $Enc(input_{sender}||Out^{+}_{key})$ and sends it to the cloud.
6. The cloud enters $Enc(input_{sender}||Out^{+}_{key})$ into the SGX program, $prog_{sgx}$. *We note here that there is no reason the cloud cannot also provide input to the program if desired.*
7. The input is sent from the cloud to the evaluator.

8. $prog_{sgx}$ is run according to the previous SGX-supported 2P-SFE protocol.
9. The sender's output, $output_{sender}$, is encrypted under Out_{key}^{+} as a final step in $prog_{sgx}$.
10. This value, $Enc(output_{sender})$, is sent from the evaluator to the sender.
11. The sender uses the output private key Out_{key}^{-} to decrypt $Enc(output_{sender})$.

Security of the Sender's Data

Input: Because the sender's input is encrypted under the evaluator's enclave private key, it can only be decrypted inside of the evaluator's enclave. Given the measurement of the evaluator's enclave, we also know that the program inside of the enclave is correct; so it will not pass the input outside the enclave.

Output: Because the sender's output is encrypted inside the enclave during evaluation and is only sent outside when it is encrypted under the sender's public key, only the sender can decrypt and read this output.

4.4 Improving the Security of 2P-SFE Protocols Using SGX

Semi-honest or honest-but-curious protocols guarantee security as long as all parties faithfully follow the protocol. Such protocols are much cheaper in terms of computational cost than those that protect against malicious adversaries, who attempt to gain additional information by any means necessary. We can use SGX for parts of the semi-honest 2P-SFE protocol to gain additional security guarantees without incurring significant overhead.

First, we replace the OT in the 2P-SFE protocol with an SGX component that acts like an OT. The SGX OT is a stripped-down version of the previously described SGX-supported 2P-SFE protocol. In this program, the 2P-SFE evaluator chooses the encrypted form of the input as in the 2P-SFE protocol. This immediately gives us greater security than the standard semi-honest OT, because we are not relying on the parties to behave correctly during the OT (*i.e.*, the SGX unit checks whether the parties are running the correct "OT" program). Note that this does not guarantee fair release of the result, because a malicious party can still cause us to abort at any point.

Similarly, we can replace the circuit generation and evaluation with an SGX component. This SGX-evaluation is the program-evaluation component described earlier. While we could use the 2P-SFE OT before this part of the protocol, using the SGX OT component gives us better security. After the input and circuit-evaluation components are replaced, we can also replace the output component with the SGX output protocol. Replacing all of these elements leaves us with a protocol that is significantly more secure than the original semi-honest 2P-SFE protocol (because the SGX protocol has checks for when a user is malicious), while remaining much cheaper than a malicious 2P-SFE protocol.

4.5 Universal Programs (Circuits)

A *universal circuit* (UC) is a program that takes another program as input (denoted as UC_{prog}) and then executes it. In a UC for two parties, one party enters UC_{prog} as input while the other party enters the input for UC_{prog}.

However, in 2P-SFE, a UC requires a massive number of array accesses because of the nature of oblivious data access. For each operation in UC_{prog} (e.g., $data[a] = data[b] + data[c]$), the inputs to the operation (i.e., $data[b]$ and $data[c]$) have to be found from all the possible values that could be entered into the instructions – i.e.. this requires a set of if statements to check whether index value v equals b – unless constraints can be added to UC_{prog}. However, in SGX-supported 2P-SFE, this would be more efficient, because array access takes $O(1)$. Thus, UC programs can be efficiently and privately executed in an enclave.

4.6   Novel Use Cases for SGX

Secure Data Storage: With the advent of cloud and multi-user systems, unauthorized data access is a greater problem than ever before. Our idea is to use SGX as a gatekeeper: If all reads and writes went through the SGX hardware, we could automatically encrypt and decrypt it based on a user-entered key without the need for a specialized drive. A keyboard could enter the enclave password while skipping the operating system and any keyloggers within. Unlike systems such as BitLocker [18], the key here would remain safe even if the operating system were compromised. For cloud storage, the SGX program would encrypt data before they are sent to the cloud server; it could be implemented so as to be transparent to the end user and obviate the need to trust cloud companies.

User Authentication: SGX offers many new avenues for user authentication. It includes MRSIGNER, which signs the enclave before it is deployed. Group authentication is also possible, using EPID (Enhanced Privacy ID) [1], an extension to the Direct Anonymous attestation scheme used in [21,22]. This allows an enclave to sign communications while maintaining privacy within a group.

There is also a "pseudonymous" mode, which relaxes the security slightly, allowing the verifier to know whether it has checked an enclave in the past while still maintaining intra-group anonymity.

Cyber-Physical Applications: Given the security concerns involved in control systems for sensitive infrastructure (e.g., a nuclear power plant or a hydroelectric dam), improving security is highly desirable. In order to prevent attacks on such systems, the controls could be made accessible only through an enclave that would require all orders to the system to be signed; the current state of the system would also be hidden. Periodic signed updates from the enclave to a "master" control system would prevent the system from being taken offline without the knowledge of the master control system. These strategies would mitigate the threat of hackers breaking into the system and altering code or stealing passwords – this information would exist only inside of the enclaves.

Online Games: Online games are played by multiple users on different machines. In order to reduce bandwidth, many games only transfer events, e.g., information for each user command. Each machine can then process events independently but at the cost of each machine's knowing the entirety of the game's data, including sensitive information about other players' positions. SGX could be used to protect private data from other gamers. If each gamer's private data are inside an enclave, a hacker (or any user who uses a tool to read information normally not available to him) is denied access to private information. The enclave would release such private information to the local machine based on triggers in the code, *e.g.*, when an enemy unit is nearby. We can periodically verify the state of each enclave to prevent cheating.

5   Previous Work on Secure-Execution Environments

In this section, we briefly discuss previous work on the use of specialized software and hardware platforms to enable secure execution of code. None of these works provides the same guarantees or addresses the same scenarios as a 2P-SFE protocol. Various levels of code and data protection have been achieved using approaches as varied as managed runtime environments (such as Java and .NET), tamper resistant software [3], and microkernels.

Haven [5] is an SGX-based system for executing Windows applications in the cloud. VC3 [42], also based on SGX, allows verifiable and confidential execution of MapReduce jobs in untrusted cloud environments.

Systems such as TrustedDB [4] and Cipherbase [2] use different kinds of trusted hardware to process database queries over encrypted data. There exist several other systems [30,39,47] that use trusted system software (usually a trusted hypervisor) along with specialized hardware to achieve various security and privacy requirements. Some, such as Virtual Ghost [15] and Flicker [34], avoid hypervisors by using specialized kernel-level hardware-isolation mechanisms and time-partitioning between trusted and untrusted operations, respectively. Super-distribution systems for transmission of protected digital data also exist [27]. They decrypt protected data using a key from an authorized clearinghouse and then re-encrypt the data with a locally generated key on the end-user system, ensuring that no one else can use the data. Secure co-processors [44] allow programs to execute securely as long as users can verify that they are dealing with untampered programs and hardware.

Intel has a number of whitepapers on SGX [1,25], as well as previous attempts in the same vein, such as the Trusted Execution Technology [20]. ARM trustzone for Cortex-A processors also provides some similar guarantees and has been used to build embedded linux platforms [49], language runtimes for mobile applications [41], and many other systems.

6   Conclusion

This paper presents the first systematic consideration of Intel's Software Guard Extensions as a platform on which to implement two-party secure function evaluation. We show that careful use of SGX primitives can facilitate extremely efficient 2P-SFE protocols, provide an outsourcing mechanism for machines without an SGX module, and discuss augmentations to SGX which provide stronger guarantees against leakage. We also use SGX to convert 2P-SFE protocols secure against semi-honest adversaries into ones secure against malicious adversaries, and discuss a number of use cases for SGX. As SGX-enabled processors eventually make their way onto the market, future work will include implementations and improvements to the efficiency and security properties of these protocols.

Acknowledgements. The first author was supported in part by DARPA contract FA8750-13-2-0058. The second and fourth authors were supported in part by NSF grants CNS-1540217 and CNS-1540218. The third author was supported in part by NSF grants CNS-1407454 and CNS-1409599. The fifth author was supported in part by NSF grants CNS-1464087 and CNS-1464088. The U.S. Government is authorized to reproduce and distribute reprints for Governmental purposes notwithstanding any copyright notation thereon. The views and conclusions contained herein are those of the authors and should not be interpreted as necessarily representing the official policies or endorsements, either expressed or implied, of DARPA, NSF, or the U.S. Government.

References

1. Anati, I., Gueron, S., Johnson, S., Scarlata, V.: Innovative technology for CPU based attestation and sealing. In: Proceedings of the 2nd International Workshop on Hardware and Architectural Support for Security and Privacy (2013)
2. Arasu, A., Blanas, S., Eguro, K., Kaushik, R., Kossmann, D., Ramamurthy, R., Venkatesan, R.: Orthogonal security with cipherbase. In: CIDR (2013)
3. Aucsmith, D.: Tamper resistant software: an implementation. In: Anderson, R. (ed.) IH 1996. LNCS, vol. 1174, pp. 317–333. Springer, Heidelberg (1996)
4. Bajaj, S., Sion, R.: TrustedDB: a trusted hardware-based database with privacy and data confidentiality. IEEE Trans. Knowl. Data Eng. **26**(3), 752–765 (2014)
5. Baumann, A., Peinado, M., Hunt, G.: Shielding applications from an untrusted cloud with haven. In: USENIX Symposium on Operating Systems Design and Implementation (OSDI) (2014)
6. Bogdanov, D., Talviste, R., Willemson, J.: Deploying secure multi-party computation for financial data analysis. In: Keromytis, A.D. (ed.) FC 2012. LNCS, vol. 7397, pp. 57–64. Springer, Heidelberg (2012)
7. Bogetoft, P., Christensen, D.L., Damgård, I., Geisler, M., Jakobsen, T., Krøigaard, M., Nielsen, J.D., Nielsen, J.B., Nielsen, K., Pagter, J., Schwartzbach, M., Toft, T.: Secure multiparty computation goes live. In: Dingledine, R., Golle, P. (eds.) FC 2009. LNCS, vol. 5628, pp. 325–343. Springer, Heidelberg (2009)
8. Burkhart, M., Strasser, M., Many, D., Dimitropoulos, X.: SEPIA: privacy-preserving aggregation of multi-domain network events and statistics. In: Proceedings of the USENIX Security Symposium (2010)
9. Carter, H., Amrutkar, C., Dacosta, I., Traynor, P.: For your phone only: custom protocols for efficient secure function evaluation on mobile devices. J. Secur. Commun. Netw. (SCN) **7**(7), 1165–1176 (2014)
10. Carter, H., Lever, C., Traynor, P.: Whitewash: outsourcing garbled circuit generation for mobile devices. In: Proceedings of the Annual Computer Security Applications Conference (ACSAC) (2014)
11. Carter, H., Mood, B., Traynor, P., Butler, K.: Secure outsourced garbled circuit evaluation for mobile devices. In: Proceedings of the USENIX Security Symposium (SECURITY 2013) (2013)

12. Carter, H., Mood, B., Traynor, P., Butler, K.: Outsourcing secure two-party computation as a black box. In: Reiter, M., et al. (eds.) CANS 2015. LNCS, vol. 9476, pp. 214–222. Springer, Heidelberg (2015). doi:10.1007/978-3-319-26823-1_15

13. Cowan, C., Wagle, P., Pu, C., Beattie, S., Walpole, J.: Buffer overflows: attacks and defenses for the vulnerability of the decade. In: DARPA Information Survivability Conference and Exposition, vol. 2, pp. 119–129. IEEE (2000)

14. Di Crescenzo, G., Feigenbaum, J., Gupta, D., Panagos, E., Perry, J., Wright, R.N.: Practical and privacy-preserving policy compliance for outsourced data. In: Böhme, R., Brenner, M., Moore, T., Smith, M. (eds.) FC 2014 Workshops. LNCS, vol. 8438, pp. 181–194. Springer, Heidelberg (2014)

15. Criswell, J., Dautenhahn, N., Adve, V.: Virtual ghost: protecting applications from hostile operating systems. ACM SIGARCH Comput. Architect. News **42**(1), 81–96 (2014)

16. Damgård, I., Geisler, M., Krøigaard, M., Nielsen, J.B.: Asynchronous multiparty computation: theory and implementation. In: Jarecki, S., Tsudik, G. (eds.) PKC 2009. LNCS, vol. 5443, pp. 160–179. Springer, Heidelberg (2009)

17. Erlingsson, Ú., Abadi, M.: Operating system protection against side-channel attacks that exploit memory latency. Technical report, MSR-TR-2007-117, Microsoft Research (2007)

18. Ferguson, N.: AES-CBC+ elephant diffuser: A disk encryption algorithm for windows vista. Technical report, Microsoft (2006)

19. Goldreich, O., Ostrovsky, R.: Software protection and simulation on oblivious RAMs. J. ACM (JACM) **43**(3), 431–473 (1996)

20. Greene, J.: Intel trusted execution technology. Intel Technology White Paper (2012)

21. Group, T.C.: Trusted platform module main specification (tpm1.0) (2011). http://www.trustedcomputinggroup.org/resources/tpm_main_specification

22. Group, T.C.: Trusted platform module library specification (tpm2.0) (2013). http://www.trustedcomputinggroup.org/resources/tpm_library_specification

23. Gupta, D., Segal, A., Panda, A., Segev, G., Schapira, M., Feigenbaum, J., Rexford, J., Shenker, S.: A new approach to interdomain routing based on secure multiparty computation. In: Proceedings of the 11th ACM Workshop on Hot Topics in Networks, pp. 37–42. ACM (2012)

24. Henecka, W., Kogl, S., Sadeghi, A.R., Schneider, T., Wehrenberg, I.: Tasty: tool for automating secure two-party computations. In: Proceedings of the Conference on Computer and Communications Security. ACM (2010)

25. Hoekstra, M., Lal, R., Pappachan, P., Phegade, V., Del Cuvillo, J.: Using innovative instructions to create trustworthy software solutions. In: Proceedings of the 2nd International Workshop on Hardware and Architectural Support for Security and Privacy, p. 11. ACM (2013)

26. Holzer, A., Franz, M., Katzenbeisser, S., Veith, H.: Secure two-party computations in ANSI C. In: Proceedings of the Conference on Computer and Communications Security. ACM (2012)

27. Kawahara, M.: Superdistribution: the concept and the architecture. IEICE TRANSACTIONS (1976–1990) **73**(7), 1133–1146 (1990)

28. Kreuter, B., Mood, B., Shelat, A., Butler, K.: PCF: a portable circuit format for scalable two-party secure computation. In: Proceedings of the USENIX Security Symposium (2013)

29. Libicki, M., Tkacheva, O., Feng, C., Hemenway, B.: Ramifications of DARPA's PROCEED Program. RAND, Santa Monica (2014)

30. Lie, D., Thekkath, C., Mitchell, M., Lincoln, P., Boneh, D., Mitchell, J., Horowitz, M.: Architectural support for copy and tamper resistant software. ACM SIGPLAN Not. **35**(11), 168–177 (2000)
31. Lindell, Y., Riva, B.: Blazing fast 2PC in the offline/online setting with security for malicious adversaries. In: Proceedings of the 2015 ACM SIGSAC Conference on Computer and Communications Security. ACM (2015)
32. Malkhi, D., Nisan, N., Pinkas, B., Sella, Y.: Fairplay-a secure two-party computation system. In: Proceedings of the USENIX Security Symposium (SECURITY 2004) (2004)
33. Martin, R., Demme, J., Sethumadhavan, S.: Timewarp: rethinking timekeeping and performance monitoring mechanisms to mitigate side-channel attacks. In: Proceedings of the 39th Annual International Symposium on Computer Architecture ISCA 2012, pp. 118–129. IEEE Computer Society, Washington, DC (2012)
34. McCune, J.M., Parno, B.J., Perrig, A., Reiter, M.K., Isozaki, H.: Flicker: an execution infrastructure for TCB minimization. ACM SIGOPS Oper. Syst. Rev. **42**, 315–328 (2008)
35. Mood, B., Gupta, D., Butler, K., Feigenbaum, J.: Reuse it or lose it: more efficient secure computation through reuse of encrypted values. In: Proceedings of the ACM SIGSAC Conference on Computer and Communications Security (2014)
36. Mood, B., Gupta, D., Carter, H., Butler, K., Traynor, P.: Frigate: a validated, extensible, and efficient compiler and interpreter for secure computation. In: Proceedings of the 1st IEEE European Symposium on Security and Privacy (2016)
37. Mood, B., Letaw, L., Butler, K.: Memory-efficient garbled circuit generation for mobile devices. In: Keromytis, A.D. (ed.) FC 2012. LNCS, vol. 7397, pp. 254–268. Springer, Heidelberg (2012)
38. Osvik, D.A., Shamir, A., Tromer, E.: Cache attacks and countermeasures: the case of AES. In: Pointcheval, D. (ed.) CT-RSA 2006. LNCS, vol. 3860, pp. 1–20. Springer, Heidelberg (2006)
39. Owusu, E., Guajardo, J., McCune, J., Newsome, J., Perrig, A., Vasudevan, A.: OASIS: On achieving a sanctuary for integrity and secrecy on untrusted platforms. In: Proceedings of the 2013 ACM SIGSAC Conference on Computer and Communications Security, pp. 13–24. ACM (2013)
40. Perry, J., Gupta, D., Feigenbaum, J., Wright, R.N.: Systematizing secure computation for research and decision support. In: Abdalla, M., De Prisco, R. (eds.) SCN 2014. LNCS, vol. 8642, pp. 380–397. Springer, Heidelberg (2014)
41. Santos, N., Raj, H., Saroiu, S., Wolman, A.: Using arm trustzone to build a trusted language runtime for mobile applications. ACM SIGARCH Comput. Archit. News **42**, 67–80 (2014)
42. Schuster, F., Costa, M., Fournet, C., Gkantsidis, C., Peinado, M., Mainar-Ruiz, G., Russinovich, M.: Vc 3: trustworthy data analytics in the cloud using SGX. In: 36th IEEE Symposium on Security and Privacy - S & P 2015. IEEE, New York (2015)
43. Shelat, A., Shen, C.: Two-output secure computation with malicious adversaries. In: Paterson, K.G. (ed.) EUROCRYPT 2011. LNCS, vol. 6632, pp. 386–405. Springer, Heidelberg (2011)
44. Smith, S.W., Weingart, S.: Building a high-performance, programmable secure coprocessor. Comput. Netw. **31**(8), 831–860 (1999)
45. Standaert, F.-X., Rouvroy, G., Quisquater, J.-J., Legat, J.-D.: Efficient implementation of Rijndael encryption in reconfigurable hardware: improvements and design tradeoffs. In: Walter, C.D., Koç, Ç.K., Paar, C. (eds.) CHES 2003. LNCS, vol. 2779, pp. 334–350. Springer, Heidelberg (2003)

46. Stefanov, E., Van Dijk, M., Shi, E., Fletcher, C., Ren, L., Yu, X., Devadas, S.: Path oram: an extremely simple oblivious RAM protocol. In: Proceedings of the 2013 ACM SIGSAC Conference on Computer and Communications Security, pp. 299–310. ACM (2013)
47. Suh, G.E., Clarke, D., Gassend, B., Van Dijk, M., Devadas, S.: Aegis: architecture for tamper-evident and tamper-resistant processing. In: Proceedings of the 17th Annual International Conference on Supercomputing, pp. 160–171. ACM (2003)
48. Vipindeep, V., Jalote, P.: List of common bugs and programming practices to avoid them (2005)
49. Winter, J.: Trusted computing building blocks for embedded Linux-based arm trustzone platforms. In: Proceedings of the 3rd ACM Workshop on Scalable Trusted Computing, pp. 21–30. ACM (2008)
50. Yao, A.C.: Protocols for secure computations. In: Proceedings of the IEEE Symposium on Foundations of Computer Science (FOCS 1982) (1982)

CallForFire: A Mission-Critical Cloud-Based Application Built Using the Nomad Framework

Mamadou H. Diallo(✉), Michael August, Roger Hallman, Megan Kline,
Henry Au, and Vic Beach

US Department of Defense, SPAWAR Systems Center Pacific, San Diego, USA
{mamadou.h.diallo,michael.august,roger.hallman,megan.kline,henry.au,
vic.beach}@navy.mil

Abstract. In this demo paper we describe *CallForFire*, a GIS-based mission-critical defense application that can be deployed in the cloud. *CallForFire* enables secure computation of enemy target locations and selection of firing assets. It is built using the Nomad framework, which enables the development of secure cloud-based applications. Our experimental results validate the feasibility of this application within the Nomad framework.

1 Introduction

Cloud computing provides many benefits for organizations, including improved IT cost efficiencies, scalability, flexibility, and accessibility. However, the confidentiality of data stored within public clouds is not guaranteed due to the multiple cloud security threats identified by the Cloud Security Alliance [2] as well as other surveys [1]. As a result, organizations with sensitive data, especially government agencies, are hesitant to make use of public clouds.

Various technologies have been suggested to address the security concerns associated with storing and processing sensitive data in off-premise public clouds. One such technology is Fully Homomorphic Encryption (FHE), which enables computations to be performed directly on encrypted data. Over the past few years, the cryptographic research community has introduced efficient FHE schemes [5,9]. The Nomad Framework [4] takes advantage of these efficiencies, thereby enabling developers to build applications that leverage FHE for secure computation.

In this demo paper, we describe *CallForFire*, a prototype cloud-based application that uses the Nomad framework to implement the "Call for Indirect/Supporting Fire" protocol [7]. Nomad's underlying storage system is a FHE-based key/value store, which enables storage, computation, and retrieval of encrypted data in the cloud. The use of FHE ensures the confidentiality of the data that is stored and processed in the cloud by mission-critical applications. Nomad uses HElib, an open source FHE library [6] that implements the Brakerski, Gentry, and Vaikuntanathan (BGV) FHE scheme [3]. While *CallForFire* runs slowly due to the intensive FHE operations, the experimental results show that it is feasible for interactive applications.

© International Financial Cryptography Association 2016
J. Clark et al. (Eds.): FC 2016 Workshops, LNCS 9604, pp. 319–327, 2016.
DOI: 10.1007/978-3-662-53357-4_21

2   Nomad Framework Overview

The Nomad framework provides building blocks for ensuring the confidentiality of the data stored and processed in the cloud by using *FHE*. It abstracts out the underlying mechanisms for protecting the data so that developers can focus on building the value-added capabilities of their applications. This framework has the benefits of speeding up and simplifying the development of secure applications deployed in the cloud.

Nomad is designed using the client/server architecture paradigm. The design is modular, which enables extensibility and customization of the framework. The architecture of the framework is depicted in Fig. 1, which is composed of two main components: the Client Management Service and the Cloud Storage Service. It is assumed that the Client Management Service will be deployed in a trusted infrastructure, and that insider attacks are still a threat. The Cloud Storage Service is assumed to be deployed in a semi-trusted cloud infrastructure. In the following sections, we describe the Client Management Service, the Cloud Storage Service, and the Operational Overview of Nomad.

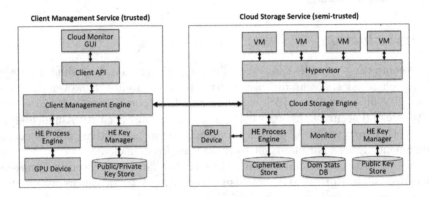

Fig. 1. Nomad framework high-level architecture

2.1   Client Management and Storage Services

The Client Management Service provides both the client management and graphical user interfaces for the system. It consists of multiple components (see Fig. 1). The Client Management Engine orchestrates the client operations, which include encryption, decryption, homomorphic arithmetic operations, key generation, and key management. The client-side FHE Processing Engine is used for encrypting and decrypting the application's data. In order to store the data in the FHE-based storage, the following steps are performed: (1) homomorphic encryption is performed on the data using the public key, and (2) the public key is sent along with the ciphertext to the server for storage. Note that the public key is needed by the server-side FHE Processing Engine in order to perform re-encryption (i.e. bootstrapping) and operations on the ciphertext. The Public/Private Key Store persists both the public and private keys associated with each user of the system. The client-side FHE Key Manager is responsible for generating public/private key pairs, storing/retrieving them in the Public/Private Key Store, and encrypting/decrypting data. The Client API is used for exposing these services to applications, and the Cloud Monitor GUI is used for monitoring the resource usage of the virtual machines in the cloud.

The Cloud Storage Service enables the deployment of trusted storage and computation services within a semi-trusted cloud environment. The Cloud Storage Engine orchestrates all of the operations of the Cloud Storage Service and provides the server-side interface to the storage system. The cloud service provider's underlying hypervisor generates and manages the Virtual Machines (VMs) which host Nomad's cloud services. The Monitor collects the resource usage of each VM periodically and stores it in the Dom Stats DB (i.e., the domain statistics database). The server-side FHE Processing Engine is used for processing the homomorphically encrypted data, and stores the results along with the original ciphertexts in the Ciphertext Store. The server-side FHE Key Manager keeps track of the public keys used to encrypt the data.

2.2 Nomad Operational Overview

The operations performed by the Nomad framework include encryption/ decryption, storage, retrieval, deletion, and processing of the data. The Cloud Storage Service functionality is exposed to the client application via the Client API. The Client Management Service manages all of the keys, data, and operations on behalf of the client. At a high level, the client application data is stored and processed in the cloud in encrypted form, then returned to the client application and decrypted for display to the end-user. When first using the system, the user must initialize the client and generate their own public/private key pair (Key_{public}, $Key_{private}$). Note that, in a deployment environment, key generation must be done by a trusted third party, as it is done with current certificate authorities. Alternatively, key management/distribution could be done using homomorphic encryption, as is being done by Porticor [10].

Data Storage Workflow. In this data storage workflow, we assume that each user has a single public/private key pair used for encrypting and decrypting their data.

1. System Initialization: Upon first using the system, the user sends a request to the *Client Management Engine* to generate a public/private key tuple ($<ID_{user}, Key_{public}, Key_{private}>$). The *Client Management Engine* forwards the request to the *HE Key Manager* to generate the key pair and store it in the *Public/Private Key Store*. The *Client Management Engine* also sends the tuple ($< ID_{user}, Key_{public} >$) to the *Cloud Storage Engine* for later usage. The *Cloud Storage Engine* calls on the *HE Key Manager* to store the tuple ($< ID_{user}, Key_{public} >$) in the *Public Key Store*.

2. The user initiates a request to store their $Data_{plaintext}$ in the cloud storage.
3. The *Client Management Engine* submits a request to encrypt the data to get the ciphertext ($Enc(Data_{plaintext}, Key_{public}) = Data_{ciphertext}$).
4. The *Client Management Engine* submits a request to the *Cloud Storage Engine* to store the ID/data tuple ($< ID_{user}, ID_{data}, Data_{ciphertext} >$).
5. The *Cloud Storage Engine* receives the storage request and calls on the *HE Processing Engine* to store the data ($ID_{user}, < ID_{data}, Data_{ciphertext} >$) in the *Ciphertext Store*.

3   Application: Call For Fire

In this section, we describe the design of the *CallForFire* prototype. Defense organizations may call for indirect/supporting fire during combat operations when an infantry unit is impractical for engagement with a target. *CallForFire* places the sensitive computations involved in calling for indirect or supporting fire, specifically computation of a target location, into a secure, homomorphically encrypted cloud environment.

In a tactical environment, the call for indirect/supporting fire procedure involves multiple players. The Forward Observer (FO) observes an adversary target, or "High Value Target" (HVT). The FO determines the Observer-Target distance ($OT_{distance}$) and bearing ($OT_{direction}$) using technology such as a laser range finder or other means. The FO then homomorphically encrypts the ($OT_{distance}, OT_{direction}$) and transmits the information to the "Fire Direction Center" (FDC). Since the FO location is already known, the FDC uses the FO's position and the ($OT_{distance}, OT_{direction}$) to calculate the HVT location. Once calculated, the information is sent to the "Firing Unit" (FU), which "fires for effect" on the HVT. Note that the FDC is not fully trusted due to insider threats, which is the main reason FHE is used to enforce the "need to know" restriction. FHE is also needed to securely outsource the computation to the cloud.

CallForFire uses the Military Grid Reference System (MGRS) [8] rather than the more widely known latitude/longitude coordinate system. The reasons for choosing MGRS are twofold: (1) it is the geocoordinate standard used by all NATO militaries, and (2) all MGRS coordinates are alpha-numeric with letters and integers which are easily handled by all FHE schemes. MGRS coordinates consist of a grid zone designator (GZD)–a double digit integer followed by a letter, a 100,000-meter square identifier (SQ_{ID})–two letters, followed by the numerical location (*easting* and *northing*) within the 100,000 m^2–both with the same number of digits, which varies from 1 to 5 depending on the MGRS precision/resolution level. The lowest value 1 corresponds to precision level 10 km, while the highest value 5 corresponds to precision level 1 m. The precision level of 1 m is used in the *CallForFire* application. Given a reference point, distance, and bearing, the numerical location of any position can be computed.

To compute the HVT location in MGRS, it is assumed that the GZD and SQ_{ID} are known. Also assumed is that the FO location within the 100,000-meter square is known and the HVT is within the same square. Let $FO_{easting}$

and $FO_{northing}$ be the FO's easting and northing. Similarly, let $HVT_{easting}$ and $HVT_{northing}$ be the HVT's easting and northing. The $OT_{direction}$, θ, is referenced from 0° north, moving clockwise. Note that the trigonometric function values are pre-computed to four decimal places, appropriately scaled for computation as integers, and then stored in the FHE-based storage. The HVT's location is calculated as follows:

$$HVT_{easting} = FO_{easting} + OT_{distance} \times \sin(\theta)$$

$$HVT_{northing} = FO_{northing} + OT_{distance} \times \cos(\theta)$$

Initially, *CallForFire* was tested using only a single FO and HVT [4]. In an actual combat environment, there are likely to be multiple FOs, HVTs, and FUs, and a single FDC would need to process many calls for indirect/supporting fire simultaneously. Therefore, *CallForFire* has been expanded to handle multiple FOs requesting indirect/supporting fire on adversary HVTs, and selectively assigning the HVTs to different FUs based on predefined criteria (i.e. firing asset selection). The firing asset selection process involves computing the distances between all FUs and a given HVT, and selecting which FU to direct fire on the HVT. In a real world scenario, asset selection would consist of more criteria than just the distance between the FU and the HVT. It will be assumed that the positions of the FOs and FUs will be known to the FDC. Multiple FOs may call for fire support on the same HVT. The distance is calculated as follows:

$$Distance_{FU-HVT}^2 = (FU_{easting} - HVT_{easting})^2 + (FU_{northing} - HVT_{northing})^2$$

Figure 2 is a screenshot of the actual *CallForFire* GUI in a web browser. It shows an example scenario with the following players: 1 FDC, 4 FOs, 5 FUs, and 3

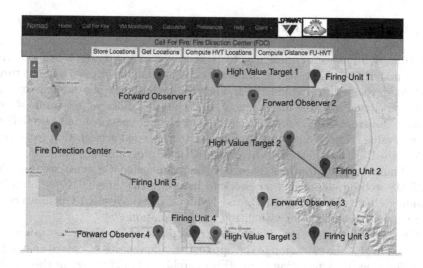

Fig. 2. Screenshot of the CallForFire application in a web browser.

*HVT*s. In this scenario, the *FDC* has computed the locations of the three *HVT*s using the information given by the *FO*s. It has also selected the nearest *FU* for each *HVT* as indicated by the lines between them on the map.

CallForFire Operational Workflow. The CallForFire operational workflow describes how the call for indirect/supporting fire procedure is simulated by the CallForFire application. Nomad currently supports the following integer operations in the encrypted domain: addition, subtraction, multiplication, and negation. For this simple scenario, we assume that all locations (except the *FDC*) are inside of the same MGRS zone.

1. The *FO* detects an *HVT* in the field, estimates its distance and bearing, and enters the data into the *FO* client application.
2. The *FO* client application uses the *FDC* public key to homomorphically encrypt the *FO*'s location (easting and northing) and the *HVT*'s distance and bearing, and sends them to the *FDC*.
3. The *FDC* outsources the computation of the *HVT*'s location to the Nomad cloud service by sending the homomorphically encrypted *FO*'s location, the *HVT*'s bearing and distance, and locations of the available *FU*s over to the cloud.
4. The cloud homomorphically computes the *HVT*'s absolute location and selects the nearest *FU* to direct fire on the *HVT*.
5. The cloud sends the *HVT*'s location and *FU* selection back to the *FDC*.
6. The *FDC* decrypts the *HVT*'s location and the *FU* selection, then makes the final decision to initiate the firing operation.
7. The *FDC* encrypts the *HVT*'s location using the *FU* public key and sends the firing command to the selected *FU*.
8. The selected *FU* decrypts the *HVT*'s location and directs fire on the *HVT*.

4 Implementation and Experiments

The Nomad framework is designed to be modular and extensible, using Thrift as the underlying client/server framework. This enables an open architecture, allowing developers to extend the framework, including using different hypervisors for virtual machine management, and choosing different key/value stores for back-end storage. We used Xen as the underlying hypervisor and LevelDB as the key/value store. We implemented the GPGPU-based acceleration technique as described in [4], which uses the Nvidia CUDA programming platform, for a limited number of subroutines. For the Client Management Service, we used the CppCMS web development framework to integrate the different C++ libraries including HElib, Thrift, LevelDB, and Nvidia CUDA. We used OpenLayers as the mapping technology for visualizing the information.

We have extended the *CallForFire* application, which was originally described in [4]. The extension of the application allows us to examine the performance improvement resulting from HElib batching of operations. In this extension, we have increased the number of Forward Observers (*FO*s), Firing Units

(*FU*s), and observed targets (*HVTs*). We compute the locations of all the *HVTs* using the information given by the *FOs*. Once the locations of all the *HVTs* are known, then we identify which *FU* to assign to each *HVT*. This determination is based on the distance between the *HVT* and the *FU*. We can then compare the performance between batched and non-batched (individual) calculations. We performed experiments to analyze the performance of *CallForFire* with respect to the overhead associated with Computation, Storage, and Data Transmission. We ignored the latency between browser and server.

HElib uses the following main parameters: R (number of rounds), p (plaintext base), r (lifting), d (degree of the field extension), c (number of columns in the key-switching matrices), k (security parameter), L (number of levels in the modulus chain), s (minimum number of slots), and m (modulus). For all the experiments, the following parameters are fixed: $R = 1$, $r = 1$, $d = 1$, $c = 2$, and $s = 0$. We adjusted the parameters p and k in order to evaluate the performance tradeoffs associated with having a larger integer space and a higher security level, respectively. The parameters L and m are automatically generated by HElib based on the other parameters.

The experiments were performed using two HP Z420 desktops with 16 GB RAM and 500 GB storage, and one MacBook Pro with 2.6 GHz Intel Core i7, 16 GB RAM, and 500 GB storage. The setup is as follows: *FO* (MacBook), *FDC* (Z420), Cloud (Z420).

Table 1. Average computation overhead in sec. with fixed p = 9576890767 (10 digits)

k: Security parameter	80 (L = 11, m = 11021)		100 (L = 11, m=12403)		120 (L=11, m=13019)	
Type	Individual	Batched	Individual	Batched	Individual	Batched
Location encryption	702.3990	63.0778	782.6890	71.8735	831.9190	77.1963
Location decryption	600.7040	165.2790	692.3490	217.0520	760.9390	217.0620
Location computation	212.1974	21.3238	221.7478	27.3559	237.1199	23.2551
Distance computation	271.2946	26.3864	283.7557	28.7946	331.0418	33.2885
Storing location	2.4743	0.2498	2.7999	0.2847	2.8119	0.2824
Retrieving location	16.3833	1.5589	18.0937	1.8003	21.8311	1.9645

CallForFire Computation Overhead. To measure the computation overhead, we performed two sets of computations: (1) calculation of the *HVT*'s location and, (2) firing asset selection. In the *HVT* location calculation, we measured the time it took to homomorphically encrypt 10 individual locations consisting of 6 parameters (GZD, SQ_{ID}, $FO_{easting}$, $FO_{northing}$, $OT_{distance}$, $OT_{direction}$) each, computed the numerical location (easting and northing) of the *HVT* for each *FO*, and decrypted the *HVT* locations. We also measured the time it took to store and retrieve 10 encrypted locations from the storage. In the firing asset selection, we measured the time it took to compute the distance between 10 *FUs* and 10 *HVTs* pairwise. We repeated both experiments 100 times and computed the averages. Tables 1 and 2 summarizes the results of

Table 2. Average computation overhead in sec. with Fixed p = 1000000000039 (13 digits)

k: Security parameter	80 (L = 12, m = 11639)		100 (L = 12, m = 12851)		120 (L = 12, m = 14279)	
Type	Individual	Batched	Individual	Batched	Individual	Batched
Location encryption	818.4560	72.2017	850.1300	72.3850	939.4530	84.5170
Location decryption	696.9510	181.3630	738.4030	220.9120	931.8070	303.4390
Location computation	227.4829	23.1525	253.9844	25.3798	262.6284	26.6340
Distance computation	287.5192	28.1036	295.7541	27.7043	354.8627	34.4122
Storing location	2.5129	0.2454	2.7538	0.2922	3.1536	0.3925
Retrieving location	16.5563	1.7040	18.2733	1.9397	20.7723	2.1635

these experiments and gives a comparison between the performance of *individual* and *batched* operations. When performing operations in *batched* mode, an input array with multiple elements is passed in to the storage system. The homomorphic encryption operations can then be performed on all of the elements of the array within the same operation. With *individual* operations, one data element (i.e. an integer) is placed into the input array, which is then passed to the storage system. Based on the results of these experiments, it is best to use *batch* mode when possible, which can reduce the overhead significantly.

Transmission and Storage Overhead. For the transmission and storage overhead, we measured the time it took for the FO to encrypt and transmit the location information to the FDC, and for the FDC to store the information in its database. We considered scenarios for 100 FOs and calculated the averages. The time it takes to transmit an encrypted location and store it in the database is about 22 times longer than when the location is not encrypted. For the storage space overhead, the average space used to store a location using HE is 8.96 megabytes, whereas the average for a location without using HE is 17.6 bytes. This significant storage space overhead is a limitation common to all lattice-based homomorphic encryption schemes.

5   Conclusion

In this paper, we presented *CallForFire*, a cloud-based mission-critical defense application built using the Nomad framework. *CallForFire* takes advantage of Nomad's Cloud Storage Service to encrypt and compute enemy target locations in the battlefield. In order to accelerate FHE operations, we investigated the use of GPGPU programming techniques to parallelize some of the HElib subroutines. Our preliminary results show some improvement in the performance of HElib. While the overall performance of HElib may still be impractical for many applications, certain interactive applications, such as *CallForFire*, can still make use of HElib in a limited context to enhance data confidentiality. Further development of HE libraries such as HElib will likely accelerate the adoption of cloud computing by organizations with sensitive data.

References

1. GCN: Like it or not, cloud computing is here to stay (2011). http://gcn.com/ microsites/2011/cloud-computing-download/cloud-computing-application-develop ment.aspx
2. Alliance, C.S.: The notorious nine: cloud computing top threats in 2013. In: Top Threats Working Group (2013)
3. Brakerski, Z., Gentry, C., Vaikuntanathan, V.: Fully homomorphic encryption without bootstrapping. Cryptology ePrint Archive, Report 2011/277 (2011)
4. Diallo, M.H., August, M., Hallman, R., Kline, M., Au, H., Beach, V.: Nomad: a framework for developing mission-critical cloud-based applications. In: 10th International Conference on Availability, Reliability and Security, ARES, Toulouse, France, 24–27 August 2015
5. Gentry, C.: Fully homomorphic encryption using ideal lattices. In: Proceedings of the Forty-first Annual ACM Symposium on Theory of Computing, STOC 2009. ACM (2009)
6. Halevi, S., Shoup, V.: Design and implementation of a homomorphic-encryption library (2013)
7. Headquarters, Department of the Army: Tactics, Techniques, and Procedures for Observed Fire, Field Manual 6-30 (1991)
8. Headquarters Department of the Army Washington, D.C: FM 3–25.26 Map Reading and Land Navigation (2001)
9. Parmar, P.V., Padhar, S.B., Patel, S.N., Bhatt, N.I., Jhaveri, R.H.: Survey of various homomorphic encryption algorithms and schemes. Int. J. Comput. Appl. **91**(8), 26–32 (2014). Published by Foundation of Computer Science, New York, USA, April 2014
10. Porticor: Securing data in the cloud (2013). https://www.porticor.com/ homomorphic-encryption/

Cryptographic Solutions for Genomic Privacy

Erman Ayday[⊠]

Computer Engineering Department, Bilkent University,
06800 Bilkent, Ankara, Turkey
erman@cs.bilkent.edu.tr

Abstract. With the help of rapidly developing technology, DNA sequencing is becoming less expensive. As a consequence, the research in genomics has gained speed in paving the way to personalized (genomic) medicine, and geneticists need large collections of human genomes to further increase this speed. Furthermore, individuals are using their genomes to learn about their (genetic) predispositions to diseases, their ancestries, and even their (genetic) compatibilities with potential partners. This trend has also caused the launch of health-related websites and online social networks (OSNs), in which individuals share their genomic data (e.g., OpenSNP or 23andMe). On the other hand, genomic data carries much sensitive information about its owner. By analyzing the DNA of an individual, it is now possible to learn about his disease predispositions (e.g., for Alzheimer's or Parkinson's), ancestries, and physical attributes. The threat to genomic privacy is magnified by the fact that a person's genome is correlated to his family members' genomes, thus leading to interdependent privacy risks. In this work, focusing on our existing and ongoing work on genomic privacy, we will first highlight one serious threat for genomic privacy. Then, we will present the high level descriptions of our cryptographic solutions to protect the privacy of genomic data.

1 Kin Genomic Privacy

A recent New York Times' article [1] reports the controversy about sequencing and publishing, without the permission of her family, the genome of Henrietta Lacks (who died in 1951). On the one hand, the family members think that her genome is private family information and it should not be published without the consent of the family. On the other hand, some scientists argued that the genomes of current family members have changed so much over time (due to gene mixing during reproduction), that nothing accurate could be told about the genomes of current family members by using Henrietta Lacks' genome. As we shown in [10] (that we briefly describe in the latter), they are wrong. Minutes after Henrietta Lacks' genome was uploaded to a public website called SNPedia, researchers produced a report full of personal information about Henrietta Lacks. Later, the genome was taken offline, but it had already been downloaded by several people, hence both her and (partially) the Lacks family's genomic privacy was already lost.

© International Financial Cryptography Association 2016
J. Clark et al. (Eds.): FC 2016 Workshops, LNCS 9604, pp. 328–341, 2016.
DOI: 10.1007/978-3-662-53357-4_22

Unfortunately, the Lacks, even though possibly the most publicized family facing this problem, are not the only family facing this threat. Genomes of thousands of individuals are available online. Once the identity of a genome donor is known, an attacker can learn about his relatives (or his family tree) by using an auxiliary side channel, such as an OSN, and infer significant information about the DNA sequences of the donor's relatives. We will show the feasibility of such an attack and evaluate the privacy risks by using publicly available data on the Web.

Although the researchers took Henrietta Lacks' genome offline from SNPedia, other databases continue to publish portions of her genomic data. Publishing only portions of a genome does not, however, completely hide the unpublished portions; even if a person reveals only a part of his genome, other parts can be inferred using the statistical relationships between the nucleotides in his DNA. For example, James Watson, co-discoverer of DNA, made his whole DNA sequence publicly available, with the exception of one gene known as Apolipoprotein E (ApoE), one of the strongest predictors for the development of Alzheimer's disease. However, later it was shown that the correlation (called *linkage disequilibrium* by geneticists) between one or multiple polymorphisms and ApoE can be used to predict the ApoE status [13]. Thus, an attacker can also use these statistical relationships (which are publicly available) to infer the DNA sequences of a donor's family members, even if the donor shares only part of his genome. It is important to note that these privacy threats not only jeopardize kin genomic privacy, but, if not properly addressed, these issues could also hamper genomic research due to untimely fear of potential misuse of genomic information.

In this work, we evaluate the genomic privacy of an individual threatened by his relatives revealing their genomes. Focusing on the most common genetic variant in human population, single nucleotide polymorphism (SNP), and considering the statistical relationships between the SNPs on the DNA sequence, we quantify the loss in genomic privacy of individuals when one or more of their family members' genomes are (either partially or fully) revealed.[1] To achieve this goal, first, we design a reconstruction attack based on a well-known statistical inference technique. The computational complexity of the traditional ways of realizing such inference grows exponentially with the number of SNPs (which is on the order of tens of millions) and relatives. Therefore, in order to infer the values of the unknown SNPs in linear complexity, we represent the SNPs, family relationships and the statistical relationships between SNPs on a factor graph and use the belief propagation algorithm [12,14] for inference. Then, using various metrics, we quantify the genomic privacy of individuals and show the decrease in their level of genomic privacy caused by the published genomes of their family members. We also quantify the health privacy of the individuals by considering their (genetic) predisposition to certain serious diseases. We evaluate the proposed inference attack and show its efficiency and accuracy by using real genomic data of a pedigree. Figure 1 gives an overview of the framework.

---

[1] SNPs carry privacy-sensitive information about individuals' health. Recent discoveries show that the susceptibility of an individual to several diseases can be computed from his SNPs.

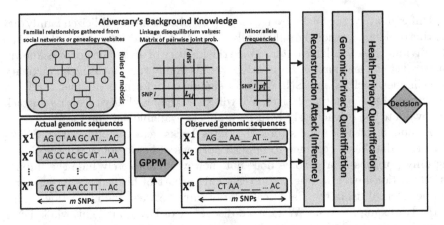

Fig. 1. Overview of the proposed framework to quantify kin genomic privacy. Each vector $\mathbf{X}^i$ ($i \in \{1,\ldots,n\}$) includes the set of SNPs for an individual in the targeted family. Furthermore, each letter pair in $\mathbf{X}^i$ represents a SNP x^i_j; and for simplicity, each SNP x^i_j can be represented using $\{BB, Bb, bb\}$ (or $\{0, 1, 2\}$). Linkage disequilibrium (LD) can be thought as a correlation between two variables (SNPs) and minor allele frequency can be considered as the probability of observing a SNP in the population. Once the health privacy is quantified, the family should ideally decide whether to reveal less or more of their genomic information through the genomic-privacy preserving mechanism (GPPM).

In a nutshell, the goal of the adversary is to infer the unknown (unobserved) SNPs of a member (or multiple members) of a *targeted family*. For the evaluation, we use the *CEPH/Utah Pedigree 1463* that contains the partial DNA sequences of 17 family members (4 grandparents, 2 parents, and 11 children) [7]. As shown in Fig. 2 that we only use 5 (out of 11) children for our evaluation.

We consider 100 SNPs on chromosome 1. We define a target individual from the CEPH family and sequentially reveal other family members' SNPs (excluding the target individual) to observe the decrease in the genomic privacy of the target individual. We start revealing from the most distant family members to the target individual (in terms of number of hops in Fig. 2) and we keep revealing relatives until we reach his/her closest family members.[2] We observe that individuals sometimes reveal different parts of their genomes (e.g., different sets of SNPs) on the Internet. Thus, we assume that for each family member (except for the target individual), the adversary observes 50 random SNPs out of 100 only, and these sets of observed SNPs are different for each family member. In Fig. 3, we show the evolution of genomic privacy of one target individual (P5). We quantify the genomic privacy based on (i) attackers in correctness (red plot), (ii) attacker's uncertainty (green plot), and (iii) an entropy-based metrics that quantifies the mutual dependence between the hidden genomic data that

---

[2] The exact sequence of the family members (whose SNPs are revealed) is indicated for each evaluation.

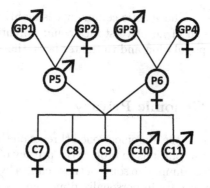

Fig. 2. Family tree of *CEPH/Utah Pedigree 1463* consisting of the 11 family members that were considered. The symbols ♂ and ♀ represent the male and female family members, respectively.

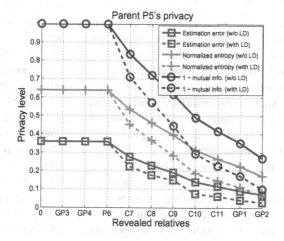

Fig. 3. Evolution of the genomic privacy of the parent (P5), with and without considering LD. For each family member, we reveal 50 randomly picked SNPs (out of 100 SNPs on chromosome 1), starting from the most distant family members, and the *x*-axis represents the exact sequence of this disclosure. Note that $x = 0$ represents the prior distribution, when no genomic data is revealed.

the adversary is trying to reconstruct (blue plot). We observe that LD decreases genomic privacy, especially when few individuals' genomes are revealed. As more family member's genomes are observed, LD has less impact on the genomic privacy.

As we already mentioned, the Lacks family is just one (albeit famous) example. In the future (and already today), people of the same family might have very different opinions on whether to reveal genomic data, and this can lead to disagreement: relatives might have divergent perceptions of possible consequences. It is high time for the security research community to prepare itself for this formidable challenge. The genetic community is highly concerned about the fact that the proliferation of negative stories could potentially lead to a negative perception by the population and to tighter laws, thus hampering scientific progress in this field.

2 Solutions for Genomic Privacy

In order to prevent some of the aforementioned threats on the privacy of genomic data, we proposed several solutions to protect the privacy of such data in various domains. In this part, we summarize some of those efforts by focusing on privacy-preserving use of genomic data in personalized medicine and post-quantum privacy for storage of genomic data, and protecting kin genomic privacy.

2.1 Private Use of Genomic Data in Personalized Medicine

As we have shown in [5], our goal is to protect the privacy of users' genomic data while enabling medical units to access the genomic data in order to conduct medical tests or develop personalized medicine methods. In a medical test, a medical unit checks for different health risks (e.g., disease susceptibilities) of a user by using specific parts of his genome. Similarly, to provide personalized medicine, a pharmaceutical company tests the compatibility of a user with a particular medicine. It is important to note that these genetic tests are currently done by different types of medical units, and the tools we propose in this work aim to protect the genomic privacy of the patients in such tests. In both medical tests and personalized medicine methods, in order to preserve his privacy, the user does not want to reveal his complete genome to the medical unit or to the pharmaceutical company. In addition, in some scenarios, it is the pharmaceutical companies who do not want to reveal the genetic properties of their drugs. To achieve these goals, we introduce the *privacy-preserving disease susceptibility test* (PDS).

Most medical tests and personalized medicine methods (that use genomic data) involve a patient and a medical unit. In general, the medical unit can be a physician in a medical center (e.g., hospital), a pharmacist, a pharmaceutical company, or a medical council. In this study, we consider the existence of a malicious entity in the medical unit as the potential attacker. That is, a medical unit might contain a disgruntled employee or it can be hacked by an intruder that is trying to obtain private genomic information about a patient (for which it is not authorized).

In addition, extreme precaution is needed for the storage of genomic data due to its sensitivity. Thus, we claim that a storage and processing unit (SPU) should be used to store the genomic data. We assume that the SPU is more "security-aware" than a medical unit, hence it can protect the stored genomic data against a hacker better than a medical unit (yet, attacks against the SPU cannot be ruled out, as we discuss next). Recent medical data breaches from various medical units also support this assumption. Furthermore, instead of every medical unit individually storing the genomic data of the patients (in which case patients need to be sequenced by several medical units and their genomic data will be stored at several locations), a medical unit can retrieve the required genomic data belonging to a patient directly from the SPU. We note that a private company (e.g., cloud storage service), the government, or a non-profit organization could play the role of the SPU.

We assume that the SPU is an honest organization, but it might be curious. In other words, the SPU honestly follows the protocols and provides correct information to the other parties, however, a curious party at the SPU could access or infer the stored genomic data. Further, it is possible to identify a person only from his genomic data via phenotyping, which determines the observable physical or biochemical characteristics of an organism from its genetic makeup and environmental influences. Therefore, genomic data should be stored at the SPU in encrypted form. Similarly, apart from the possibility of containing a malicious entity, the medical unit honestly follows the protocols. Thus, we assume that the medical unit does not make malicious requests from the SPU. We consider the following models for the attacker:

- A curious party at the SPU (or a hacker who breaks into the SPU), who tries to infer the genomic sequence of a patient from his stored genomic data. Such an attacker can infer the variants (i.e., nucleotides that vary between individuals) of the patient from his stored data.
- A semi-honest entity in the medical unit, who can be considered either as an attacker that hacks into the medical unit's system or a disgruntled employee who has access the medical unit's database. The goal of such an attacker is to obtain private genomic data of a patient for which it is not authorized. The main resource of such an attacker is the results of the genetic tests the patient undergoes.

For the simplicity of presentation, in the rest of this section, we will focus on a particular medical test (namely, computing genetic disease susceptibility). Similar techniques would apply for other medical tests and personalized medicine methods. In a typical genetic disease-susceptibility test, a *medical center* (MC) wants to check the susceptibility of a patient (P) for a particular disease X (i.e., the probability that patient P will develop disease X) by analyzing particular SNPs of the patient.[3]

For each patient, we propose to store only the real SNPs (around 4 million SNP positions on the DNA at which the patient has a mutation) at the SPU. At this point, it can be argued that these 4 million real SNPs (nucleotides) could be easily stored on the patient's computer or mobile device, instead of at the SPU. However, we assert that this should be avoided due to the following issues. On one hand, types of variations in human population are not limited to SNPs, and there are other types of variations such as *copy-number variations*

---

[3] In this study, we only focus on the diseases which can be analyzed using the SNPs. We admit that there are also other diseases which depend on other forms of mutations or environmental factors.

(CNVs), rearrangements, or translocations, consequently the required storage per patient is likely to be considerably more than only 4 million nucleotides. This high storage cost might still be affordable (via desktop computers or USB drives), however, the genomic data of the patient should be available any time (e.g., for emergencies), thus it should be stored at a reliable source such as the SPU. On the other hand, leaving the patient's genomic data in his own hands and letting him store it on his computer or mobile device is risky, because his mobile device can be stolen or his computer can be hacked. It is true that the patient's cryptographic keys (or his authentication material) to access his genomic data at the SPU can also be stolen, however, in the case of a stolen cryptographic key, his genomic data (which is stored at the SPU) will still be safe. This can be considered like a stolen credit card issue. If the patient does not report that his keys are compromised as soon as possible, his genomic data can be accessed by the attacker.

It is important to note that protecting only the states (contents) of the patient's real SNPs is not sufficient in terms of his genomic privacy. As the real SNPs are stored at the SPU, a curious party at the SPU can infer the nucleotides corresponding to the real SNPs from their positions and from the correlation between the patient's potential SNPs and the real ones. That is, by knowing the positions of the patient's real SNPs, the curious party at the SPU will at least know that the patient has one or two minor alleles at these SNP positions (i.e., it will know that the corresponding SNP position includes either a real homozygous or heterozygous SNP), and it can make its inference stronger using the correlation between the SNPs. Therefore, we propose to encrypt both the positions of the real SNPs and their states. We assume that the patient stores his cryptographic keys (public-secret key pair for asymmetric encryption, and symmetric keys between the patient and other parties) on his smart card (e.g., digital ID card). Alternatively, these keys can be stored at a cloud-based password manager and retrieved by the patient when required.

In short, the whole genome sequencing is done by a *certified institution* (CI) with the consent of the patient. Moreover, the real SNPs of the patient and their positions on the DNA sequence (or their unique IDs) are encrypted by the same CI (using the patient's public and symmetric key, respectively) and uploaded to the SPU, so that the SPU cannot access the real SNPs of the patient (or their positions). We are aware that the number of discovered SNPs increases with time. Thus, the patient's complete DNA sequence is also encrypted as a single vector file (via symmetric encryption using the patient's symmetric key) and stored at the SPU, thus when new SNPs are discovered, these can be included in the pool of the previously stored SNPs of the patient. We also assume the SPU not to have access to the real identities of the patients and data to be stored at the SPU by using pseudonyms; this way, the SPU cannot associate the conducted genetic tests to the real identities of the patients.

Depending on the access rights of the MC, either (i) the MC computes $\Pr(X)$, the probability that the patient will develop disease X by checking a subset of the patient's encrypted SNPs via homomorphic encryption techniques [6], or (ii) the SPU provides the relevant SNPs to the MC (e.g., for complex diseases that cannot be interpreted using homomorphic operations). These access rights are defined either jointly by the MC and the patient, or directly by the medical authorities. We note that homomorphic encryption lets the MC compute $\Pr(X)$ using encrypted SNPs of patient P. In other words, the MC does not access P's SNPs to compute his disease susceptibility. We use a modification of the Paillier cryptosystem [2, 6] to support the homomorphic operations at the MC. We show our proposed protocol in Fig. 4.

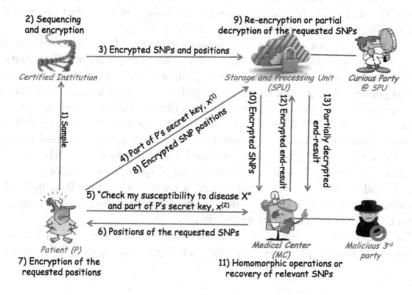

Fig. 4. Proposed privacy-preserving disease susceptibility test (PDS).

Following the steps in the figure, initially, the patient (P) provides his sample (e.g., his blood or saliva) to the certified institution (CI) for sequencing. After sequencing, the CI first determines the positions of P's real SNPs and the set positions at which P has real SNPs. Then, CI encrypts the SNPs (with Paillier cryptosystem using the public key of the patients) and their positions (using the symmetric key shared between the patient and the CI). Next, the CI sends the encrypted SNPs and positions to the SPU and the patient provides a part of his secret key ($x^{(1)}$) to the SPU. This finalizes the initialization phase of the protocol. Then, the MC wants to conduct a susceptibility test on P for a particular disease X, and P provides the other part of his secret key ($x^{(2)}$) to the MC. The MC tells the patient the positions of the SNPs that are required for the susceptibility test or requested directly as the relevant SNPs (but not the individual contributions of these SNPs to the test). The patient encrypts each requested position with the symmetric key and sends the SPU the encrypted positions of the requested SNPs. Next, the SPU re-encrypts the requested SNPs and sends then to the MC. MC computes P's total susceptibility for disease X by using the homomorphic properties (i.e., homomorphic addition and multiplication with a constant) of the modified Paillier cryptosystem. The MC sends the encrypted end-result to the SPU. The SPU partially decrypts the end-result using $x^{(1)}$ by following a proxy re-encryption protocol and sends it back to the MC. Finally, the MC decrypts the message received from the SPU by using $x^{(2)}$ and recovers the end-result.

Even though this proposed approach provides a secure algorithm, there is still a privacy risk in case the MC tries to infer the patient's SNPs from the end-result of a test. We also show that such an attack is indeed possible and one way to prevent such an attack is to obfuscate the end-result before providing it to the MC. Obviously, this causes a conflict between privacy and utility and this conflict is still a hot research topic for genomic privacy.

In a follow up work [4], we also propose a system for protecting the privacy of individuals' sensitive genomic, clinical, and environmental information, while enabling medical units to process it in a privacy-preserving fashion in order to perform disease risk tests. We introduce a framework in which individuals' medical data (genomic, clinical, and environmental) is stored at a storage and processing unit (SPU) and a medical unit conducts the disease risk test on the encrypted medical data by using homomorphic encryption and privacy-preserving integer comparison. The proposed system preserves the privacy of the individuals' genomic, clinical, and environmental data from a curious party at the SPU and from a malicious party (e.g., a hacker) at the medical unit when computing the disease risk. We also implement the proposed system and show its practicality via a complexity evaluation.

The general architecture of the proposed system is illustrated in Fig. 5. In summary, the patient provides his sample for sequencing to the CI. Meanwhile,

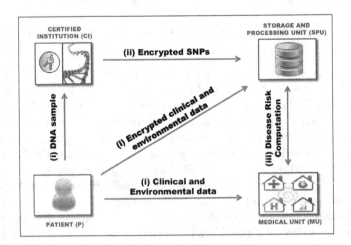

Fig. 5. Proposed system model for the privacy-preserving computation of the disease risk.

he also provides his clinical and environmental data to the SPU and the MU.[4] The CI is responsible for sequencing and encryption of the patient's genomic data. Then, the CI sends the encrypted genomic data to the SPU. Finally, the privacy-preserving computation of the disease risk takes place between the MU and the SPU.

2.2 Coping with Weak Passwords for the Protection of Genomic Data

Appropriately designed cryptographic schemes can preserve the utility of data, but they provide security based on assumptions about the computational limitations of adversaries. Hence they are vulnerable to brute-force attacks when these assumptions are incorrect or erode over time. Given the longevity of genomic data, serious consequences can result. Compared with other types of data, genomic data has especially long-term sensitivity. A genome is (almost) stable over time and thus needs protection over the lifetime of an individual and even beyond, as genomic data is correlated between the members of a single family. It has been shown that the genome of an individual can be probabilistically inferred from the genomes of his family members [10].

In many situations, though, particularly those involving direct use of data by consumers, keys are weak and vulnerable to brute-force cracking *even today*. This problem arises in systems that employ password-based encryption (PBE), a common approach to protection of user-owned data. Users' tendency to choose weak passwords is widespread and well documented [8].

Recently, Juels and Ristenpart introduced a new theoretical framework for encryption called *honey encryption* (HE) [11]. Honey encryption has the property that when a ciphertext is decrypted with an incorrect key (as guessed by an adversary), the result is a plausible-looking yet incorrect plaintext. Therefore, HE gives encrypted data an additional layer of protection by serving up fake data in response to every incorrect guess of a cryptographic key or password. Notably, HE provides a hedge against brute-force decryption in the long term, giving it a special value in the genomic setting.

However, HE relies on a highly accurate distribution-transforming encoder (DTE) over the message space. Unfortunately, this requirement jeopardizes the practicality of HE. To use HE in any scenario, we have to understand the corresponding message space quantitatively, that is, the precise probability of every possible message. When messages are not uniformly distributed, characterizing and quantifying the distribution is a highly non-trivial task. Building an efficient and precise DTE is the main challenge when extending HE to a real use case, and it is what we do in this work. Hopefully, the techniques proposed in this work are not limited to genomic data; they are intended to inspire those who want to apply HE to other scenarios, typically when the data shares similar characteristics with genomic data.

---

[4] Depending on the privacy-sensitivity of the clinical and environmental data, the patient can choose which clinical and environmental attributes to reveal to the MU, and which ones to encrypt and keep at the SPU.

As we have shown [9], we propose to address the problem of protecting genomic data by combining the idea of honey encryption with the special characteristics of genomic data in order to develop a secure genomic data storage (and retrieval) technique that is (i) robust against potential data breaches, (ii) robust against a computationally unbounded adversary, and (iii) efficient.

In the original HE paper [11], Juels and Ristenpart propose specific HE constructions that rely on existing generation algorithms (e.g. for RSA private keys), or operate over very simple message distributions (e.g., credit card numbers). These constructions, however, are inapplicable to plaintexts with considerably more complicated structure, such as genomic data. Thus substantially new techniques are needed in order to apply HE to genomic data. Additional complications arise when the correlation between the genetic variants (on the genome) and phenotypic side information are taken into account. This work is devoted mainly to addressing these challenges.

We propose a scheme called GenoGuard. In GenoGuard, genomic data is encoded, encrypted under a patient's password[5], and stored at a centralized biobank. We propose a novel tree-based technique to efficiently encode (and decode) the genomic sequence to meet the special requirements of honey encryption. Legitimate users of the system can retrieve the stored genomic data by typing their passwords.

A computationally unbounded adversary can break into the biobank protected by GenoGuard, or remotely try to retrieve the genome of a victim. The adversary could exhaustively try all the potential passwords in the password space for any genome in the biobank. However, for each password he tries (thanks to our encoding phase), the adversary will obtain a plausible-looking genome without knowing whether it is the correct one. We also consider the case when the adversary has side information about a victim (or victims) in terms of his physical traits. In this case, the adversary could use genotype-phenotype associations to determine the real genome of the victim. GenoGuard is designed to prevent such attacks, hence it provides protections beyond the normal guarantees of HE.

We show the main steps of the GenoGuard protocol in Fig. 6. We represent the patient and the user as two separate entities, but they can be the same individual, depending on the application.

GenoGuard is highly efficient and can be used by the service providers that offer DTC services (e.g., 23andMe) to securely store the genomes of their customers. It can also be used by medical units (e.g., hospitals) to securely store the genomes of patients and to retrieve them later for clinical use. The general protocol in Fig. 6 can work in a healthcare scenario without any major changes. In this scenario, a patient wants a medical unit (e.g., his doctor) to access his genome and perform medical tests. The medical unit can request for the encrypted seed on behalf of (and with consent from) the patient. Hence, there is a negotiation phase that provides the password to the medical unit. Such a phase can be

---

[5] A patient can choose a low-entropy password that is easier for him/her to remember, which is a common case in the real world [8].

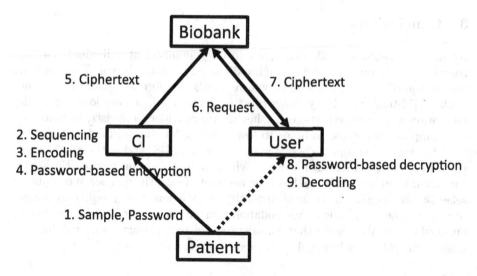

Fig. 6. GenoGuard protocol. A patient provides his biological sample to the CI, and chooses a password for honey encryption. The CI does the sequencing, encoding and password-based encryption, and then sends the ciphertext to the biobank. During a retrieval, a user (e.g., the patient or his doctor) requests for the ciphertext, decrypts it and finally decodes it to get the original sequence.

completed automatically via the patient's smart card (or smart phone), or the patient can type his password himself. In this setup, the biobank can be a public centralized database that is semi-trusted. Such a centralized database would be convenient for the storage and retrieval of the genomes by several medical units.

For direct-to-customer (DTC) services, the protocol needs some adjustments. For instance, Counsyl[6] and 23andMe[7] provide their customers various DTC genetic tests. In such scenarios, the biobank is the private database of these service providers. Thus, such service providers have the obligation to protect customers' genomic data in case of a data breach. In order to perform various genetic tests, the service providers should be granted permission to decrypt the sequences on their side, which is a reasonable relaxation of the threat model because customers share their sequences with the service providers. Therefore, steps 8 and 9 in Fig. 6 should be moved to the biobank. A user (customer) who requests a genetic test result logs into the biobank system, provides the password for password-based decryption and asks for a genetic test on his sequence. The plaintext sequence is deleted after the test.

---

[6] https://www.counsyl.com/.
[7] https://www.23andme.com/.

3   Conclusions

Advances in genomics will soon result in large numbers of individuals having their genomes sequenced and obtaining digitized versions thereof. This poses a wide range of technical problems, which we also explore in detail in a recent work [3]. Mitigating privacy issues of genomic data will require long-term collaboration among geneticists, other healthcare providers, ethicists, lawmakers, and computer scientists. In order to foster this collaboration, funding agencies need to target this topic. There are numerous EU, US, and nationally funded projects focusing on e-health, some of which address data protection. However, the genomic privacy challenge has been overlooked, and the number of computer scientists working on the topic is currently low. We hope that the privacy issues highlighted here will encourage collaboration among researchers in the fields outlined above. We believe that consideration of such privacy issues will have a positive benefit to society and individuals in their daily lives.

References

1. http://www.nytimes.com/2013/03/24/opinion/sunday/the-immortal-life-of-henrietta-lacks-the-sequel.html?pagewanted=all
2. Ateniese, G., Fu, K., Green, M., Hohenberger, S.: Improved proxy re-encryption schemes with applications to secure distributed storage. ACM Trans. Inf. Syst. Secur. **9**, 1–30 (2006)
3. Ayday, E., Cristofaro, E.D., Tsudik, G., Hubaux, J.-P.: Whole genome sequencing: revolutionary medicine or privacy nightmare. IEEE Comput. Mag. **48**(2), 58–66 (2015)
4. Ayday, E., Raisaro, J.L., Mclaren, P.J., Fellay, J., Hubaux, J.-P.: Privacy-preserving computation of disease risk by using genomic, clinical, and environmental data. In: Proceedings of USENIX Security Workshop on Health Information Technologies (HealthTech) (2013)
5. Ayday, E., Raisaro, J.L., Rougemont, J., Hubaux, J.-P.: Protecting and evaluating genomic privacy in medical tests and personalized medicine. In: WPES 2013 (2013)
6. Bresson, E., Catalano, D., Pointcheval, D.: A simple public-key cryptosystem with a double trapdoor decryption mechanism and its applications. In: Proceedings of Asiacrypt (2003)
7. Drmanac, R., Sparks, A.B., Callow, M.J., Halpern, A.L., Burns, N.L., Kermani, B.G., Carnevali, P., Nazarenko, I., Nilsen, G.B., Yeung, G., et al.: Human genome sequencing using unchained base reads on self-assembling DNA nanoarrays. Science **327**(5961), 78–81 (2010)
8. Florencio, D., Herley, C.: A large-scale study of web password habits. In: Proceedings of the 16th International Conference on World Wide Web, WWW 2007, pp. 657–666. ACM, New York (2007)
9. Huang, Z., Ayday, E., Hubaux, J.-P., Fellay, J., Juels, A.: Genoguard: protecting genomic data against brute-force attacks. In: Proceedings of IEEE Symposium on Security and Privacy (2015)
10. Humbert, M., Ayday, E., Hubaux, J.-P., Telenti, A.: Addressing the concerns of the Lacks family: quantification of kin genomic privacy. In: CCS 2013 (2013)

11. Juels, A., Ristenpart, T.: honey encryption: security beyond the brute-force bound. In: Nguyen, P.Q., Oswald, E. (eds.) EUROCRYPT 2014. LNCS, vol. 8441, pp. 293–310. Springer, Heidelberg (2014)
12. Kschischang, F., Frey, B., Loeliger, H.A.: Factor graphs and the sum-product algorithm. IEEE Trans. Inf. Theor. **47**, 498–519 (2001)
13. Nyholt, D., Yu, C., Visscher, P.: On Jim Watson's APOE status: genetic information is hard to hide. Eur. J. Hum. Genet. **17**, 147–149 (2009)
14. Pearl, J., Reasoning, P.: Probabilistic Reasoning in Intelligent Systems: Networks of Plausible Inference. Morgan Kaufmann Publishers Inc., San Francisco (1988)

Author Index

Printed in the United States
By Bookmasters